In *Theorizing the Avant-Garde: Modernism, Expressionism, and the Problem of Postmodernity*, Richard Murphy mobilizes theories of the postmodern to challenge our understanding of the avant-garde. He assesses the importance of the avant-garde for contemporary culture and for the debates among theorists of postmodernism such as Jameson, Eagleton, Lyotard and Habermas. Murphy reconsiders the classic formulation of the avant-garde in Lukács, Bloch and Bürger, especially their discussion of aesthetic autonomy, and investigates the relationship between art and politics via a discussion of Marcuse, Adorno and Benjamin. Combining close textual readings of a wide range of works of literature as well as films, it draws on a rich array of critical theories, such as those of Bakhtin, Todorov, MacCabe, Belsey and Raymond Williams. This interdisciplinary project will appeal to all those interested in modernist and avant-garde movements of the early twentieth century, and provides a critical rethinking of the present-day controversy regarding postmodernity.

RICHARD MURPHY has taught at Columbia University and at the University of Freiburg, and is Associate Professor in the Literature Department at the University of California, Santa Cruz. He has published numerous essays on literary theory, film and twentieth-century culture.

D1284166

# Theorizing the Avant-Garde

# Literature, Culture, Theory

*General editors*

ANTHONY CASCARDI, *University of California, Berkeley*

RICHARD MACKSEY, *The Johns Hopkins University*

Recent titles include

Paratexts: Thresholds of interpretation
GERARD GENETTE

Chronoschisms: Time, narrative, and postmodernism
URSULA HEISE

Cinema, theory, and political responsibility
PATRICK MCGEE

The practice of theory: Rhetoric, knowledge, and pedagogy in the academy
MICHAEL BERNARD-DONALS

Singularities: Extremes of theory in the twentieth century
TOM PEPPER

Ideology and inscription: "Cultural studies" after de Man, Bakhtin, and Benjamin
TOM COHEN

Consequences of Enlightenment
ANTHONY CASCARDI

# Theorizing the Avant-Garde

## Modernism, Expressionism, and the Problem of Postmodernity

❖❖❖❖❖❖❖❖❖❖❖❖❖❖❖❖❖❖❖❖❖❖❖❖❖❖❖❖❖❖❖❖❖❖❖❖❖❖❖❖❖

### RICHARD MURPHY

CAMBRIDGE
UNIVERSITY PRESS

PUBLISHED BY THE PRESS SYNDICATE OF THE UNIVERSITY OF CAMBRIDGE
The Pitt Building, Trumpington Street, Cambridge CB2 1RP, United Kingdom

CAMBRIDGE UNIVERSITY PRESS
The Edinburgh Building, Cambridge CB2 2RU, UK   http://www.cup.cam.ac.uk
40 West 20th Street, New York, NY 10011-4211, USA   http://www.cup.org
10 Stamford Road, Oakleigh, Melbourne 3166, Australia

First published 1999

Printed in the United Kingdom at the University Press, Cambridge

Typeset in Palatino 10/12.5 pt. [VN]

*A catalogue record for this book is available from the British Library*

ISBN 0 521 63291 9 hardback
ISBN 0 521 64869 6 paperback

# Contents

# Contents

# 1

❖❖❖❖❖❖❖❖❖❖❖❖❖❖❖❖❖❖❖❖❖❖❖❖❖❖❖❖❖❖❖❖❖❖❖❖❖❖❖❖❖

# Theories of the avant-garde

❖❖❖❖❖❖❖❖❖❖❖❖❖❖❖❖❖❖❖❖❖❖❖❖❖❖❖❖❖❖❖❖❖❖❖❖❖❖❖❖❖

> It has been said that the degree to which a revolution is developing *qualitatively* different social conditions and relationships may perhaps be indicated by the development of a different language: the rupture with the continuum of domination must also be a rupture with the vocabulary of domination.
>
> Herbert Marcuse[1]

## Introduction

In his *Theory of the Avant-Garde* (1974) Peter Bürger sets himself the task of producing a definition of the progressive artistic movements of the early twentieth century that will both distinguish them from earlier avant-garde phenomena as well as from other contemporary artistic movements of the modernist period such as aestheticism.[2] Although Bürger's model offers what purports to be a general definition of the historical avant-garde it is clear that for the most part his theoretical descriptions and analyses are oriented specifically towards dada and surrealism, his examples being drawn almost exclusively from these movements and in particular from the plastic arts rather than from literary texts. Notably absent from Bürger's analysis of the movements of the avant-garde, for example, is one of the seminal phenomena of early twentieth-century literature, film and art, namely German expressionism. Bürger adds a suggestive note to the effect that one

---

[1] *An Essay on Liberation* (Boston: Beacon, 1969), 33.

[2] Peter Bürger, *Theorie der Avantgarde*, (Frankfurt: Suhrkamp, 1974). Here I refer wherever possible to the English translation by Michael Shaw, (Minneapolis: University of Minnesota Press, 1984). Unless otherwise noted, all other translations throughout are my own.

might, within certain limitations, discover a number of essential avant-garde features in expressionism, such as its critique of the institutionalized character of art and its characteristic rejection not simply of previous movements but of the tradition of art in its entirety.[3] Yet having noted that these similarities remain to be worked out concretely in future analyses Bürger himself skirts the central problem of expressionism and its relationship to the avant-garde.

In the light of the current debates on postmodernism there has been renewed interest both in modernism and the avant-garde and, more particularly, in the nature of their mutual relationship. Postmodernism has frequently been seen for example as a phenomenon which is neither totally new nor a movement constituting a radically innovative stylistic breakthrough, but rather as the attempt to reconfigure in contemporary terms some of the questions already faced by modernism and the avant-garde.[4] In this sense, any definition of postmodernism must inevitably depend upon a prior understanding of those earlier phenomena. Postmodernism might then be thought of as a change of "dominant" within modernism,[5] or as a realignment of a constellation of meaning mapped out in the shifting relations between the reference-points denoted by modernism, the contemporary and the avant-garde.

Given this configuration of terms, the issues dealt with by Bürger's book become especially important in helping to establish the various distinctions and interdependencies operating between modernism and the avant-garde. The omission of expressionism from Bürger's discussion is then all the more surprising in view of its importance as a crucial space in which the avant-garde confronts modernism and in which the differences between the

---

[3] Bürger, *Theory of the Avant-Garde*, 109, note 4.

[4] See for example Andreas Huyssen, *After the Great Divide: Modernism, Mass Culture, Postmodernism* (Bloomington: Indiana University Press, 1986) 168.

[5] Brian McHale employs the Formalist concept of the "dominant" (derived from Tynjanov and Jakobson) in order to describe the transition from modernism to postmodernism. McHale sees a shift from a period dominated by epistemological issues to one concerned more with ontological matters (such as the confrontation between different realities). See McHale's article "Change of Dominant from Modernist to Postmodernist Writing," *Approaching Postmodernism*, ed. Hans Bertens and Douwe Fokkema (Philadelphia and Amsterdam: John Benjamins, 1986), 53–78, and also his book *Postmodernist Fiction* (London: Methuen, 1987) where this idea forms the central thesis.

two are negotiated. For although expressionism has been labeled the "historical modernist movement par excellence,"[6] besides its modernist characteristics – such as its shift from transparent, realist representations of a common world, towards abstraction, obscurity, and the investigation of subjectivity and the unconscious[7] – it also shares many of those key features, in particular the revolutionary, counter-discursive and anti-institutional functions, by which Bürger defines the historical avant-garde.

This overlap is itself significant. For the various contradictory impulses within expressionism illustrate that the avant-garde is a much more ambiguous and heterogeneous phenomenon than Bürger – with his narrow focus on dada and surrealism – would sometimes have us believe. More typically the avant-garde serves as the political and revolutionary cutting-edge of the broader movement of modernism, from which it frequently appears to be trying with difficulty to free itself. Modernism and the avant-garde often seem to be locked into a dialectical relationship in which the avant-garde questions the blind spots and unreflected presuppositions of modernism, while modernism itself reacts to this critique, at least in its later stages, by attempting to take into account its own poetics some of the spectacular failures and successes of the historical avant-garde.

The current debates on postmodernism and its relation to modernism and the avant-garde have not only renewed interest in early twentieth-century art then, but have provided both fresh perspectives with which to re-read the texts of this period, as well as new questions and theoretical strategies with which to approach their characteristic problematics. The goal in re-reading expressionism through Bürger's *Theory of the Avant-Garde* and in the light of the recent discussion on the modern (and postmodern) period is thus twofold.

Firstly, it is important to interrogate Bürger's influential work and to develop his argumentation by testing it against a broader range of avant-garde and modernist phenomena than Bürger's own examples provide in order to discover the extent to which the

---

[6] For example by David Bathrick and Andreas Huyssen, "Modernism and the Experience of Modernity," *Modernity and the Text: Revisions of German Modernism*, ed. Huyssen and Bathrick (New York: Columbia University Press, 1989), 8.

[7] See Walter Sokel's definition of expressionism in terms of modernism in his book *The Writer in Extremis* (Stanford: Stanford University Press, 1959), 18.

various methodological categories which make up his theory are capable of distinguishing between the contemporaneous phenomena within the modernist period. For example, to what degree does expressionism fulfill the avant-garde's role of producing a fundamental re-thinking of the artist's social practice, together with a full-scale interrogation of the social and institutional conditions of art? To what extent does it remain caught within modernism's predilection for aesthetic autonomy and its drive for purely technical and formal progress?

Secondly, by re-reading the texts of expressionism in the context of some of the new questions which have been thrown up recently by the postmodernism debate as well as by the related discussion surrounding Bürger's theoretical model, it is possible to observe the extent of the "epistemic" or "paradigmatic" shift which has taken place between the progressive movements of the early twentieth century and the contemporary culture of postmodernity. Re-examining expressionism in this light forces us to reconsider both the degree of real innovation brought about by postmodernism, as well as allowing us to appreciate the extent to which the expressionist avant-garde preempts postmodernism in deconstructing and re-writing the established images and constructions of the world – the anticipatory effect that Jochen Schulte-Sasse has called a "postmodern transformation of modernism."[8]

In this respect my investigation into expressionism and its relationship to modernism and the avant-garde is also intended as a contribution towards the ongoing debate on modernism and the postmodern by undertaking precisely the kind of concrete analysis of individual texts that has become rather rare in the discussion. It has become a pressing obligation to focus in detail again upon some of the important literary texts which subtend the theoretical categories employed in this discussion, since their specificity has frequently been lost from view at the level of generalization on which much of the theoretical debate has been conducted.

German expressionism is itself notoriously difficult to define, and one hesitates even to use the term "movement" in connection with this multi-faceted phenomenon, given that term's implica-

---

[8] Jochen Schulte-Sasse, "Carl Einstein; or, the Postmodern Transformation of Modernism," *Modernity and the Text*, ed. Huyssen and Bathrick.

tion of a cooperative endeavor or single-minded tendency. The expressionist generation was such a broad and varied group of writers and artists, that it is unlikely to yield to any single definition or generalization. Since conventional categorizations of such literary movements frequently have the tendency to obscure differences by reducing a diverse and varied phenomenon to the terms of a broad homogeneity, it would seem more appropriate to describe the position of expressionism by locating it instead through its relations to the reference-points of modernism and the avant-garde. The central principles and functions that these categories embody would then figure as the points between which is mapped out the area occupied by the art of expressionism.

Given that *Theory of the Avant-Garde* tends to confine the heterogeneity of the avant-garde within certain narrow limits, expressionism as a diverse and multidisciplinary cultural event is perhaps the ideal example with which to test Bürger's theses. At the same time Bürger's criteria concerning the avant-garde bring to the existing scholarship on expressionism important alternatives to those traditional approaches to the movement which have frequently obscured its radical and oppositional characteristics.

Let us now examine in detail some of the central categories of Bürger's model (in particular the notions of montage and aesthetic autonomy), and propose certain revisions to Bürger's theory which will be important in describing some of the essential features of German expressionism in the chapters ahead.

## Bürger's *Theory of the Avant-Garde*: ideology-critique, affirmative culture and the institution of art

Previous studies of the avant-garde such as Matei Calinescu's *Faces of Modernity* have frequently defined it merely as a later, more radical and more "advanced" phase of modernism, distinguished by its ideological and overtly political orientation from the more formal, aesthetically purist and "subtly traditional" character of mainstream modernism.[9] Bürger's study is unique in trying to define the nature of the avant-garde not only by relating it to the literary-historical context but with regard to certain changes in the perception of the *social* functions of art.

[9] Matei Calinescu, *Faces of Modernity: Avant-Garde, Decadence, Kitsch* (1977; Bloomington: Indiana University Press, 1987), 96, 149.

Bürger sees the development of art within bourgeois society as characterized by its historical shift towards increasing aesthetic autonomy, a condition he defines with Habermas as the "independence of works of art from extra-aesthetic uses."[10] This process of liberating art from all practical demands external to it culminates in the movement of aestheticism or "l'art pour l'art." Nineteenth-century aestheticism figures as a radical attempt firstly to turn art in upon itself, and secondly – as with modernism's characteristic interest in issues such as the poetics of silence and the crisis of language – to concern itself largely with the medium itself. It is consequently through the excesses of aestheticism, its extremes of hermeticism and aesthetic self-centeredness, that "the other side of autonomy, art's lack of social impact also becomes recognizable."[11] And it is in response to this recognition that the "historical avant-garde" emerges as a movement defined by its opposition to this shift towards hermeticism.

To extend Bürger's argument, one could say that it is not the emergence of the phenomenon of aestheticism in itself that suddenly and miraculously reveals the practice of autonomy and which consequently calls down upon itself the wrath of the avant-garde. Art's claim to autonomy had existed in bourgeois society in Germany for example at least since Kant and Schiller. If we look beyond the narrow confines of the immanent theory of the development of art – from which Bürger uncharacteristically appears to be arguing at this point – we can see that the crucial moment of change to which the avant-garde responds is not only the extremism of the aestheticist movement and its characteristic gesture of turning its back on the real world. Rather, it is the fact that the aestheticist movement should take this course at this particular *historical* juncture, in other words, at the beginning of twentieth-century "modernity," and in a period of unprecedented and momentous economic and technological revolution in society. Aestheticism's characteristic reaction of retreating into hibernation and hermeticism is all the more shocking since it contrasts with the kind of artistic response one *might* have expected, namely

---

[10] "(Die) Selbständigkeit der Kunstwerke gegenüber kunstexternen Verwendungsansprüchen." Jürgen Habermas, "Bewußtmachende oder rettende Kritik," *Zur Aktualität Walter Benjamins*, ed. Siegfried Unseld (Frankfurt: Suhrkamp, 1972). Quoted by Bürger, *Theorie der Avantgarde*, 46 note 13; *Theory of the Avant-Garde*, 110, note 13. I have used my own translation in this case.

[11] Bürger, *Theory of the Avant-Garde*, 22.

a more socially oriented response in art, or at least the attempt to formulate these new socio-historical experiences in contemporary aesthetic terms. The historical significance of aestheticism for the emergence of the avant-garde lies then in the conjunction of historical factors: the extreme turmoil of contemporary society combined with the crassness of aestheticism's blank rejection of any need to react to it. It is this response that begins to raise doubts concerning the legitimacy of such autonomous art forms, and so ultimately mobilizes the avant-garde.

According to Bürger, it is the particular character of the avant-garde's response to aestheticism that is important. For with the historical avant-garde movements the social sub-system of art enters a new stage of development. Dada, the most radical movement within the European avant-garde no longer criticizes the individual aesthetic fashions and schools that preceded it, but criticizes art as an institution: in other words with the historical avant-garde art enters the stage of "self-criticism."[12] In order to

---

[12] Bürger, *Theory of the Avant-Garde*, 22. Although dada's "self-criticism" of the institution of art is indeed very powerful, Bürger is quite wrong in assuming that dada is not equally concerned to attack its "rival" movements, including its most immediate predecessor, expressionism. Indeed, this onslaught on expressionism is an essential feature of much of the early writing of both the Zürich and Berlin phases of dada, and expressionist idealism forms a favorite target for dada's familiar vitriolic attacks. The first dada manifesto (1918) for example takes as its starting point its own distance from expressionism's "pretense of intensification" ("Vorwand der Verinnerlichung") which allegedly stifled any progressive tendencies and served merely to hide the expressionists' own bourgeois leanings. See Richard Huelsenbeck, ed., *Dada. Eine literarische Dokumentation* (Hamburg: Rowohlt, 1984), 31–33. Similarly, in Raoul Hausmann's text "The Return to Objectivity in Art" ("Rückkehr zur Gegenständlichkeit in der Kunst") Expressionism is described as "the culture of hypocritical stupidity " ("die Kultur der verlogener Dummheit," Huelsenbeck, *Dada*, 115). Meanwhile Richard Huelsenbeck's various ironic attacks in "En avant Dada" (1920) describe expressionism's critical response to modernity as merely "that sentimental resistance to the times" ("jener sentimentale Widerstand gegen die Zeit") and illustrate its alleged naivity – thereby tarring the entire movement with the same brush – by citing Leonhard Frank's "Der Mensch ist gut" (*dada*, 118–119). In the context of our discussion it is interesting to note that dada's proponents see themselves in an explicitly avant-garde role, "gathered together to provide propaganda for a form of art from which they look forward to the realization of new ideals" ("zur Propaganda einer Kunst gesammelt, von der sie die Verwirklichung neuer Ideale erwarten," *Dada*, 120). Consequently, dada sees itself as having given up any remnants of the "l'art pour l'art Charakter" and having changed its goal: "instead of continuing to create art, Dada has sought out an enemy . . . The movement, the stuggle was uppermost" ("anstatt weiter Kunst zu machen, hat sich Dada einen Gegner gesucht . . . Die Bewegung, der Kampf wurde betont," *Dada*, 120).

appreciate the full significance for the avant-garde of this development towards "self-criticism" it is important to understand here exactly what Bürger means by the term and how it relates to other analytical approaches in progressive art, in particular to "ideology-critique."

Bürger takes as the starting point for his discussion of "self-criticism" firstly Marx's analysis of religion as ideology and of the twofold character of such ideology; and secondly Marcuse's application of this analysis to the field of art.[13] From Marx's analysis Bürger draws the following conclusions for his own model:

1. Religion is an illusion. Man projects into heaven what he would like to see realized on earth. To the extent that man believes in God who is no more than an objectification of human qualities, he succumbs to an illusion. 2. But religion also contains an element of truth. It is "an expression of real wretchedness" (for the realization of humanity in heaven is merely a creation of the mind and denounces the lack of real humanity in human society). And it is "a protest against real wretchedness" for even in their alienated form, religious ideals are a standard of what ought to be. (7)

The social function of religion, like art, is therefore characterized above all by its twofold character, that is, by what we can call its "duplicity": it permits the experience of an "illusory happiness" but to the extent that it alleviates misery through illusion, it makes less pressing (and thus less likely) the possibility of any *genuine* change leading to the establishment of "true happiness."

Herbert Marcuse's famous essay "On the Affirmative Character of Culture" (1937) precedes Bürger both in adopting Marx's method of analyzing the duplicitous character of religion and in reapplying it to the similarly ambiguous ideological function of art in society.[14] Marcuse maintains that, like religion, art has the positive function of preserving society's unfulfilled ideals and "forgotten truths."[15] It thus contains an important critical element: it protests against the deficiencies of a reality in which these ideals have disappeared. But on the other hand, in as far as art serves to compensate in the realm of aesthetic illusion

---

[13] Karl Marx, *Critique of Hegel's Philosophy of Right* (Cambridge: Cambridge University Press, 1970). Herbert Marcuse, "The Affirmative Character of Culture," *Negations*, trans. J. Shapiro (Boston: Beacon, 1968), 88–133.

[14] Marcuse, "The Affirmative Character of Culture," 120–122.

[15] Bürger, *Theory of the Avant-Garde*, 11.

*Introduction*

("Schein") for these real-life deficiencies, it simultaneously sublimates and defuses this protest. Paradoxically then in preserving
life's unfulfilled ideals art may take on a quietist and "affirmative
character" in as far as it serves merely to stabilize and legitimize
that reality against which it protests.

In both of these analytical models the practice of "ideology-
critique" lays bare the grain of truth contained within the illusion
created by religion and art, while simultaneously demonstrating
the ideological constraints on implementing this truth which are
imposed by these institutions themselves. If the emergence of the
avant-garde marks art's entry into the "stage of self-criticism," it
also signifies the beginning of a similar form of "ideology-critique" through which artistic practice is turned against art itself as
an institutional formation. It means that art's critical power no
longer operates merely in an "immanent" fashion, that is, as the
kind of criticism that remains enclosed within the social institution (such as when one type of religion criticizes another) and
within which it would consequently be blind to the institutional
restraints operating upon it. In as far as it analyzes the overall
functioning of the institution itself – and especially its social and
ideological effects rather than the individual elements of the system – self-criticism operates as a form of ideology-critique performed from *within* the limits of the institution, yet directed
*against* its institutional functions. What this self-criticism means in
practical terms for the "historical" avant-garde of the early twentieth century is that, unlike previous avant-garde movements, its
subversive or revolutionary character is demonstrated by the way
that it turns its attention increasingly to the institutional framework through which art is produced and received, and to the
"dominant social discourses" which emerge in art through these
institutional mediations.

As we have seen, the institutionalization of art reaches a crucial
stage where those seemingly perennial conditions of art, namely
autonomy and the absence of social consequence, are valorized as
goals in their own right, in particular by the movement of aestheticism. The "historical" avant-garde's critical response to this situation takes two forms.

Firstly, it deconstructs the claim that these "universal" principles of autonomy constitute the inevitable conditions of the
possibility of art. Similar to the way in which the avant-garde

reveals that even realism or mimetic representation – long thought of as perennial and unchanging criteria of value in the Aristotelian tradition – are actually merely a set of culturally-privileged codes which have simply attained a special institutional status, so it also exposes the notion of autonomy as an arbitrary value which is *institutionally* imposed upon art.

Secondly, the self-critical response of the avant-garde leads to an awareness of the fact that with the progressive detachment of the "sub-system" of art from the practice of life – a separation that is part of a more general process of what Max Weber calls the differentiation or "rationalization" in modern society – art's duplicitous or "affirmative" function is reinforced. Although autonomy offers a degree of independence and critical distance from society, art simultaneously suffers from this isolation. For any social or political content is instantly neutralized when the work of art is received as a purely "imaginative" product, an aesthetic illusion that need not be taken seriously.

In connection with this self-critical impulse of the avant-garde the concept of the "institution of art" becomes one of the key notions used by Bürger to analyze the social administration of the aesthetic sphere. He uses this term to refer both to the "productive and distributive apparatus" of art but also more particularly to the "ideas about art that prevail at a given time and that determine the reception of works."[16] Bürger further defines the institution of art in a later article as that set of social conditions which determine the particular functions of art in a given historical period, and he emphasizes further that although alternative conceptions of art may exist, the institution of art at any given time is always predisposed towards the dominance of one conception of art in particular.[17] Thus, the term describes both the attitudes taken up towards art in society as well as the ideological and institutional limitations imposed upon art's possible effects.

The importance of the institution of art may be measured by the vehemence of the avant-garde's attacks upon it. These attacks also illustrate the degree to which the more progressive artists and

[16] Bürger, *Theory of the Avant-Garde*, 22.
[17] Peter Bürger, "Institution Kunst als literatursoziologische Kategorie. Skizze eine Theorie des historischen Wandels der gesellschaftlichen Funktion der Literatur," *Vermittlung – Rezeption – Funktion* (Frankfurt: Suhrkamp, 1979), 173–174; 177.

writers of the early twentieth century had become aware of the significance of general institutional conditions on the reception of their art, and as we shall see later, it also indicates their growing awareness of the institution's ideological influence and of its dominant social discourses in determining the extent of each work's *social* effect. Consequently the central goal of the avant-garde's attack according to Bürger is not only to explode the institution of art but to lead aesthetic experience out of its isolation – imprisoned by autonomy – in order to drive it back into the real world, where it can play its part in the transformation of everyday life.

In its opposition to an institution of art characterized by its detachment from everyday experience, the avant-garde consequently champions a form of art whose central goal becomes the reintegration and "sublation" of art and life. With this "reintegration of art into life" ("Rückführung der Kunst in Lebenspraxis") the avant-gardists aim at a more practical kind of art with a clear social significance.[18] However, this does not mean that the art of the avant-garde was simply to integrate itself neatly into the existing, goal-oriented and rationally organized world of modernity. On the contrary, the intention was to create a new art, from within which it would become possible to conceive of an entirely new basis for social practice (49).

As Bürger concedes, the avant-gardists failed to achieve their ultimate goal of dissolving the borders between art and life. Yet in their critique of the institution of art they were more successful. For despite the fact that they did not manage to dismantle the cultural apparatus as a whole, the various forms of protest which they employed succeeded both in making the general categories of the work of art recognizable, and in revealing the extent to which these categories needed constantly to be underwritten by the institution of art. Thus without destroying the institution of art the avant-garde did succeed in raising important questions concerning the validity of "conventional" artistic norms and criteria, both with respect to the way they are held in place by the institution and the way that the work of art in turn fulfills an affirmative or legitimizing function within the society from which it emerges. As proof of this success of the avant-garde in

---

[18] Bürger, *Theorie der Avantgarde*, 121.

revealing the institutionalized character of art Bürger points to the subsequent impossibility of any particular form or movement claiming universal validity (87). In the light of the debate on the postmodern, one might now add that the lasting achievement of the avant-garde is also borne out by the heterogeneous or pluralistic character of the contemporary art of postmodernism which makes a virtue out of the absence of any such binding norms and universal criteria.

## Benjamin, Lukacs and Bloch: the "expressionism debates" and the problem of montage

With the avant-garde's insights into the institutional constraints upon art's reception comes a corresponding awareness of the ways in which the institution of art conditions the very form and techniques employed in the work of art. In this regard Walter Benjamin's important article "The Author as Producer" (1934), although not discussed by Bürger, clearly forms a central point of reference throughout the book for his thinking on the avant-garde's formal revolution and for the very notion of the "institution of art."

In the article Benjamin warns against the danger of writers merely producing works for what he terms the "apparatus" of art without their being prepared to exert direct influence upon this apparatus. He points to the way in which this bourgeois "publication apparatus" is capable of assimilating all manner of revolutionary material in its search for ever more spectacular effects with which to entertain its insatiable public.[19] He maintains that, as a consequence artists should generate their aesthetic techniques and formal strategies with an awareness both of their work's relation to the conditions of its production and of its implication within the wider institutional networks of power.

Benjamin offers as an example of the way this institutional recuperation operates an image which also serves as a reminder of the importance for art of finding the appropriate "Technik" ("technique") of ideological resistance. He explains how even a socially-engaged work, a photograph of a slum for example, if produced without regard for the appropriate technical and formal

---

[19] Walter Benjamin, "Der Autor als Produzent," *Gesammelte Schriften*, II, 2, ed. R. Tiedemann and H. Schweppenhäuser (Frankfurt: Suhrkamp, 1980), 692.

# Introduction

strategies needed to accompany its critical intentions, risks being transformed unthinkingly through the artistic gloss of technical perfection solely into an object of aesthetic enjoyment.[20] Consequently he maintains that the artist should pay attention not just to the political "tendency" or "Tendenz," that is, to the *social* goals of the work, but also to the "Technik," the technical and formal means he or she employs in it – the implication being that the artist needs to maintain a heightened awareness of the broader institutional and ideological factors affecting the reception of the work. Recommending that the artist choose only such formal means as are ideologically appropriate to the task, Benjamin cites as a specific example the technique of montage and the progressive uses to which such discontinuous forms are put in Brecht's "epic theater."[21] In his view such strategies of fragmentation counter any false reconciliations at the level of form that might threaten to neutralize the work's progressive intentions at the level of content.[22]

Himself an early commentator on the avant-garde (in particular with regard to surrealism as well as to Brecht's theater) Benjamin clearly provides the inspiration here for Bürger's analysis of the centrality of montage for the poetics of the avant-garde. For Bürger the central feature linking together the various formal and technical strategies of the avant-garde is their common opposition to the convention of the *organic* work of art. The various component parts of the organic work form a rounded and continuous whole, and in imitating the appearance of a natural phenomenon or "work of nature" the organic work covers up the traces of its own construction, producing artificially the appearance of the "givenness" of nature. The danger with this attempt to produce a harmonious appearance by covering over the traces of discontinuity is that it produces the "false reconciliations" that Benjamin also warns against: the creation of an imaginary sense of social unity. Bürger too is aware of this danger and warns that, "instead of baring the contradictions of society in our time, the organic work promotes, by its very form, the illusion of a world that is whole, even though the explicit contents may show a wholly different intent" (86).

[20] Benjamin, "Der Autor," 693.
[21] Brecht's use of montage is discussed in detail below, 21.
[22] Benjamin, "Der Autor," 697.

Given these potential pitfalls one of the clearest examples in the avant-garde of a progressive poetics focusing on a fragmentary, non-organic notion of form may be found in expressionism. The expressionists showed a definite preference for non-organic forms, as in the paratactically-listed one-line images of the "Simultangedicht" or "simultaneous poem," in the anti-linear "epic" structure, or in the disjointed and discontinuous montage style, as well as in their widespread practice of a multitude of related strategies of abstraction, interruption and fragmentation. Yet it is important to note that it is not just their formal strategies which clearly link them to the avant-garde. For this formal vanguardism is also underpinned in the poetics of expressionism by ideological conviction. In all but the most "naive" of the expressionists the principle of non-organic form has two important (and highly contentious) avant-garde functions: the abjuration of conventionally harmonious formal structures and the disruption of any artificial sense of unity which might offer the subject a sense of reconciliation within the social imaginary.

Interestingly, it was precisely the avant-garde quality of expressionism's use of such progressive strategies, and particularly of montage, which became a defining issue and a central bone of contention during the famous "expressionism debates" of the thirties – a series of discussions which have had a lasting influence upon twentieth-century thinking regarding the problem of ideology, realism and representation.[23] Although two of the main protagonists in the debate, Georg Lukacs and Ernst Bloch, were united for example in arguing in favor of the principle of progressive and committed forms of art, their views on how this should be achieved in terms of literary strategies were diametrically opposed. This conflict was articulated precisely in terms of their differing attitudes towards the avant-garde, and in particular towards Expressionism's use of montage and of other non-organic forms.

Lukacs for example supports a particular tradition of realism which attempts to penetrate the chaos of the world and open it up

[23] Most of the essays which made up these debates have been collected in *Die Expressionismusdebatte. Materialien zu einer marxistischen Realismuskonzeption*, ed. Hans-Jürgen Schmitt (Frankfurt: Suhrkamp, 1973). Translations of some of these essays, together with commentaries (and an essay by Fredric Jameson on the Brecht–Lukacs debate) appear in the volume *Aesthetics and Politics*, ed. Ronald Taylor et al. (London: New Left Books, 1979).

("Aufdecken")[24] in order to "grasp reality as it really is" (198). Having exposed the essence of "reality," Lukacs' version of realism would construct a rounded version of the real by reworking this material in such a way that, through an act of artificial "closure" or "covering over" ("Zudecken") (205), it would synthetically give to the image the appearance of a smooth and natural surface. In other words, Lukacs demands a form of realism that would reconstitute the unified appearance of nature and create what would amount to an *organic* work. He is consequently highly critical of the expressionists – and of their technique of montage in particular – for "abandoning the objective representation of reality" (211). He maintains that the avant-garde's central tendency is towards "an ever more pronounced *distancing from realism*, an ever more energetic *liquidation* of realism" (193, Lukacs' emphasis) and he criticizes the expressionists' use of montage forms as the "high-point of this development" (210).

However, expressionism's attempt to "distance" itself from conventional forms of realism constitutes only one of its many avant-garde characteristics. Also important are the strategies to which Bloch points, for example the way in which expressionism refines and develops a whole range of non-organic and ambiguous forms alongside montage, whose function is not only to destabilize realistic representation, but more to the point, to subvert the *epistemological and ideological assumptions* which underpin it.[25] For it is in this manner that expressionism pursues the avant-garde's broader goal of critiquing the institution of art: it exposes realism as an institutionally-supported code which serves to legitimize only a certain concept of reality, and which leaves out of account large areas of human experience that fall outside of this sanctioned category.

If Lukacs' position in the debate is defined by his valorization of an archaic form of classic realism, Bloch's position by contrast demonstrates a much more progressive understanding of the avant-garde (and of expressionism's role within it) as a critical movement characterized by this fundamental ideological and epistemological skepticism. For example, his interpretation of the avant-garde overlaps at many points both with Bürger's later

---

[24] Lukacs, "Es geht um den Realismus," *Expressionismusdebatte*, 205.
[25] I will show this in the later chapters on Kafka, expressionist poetics, melodrama and on the anti-mimetic structure of *The Cabinet of Dr. Caligari*.

description of the non-organic work, as well as with Benjamin's demand that the avant-garde's progressive "Tendenz" be matched by an appropriate and corresponding "Technik." And whereas Lukacs criticizes the expressionists for reproducing the chaotic quality of modern reality with similarly fragmented and discontinuous forms (211), Bloch welcomes these destructive (or "deconstructive") forms of "decomposition" and "disintegration" ("Zerfall" and "Zersetzung") precisely because they avoid the kind of organic representationalism which risks covering up the real discontinuities in the world. Consequently he asks Lukacs ironically, "would it have been better if [the expressionists] had served as doctors at the sick-bed of capitalism? If they had stitched together the surface of 'reality' rather than ripping it open even further?"[26]

## The avant-garde vs. affirmative culture: the aesthetic construction of subjectivity

The expressionist movement's exploration of these destructive, non-organic procedures involves the creation of many different progressive artistic forms, some of which would not be immediately recognizable under the concept of "montage." Before returning to the discussion of the theories of the avant-garde, it is worth looking briefly at some of these alternative forms of purposeful aesthetic discontinuity in order to understand the variety of critical functions they take on within expressionism's avant-garde poetics.

As we have seen, the convention of organic artistic form is associated with the affirmative function of culture, and the creation of "false reconciliations" by producing the aesthetic illusion of a harmonious world. According to Bürger, this affirmative and compensatory function of conventional art is also crucial with regard to the aesthetic construction of subjectivity: "The individual who in the rationalized and means-oriented everyday world has been reduced to a partial function re-experiences himself in art as a human being. Here he can develop the full range of his abilities ..."[27] As Bürger points out in his essay on the "Institution of Art," it

[26] Ernst Bloch, "Diskussionen über Expressionismus," *Expressionismusdebatte*, 187 (my translation).
[27] Bürger, *Theory of the Avant-Garde*, 48–49. Translation modified.

is for this reason that art played an essential role in Schiller's classical conception of "Bildung" (the education and formation of the personality). For it helped to "recover the lost totality of the human being after the harmony of the human personality had been destroyed by the rigidly rational organization of everyday life and by the division of labor prevalent in developing bourgeois society."[28] Through its very form the organic work may serve as a means of socialization, presenting the illusion of a harmonious world into which the individual can be integrated effortlessly. At the same time it offers compensatory images in which for example the decentered modern subject – victim of what Benjamin calls the "Erfahrungsverlust" or "atrophy of experience" typical of modernity – can discover an artificial sense of unity.

To extend Bürger's argument here we might say that the avant-garde's opposition to the conventional organic work is directed then not only against its ideologically affirmative function but also against its reconciliatory use as an instrument of social integration or "subject-positioning." For if the traditional organic text allows the subject to experience an "ideal" and harmonious realization of centered selfhood within a unified world, expressionism's goal – one which again fulfills a central premise of the avant-garde – is purposefully to disrupt this harmony.[29]

It can be argued that the modern individual's alienated and decentered position in the anomic social structure of the early twentieth century produces an intensified need for a compensatory staging of the self as a unified entity.[30] If this is so then the expressionist text may be characterized by its denial of such needs and by its tendency to forestall precisely such reconciliatory functions in the text. Instead, expressionism takes up this experiential complex of alienation and decentering not as an abstraction, a

[28] Bürger, "Institution Kunst," 178. My translation.
[29] As we shall see (especially in the chapter below on Döblin, Benn and expressionist poetics) expressionism develops various narratological strategies which "decenter" the reader, either by denying him or her the conventional privilege of a clear and well-defined position as "implied reader," or alternatively by undermining the text's narrative continuity in such a manner that the possibility of easy identification with the comfortable perspective of a knowledgeable narrator is withheld. Instead the reader is stretched between contradictory perspectives and irreconcilable subject-positions which preclude any illusory sense of integration within the fictional world presented by the text.
[30] On this point see Wolfgang Iser, *Prospecting: From Reader Response to Literary Anthropology* (Baltimore: Johns Hopkins University Press, 1989), 244.

literary topos or describable "content" – such as the way that the "theme" of "dehumanization" is frequently treated in modernism – but as an unavoidable *effect* of the literary text which the reader is made to experience at first hand.[31]

It is in this regard that the various forms of montage and discontinuity occurring throughout the prose and drama of expressionism are important. These non-organic textual structures dramatize subjectivity not by channeling it into the traditional format, namely a combination of plot and characterization based on the notion of the individual as a single, unified and unique Cartesian entity – in other words not into the form which Bürger sees as providing an aesthetic compensation for the "lost totality of the human being." Instead, the avant-garde text stages subjectivity as fragmented and discontinuous, for example as a constellation of personae, a series of mutually conflicting and contradictory roles played out by seemingly separate figures in the texts. The world which the central figure encounters is frequently the realm of reflected selfhood, the other figures becoming mere refractions of the ego – as can be seen most obviously in works as varied as Kafka's "A Country Doctor" and "Description of a Struggle," Einstein's *Bebuquin*, or the expressionist "dramas of selfhood" ("Ich-Dramen") such as Sorge's *The Beggar* and Becker's *The Last Judgment*.

Whereas the reader could previously discover in the organic text a sense of self as a knowable entity which could be embraced, the conventional understanding of self gives way in the avant-garde to the experience of subjectivity as an ongoing process, fundamentally ungraspable. The reader who brings to the expressionist text the expectation of finding the illusion of unity, or a sense of harmony between self and world, will be disappointed to discover instead discontinuity and decenteredness.

This association between the development of non-organic structures and the attempt to deconstruct the notion of subjectivity as fundamentally decentered can be seen in two areas of expressionist prose and drama. Firstly, at the level of *characteriz-*

---

[31] An example of this would be Benn's expressionist text *Gehirne* which suppresses the traditional "realist" signposts orienting the reader and so effaces the temporal and spatial boundaries not just for the protagonist, but also for the reader. This produces a sense of disorientation in the latter analogous to that described by the text in the case of the former. See chapter 3 on Benn and Döblin.

*ation* the individual figure frequently becomes a mere montage of separate characteristics or an amalgam of roles, rather than a complete individual with whom the audience might identify (a strategy which Brecht's drama later adopts with its various "alienation effects" and strategies of discontinuity). At the same time the other dramatis personae frequently become mere functions of the distorted central subjective standpoint from which the protagonist sees them. This "anti-objective" bias occurs for example in Hasenclever's play *The Son* (*Der Sohn*), where according to a contemporary review by Kurt Pinthus, the three secondary figures of the father, the friend and the governess are correspondingly exaggerated and "not depicted objectively by the writer, according to convention, but rather as the son sees them."[32]

Secondly, besides its effect on characterization, the avant-garde model of fragmented form also affects the text's *dramatic* structure in a similar way. In the same review of *Der Sohn* Pinthus goes on to describe the "undramatic" plot-structure in precisely the terms we have employed in our discussion of the avant-garde, namely as "non-organic": "The conflict does not develop, but is threateningly present from the first scene to the last, without being connected or resolved. It is *inorganic*, since the figures are sometimes realistic persons, sometimes abstract types, at one moment frantically discussing in dialectics, then indulging in lyrical monologs."[33] Pinthus' use of the term "inorganic" is significant here, not least since this formulation demonstrates the play's rootedness in the avant-garde and in its typical strategy of using certain radical forms of discontinuity to promote a sense of *representational instability*: firstly, instead of the conventional organic presentation of character the depiction of the figures is anything but "holistic" and alternates between realism and abstraction; sec-

[32] "nicht nach bisherigem Brauch, vom Dichter objektiv umrissen, sondern so, wie der Sohn sie sieht." Kurt Pinthus, "Versuch eines zukünftigen Dramas," *Schaubühne* 10.14 (April 2, 1914): 391–394. Rpt. *Expressionismus. Manifeste und Dokumente zur deutschen Literatur 1910–1920*, ed. Thomas Anz and Michael Stark (Stuttgart: Metzler, 1982), 681.

[33] "Der Konflikt entwickle sich nicht, sondern sei von der ersten Szene bis zur letzten drohend vorhanden, ohne geknüpft, ohne gelöst zu werden. Auch *unorganisch* sei es, da die Darsteller bald realistische Menschen, bald abstrahierte Typen seien, jetzt in rasender Dialektik diskutierten, dann in lyrisierenden Monologen einherschwelgten." Pinthus, "Versuch." *Manifeste und Dokumente*, 680, my emphasis.

ondly it ignores the conventions of linear plot development by refusing either to define or resolve the dramatic conflict.

The characteristically dissonant expressionist structure described by Pinthus clearly hinders any possibility that the text might serve in Schiller's sense as a means by which the fragmented modern subject might recover the lost sense of a totality in human existence through an aesthetic reconstruction of subjectivity. Firstly, rather than presenting an integrating and unified perspective on reality, such expressionist texts offer a "monoperspective," a skewed and idiosyncratic view, in which the spectator is unlikely to find either an accommodating "subject-position" or any other source of compensation within a unified imaginary.[34] Secondly, the reduction of plot to a series of shifting scenes without a vital and dramatic relation to a central conflict reinforces the idea that any sense of a harmonious world has also vanished, along with the conventional orienting notions of time, space and causality.

## Montage and the epic form: Brecht and Döblin

Besides the destabilizing effects of expressionism's progressive poetics upon the aesthetic construction of subjectivity the avant-garde is important in many other aspects of the movement's oppositional discourses. In both the drama and the prose of expressionism one of the paradigms of the non-organic or montage form is the "epic." Here the text's various component parts begin to take on a degree of structural and semantic autonomy, rather than being subordinated to the meaning of the whole. Similarly, the work may even adopt a loose or "open" structure in which individual components are entirely indispensable and can be discarded without loss to the sense of the whole.[35]

---

[34] In the case of *Der Sohn* the dominant point of view is "das Abbild der Realität im Geiste des Sohnes" ("the reflection of reality in the mind of the son," Pinthus, "Versuch." *Manifeste und Dokumente*, 682). This perspective embodies the marginalized and alienated point of view of the isolated intellectual in patriarchal society – corresponding to the general position of the expressionist intellectual in the bourgeois social order of the Wilhemine period.

[35] The paradigmatic forms of expressionist theater here are the "Ich-Dramen" ("dramas of the self") and "Stationen drama," (those plays patterned after the Strindberg's *To Damascus* and its movement through various 'stations of the cross'). These are structured according to the montage-principle and are clearly related to avant-garde thought in this respect. They either present a causally

Probably the best known examples of such an open or "non-organic" structure are to be found in the "epic" work associated with Brecht and Döblin.[36] With both of these writers a central goal of the epic is to problematize the status of the traditional organic structure: firstly by defusing the dramatic tension produced by the convention of a tight linear organization and secondly by loosening the sense of causality that in the organic work gives each aspect of the plot the aura of indispensability.

Both Brecht and Döblin aim to release individual scenes and images from their subordination to the organic whole. Brecht for example believes that, "in contrast to classical drama the structure of the epic should allow one to cut it into separate pieces which nevertheless remain individually viable."[37] Similarly Döblin remarks that, "If a novel cannot be cut up like a worm into ten pieces so that each bit moves independently, then it is no good."[38] In the case of Döblin the conception of the "epic" as an accumulative or aggregate form problematizes plot and suppresses dramatic tension, producing instead a more "difficult" structure that demands of the audience a more considered and reflective approach towards each individual component of the text, rather than the kind of reading that treats each segment merely as the subsidiary means to an ending.

To the extent that this epic structure makes the avant-garde work less accessible, it appears to be linked with one of the most pronounced features of modernism, namely its alleged "elitism,"

unconnected group of scenes representing the various stations passed through by the protagonist on the path towards a vaguely defined state of enlightenment, or juxtapose a series of scenarios each of which dramatizes one aspect of the central figure's experience and defining relationship with others.

[36] Brecht's close relations with expressionism early on in his career are fruitfully explored in Walter Sokel's "Brecht und der Expressionismus," *Die sogenannten zwanziger Jahre*, ed. R. Grimm and J. Hermand (Bad Homburg: Gehlen Verlag, 1970), 47–74. On the relationship between the work of Brecht and Döblin and the links between their conceptions of the "epic," see Viktor Zmegac's essential article "Alfred Döblins Poetik des Romans," *Deutsche Romantheorien*, ed. R. Grimm (Frankfurt: Fischer-Athenäum, 1968), 341–364.

[37] "zur Struktur der Epik gehöre es, daß man sie, im Gegensatz zur (klassischen) Dramatik, gleichsam mit der Schere in einzelne Stücke schneiden könne, die trotzdem lebensfähig bleiben." Brecht, *Schriften zum Theater*, vol. 3 (Frankfurt: Suhrkamp, 1963), 53. See also Viktor Zmegac, "Alfred Döblin's Poetik des Romans," 349.

[38] "Wenn ein Roman nicht wie ein Regenwurm in zehn Stücke geschnitten werden kann und jeder Teil bewegt sich selbst, dann taugt er nichts." Alfred Döblin, "Bemerkungen zum Roman," *Aufsätze zur Literatur*, ed. Walter Muschg (Olten and Freiburg: Walter Verlag, 1963), 21.

most visible in modernism's attempt to define itself as "high culture" and so distance itself from the encroachments of popular culture. Yet in the case of the avant-garde one can also understand this shift away from the more accessible organic structures more readily as the attempt to resist what the Frankfurt School would later call the "culture industry" and the commodification of the work of art without pitching its appeal exclusively towards an elitist or aestheticist reception. Assuming for example that the typical work of mass culture is geared to a more "consumerist" approach – a mode of reception frequently oriented exclusively towards the final outcome of the plot – then the effect is that the rest of the text is merely "consumed" as a means to this end.[39] In the epic work by contrast, this tension is defused in advance, so that the reader or spectator is forced to reflect instead on the individual scenes as they develop. As Döblin explains,

Characters and events in the epic work attract our sympathy in themselves and quite apart from any suspense. They grip us on their own account. In a good epic work individual characters and individual events live a life independently, whereas the novelistic work ["Schriftstellereiroman"] rushes past us with the greatest suspense, yet after a couple of days one can remember nothing and the whole thing was a deception.[40]

Instead of building dramatic tension and subordinating individual scenes and images to the plot in its entirety, the epic promotes the metonymic accumulation or aggregation of scenes and images. As a result each of these may be interpreted in its own right, rather than gaining significance merely to the extent that it contributes to the overall image, or to the text's general sense of closure.

With its montage-like construction the epic thus corresponds both formally and functionally to the avant-garde's demand that art enter into a new relationship with reality, "the sublation of art

[39] Fredric Jameson describes this commodified reading process as oriented towards "an end and a consumption-satisfaction around which the rest of the work is then 'degraded' to the status of sheer means." See "Reification and Utopia in Mass Culture," *Social Text* (Winter 1979): 132.

[40] "Figuren und Vorgänge des epischen Werks erwecken an sich und außerhalb jeder Spannung unsere innere Teilnahme. Sie fesseln an sich. Im guten epischen Werk haben auch die einzelnen Figuren oder einzelnen Vorgänge herausgenommen ihr Leben, während der Schriftstellereiroman vorüberrauscht mit der schärfsten Spannung, und man kann sich nach ein paar Tagen auf nichts besinnen und das Ganze war ein Betrug." Döblin, "Bemerkungen zum Roman," *Aufsätze zur Literatur*, 96.

and life." For whereas organic work tends to subordinate its individual components and to seal them into its closed referential structure, the non-organic text – and in particular the epic work – opens them up and confronts them directly and individually with the real.[41] This is significant both for the aesthetics of representation and for the ontology of the work of art. It means that the representation of the real undergoes a radical change, since the new, discontinuous mode of depiction is no longer in danger of transmitting automatically – through its very form – a sense of reality's immovable solidity or of the unchangeable quality of "nature." At the same time the previously sacrosanct space of the work of art is now transgressed more frequently in the avant-garde as unreconstructed fragments of the real find their way directly into the body of the non-organic text. Consequently, as Bürger says, "the work no longer seals itself off from (the world)" but is brought into closer proximity with reality, relating to the social context with a new immediacy (91–92).

## The avant-garde poetics of negation and meaninglessness

This mutual interpenetration of art and reality occurs in other areas besides the montage. According to Bürger, one of the most extreme realizations of this principle of sublation occurs in the "objet trouvé" or real-life object, and he cites the example of Marcel Duchamp's "fountain," a urinal which the artist signed and presented to museums as an ironic work of art (51–52). Like the montage, the avant-garde's "ready-mades" and other related forms (such as the Surrealists' "automatic writing" and their mechanical "recipes" for creating literary texts) function according to a poetics of negation and meaninglessness.

These "meaningless" objects confront the conventions and expectations pertaining to the institution of art in a variety of ways. Firstly, they brazenly contradict the principle that the "work" should be an original and inspired creation, crafted in its entirety by the genius of the artist. Secondly, in frustrating expectations and conventions they shift attention away from the search for the work's self-contained meaning. Thus whereas the enigmatic texts of modernism tend, according to Terry Eagleton, to promote this

[41] Bürger, *Theory of the Avant-Garde*, 91–92.

autotelic and self-absorbed attitude to meaning,[42] the avant-garde redirects the search towards the external, "institutional" criteria by which meaning is created within the "sub-system" of art.

Examples of the kind of institutional conditions targeted by the avant-garde include the conventions of the artistic context (for example, the fact that the work is exhibited in a museum may lead automatically to its being pre-defined as a "work of art," and so viewed correspondingly); the notion of authenticity and original-ity (customarily indicated by the signature of the artist); and the "Werkbegriff" (the concept of the "work" as a definable entity or frameable "thing" with a definite set of limits – as opposed to an avant-garde event or abstract "happening").

As with the avant-garde's use of montage, its poetics of nega-tion aims to question and ultimately to realign the relationship between art and life. By reducing art to its minimal conditions the avant-garde succeeds in pointing up the limits of art, as well as indicating those factors not intrinsic to the work itself – the social and ideological context.[43] The avant-garde's interrogation of the institutional definition and function of art reveals the pervasive influence of the institution upon the work's reception, upon its meaning and upon its production. And in revealing the arbitrari-ness of both of these institutionally imposed definitions and of the generally accepted aesthetic values, the avant-garde points to the institution's tendency to legitimize only *certain* meanings, truths and codes to the exclusion of other possible values: in short the avant-garde demonstrates the institution's use of convention to privilege a particular set of dominant social discourses.[44]

The apparent "meaninglessness" of art-objects such as Duchamp's "fountain" is linked to the similarly enigmatic quality of the montage (which also frequently lacks any obvious "inten-tion" or explicit unifying meaning as a mode of joining its individ-ual components). Clearly the goal of such meaninglessness is to negate *specific* expectations and so reveal the presence of the

[42] See Terry Eagleton, "Capitalism, Modernism and Postmodernism," *New Left Review* 152 (1985), 60–79.

[43] This play with the institutionally-produced limits and conventions of art has the effect not only of critiquing but also of *expanding* the prevailing concept of art. Arguably, Duchamp's avant-garde principle of the "ready-made" has long since been recuperated by the institution of art and has become one of its staples – as in Warhol's work.

[44] The concept of the "dominant social discourse" will be explored in detail in chapter 3.

institution of art as its hidden context and as the pre-condition for its unsettling effect.[45] These avant-garde forms are consequently revealed to be entirely meaningful at another level, namely at the meta-aesthetic level, where art practices self-criticism and reflects upon the conditions of its own possibility.

Bürger suggests that with the *objet trouvé* and other "meaning-less" works, it is the act of provocation itself which takes the place of the "work." If this is so then this displacement of conventional signification can have any impact only on the basis of all of those unspoken criteria that the work's meaninglessness calls up and negates, but which it nevertheless continues to depend upon for its effect. Through this shift, the avant-garde enforces a major reorientation in the interpretational approaches towards its art. For whereas in the organic work individual components harmon-ize with the whole, in the case of the montage or non-organic work the contradiction or disjuncture between parts not only provokes the impression of "meaninglessness" but frequently introduces ambiguity and – in some of the instances I will examine in later chapters – epistemological doubt. This uncertainty calls for a corresponding shift in interpretative strategies. For instead of attempting to discover the meaning from the interrelation of the parts and the whole, according to Bürger the interpreter will suspend this search and concentrate instead upon the constitution of the work and the principles of construction underlying it: interpretation shifts to the meta-aesthetic or meta-interpretational level.[46]

Again we can extend Bürger's argument here by observing that where the contradictions in the work take the form of a series of conflicting perspectives or levels of narration (as we shall see in chapter 6 on the expressionist film *The Cabinet of Dr. Caligari*), the recipient will frequently find it difficult to continue to believe in the possibility of a single, unambiguous and "intended" meaning arising out of the whole, and will turn his or her attention away from the search for such a meaning and instead take up as the new theme the problem of interpretation, or of epistemological uncer-tainty, or of the production of meaning itself. In other cases, the

[45] Frank Kermode makes the point that a certain intentionality is always present, and that even Duchamp obviously did not simply pick up any object arbitrarily and sign it. See "The Modern," *Modern Essays* (London: Routledge, 1971), 57–58.
[46] Bürger, *Theory of the avant-garde*, 81.

process of interpreting the non-organic work will tend to displace its focus onto the fact of the work's decentering, onto its denial of meaning and its sabotaging of the conventional means of producing such meaning. Interpretation will be forced to take a step back, and rather than merely searching for a traditional "implied" or "hidden" meaning – a "figure in the carpet" – it will also consider the conventions by which meaning is produced in general and the ways in which the avant-garde work subverts them.[47]

## Revisions of Bürger's theory

### Aesthetic autonomy in modernism and the avant-garde

Where Bürger discusses the avant-garde's dismantling of the concept of the "work" and its creation instead of a poetics of shock, provocation and meaninglessness a key problem of the *Theory of the Avant-Garde* comes into focus, which is of central importance for any discussion of expressionism. This is the avant-garde's central principle of undermining aesthetic autonomy and

---

[47] In important respects this shift already occurs for example in many of Kafka's texts of the expressionist period, where the theme becomes the interpretation itself and the impossibility of discovering stable meanings in a world in which the conventional guides to interpretation have been called into question. In Kafka's work this occurs through a very specific form of ambiguity: through the contradiction between different possible perspectives on the real; through the clash between the "inhabited worlds" corresponding to them (for example, those very different realities inhabited by the father and son in "The Judgement"); or through the conflict between juxtaposed orders of reality (such as the interpenetration of the real and the fantastic in *The Metamorphosis* discussed in chapter 5). The resulting "meaninglessness" parallels the effects of shock and provocation described by Bürger as ensuing from the violation of institutional conventions by the avant-garde's strategies of discontinuity. With Kafka however, it is a most carefully delineated form of meaninglessness that is constructed, one which cries out to be interpreted. For those indeterminacies and "semantic vacuums" occupying the center of Kafka's texts (for example, the meaning of the "trial," of the "judgement" or of the peculiar "metamorphosis") are at the same time polysemous symbolic constructions, created in such a way that they appear to articulate and organize a vast number and variety of unspecified anxieties in the minds of Kafka's readers and hence to invite a multitude of interpretations. It is precisely on account of the personal character of the response they call forth that they tend also to encourage a particular kind of interpretation and analysis which almost invariably wants to bring about a final and absolute resolution of the problems and thus a resolution of the anxieties these semantic constructions appear to formulate. Yet it is the text's simultaneous undercutting of any such harmonious illusion of interpretational closure and its resolute refusal to sanction any such hermeneutical consolations which clearly places Kafka's work in close proximity to the avant-garde, and to its characteristic projection of epistemological uncertainty.

reintegrating art and reality ("das Prinzip der Aufhebung der Kunst in der Lebenspraxis," 69). One commentator, Richard Wolin, has complained that Bürger's use of the latter concept "remains precipitate and overly simplistic" and it is true that its use is indeed surrounded by ambiguities throughout the book.[48]

For example, if we understand this principle of sublation in its most obvious sense, namely as the attempt to instrumentalize art for social and revolutionary causes, it would fail to distinguish the "historical" avant-garde from previous avant-gardes as well as from other forms of "engagement" in art. Not surprisingly, Bürger himself is clearly against such a connotation of the term.[49] Yet if alternatively this central tenet is to be understood in the way Bürger suggests, namely to indicate art's function as an important free space in which reality and social practice may be theorized and reconceptualized,[50] then, as we shall see later, the avant-garde would appear merely to be sharing a critical function common to many different forms and movements throughout the history of art, a function in other words which is certainly not the prerogative of the historical avant-garde.

This brings us to the blind spot at the heart of Bürger's model, namely his fundamental ambiguity with regard to the category of aesthetic autonomy. For surely the possibility of reconceptualizing social practice is itself predicated upon the privilege of attaining a certain independence from the real (rather than being merged with it) and upon a sense of *critical distance* from the object to be criticized. In other words, the possibility for criticism and social change appears to be predicated upon precisely that aesthetic autonomy which the avant-garde according to Bürger is supposed to overcome. It is as a result of Bürger's ambiguity in this regard that his treatment of the avant-garde's central principle, its goal of "overcoming art in the realm of life-praxis," remains rather vague. Bürger is well aware of the duplicity or double-edged quality that is associated with aesthetic autonomy, and he himself points out that "the detachment of art as a special

---

[48] Richard Wolin, "Modernism vs. Postmodernism," *Telos* 62 (1984–85): 14.

[49] For as Bürger himself says, "[w]hen the avantgardists demand that art become practical again, they do not mean that the contents of works of art should be socially significant." *Theory of the Avant-Garde*, 49.

[50] See the quotation discussed below: "An art no longer distinct from the praxis of life but wholly absorbed in it will lose the capacity to criticize it, along with its distance." See Bürger, *Theory of the Avant-Garde*, 50.

sphere of human activity from the nexus of the praxis of life" (36), that is, the differentiation of art as a seemingly autonomous sub-system, not only has a positive effect, namely the development of "art's independence from society" (35), but also contributes towards the dangerous illusion that art is in some manner both free from determination by social and historical forces while also remaining free from social responsibility. Nevertheless, despite his awareness of the contradiction, it is this ambiguity which undermines his central thesis that the avant-garde intended to destroy art's autonomous status and reintegrate it with life. For as Bürger himself concedes, in as far as aesthetic autonomy shares that ambivalent status linked with affirmative culture, namely the function of both promoting criticism and hindering its implementation, this avant-garde attack on autonomy remains a "profoundly contradictory endeavor. For the (relative) freedom of art vis à vis the praxis of life is at the same time the condition that must be fulfilled if there is to be a critical cognition of reality. And art no longer distinct from the praxis of life but wholly absorbed in it will lose the capacity to criticize, along with its distance" (50). One should consider too the various failures resulting from the abandonment of autonomy, such as the false reconciliations of art and life exemplified by the "aestheticized politics" of fascism, by Soviet and socialist realism, by the culture industry and by the aesthetics of consumerism ("Warenästhetik"). In this light the advantages offered by autonomy (in terms of providing art with a degree of independence and critical distance) seem to outweigh the disadvantages. Having based his theory then on the idea that the historical avant-garde sets out to criticize aesthetic autonomy Bürger himself then ends up questioning "whether a sublation of the autonomy-status can be desirable at all, whether the distance between art and the practice of life is not requisite for that free space within which alternatives to what exists become conceivable" (54).

Bürger's own ambiguity in attempting to distinguish the avant-garde's position on autonomy is thus the central weakness that affects the main concepts throughout his analysis. The vagueness of some of his explanations of the central avant-garde tenet concerning art's sublation with life stems precisely from this unresolved problem. At another level however Bürger's theoretical ambiguity here is itself significant since it directly reflects a similar contradiction within the avant-garde. For where Bürger would maintain that the failure of the avant-garde lies in its vain attempt to integrate art and life, it seems clear that the reason for this failure lies at a prior stage: within the avant-garde there is an ongoing and unresolved negotiation between the desire to create a new form of art with a direct bearing upon life, and the need to retain for art a degree of autonomy in order to preserve a distance to reality and thus a vantage point from which art might formulate its social critique. Clearly Bürger's model stands in need of a substantial revision on this point.

Before outlining the direction such a revision might take however, there is a further difficulty to be taken into account with regard to this same question of autonomy. Bürger maintains that "the separation of art from the praxis of life becomes the decisive characteristic of the autonomy of *bourgeois* art" (49, my emphasis). But if, as Adorno pointed out, a truly oppositional aesthetics can exist only where art is autonomous and "an entity unto itself," then aesthetic autonomy also becomes the last guarantee that art's critical capacity is safe from recuperation by bourgeois society. As a result Adorno sees art's separation from life-praxis in a much more positive light, for it means that "rather than obeying existing social norms and thus proving itself to be 'socially useful' – art criticizes society just by being there."[51] Consequently aesthetic autonomy appears to be just as crucial as a precondition of critical distance for the avant-garde as it is for the heirs to the tradition of *l'art pour l'art* in modernism. And in as far as Bürger is forced to concede that the avant-garde like modernism also relies on a degree of aesthetic autonomy, his definition of the avant-garde – in this respect, at least – must then admit an overlap with modernism.

This is not to say that there are not important differences between modernism and the avant-garde with regard to the question of aesthetic autonomy, and I will presently examine an important category for distinguishing the two. For the moment, however, one should note one simple distinguishing feature: unlike the avant-garde, modernism tends to embrace aesthetic autonomy. Consequently in modernism – as in aestheticism – autonomy frequently takes on a vastly different and questionable character as a goal or value in its own right. For as Terry Eagleton

---

[51] Theodor Adorno, *Aesthetic Theory* (London: Routledge & Kegan Paul, 1984), 321.

argues, "by removing itself from society into its own impermeable space, the modernist work paradoxically reproduces – indeed intensifies – the very illusion of aesthetic autonomy which marks the bourgeois humanist order it also protests against."[52] In modernism aesthetic autonomy – the condition of the progressive work's critical possibilities – is itself made an important term of dominant cultural discourse and becomes instrumental in substantiating affirmative culture.

According to Eagleton's way of thinking autonomy would also have a different value in the modernist work since, as with aestheticism, it typically demonstrates a "chronic failure to engage the real" and becomes instead an end in itself (66). In modernism the emphasis lies on the work as a signifier, rather than as the medium pointing to a referent in the real world. For as Eagleton observes: "Modernist works are after all 'works,' discrete and bounded entities for all the free play within them, which is just what the bourgeois art institution understands" (68). Rather than the real it is thus the modernist text itself which becomes the enigma demanding interpretation: rather than providing a degree of critical distance, in modernism aesthetic autonomy frequently becomes a means of supporting and enhancing this enigmatic status.

Modernism's conservative relationship to autonomy is thus deeply ingrained in the ideological make-up of its works in a variety of ways. The modernist work is wary firstly of that sense of ideological commitment characteristic of the avant-garde, since instrumentalization by a political cause or annexation by any particular interpretation of reality or "Weltbild" would risk encroaching upon its ambiguity and limiting its semantic horizons. For modernism political solutions appear merely to be part of the problem rather than part of the cure.[53] Instead, it clings to various autotelic forms of aesthetic autonomy and hermeticism in order to resist any kind of co-option which would limit the work's meaning. As a result it frequently becomes a bastion of high-culture: elitist, arcane and inaccessible.

Secondly, modernism becomes particularly protective of its

---

[52] Eagleton, "Capitalism, Modernism and Postmodernism," 68.
[53] In this respect postmodernism's adoption of a similar skepticism regarding the political realm is a throwback to modernism's general wariness of direct ideological allegiances and concrete political strategies.

autonomous status because it is constantly obliged to resist the encroachments of mass culture.[54] Its forms may be inaccessible and elitist, but in separating itself off with a self-enclosed, enigmatic meaning which invites but resists decipherment, it not only excludes itself from the historical world, but more importantly, it resists commodification. Thus, according to Eagleton, it "forestalls [that] instant consumability" associated with the products of the culture industry which develops rapidly throughout modernity and which poses a direct threat to modernist "high" culture (67).

In this respect modernism's relationship to autonomy, unlike that of the avant-garde, becomes a defining feature which keeps even its more progressive tendencies squarely within the sphere of affirmative culture. For example, its search for innovation and technical perfection, and its attempt to refine art to its very essence becomes such a self-sufficient and entirely self-absorbing aesthetic practice that it always risks devolving merely into a formal correlative of bourgeois society's myth of progress. Similarly modernism's formal revolts seem to suggest a sanitized revolution, often lacking that sense – central to the avant-garde by contrast – that behind the struggle in the secluded realm of the aesthetic lies the much more important goal: the struggle for a fundamental transformation in society.

## "De-aestheticized autonomous art"

From this discussion it is clear that although modernism and the avant-garde appear to overlap in sharing a reliance on aesthetic autonomy, they differ in one major respect, namely the ideology-

---

[54] Fredric Jameson has described the genesis of modernism in relation to mass culture in his article "Reification and Utopia in Mass Culture." Similarly Andreas Huyssen's central thesis in his book *After the Great Divide* is that whereas modernism with its "anxiety of contamination" always "insisted on the inherent hostility between high and low [culture]," the avant-garde aimed at developing an alternative relationship between the two. Although it is clear that the avant-garde did indeed support a vastly expanded concept of art, which would also embrace many mass-cultural forms, it must also be said that this by no means implies that the historical avant-garde was willing to embrace mass culture "tout court," including the commodified forms, and the affirmative and legitimizing functions of the culture industry within society. In contrast to Huyssen, I would maintain that it is this awareness of the social and institutional functioning of art that always defines the cultural politics of the avant-garde, even to the exclusion, in many cases, of its recourse to mass culture. See *After the Great Divide*, viii.

critical uses to which they put autonomy. For the central principle which divides the avant-garde from modernism is its concern always for the "way art functions *in society*, a process that does as much to determine the effects that works have as does the particular content."[55] In other words what distinguishes the avant-garde is always its awareness of the social and institutional constraints which influence the form and content of the work of art, and which limit its possible effects.

It is this crucial component which Benjamin points to so forcefully in his essay on "The Author as Producer" where, as we have seen, he places the emphasis not so much on the work's political orientation – for "political tendency alone is not sufficient"[56] – as firstly on the author's awareness of the apparatus and conditions of artistic production, and secondly on the need for an appropriate formal response or "Technik" taking this situation into account. For even where the avant-garde shares with modernism the benefits of autonomy, it always distinguishes itself in precisely this aspect: it takes up a certain critical distance in order to see through the duplicities and hidden social functions of affirmative culture, and in order to articulate an awareness of the social and historical conditions of art.

Since both modernism and, to a large extent, the avant-garde share a dependency upon aesthetic autonomy, Richard Wolin has proposed a new formulation in order to make this crucial distinction explicit. He suggests that Bürger's "theoretical framework would be in need of a [further] term: de-aestheticized autonomous art." This category would refer to those movements such as surrealism (and, I would maintain, expressionism too) which have "simultaneously negated the aura of affirmation, characteristic of art for art's sake, while remaining consistent with the 'modern' requirement of aesthetic autonomy." The category of "de-aestheticized autonomous art" describes that essential characteristic of avant-garde art through which it "self-consciously divests itself of the beautiful illusion, the aura of reconciliation, projected by art for art's sake, while at the same time refusing to overstep the boundaries of aesthetic autonomy, beyond which art degenerates to the status of merely a 'thing among things'."[57]

---

55 Bürger, *Theory of the Avant-Garde*, 49. My emphasis.
56 "[D]ie Tendenz allein tut es nicht." Benjamin, "Der Autor," 696.
57 Richard Wolin, "Modernism vs. Postmodernism," *Telos* 62 (1984–85), 16.

Wolin's term "de-aestheticized autonomous art" describes the way in which the avant-garde articulates its self-criticism of art: it sets out not only to disrupt aesthetic convention but – acknowledging the balance between "Tendenz" and "Technik" – also to dismantle any lingering consolations of "aestheticized" form. Yet in doing so it nevertheless retains its critical distance within the sphere of aesthetic autonomy.[58]

Peter Uwe Hohendahl has proposed a similar revision of Bürger's model which explains in more detail the rationale for this retention of the category of aesthetic autonomy. He observes that we need "to reexamine the theory of the avant-garde by de-emphasizing the negation of aesthetic autonomy and stressing the ideologically charged continuation of this problematical category."[59] With Wolin he shares the view then that the category of autonomy in itself need not be inconsistent with the aims of the avant-garde. However, he cautions that autonomy must first be freed from its traditionally "affirmative" functions which mask real social contradictions by aestheticizing or sublimating them. In this way, rather than becoming a goal in its own right (as in the more autotelic and hermetic movements, such as aestheticism and, as we have seen, modernism) and rather than providing an aesthetic refuge, this "ideologically charged" notion of autonomy gives art the distance to society necessary to produce its critical and ideological force while its "de-aestheticizing" edge ensures that art does not merely degenerate into affirmative culture or another version of "aestheticized politics."

## From the sublime to the historical avant-garde: the cynical sublation of art and life

This issue of "de-aestheticized" art points to a crucial distinction between two central and defining conceptions of the avant-garde.

---

[58] In a commentary on Marcuse's theories of art and revolution, Jürgen Habermas largely prefigures Richard Wolin's modification of the theory of the avant-garde. He describes a variety of progressive and experimental artistic strategies in terms of a "de-aestheticization of art" (349). These cultural-revolutionary activities have the goal of a "removing of the differences" ("Entdifferenzierung") between art and life (349). See Habermas, "Herbert Marcuse über Kunst und Revolution," *Kultur und Kritik. Verstreute Aufsätze* (Frankfurt: Suhrkamp, 1973), 345–351.

[59] Peter Uwe Hohendahl, "The Loss of Reality: Gottfried Benn's Early Prose," *Modernity and the Text*, 92.

For if as Bürger maintains, all avant-garde art intends in some manner to bring together art and life, or at least to coordinate artistic and social progress,[60] then I would propose that two major options present themselves. Art may serve as an *ideal* model for life: it can offer a prototype of harmony and order, a utopian pattern for the way in which the chaotic, violent or tragic aspects of life may be "mastered" by the form of the work of art, so that in this way the mundane world is "sublimated" or raised up to the sublime and ideal level of the aesthetic sphere. This is the goal characterizing the "idealist" wing of the avant-garde. Alternatively art and life can be brought together by a shift in the *opposite* direction: by what I would call a "cynical" sublation of art and life bringing art down to the banal level of reality, fragmenting artistic form, dismantling the syntax of poetic language and destroying any lingering sense of aesthetic harmony and of organic structuring, so that the work of art leaves the realm of ideal and harmonious forms, and descends to the disjointed world of modernity. And I would suggest that it is this that characterizes the "historical" avant-garde.[61]

Richard Wolin does not offer any concrete examples of what his "de-aestheticized" avant-garde art would look like. Yet this "cynical" sublation of art and life, as a strategy of "desublimation," of bringing art down from the sublime to the mundane, responds to a set of concerns similar to those that Wolin's concept is intended to counter: the danger involved in creating utopian works which end up producing a self-sufficient form of aesthetic autonomy issuing in further works of "affirmative culture." The notion of "desublimation," as Marcuse describes it for example, involves creating a form of "anti-art" which aims firstly at "undoing the aesthetic form" that is, "the total of qualities (harmony, rhythm, contrast) which make an oeuvre a self-contained whole . . ."[62] In other

---

[60] Edgar Lohner describes this goal as the "Gleichsetzung von politischem und künstlerischem Fortschritt." See his article, "Die Problematik des Begriffes der Avantgarde," *Literarische Avantgarden*,, ed. Manfred Hardt (Darmstadt: Wissenschaftliche Buchgesellschaft, 1989), 116.

[61] My description of the opposition between the "idealist" and the "historical" avant-garde is indebted to two pathbreaking articles: Edgar Lohner, "Die Problematik des Begriffes der Avantgarde," and Manfred Hardt, "Zu Begriff, Geschichte und Theorie der literarischen Avantgarde," both reprinted in the excellent collection *Literarische Avantgarden*, ed. Manfred Hardt (Darmstadt: Wissenschaftliche Buchgesellschaft, 1989), 113–127, 145–71.

[62] Herbert Marcuse, *Counterrevolution and Revolt* (Boston: Beacon, 1972), 81.

words, it involves overcoming precisely that illusionistic quality of harmony and order which is always present in the very form of the conventional organic work of art, and even in previous idealist versions of the avant-garde. Secondly, desublimated art involves reappropriating those sublime images and concepts of Western culture whose critical potential has been neutralized as cliché in affirmative culture and then re-writing them in such a way that their radical sense can resurface.[63]

## The "Romantic avant-garde" and the "Aktivisten"

In order to appreciate the way in which the tension between these two diametrically opposed conceptions of the avant-garde continues to define the expressionists' understanding of progressive art we must look briefly at the history of the term.

The earliest use of the term "avant-garde" as applied to a progressive artistic group occurs around 1825, toward the later phase of the European Romantic movements, and is associated with the followers of the proto-socialists Saint-Simon and Fourier.[64] The Saint-Simonist Olinde Rodrigues, for example, expressly calls upon artists "to serve as an avant-garde" for social change and for a "glorious future," arguing that it is above all art, with its unique qualities, that has the power through "fantasy and emotion" to affect its audience most directly, vitally and decisively. It is art which "supports reason" and produces in humankind both those sensations conducive to "noble thoughts"[65] as well as the energy needed to change the direction of society for the good of all.[66]

---

[63] One should note that Marcuse is also sceptical regarding the prospects for "anti-art." He fears that in undermining artistic form, the new works will simultaneously destroy the very basis for art's effect. See Herbert Marcuse, *An Essay on Liberation* (Boston: Beacon, 1969), 34–35.

[64] On the early history of the avant-garde, see D. D. Egbert, *Social Radicalism and the Arts* (New York: Knopf, 1970); also Matei Calinescu, *Faces of Modernity: Avant-Garde, Decadence, Kitsch* (1977: Bloomington: Indiana University Press, 1987), 100–104.

[65] See Olinde Rodrigues "L'artiste, le savant et l'industriel," *Oeuvres de Saint-Simon et d'Enfantin* (Aalen: Otto Zeller, 1964), 207–213.

[66] This "avant-gardist" conviction is shared, for example, by many of the progressive English writers of the Romantic period, who similarly hold the belief that the central social goal of poetry is less the propagation of concrete political goals or social policies, than the more general ideal of a moral and spiritual "elevation" through art. With Wordsworth, for example, the work of art is to

Both the early progressive social movements of the first half of the nineteenth century and many of the Romantic writers clearly share the same concern both to purify the individual's sensations and refine his or her processing of experience by looking towards art and the instructive example of the aesthetic sphere.[67] Artistic and social practice are thus coordinated to the extent that art is to serve life both as the repository of eternal virtues and as the guide and the model of experience, thereby elevating mundane reality to the sublime level of art while preserving its own distance as a transcendent and autonomous realm. Where art takes on this leadership function, the image of the artist too begins to change and comes to be linked to that of the seer or priest.[68] Indeed, the role of art is viewed by many as so important, and the elite character of the artistic avant-garde becomes so pronounced that in some instances its original goals of meliorism and the stimulation of a social conscience are abandoned in favor of more self-seeking forms of art, such as aestheticism and *l'art pour l'art*.[69]

generate those civilizing and enlightening emotions which bind people together, strengthening and purifying the affections and so enlarging the individual's capacity to resist early modernity's negative effects – most notably those of alienation – which occur with the "increasing accumulation of men in cities" and the "uniformity of occupations." (See Wordsworth, "Observations Prefixed to the Second Edition," *Lyrical Ballads*). Shelley echoes this humanitarianism and "passion for reforming the world." He maintains that his "purpose has hitherto been simply to familiarise the highly refined imagination of the more select classes of poetical readers with beautiful idealisms of moral excellence . . ." However, the goal of "refining" the human imagination through art's "idealisms" should not mean dedicating "poetical compositions solely to the direct enforcement of reform . . ." For Shelley also stoutly defends aesthetic autonomy and attempts to relieve art both of the danger of political or pedagogical instrumentalization ("Didactic poetry is my abhorrence"), and of entanglement within concrete historical situations and material circumstances: "For my part I had rather be damned with Plato and Lord Bacon than go to heaven with Paley and Malthus." See Shelley, "Preface to Prometheus Unbound," *Shelley's Poetry and Prose*, ed. D. Reiman and S. Powers (New York: Norton, 1977), 135. This autonomy ensures that art's crucial separation from everyday reality and its elevation to autonomous status also turns it into a transcendent repository of moral and spiritual values: "A Poet participates in the eternal, the infinite, and the one" rather than in "time and place and number." See Shelley, "A Defence of Poetry," *Shelley's Poetry and Prose*, 483.

[67] D. D. Egbert describes the relationship between these two early avant-garde movements in his history *Social Radicalism and the Arts*.

[68] See D. D. Egbert, "The Idea of 'Avant-Garde' in Art and Politics," *Literarische Avantgarden*, ed. Manfred Hardt (Darmstadt: Wissenschaftliche Buchgesellschaft, 1989), 49; also Calinescu, *Faces of Modernity*, 105.

[69] On this point see D. D. Egbert "The Idea of 'Avant-Garde' in Art and Politics," 50. This fundamental historical link between aestheticism and the avant-garde provides an interesting alternative viewpoint to that offered by Bürger on the

Now if the "idealist" avant-garde of the early nineteenth century is characterized by the goal of reducing the distance between art and life, and by the elevation of the worldly to the ideal sphere of art, I would maintain, in contrast to Bürger, that the historical avant-garde of the early twentieth century is defined precisely by its attack on this previously progressive function of sublimation and by its attempt to reverse the direction by which art and life are brought together. For, as we saw earlier in this chapter, although idealist art has the critical function of preserving in the aesthetic sphere those ideals which have not been realized in life, as Marcuse notes, such sublimated art also constitutes a form of "affirmative culture" which simultaneously postpones their fulfillment, since it offers on an aesthetic level a false reconciliation of real contradictions and conflicts, in other words, a purely illusory or "aesthetic" satisfaction of real needs.

Consequently far from "sublimating" or idealizing life through art, the historical avant-garde's attempt to reconcile art and life takes the opposite tack, as we have seen. It responds to the idealizing conventions of artistic form, and in particular to previous utopian versions of the avant-garde, by desublimating art and bringing it sharply down to earth, to the level of the banal and the everyday. It responds by destroying art's beautifying structures, and with them the illusory sense of mastery and closure that artistic form can bring. By rummaging through the debris of modernity for its new forms, and by seeking out the marginalized, the grotesque, the deformed and the discarded, the avant-garde creates instead a program of de-aestheticization. Through its de-aestheticized forms it produces a new aesthetics (or "anti-aesthetics") of the ugly, the fragmentary and the chaotic in order to subvert precisely this illusory sense of mastery,

---

question of aestheticism's role in the genesis of the historical avant-garde. It allows us to reassess a similar contradiction among many expressionists concerning their leadership role in society. For their self-appointed position as the intellectual and cultural leaders of the public is frequently colored by an odd mixture of concern for the spiritual welfare of their fellow man and disgust for his bourgeois philistinism. Rudolf Leonhard owns up to this ambivalence, saying that the poet has "despite his love for humanity in general a good degree of contempt for each individual among the masses . . . " ("bei aller etwaiger Liebe zum allgemeinen Menschen ein gut Teil Verachtung gegen jeden einzelnen aus der Masse . . . "). See Rudolf Leonhard, "Die Politik der Dichter," *Die weißen Blätter*, 2 (1915), Heft 6 (June): 814–816. Rpt. *Manifeste und Dokumente*, 364.

artificial closure and aesthetic control which clings to the traditional, organic notion of form, and not least to those sublimating
forms employed by the idealist avant-garde.

Expressionism is clearly caught between these diametrically
opposed conceptions of the avant-garde. Indeed, one of the diffi-
culties for the literary historian in attempting to define the expressionist movement derives precisely from the fact that its various
groupings frequently follow completely contradictory notions of
what constitutes "progressive" art. Consequently in many of their
manifestos and theoretical statements the expressionists are primarily engaged in the attempt to sort out these major differences
in their approach towards oppositional forms of aesthetic discourse.[70]

The "activists" for example (writers such as Hiller, Rubiner,
Pinthus, Wolfenstein and Heinrich Mann) tended to take their
lead from the older, Romantic-utopian and socially engaged versions of avant-garde art. The activists were characterized by a
"fervid revolutionary optimism"[71] and by the strong conviction
that art needed to become an instrument of social meliorism.[72]
Although they refused to adopt specific dogmas and orthodoxies,
they did hold certain progressive, cherished values in common
with some of the early utopian avant-gardes, such as a belief in
fraternity (conceiving of themselves as "comrades of humanity")
and in a "community of the spirit," while at the same time
privileging a form of benevolent dictatorship by an intellectual
and cultural elite that was to be "a leadership by the best."[73] This
particular role for the writer was the one which Ludwig Rubiner
famously endorsed in his polemic "The Writer Engages in Politics": "The writer's effect is a thousand times more powerful than
that of the politician . . . The writer is the only one who possesses
that which really shakes us: intensity . . . He speaks of the catas-

---

[70] For an interesting description of the various attitudes of the expressionists
towards the relationship between art and society, see Augustinus Dierick,
*German Expressionist Prose* (Toronto: University of Toronto Press, 1987),
74–93.
[71] See H. Maclean, "Expressionism," *Periods in German Literature,* ed. J. M. Richie
(London: Wolff, 1966), 264.
[72] See Wolfgang Paulsen, *Expressionismus und Aktivismus. Eine typologische Untersuchung* (Bern und Leipzig: Gotthelf, 1935), 14.
[73] "Führung durch die Besten". See the manifesto of the "Council of Spiritual
Workers" ["Rat geistiger Arbeiter"] *Die Weltbühne* 14 (November 21, 1918), no.
47. Rpt. *Manifeste und Dokumente* 291.

trophes that he has taught us to see."[74] As with the utopianists of the early nineteenth century this leadership was to be spearheaded by the visionary poet, as the foremost representative of the category of the so-called "spiritual type" ("geistigen Typus").[75]

Similarly indicative of the close connection between the activists' thought and the early avant-garde's idealist aesthetics of sublimation is the activists' utopian belief in their cultural politics as a means of reconciling society. The omnipresence of the activists' central watchword "Geist" (spirit, mind) is symptomatic of this attitude. For this mystical force was seen by the activists as having the power to achieve exactly what their avant-garde predecessors had hoped for with their progressive cultural project: the power to purify ("läutern") individuals, harmonize society, and so raise reality up to the level of sublime perfection.[76]

On the other side of the expressionist movement to the activists are those who completely reject this utopian mode of thought and who, instead of raising up society to the level of art, pursue an iconoclastic poetics of "cynical sublation": deformation, de-aestheticization and desublimation with the goal of moving art down into realms it had not previously occupied. These are the expressionists whom I describe as the "expressionist avant-garde" throughout this book, and in the chapters that follow I want to explore in particular their creation of various oppositional discourses aimed at the disruption of convention, of form, of mimesis and of representational stability in general.

The expressionist avant-garde's various modes of de-aestheticization preempt any sense in which poetic form might serve as an illusory consolation at the level of the aesthetic for that which is missing in the real. Clearly with this form of avant-garde practice,

---

74 "Der Dichter wirkt tausendmal stärker als der Politiker . . . Der Dichter ist der einzige, der hat, was uns erschüttert, Intensität . . . Er spreche von den Katastrophen, die er zu sehen uns gelehrt hat." Ludwig Rubiner "Der Dichter Greift in die Politik" *Die Aktion* 21, 22 (May, 1912): 713–714.

75 See *Der Aktivismus*, ed. Wolfgang Rothe (Munich: DTV, 1969), 13.

76 An example of this progressive vision of art – and of the role of "Geist" within it – may be seen in Heinrich Mann's famous polemic "Geist und Tat" ("Spirit and Action"). Here he regrets that, unlike the French who looked to art for the goals and ideals which supported their revolution, the Germans are "not gifted with enough imagination to pattern life according to the spirit" ("nicht bildnerisch genug begabt, um durchaus das Leben formen zu müssen nach dem Geist"). *Manifeste und Dokumente*, 269, 271.

there can be no flight for the reader of expressionism into forgetful admiration of the poets' formal techniques – Benjamin's fear in his "Producer"-essay – at the expense of acknowledging the critical thrust of their explicit and shocking content.[77]

Although not a "revolutionary" art in the political and pragmatic sense of the term, by re-writing the dominant discursive constructions of the real in a de-aestheticized or desublimated form, the expressionist avant-garde brings about what Marcuse calls a "revolution in perception."[78] In other words it uses the cognitive power of art to defamiliarize a very specific set of institutional conventions: those modes of seeing that have been canonized by the power of dominant social discourse and the pervasive institution of art.[79] Thus the program of de-aestheticiz-ation produces an art form whose central function involves questioning both the "affirmative" function of traditional culture, and the inherent, institutionally-conditioned ideological effects associated with it.

The expressionist avant-garde thus goes a long way to fulfilling Hohendahl's demand[80] for an "ideologically-charged continuation of this problematical category (aesthetic autonomy)."[81] It also fulfills the definition of a critical, autonomous form of art outlined by Wolin, since it negates the "aura of affirmation" while

---

[77] Similarly since the "metaphors" the expressionist poets employ are distorted and forced, they can clearly no longer derive their power from the individual "genius" of the artist's metaphorical imagination, nor rest on the intuition – conventionally accessible only to the poet's finer sensibilities – of an ordered cosmos in which part relates to part, just as tenor relates to vehicle (as was still the case, for example, with Baudelaire's "correspondences" or even with Hofmannsthal's "interconnecting world" or "Welt der Bezüge").

[78] Marcuse, *An Essay on Liberation*, 37.

[79] Marcuse's conception of progressive art is similarly constituted in terms of this art's ability to oppose a restrictive or hegemonic ideological formation, such as the dominant social discourses: "The senses must learn not to see things anymore in the medium of that law and order which has formed them; the bad functionalism which organizes our sensibility must be smashed." See Marcuse, *An Essay on Liberation*, 39.

[80] Peter Uwe Hohendahl, "The Loss of Reality: Gottfried Benn's Early Prose," *Modernity and the Text*, 92.

[81] In this respect I would maintain – despite Marcuse's cautions regarding "anti-art" – that although this avant-garde art is destructive with regard to artistic form, it nevertheless remains within the boundaries of his definition of art since its radical or "progressive" effect still depends upon its ability to defamiliarize established aesthetic forms. At the same time this art "insists on its radical autonomy" and so preserves a critical and "ideologically charged" distance to life.

simultaneously remaining largely free of the kind of direct political or pedagogical interventions which would jeopardize its autonomy and its critical capacity for negation. For like the progressive art which Marcuse envisages, this avant-garde is "alien to the revolutionary practice by virtue of the artist's commitment to Form: Form as art's own reality, as *die Sache selbst*."[82] And precisely on account of this commitment it remains an autonomous and yet entirely critical form of oppositional discourse.

These modifications of Bürger's theory not only help to establish expressionism's close relationship to the general thinking behind the avant-garde, they help at the same time to differentiate between the different factions within the expressionist movement. For example the preservation of aesthetic autonomy as a critical and ideologically oriented category rather than as a privileged shelter for art would allow us to distinguish the expressionist avant-garde from those other formations associated with the movement whose progressiveness, as with modernism, lies primarily in their self-sufficient, formal experimentation.

As I will argue later, some of the most challenging expressionist writers are those, such as Döblin, Benn and Kafka, who clearly distance themselves from the bandwagon of "revolutionary" excesses in Expressionism (such as those practiced by the activist, the utopian or the "O Mensch" ["Oh Man"] groups). Like many of their modernist counterparts they scarcely question the necessity for aesthetic autonomy in their individualist search for style. Nevertheless, they are clearly linked primarily to the historical avant-garde rather than to modernism as a whole by their fundamental questioning of the "dominant social discourses," the ideological and epistemological premises of conventional concepts of rationality and subjectivity which the institution of art supports. They are "avant-garde" not only in their interrogation of the way that these conventions support the idea of the "normalcy" of the bourgeois world, but in their creation of a set of "oppositional discourses" intended to overhaul the institutionalized artistic means through which certain values are privileged.

Consequently, it is no coincidence that the expressionist works which have had the most lasting and profound impact come from precisely those writers who avoided nailing their colors directly to

---

[82] Marcuse, *An Essay on Liberation*, 39. Emphasis in original.

the mast of a determinate and historical social program and who avoided associating themselves wholly with a clearly definable *collective* "style" and rhetoric. The writers of the expressionist avant-garde differ for example from those "epigonal" or "naive"[83] expressionists, who merely take up the *spirit* of the "expressionist revolution," but who are not interested in creating the kind of vital and progressive new forms through which their innovative ideological orientation might be conveyed. The latter lack that crucial understanding of the need to balance "Tendenz" and "Technik," in other words, the need to match their progressive social goals with a correspondingly progressive set of formal strategies created with an historical awareness of the social and institutional constraints within which art functions.[84] Lacking this institutional insight they are often content instead simply to reproduce tiredly expressionism's characteristic rhetorical gestures and outward flourishes – and as a result they risk being recuperated by the institution of art, or ending up as forgotten cultural fashion victims.

On the other hand, the expressionist avant-garde differs from those whose commitment was *exclusively* to extra-aesthetic goals (such as the political merging of art and life-praxis) and who consequently suffered from their abandonment of aesthetic autonomy. Their works have consequently taken on that "ephemeral quality," which according to Adorno, is the fate of those works that "merely assimilate themselves sedulously to the brute existence against which they protest" so that "from the very first day they belong to the seminars in which they inevitably end."[85]

---

[83] See Walter Sokel's definition of "naive" or "rhetorical" expressionism in his book *The Writer in Extremis* 18–20.

[84] Against other politically engaged expressionists the "expressionist avant-garde" would then be distinguished from those expressionist writers, whose "commitment" at the level of content (or "Tendenz") is not matched by "Technik" and by a corresponding rejection of the institution of art and its conventions. An example would be the plays of Carl Sternheim, whose radical satires on the conventions of bourgeois life largely preserve the inherited codes of bourgeois theater as well as the conventions of organic form. In this sense the avant-garde antithesis of Sternheim would be Brecht's theater.

[85] Adorno, "Commitment," *The Essential Frankfurt School Reader*, ed. A. Arato and E. Gebhardt (New York, 1978), 30. Also quoted by Wolin, "Modernism vs. Postmodernism," 15.

Prospectus.
The reaction against realism: counter-discourse and the
avant-garde

In the chapters that follow my intention is not to debate the
various definitions of expressionism nor to discuss which texts are
to be considered "expressionist" and which are not. As I have
already indicated, the most challenging writers of the expressionist generation were those who were not content merely to
follow a predetermined set of stylistic or thematic criteria – as did
the more epigonal and "naive" expressionists – but who tended
rather to break all the rules, not least their own.[86] Consequently,
the search for an all-inclusive definition is problematic to the
extent that the most challenging expressionists such as Kafka,
Benn and Döblin were simultaneously the most vociferous "anti-
expressionists."

It is also not my goal here to offer an exhaustive account of the
entire expressionist movement in all its complexities and variations, or to cite a series of expressionist texts that can be matched
point by point to the precise theoretical categories which have
been elucidated in this discussion of the avant-garde. This would
be to efface the heterogeneity of the expressionist movement[87] and
at the same time to reduce the scope of my working definition of
the avant-garde. Instead I shall focus on a group of texts that seem
to embody the primary avant-garde functions of expressionism
that I have discussed here.

For example, one of the central means by which expressionism
identifies itself as an avant-garde movement, and by which it
marks its distance to tradition and the cultural institution as a
whole is through its relationship to realism and the dominant
conventions of representation. The discussion of this relationship
to realism will constitute one of the means by which I will show in

---

[86] This is the case for example with Döblin, who rejects other practices and other
"-isms" in favor of his own "Döblinismus." His theories of "cinematic style" in
prose ("Kinostil") and "logical naturalism" ("konsequenter Naturalismus")
and the rules that he sets up are observed only where he breaches them or
subverts their obvious meaning. See Alfred Döblin, "Futuristische Worttechnik," *Aufsätze zur Literatur*, ed. Walter Muschg (Freiburg: Walter, 1963), 15. See
also chapter 3 below.

[87] Gerhard Knapp's warnings in this regard are very much to the point, in
particular his observation that with the term "expressionism" there is the
suggestion of "a unified epochal style which, in reality never existed." See
Gerhard Knapp, *Die Literatur des Expressionismus* (Munich: Beck, 1979), 13–16.

the following chapters that the expressionist texts examined here have a common basis in the thinking of the avant-garde. Since modernism too has an iconoclastic relationship to this tradition – even though as I have indicated, it often remains subtly conservative – it is worth making some preliminary distinctions between these two cultural formations with regard to realism.

In various analogous ways, both modernism and the avant-garde oppose realism's characteristic gesture of pretending to offer a comprehensive survey and rational explanation of the world. Both challenge the narrative structures and conventional rationalist constructions through which reality is interpreted, in order that they can make the inherited realist models of the world less self-evident or "natural." Through their emphasis on the disclosure of a new multiplicity of consciousness and perspective they present an awareness of areas previously excluded from that view of the world which is ideologically sanctioned by the dominant social discourses, and they offer instead the sense of an underlying disorder, anarchy and the instability of conventional values. In place of realism's claim to present an abiding truth, modernism and the historical avant-garde both offer mere perspectives, conjectures and provisional meanings which are foregrounded as ambiguous, unstable and open to doubt. It is this "epistemological uncertainty" and anomic doubt that characterize the modernist period as a whole and set it off from the nineteenth century.[88]

However, despite the similarities in their response to modernity, there is a fundamental difference between the two. In the case of modernism, there is the sense that the inherited models and artistic forms are rejected largely because of the outdatedness and inadequacy of nineteenth-century realism in accounting for the new areas of experience being explored. In its technical development of new methods and aesthetic forms with the function of assisting the intellectual adjustment to social changes, Modernism thus reflects the confident faith of the bourgeois in technology and

---

[88] Douwe Fokkema and Elrud Ibsch have described "epistemological doubt" as the central characteristic of modernism in their *Modernist Conjectures* (London: Hurst, 1987), 38–39. See also Brian McHale, "Change of Dominant from Modernist to Postmodernist Writing," *Approaching Postmodernism*, ed. Hans Bertens and Douwe Fokkema (Philadelphia and Amsterdam: John Benjamins, 1986), 53–78; see also his *Postmodernist Fiction* (London: Methuen, 1987).

social progress, and the belief that, as the world of modernity becomes more complex, so updated means will be developed for its accurate representation. In this regard, modernism clearly takes on an affirmative or legitimizing function as the cultural complement of bourgeois social practices.[89]

By contrast, where the expressionist avant-garde takes up similar issues connected to modernity, and adopts similar experimental artistic techniques in order to respond to them, it appears to cast off conventional realism not because the formal limitations or conventionality of its methods per se are repugnant to it (as in high modernism's reaction), but rather because of the ideological connotations of realism. For the expressionists, the goal is not only to account for the experience of modernity but more importantly to *deconstruct* this experience by exposing those seemingly self-evident epistemological categories and rational criteria through which modernity is organized – the dominant social discourses – and to do so without lapsing into sheer stylistic and technical fetishism.

In chapter 3 (on the expressionist poetics of Döblin and Benn) I will examine in detail two expressionist texts demonstrating a similar set of concerns and strategies to those of the "high" modernists, namely Döblin's "The Murder of a Buttercup" and Benn's "Rönne-Novellas." As in modernism both of these texts deal with multiple perspectives and states of consciousness, and both similarly suppress the reader's conventional points of orientation within the reality of the text (for example the causality and the time-sequence of the story, the generic rules of the "novella"

---

[89] To draw on a concrete example from chapter 3 (on the poetics of expressionism), although modernism actively rejects the mimetic tradition as exemplified in nineteenth-century realism and naturalism, its drive for technical sophistication and progress on a purely formal level leads it into the position of developing its own techniques, such as the "stream-of-consciousness" and those other strategies intended to reflect the drastic changes which had taken place in the sense of time and space in modernity. These are refined and perfected to such an extent that they could be seen as the ultimate culmination and *fulfillment* – rather than the subversion – of the realistic tendencies of the nineteenth century, whereby the "stream-of-consciousness" technique becomes the logical continuation of naturalism's "Sekundenstil" (or detailed recording of minutiae) and in a sense its extension into the realm of human thought, emotion and the unconscious. The lack of ideological and institutional awareness in modernism, as with Benjamin's example of the technically perfect photograph of a slum (see below, p. 12–13), means that in its drive for stylistic and representational refinement it risks missing the point.

and so on).[90] However, these texts adopt two important characteristics which clearly place them at center of the avant-garde, as we
have described it here.

Firstly, there is a clear attack upon the "normality" of the
bourgeois world, a questioning of its self-evident character or the
givenness of its structure. Both Döblin and Benn satirize the
"burgher's" conventionalized and normalizing reactions to an
encounter with alien realms of experience. But more than this they
reveal that this set of ordered and rationalist responses is merely
an attempt to hold in place one of the essential epistemological
premises of the bourgeois world-view: the implicit belief in an
unshakable and "organic" relationship between a clearly delineated Cartesian ego and a distinct and rationally constructed
world.[91] Secondly, through the suppression of those narrative
conventions and markers which in realism serve as signposts
orienting the reader within the world of the text, the reader is
made to experience at first hand a sense of disorientation (or
"decentering") analogous to that described as affecting the protagonist in the text.[92]

The two features are related. For in this way the reader is both
immersed in disparate impressions and made to experience at
first hand the artificiality of those conventional discursive means
of orientation and order which not only organize the realist text
but also organize experience in modernity.[93] In this way the texts

[90] Hohendahl makes a similar point in discussing this strategy of disorienting the
reader, stating that "[t]he reader finds only the fragments of a story, kept
together by a narrator who moves from factual report to the articulation of
consciousness with great ease." See "The Loss of Reality," *Modernity and the
Text*, 84–5.

[91] In place of this rationalist construction of the real both texts reveal glimpses of a
dialectical and discontinuous reality, seemingly inaccessible to conventional
forms of rationality and meaning.

[92] Benn's protagonist "Rönne" experiences the world as a montage of discontinuous phenomena that cannot be assembled into a meaningful whole, while
Döblin's figure "Fischer" experiences his relation to the world via a set of reified
linguistic formulae and moral injunctions, and his selfhood as a mere collection
of discontinuous bourgeois characteristics mediated through clichéd phrases and
attitudes. See Benn, *Gehirne* (Stuttgart: Reclam, 1974), 3.

[93] For example through the text's rapid narrational shifts between perspectives
and levels of consciousness in the two texts, the boundaries between subject and
object are effaced, thereby destabilizing the positivistic convention of a rationally ordered conception of life based on a clear dichotomy between subject
and object, and exposing it as a false and reified construction of realism. In the
article to which I am indebted here Hohendahl makes a similar point ("The Loss
of Reality," *Modernity and the Text*, 81–94). However I would go further than

do not merely attack the signifying convention of realism but simultaneously deconstruct the *ideology* of classical representational systems such as realism by calling into question those epistemological criteria which underpin it as a dominant social discourse.[94] Thus the avant-garde text becomes a kind of "oppositional discourse" which defamiliarizes the values and conventions projected by the institution of art, and which exposes the epistemological and ideological bases beneath the construction of both the bourgeois world and the realist text. As we shall see in the later chapters, it is this attempt to deconstruct not only realism itself but the particular codes and interpretations of reality on which that realism is based, that illustrates the institutional or ideological awareness defining the avant-garde and its oppositional capacity for "self-criticism." By these analogous means the more progressive expressionist texts demonstrate that their concern is not only to produce the fullest possible account of human consciousness under the impact of modernity – as is the case with the typically modernist treatment of time and space (such as with the stream-of-consciousness technique) – but that they are also tied inextricably to the fundamental critical and institutional assumptions that define the avant-garde: the critique of epistemology and ideology.

The underlying differences between the two movements can be traced back to the fact that unlike the avant-garde, modernism fails to reflect upon its own institutionalized position, or upon the possible recuperation of its iconoclastic and innovative impulses by the institution of art. Modernism assumes that its aesthetic autonomy guarantees it a position free from historical and institutional constraints, and it is consequently vulnerable to the fallacy that a social transformation can be brought about by

Hohendahl however in placing Benn's text very firmly within the overall area of concerns mapped out by the avant-garde. The deconstruction in Benn's experimental prose of the conventions both of bourgeois realism and of a corresponding set of discourses for interpreting reality that are associated with it goes beyond the mere "use of new techniques" (88) and has a very clear ideology-critical function not shared by the ironic and critical modernist works of, say Thomas Mann.

[94] This overburdening not only confounds the expectations of the reader (to the extent that these expectations are geared to interpreting a norm of realism oriented on nineteenth-century prose) thereby exposing them as being constructed by convention and the institution of art. It also assaults the rationalist attitude towards epistemology and the interpretation of reality associated with these institutionally determined horizons of expectation.

formal innovations and a revolutionary poetics alone. It is for this reason that modernism often remains covertly traditional, with its rebelliousness always locked securely into affirmative culture and its critical potential always already defused as mere aesthetic compensation.[95]

With the avant-garde by contrast, it is the awareness of the institutional constraints and social functioning of its texts which is uppermost in its concerns. The avant-garde does not presume that its autonomous status offers the basis on which it might lay claim to an ahistorical perspective, nor does it assume that it can bring about social change through formal and linguistic transformations. It is skeptical of realism's assumption of an epistemologically secure and autonomous point-of-view, and its counter-discourses are correspondingly geared to undermining this false objectivism.

The avant-garde's standpoint rests upon a form of ideology-critique that, as a mode of "self-criticism," is aware above all of its own epistemological limits and institutional conditioning. It engages the ideological and institutional status of art by attempting to deconstruct the dominant social discourses (that is, the implicit epistemology, reality-principle and social value-system) mediated by the institution, and it dismantles those representational conventions and social signifying practices through which social experience is organized and given meaning in the discursively "constructed" image of the world.

[95] Jochen Schulte-Sasse makes a similar point in "Carl Einstein," 42.

# 2

❖❖❖❖❖❖❖❖❖❖❖❖❖❖❖❖❖❖❖❖❖❖❖❖❖❖❖❖❖❖❖❖❖❖❖❖❖❖❖❖❖❖❖

# Re-writing the discursive world: revolution and the expressionist avant-garde

"Death to the Moonlight!"
(Futurist slogan)

The heterogeneous and frequently vague nature of the many manifestoes and programmatic statements produced by the numerous writers of the expressionist movement has made it a notoriously difficult phenomenon to pin down to any clear ideological line.[1] The great variety of political and religious groupings which many of its prominent associates went on to join after its official demise, such as the various socialist and communist factions, the National-Socialists, Christians and radical Zionists, may be an indication that a breadth of opinion already existed within its ranks which made the attempt at anything more than a broad and very fleeting affiliation of like-minded thinkers virtually impossible.[2]

The question of expressionism's impact as a revolutionary event in a social and ideological sense is made even more difficult to answer by the fact that any genuinely radical political agendas proposed in the literary or programmatic writings of the movement are invariably obscured or "overdetermined" by factors apparently extraneous to the issues at stake. For besides fulfilling the intellectual's need to overcome the social and spiritual isolation through engagement within the community,[3] the notion of a

---

[1] A broad selection of these writings are collected in Anz and Stark (eds.), *Manifeste und Dokumente* in the section "Literatur und Politik," (especially "Expressionismus und Revolution," 326–353). See also the collection by Paul Pörtner (ed.), *Literaturrevolution 1910–1925. Dokumente, Manifeste, Programme,* 2 vols. (Luchterhand: Neuwied, 1960). Parts of the present chapter were originally published in *German Quarterly* 64.4 (1991): 464–74.

[2] The variety of affiliations taken up by former expressionists may also be indicative of their need, long postponed, for a spiritual or ideological community. See Walter H. Sokel, *The Writer in Extremis,* 228.

[3] See the discussion and collection of texts on this theme in Anz and Stark (eds.), *Manifeste und Dokumente,* in the section "Soziale Entfremdung und Gemeinschaft," 247–250.

revolution often appears to offer the possibility merely of curing the self vicariously through the attempt to heal the world.[4] Alternatively, the ideal of revolution frequently seems to have been embraced as part of a more general desire for spiritual renewal or even as a criminal and destructive act offering a stimulating experiential "rush" or "Lebenssteigerung."[5]

It is undeniable of course that the expressionist avant-garde's "programmatic" texts present a powerful criticism of the ideological and institutional foundations of Wilhelmine bourgeois society and its culture of affirmation. It is also no coincidence that besides the shorter literary forms of the poem, novella and the one-act play, much expressionist thought was mediated via the more direct and powerful polemical forms, such as their manifestoes and pamphlets,[6] while as a generic form the expressionist broadsheet, with its shocking, terse and excessive statements had a wide-ranging influence on the movement, constituting one of the major factors behind the belligerent and provocative tone characteristic of its "expressiveness." However it is the very diversity and vagueness of the revolutionary programs, their refusal to be fixed to a determinate set of social goals and ideologies, or to adopt a single-minded sense of direction, which may turn out, paradoxically, to offer a means of understanding the revolutionary nature of expressionism as an avant-garde literary movement. As I shall show in this chapter (with reference mainly to the poetic and programmatic texts of the movement), the particular ideological tendency of any overt intentions or stated political goals of the expressionists is ultimately much less significant for their consideration as an avant-garde[7] than the

---

[4] Sokel, *The Writer in Extremis*, 218.

[5] Richard Hamann and Jost Hermand, *Expressionismus* (Munich: Nymphenberger Verlagshandlung, 1976), 114.

[6] It is worth noting for example that the dadaist manifestations and "happenings" which Bürger cites as typically avant-gardistic forms (through which art is "confronted" directly with life and with the shocked reactions of the audience) took as their precedent the expressionists' provocative and often shocking "literary cabarets," in which their fantastic stories, dissonant poetry, and often grotesque one-act plays were read or performed.

[7] Edgar Lohner observes that it is important to build upon Peter Bürger's theoretical analysis of the historical avant-garde by examining concretely the artists' own conceptualizations of their progressive mission. See Lohner, "Die Problematik des Begriffes der Avantgarde," 124.

oppositional edge they give to the iconoclastic poetics they develop.[8]

More important for expressionism as an avant-garde literary movement is that a "revolutionary" impulse is inscribed into its poetics of representation which ensures that the first premise of its construction of the real is the constant interrogation of all ideological and epistemological foundations, all inherited models of reality and all established structures of perception and experience: in short as an avant-garde it questions those dominant social discourses supported by the institution of art, and creates in their place a set of oppositional discourses. Hence the truly revolutionary element of these texts is their constant overturning of the inherited world and its images, so that the final aim appears to lie in the very act of revolution itself as a constant and ongoing process.

## Dominant social discourse: the prison-house of language

For many expressionists the subversion of the inherited world is perceived in part as the active participation in, and continuation of an anomic process which has already been set in motion.[9] The

---

[8] In a similar vein Wolfgang Paulsen writes "no matter how revolutionary Expressionism seemed to be, it was not a political, nor even in any sense a socially oriented movement. At best it could be deemed a literary movement with larger political and social implications." In "Expressionism and the Tradition of Revolt" *Expressionism Reconsidered*, Houston German Studies vol. 1, ed. G. B. Pickar and K. E. Webb (Munich: Fink, 1979), 8. This is not to deny, however, the genuine engagement and political praxis of many individual expressionist (and dadaist) writers, especially those associated with the November revolution such as Toller. On this question see Frank Trommler, *Sozialistische Literatur in Deutschland. Ein historischer Überblick* (Stuttgart: Kröner, 1976) in particular the section "Schriftsteller und Revolution," 412–442; Wolfgang Frühwald, "Kunst als Tat und Leben. Über den Anteil deutscher Schriftsteller an der Revolution in München 1918/1919," *Sprache und Bekenntnis. Festschrift für Hermann Kunisch*, ed. Wolfgang Frühwald and Günter Niggl (Berlin: Dinker, 1971); Hans Meyer, "Expressionismus und Novemberrevolution," *Spuren* 5 (1978): 10–13.

[9] This function of actively extending a destructive process which has already been set in motion is valorized by Ernst Bloch in his defence of expressionism over and against Lukacs' charge that these poets merely participated naively in "the ideological demise of the imperialist bourgeoisie" ("den ideologischen Verfall der imperialistischen Bourgeoisie"). As we have seen in the previous chapter, Bloch asks provocatively whether it would have been better "if they had patched up the surface of reality instead of tearing it even further apart" ("wenn sie den Oberflächenzusammenhang wieder geflickt hätten . . . statt ihn immer weiter aufzureißen?"). He thereby circumscribes the ideology-critical function of the literary movement. See Bloch, "Diskussionen über Expressionismus," *Expressionismusdebatte*, 187.

expressionist writer (and later dadaist) Hugo Ball documents a typical revolutionary response of expressionism to what was perceived as the acute crisis of modernity:

God is dead. A world broke apart . . . Religion, science, morals – phenomena which emerged from the anxieties of primitive peoples. A world breaks apart. A millenial culture breaks apart. There are no more pillars and supports, no foundations that would not have been shattered. Churches have become castles in the air. Convictions prejudices . . . The meaning of the world faded away . . . Chaos broke out . . . Man lost his heavenly face, became matter, chance, conglomerate, animal, the product of insanity, of abrupt, inadequate and convulsive thoughts. Man lost his special position, which reason had vouchsafed for him.[10]

This crisis is the experience of an epoch in which all meaning seems to have disappeared from the world, leaving a mere chaos of fragmented myths and cosmologies. The text registers the onset of chaos firstly as a decisive break in the continuity of religious and philosophical thought ("There are no more pillars and supports, no foundations") and of normative values. And as with the writing of the important predecessor of the expressionist poets and thinkers, Friedrich Nietzsche, the system's breakdown, ("the death of God") also has an important ideology-critical function: the break-up of a millennial culture is seen as bringing with it not just chaos but, more positively, the possibility of release from the constraints of conventional interpretative and orienting systems. It allows the possibility of seeing through ideologies, the reified forms of thought which have been established as objective truths ("Convictions [have become] prejudices"), and which have been set up as the foundations of meaning: "the principles of logic, of centrality, unity and reason are revealed as the postulates of a domineering theology" says Ball later in the text.[11]

[10] "Gott ist tot. Eine Welt brach zusammen . . . Religion, Wissenschaft, Moral – Phänomene, die aus Angstzuständen primitiver Völker entstanden sind. Eine Welt bricht zusammen. Eine tausendjährige Kultur bricht zusammen. Es gibt keine Pfeiler und Stützen, keine Fundamente mehr, die nicht zersprengt worden wären. Kirchen sind Luftschlösser geworden. Überzeugungen Vorurteile . . . Der Sinn der Welt schwand . . . Chaos brach hervor . . . Der Mensch verlor sein himmlisches Gesicht, wurde Materie, Zufall, Konglomerat, Tier, Wahnsinnsprodukt abrupt und unzulänglicher zuckender Gedanken. Der Mensch verlor seine Sonderstellung, die ihm die Vernunft gewährt hatte." Hugo Ball, "Kandinsky." Lecture held in Galerie Dada, Zürich, April 7, 1917. *Manifeste und Dokumente*, 124.

[11] "Die Prinzipien der Logik, des Zentrums, Einheit und Vernunft wurden als Postulate einer herrschsüchtigen Theologie durchschaut."

The prevalence in this period of such iconoclastic and revolutionary sentiments suggests that towards the end of the nineteenth century the pervasive experience of crisis, moral chaos and discontinuity documented here by Ball emerges as the symptom of a deeper and fundamental epistemological fracture. For at precisely this time a series of Copernican revolutions shake the foundations of Western thought. In particular the work of Nietzsche, but also of Mach, Vaihinger and Freud has the effect of subjecting conventional social discourse to a rigorous re-examination of its most cherished notions.[12]

The writing of these thinkers functions as a form of "ideology-critique" and "Fiktionskritik" ("critique of fictions"). Their general effect is to show that no systems of thought regarding man and social reality are anchored by any "natural law" but possess the status merely of instruments of reflection and meaning, as mere hypotheses or "useful fictions": they are patterns of meaning postulated by man which are imposed upon the phenomenal world in order to formulate it and bring it under his control. If the function of all "transcendental signifieds" (Derrida), such as those cited in the text by Ball ("Reason," "Man," "Religion") is thus to anchor those systems of meaning which are imposed upon the world of experience, then it is these that are now increasingly exposed to skepticism.

Such systems are created by a semantic activity which formulates experience and encapsulates a world by the use of fictions and language. As Nietzsche's famous aphorism has it, "What then is Truth? A mobile army of metaphors, metonymies, anthropomorphisms, in short the sum of human relations."[13] This semantic activity has the primary function then of creating a set of representational codes and ideological formations which present reality as an eminently *discursive* construction.

Now the growing awareness in this period of the discursive nature of realities – an awareness, as we have seen, that is dialecti-

[12] The nihilism and critique of fictions and ideology which were prominent at the turn of the century and which played such an important role in expressionism are dealt with extensively by Silvio Vietta and Hans-Georg Kemper in *Expressionismus*, (Munich: UTB, 1975), 134–152.

[13] "Was ist also Wahrheit? Ein bewegliches Heer von Metaphern, Metonymien, Anthropomorphismen, kurz eine Summe von menschlichen Relationen." Friedrich Nietzsche, "Über Wahrheit und Lüge im außermoralischen Sinne," *Werke III* (Frankfurt: Ullstein 1969), 1022. [Schlechta edition, vol. III, 314].

cally related to the experience of their break-up – has important consequences. Firstly, it leads to the sense that, as a centering system, discourse may serve as a self-contained and all-embracing machinery which encloses the subject within itself, separating off any other modalities of experience: the "prison-house of language" was Nietzsche's expression for this phenomenon. This awareness of being enclosed within an ideological system of fictions placing limitations on experience brings with it the pervasive sense of alienation from a more "genuine" realm of being, an alternative dimension of experience[14] which the expressionists can only gesture towards, and which they hope to attain through the pursuit of what they term "spirit," "essence" or "power" ("Geist," "Wesen"[15] or "Kraft").

Secondly, since all points of orientation are seen simply as discursive fictions which have merely been postulated, not consolidated, all values appear as relative – "There is no perspective left in the moral world. Up is down, down is up." writes Ball.[16] With the proclamation of the death of God a full-scale interrogation of the discourse of reality begins, a questioning of the fictional nature of all those "essences" (the "pillars and supports" as Ball says) which anchor systems of meaning.

## Epistemological skepticism

The literary text of this period is consequently forced to a degree to undergo a functional transformation ("Funktionswandel") if it is to respond to these changed circumstances. As a result it becomes a common practice among the Expressionist writers to create the kinds of "counter-discourse" which foreground precisely the disjunction between, on the one hand, the world of

---

[14] An example of this widespread tendency is expressed by the expressionist painter Franz Marc. He articulates his generation's search for this undefined (and undefinable) source of alterity: "Wherever we saw a crack in the crust of convention, that's what we pointed to: only there, for we hoped for a power beneath which would one day come to light" ("Wo wir einen Riß in der Kruste der Konvention sahen, da deuteten wir hin; nur dahin, da wir darunter eine Kraft erhofften, die eines Tages ans Licht kommen würde"). Franz Marc, "Der Blaue Reiter" (1914), rpt. in *Manifeste Manifeste. 1905–1933*, ed. Diether Schmidt (Dresden: Verlag der Kunst, 1956), 56.

[15] See Kurt Pinthus, "Rede für die Zukunft," *Die Erhebung* (1919), cited below.

[16] "[E]s gibt keine Perspektive mehr in der moralischen Welt. Oben ist unten, unten ist oben." Hugo Ball, "Kandinsky." *Manifeste und Dokumente*, 124.

fictions and discursive orders and on the other, the reality of the referential object. The more progressive literature of the movement consequently draws attention to the mediate nature of all discursive images of the world – such as the epistemological and ideological universes which man inhabits – and simultaneously to the contingency and instability of the (fictional) concepts which underpin them.

There are several texts, drawn from the field of expressionist poetry, which we can cite briefly as typifying this skeptical consciousness of the times. Many thematize directly the shortcomings of such fictions and the individual's inability to come to terms with the world from inside the discursive system in which he is enclosed. Gustav Sack's poem "The World" is an unusually explicit presentation of this "Erkenntniskritik" or skeptical attitude towards epistemology: " . . . it's all imagery, / which so colorfully places itself before our senses, / an X, from which the veil never falls, / yes, our senses themselves are paintings, / the world, the thing, causality, time and space / everything's a difficult and puzzling dream. / And today they scream out loudly on all the streets: / no, there it is, it's concrete reality –."[17] In conceding that the world which one experiences is actually only "imagery" or the result of "painting" ("Bilderei," or "Malerei") Sack points to the discursive and fictional nature of that "dream" one might otherwise take for "concrete reality." But his attack is not simply a logical, Kantian form of cognitive criticism. In fact, it has much in common with expressionism's resistance to such rationalism.[18] For as in the works of Benn and Döblin which I will examine in chapter 3 its real targets are precisely the logical categories underpinning the dominant discourse of rationalism upon which this counterfeit world of "images" and "veils" is constructed, such as the categories cited by Sack, namely "causality, time and space."

From a similar epistemological standpoint Ernst Stadler too warns against the danger of being convinced by simple meanings

[17] " . . . es ist alles Bilderei, / was sich so bunt vor unsre Sinne stellt, / ein X, von dem niemals der Schleier fällt, / ja unsre Sinne selbst sind Malerei, / die Welt, das Ding, die Folge, Zeit und Raum / alles ein schwerer, rätselwirrer Traum. / Und heute schreit man laut auf allen Gassen: / nein, sie ist da, ist harte Wirklichkeit . . ." Gustav Sack, "Die Welt," *Lyrik des Expressionismus* (Tübingen, 1976), 203.

[18] On this theme, see Vietta and Kemper, *Expressionismus*, esp. 144–176.

and explanations, and consequently of taking appearances for essences:

And when I . . .
Lift up to myself appearances, lies, and games instead of the essence,
If I pleasingly lie to myself with easy meanings,
As if dark were clear, as if life didn't carry a thousand wildly bolted gates.[19]

Again, what the text typifies is a historical sense of the danger which lies in wait for those who do not practice some form of epistemological skepticism with regard to what are, in effect, discursive fictions. The implication is that when these fictions ultimately evaporate, the individual will be abandoned to the experience of nothingness. From this same historical perspective Brecht writes: "And when the fallacies are all worn out? The last one keeping us company / sitting right across from us / is nothingness " [20]

## The expressionist avant-garde: the cynical sublation of art and life

With this critical shift towards an attitude of skepticism the realiz-ation grows that since there is no longer any single ideological constellation which can have an ultimate claim on the truth, alternative discourses may be created to displace the dominant ideological constructs. It becomes a widely held belief among the expressionists, for example, that if meaning and order are no longer already "given" in the world, these must be imposed by an

---

[19] "Und wenn ich . . . / Schein, Lug und Spiel zu mir anstatt des Wesens hebe, / Wenn ich gefällig mich mit raschem Sinn belüge, / Als wäre Dunkles klar, als wenn nicht Leben tausend / wild verschloßne Tore trüge." Stadler, "Der Spruch," *Menschheitsdämmerung* (hereafter *MHD*), ed. Kurt Pinthus (Hamburg: Rowohlt, 1963), 196. Wherever possible I have used the translation (hereafter *MHD-DH) Menschheitsdämmerung: Dawn of Humanity. A Document of Expres-sionism*, trs. J. M. Ratych, R. Ley, R. C. Conard (Columbia S.C.: Camden House 1994). Klemm's poem "Philosophie" shares this same epistemological caution: "We do not know what light is/ Nor what the ether and its oscillations are – / . . . Hidden from us is what the stars signify / And the solemn march of time . . . / We do not know what God is!" *MHD-DH*, 94 ("Wir wissen nicht was das Licht ist / Noch was der Äther und seine Schwingungen -- . . . Fremd ist uns, was die Sterne bedeuten / Und der Feiergang der Zeit./ . . . Wir wissen nicht was Gott ist!" *Lyrik des Expressionismus*, 202).
[20] "Wenn die Irrtümer verbraucht sind? Sitzt als letzter Gesellschafter / Uns das Nichts gegenüber." Brecht,"Der Nachgeborene," *Lyrik des Expressionismus*, 249.

act of will on the part of the subject: as Kurt Pinthus says, "Everything else outside of ourselves is unreal and first becomes reality, when we turn it into reality by virtue of the power of the mind."[21] Pinthus' stance here is paradigmatic for the expressionist urge to create the world anew. It also bears a similarity to that characteristically "animistic" attitude of the Expressionist poets and playwrights who create in their texts an alternative world of selfhood in which figures and events are meaningful only as essences[22] or as correlatives of consciousness,[23] and in which "the mind forms reality according to the idea."[24]

The urge to create an alternative reality of discourse thus becomes a powerful revolutionary drive in the expressionist movement. This new discursive heterocosm serves both to displace a previous reality (which is now perceived as having lost its legitimacy) and to open up new meanings to the individual as well as an altered relationship to experience based on the imposition of an intensely personal version of world. Lothar Schreyer, echoing Pinthus writes, "In us the old world shatters. The new world arises within."[25]

One of the primary means by which this alternative discursive reality is created is through a strategy linked intimately to the avant-garde's program of creating a set of oppositional discourses marked by desublimation, de-aestheticization and the distortion of organic form. It involves a massive re-coding of what had previously been accepted as "nature": the world is now re-interpreted and re-constituted in terms of a new discourse which liberates both the object and its perception from the conditions

---

[21] "[A]lles andere außer uns ist unwirklich und wird erst zur Wirklichkeit, wenn wir kraft der Kraft des Geistes es zur Wirklichkeit machen."Kurt Pinthus, "Rede für die Zukunft" in *Die Erhebung. Jahrbuch für neue Dichtung und Wertung*, ed. A. Wolfenstein (Berlin: Fischer 1919), 414.

[22] Gottfried Benn for example explains that he has to write in this "essential" manner, "since I never see people but only the 'I', and never events, but only existence . . . " ("da ich nie Personen sehe, sondern immer nur das Ich, und nie Geschehnisse, sondern immer nur das Dasein . . . .") See "Schöpferische Konfession" *Gesammelte Werke*, vol. 4, ed. Dieter Wellershoff (Limes: Wiesbaden, 1958), 189.

[23] Examples of this attitude would be the "Ich-" and "Stationendramen", the doubling and splitting of characters throughout the texts of the movement.

[24] "der Geist formt die Wirklichkeit nach der Idee." Pinthus, "Rede für die Zukunft," 413.

[25] "In uns zerbricht die alte Welt. Die neue Welt ersteht in uns."Lothar Schreyer, "Der neue Mensch." *Manifeste und Dokumente*, 140.

pertaining to the given. Rather than creating the kind of literary work which reproduces the natural world and which thus attempts – like the conventions of organic art that Bürger critiques – to erase the marks of its artificiality in order to assimilate itself as closely as possible to nature, the expressionist text adopts one of the central strategies of the avant-garde, the procedure embodied preeminently in the montage: it foregrounds its own artifice and constructedness.[26] Thus, far from emulating the organic – and thereby implicitly substantiating the referential realm of the determinate and the given – it appears instead to valorize the "artificial" world of human creativity, the realm of the signifier, and the sovereign autonomy of consciousness.

Now since the perspective by which nature had previously been perceived was strongly influenced and "aestheticized" by the mediation of conventional, idealist and romantic topoi (such as stars and heaven, meadow and brook), the expressionist recoding of nature takes the form of a direct onslaught on such sublimating myths. Alfred Lichtenstein writes:

> The sky is like a blue *jellyfish*.
> And all around are fields, green meadow hills –
> Peaceful world, you great *mouse trap*.
>
> The earth is like a fat *Sunday roast*,
> Nicely dipped in sweet sun-sauce.[27]

Ernst Blass describes another conventionalized topos, the moon, as like "a slime / On an enormous velour of the falling night. / The stars quiver tenderly like embryos."[28] Similarly the poet Klabund describes the "evening clouds" as "like a procession of grey tattered vagabonds / swaying threateningly like drunken coffins."[29]

[26] For example one might cite the foregrounded artificiality of the common expressionist forms of montage or "Telegrammstil," or again the artificial and seemingly purely conceptual nature of figures in the dramas and in many of the prose texts (Einstein's "Bebuquin," Kafka's "Beschreibung eines Kampfes" etc.).

[27] "Der Himmel ist wie eine blaue *Qualle*. / Und rings sind Felder, grüne Wiesenhügel – / Friedliche Welt, du große *Mausefalle* . . . . // Die Erde ist wie ein fetter *Sonntagsbraten*, / Hübsch eingetünkt in süße Sonnensauce." Lichtenstein, "Sommerfrische," *MHD* 63 (my emphasis).

[28] "ein Schleim / Auf ungeheuer nachtendem Velours. / Die Sterne zucken zart wie Embryos." *Lyrik des Expressionismus*, 48.

[29] "Gleich einem Zug grau zerlumpter Strolche, / Bedrohlich schwankend wie betrunkne Särge." Klabund, "Ironische Landschaft," *Lyrik des Expressionismus*, 208.

Significantly, the title of the latter poem, "Ironic Landscape" ("Ironische Landschaft") points to the expressionist avant-garde's oppositional strategy in creating such pointedly desublimated and de-aestheticized tropes. Traditional poetic codes – the dominant conventions of the aesthetic discourse in which tradition (and the institution of art) have imprisoned perception – are exploded by the ironic treatment they receive at the hands of the expressionist poets. This serves both to defamiliarize vision and to unlock conventionalized constructions, while encouraging the reader towards a free-play of associations and a mode of intellectual reflection quite at odds with the traditional "empathetic" reception demanded by previous schools of nature poetry, as well as by other affirmative and sublimating forms of art: rather than diverting attention away from reality towards an idealized and aestheticized realm of the sublime beyond, the avant-garde's aesthetics of "desublimation" enforces a close examination of the world and its image.

The revolutionary function of this iconoclasm lies also in its gesture of clearing the way for a radical reinterpretation of nature. For in important respects, the expressionist avant-garde's aesthetics of desublimation corresponds at the figural level to the process of cynical re-interpretation occurring at the level of ideology and discourse: in a sense, it is as if the expressionists indeed respond to the break-up of the old cosmological fictions, the "facade of the totality," in the manner that Ernst Bloch suggests, namely "by ripping it open even further."[30] If it retains any meaning at all, the organic world is now frequently reduced merely to a set of signs pointing to humankind's spiritual abandonment and "transcendental homelessness" (Lukacs).

The common eschatological orientation of the poems is also important here, since natural phenomena now take on significance not as uplifting terrestrial manifestations of a sublime, redemptive ideal world beyond but in terms of a coming catastrophe or a failure of redemption. Van Hoddis' poem "End of the World" ("Weltende") and Heym's "Umbra Vitae" – the two texts which open Pinthus' important collection of expressionist poetry *Menschheitsdämmerung* (*Dawn of Humanity*) – are outstanding examples of this tendency. The "natural" presentiments of disas-

---

[30] See Bloch, "Diskussionen über Expressionismus," *Expressionismusdebatte*, 187.

ter are for example storms: "And along the coasts – the paper says – the tide is rising. // The storm is here, the wild seas are hopping / Ashore . . ."; [31] or alternatively foreboding presents itself in the form of an uncannily becalmed sea: "The seas stagnate. In the waves / the ships hang mouldering and sullen . . . ";[32] meanwhile humankind's state of spiritual excommunication may be read in the skies: although many search the heavens for a positive sign, "all of heaven's gates are closed shut."[33]

Even in those poems in which the negative reinterpretation of nature is not foregrounded quite as obviously as in these examples, the emphasis is still frequently upon its re-reading not as an entity which constitutes an end in itself or even a source of spiritual comfort and balm, but as a mere correlative or icon for man's troubled existence in a world of pain and anxiety. For van Hoddis, birdsong for example becomes an expression of pain: "The sparrows scream" ("Die Spatzen schrein").[34] For Lichtenstein nature is frequently a sign of disease or death, and his images are of "Bloodless trees" ("Blutlose Bäume"), "the swollen night" ("die aufgeschwollne Nacht"), and "the poisonous moon, the fat fog-spider" ("Der giftge Mond, die fette Nebelspinne").[35] Such purposefully "unnatural" uses of the organic image become a central characteristic of the expressionist poem's cynical sublation of art and life by means of desublimation: through expressionism's de-aestheticization of poetry, as well as its re-writing of the world, nature is made to undergo a reductive transformation, through which it is instrumentalized as a sign, or marginalized as a mere function of human consciousness.

Typical of the revolutionary and avant-garde impulse within expressionism is that it not only reverses traditional hierarchies but subverts those conventional values associated with nature, such as the monumental and sublime, which appear to be held in place by nature's unarguable "givenness." As nature's human counterpart, the body too is subject to a similar re-coding. Where-

---

[31] *MHD-DH* 61. "Und an den Küsten – liest man – steigt die Flut. // Der Sturm ist da, die wilden Meere hupfen / An Land . . . ." Van Hoddis, "Weltende," *MHD*, 39.

[32] "Die Meere aber stocken. In den Wogen / Die Schiffe hängen modernd und verdrossen . . . " Heym, "Umbra Vitae," *MHD*, 39.

[33] "Und aller Himmel Höfe sind verschlossen." Heym, "Umbra Vitae," *MHD*, 39.

[34] Jakob v. Hoddis, "Morgens," *MHD*, 168.

[35] Lichtenstein, "Nebel," *MHD*, 59.

as the lyrical poetry of a former period had upheld the idea of the body as a criterion of beauty, with the expressionists what had been the temple of the spirit often becomes a mere heap of decaying flesh, a token of a latterday version of baroque "Vergänglichkeit" or "transience." Benn's poetry of the dissection table in the "Morgue" collection is typical of this direction in the new poetry.

Here it is again the provocative and blatant re-coding of traditional romantic themes which is prominent. Benn's poem "Schöne Jugend" for example focuses on the image of the mouth of a young girl. This is not, however, because it figures as the romantic object of a lover's desire, but rather because it "looked so gnawed-at" ("sah so angeknabbert aus") on account of the rats which found an arbor ("Laube") in her body after she drowned.[36] Typically the hierarchical relationship between humanity and the spirit on the one hand, and bestiality and materiality on the other is reversed. The avant-garde's defining feature of a "cynical sublation" of art and reality is important here: if the poem reduces the differences between art and life, then instead of elevating life to the sublime level of art in an aestheticized image (or reconstituting life in a formulation whose aesthetic necessity "masters" the horror of the real) it now joins the two by descending with art to the circle of the unredeemable: the earthly, the ugly and the profane. The "lovely childhood" ("schöne Jugend") of the title turns out to refer not to the human subject, but to the life of the young rodents. Thus the girl appears merely as an object, a store of flesh for the young rats, rather than as a vessel of the spirit. In this manner the romantic Ophelia-motif of the drowned lover is evoked but then inverted, so that any remaining idealist notions of an autonomous human subject necessarily suffer a re-interpretation, as the individual becomes mere matter, a corpse tossed carelessly onto a slab.

With this revolutionary re-coding of nature, of the body, of conventional poetic topoi and of cognitive fictions, several new perspectives are opened up. Firstly an anachronistic "Weltbild" (or "image of the world") is displaced. The subversion of those traditional "transcendental signifieds," such as God (whose heaven is now repeatedly described as "empty")[37] and the subject

---

[36] Gottfried Benn, *Gesammelte Werke*, vol. 3, 8.
[37] On this theme see the poems in the section "Gott ist tot – Gespräche mit Gott" in

(now a "dissociated" entity, a "fragmented" corpse) is accomplished by their being replaced by autonomous and indeterminate signifiers. This means that the reality which these ideological "centers" had formerly anchored, together with the codes and myths which they had legitimized and held in place, are necessarily liberated.

Secondly, besides marking the break-up of the inherited world of continuity and belief, the subversion of the natural world and the linked tendencies towards dehumanization and the re-coding of the body have a further specific target: they offer a release from the values associated with the Romantic tradition of an order close to nature and retaining a precious conception of selfhood based on an anachronistic sense of "Innerlichkeit" (or "interiority").[38]

Thirdly, it is evident that other strategies of reversal similar to the re-coding of nature are common practice in expressionist texts: for example the resurrection of the socially marginal, such as madmen, prostitutes and other outcasts, and their valorization as the new prophets, saints and heroes of the age. However, this procedure is seldom utilized with any concretely political goal in mind, such as an egalitarian class revolution. Instead, by exposing the contingency of the hierarchy within such ideologies the system's boundaries and its mechanisms of exclusion *per se* are called into question. As an onslaught on the familiar, bringing with it a de-automatizing renewal of vision, the real revolutionary goal becomes the act of reversal itself: it brings about the epistemological critique of those institutionalized codes of representation which had held the concepts of the "natural" and the "organic" so firmly in place.

There are several other means by which this radical strategy of recoding is carried over into the poetics of the expressionist text, and it is to these that we now turn.

Vietta's collection *Lyrik des Expressionismus*, 155–179. For example Oskar Loerke writes: "The house of heaven pales into uncertainty" ("Ins Ungewisse bleicht das Himmelshaus" in "Die Ebene," 159); Alfred Lichtenstein: "And over everything hangs an old rag – / The heavens . . . heathenish and without sense" "Und über allem hängt ein alter Lappen – / Der Himmel . . . heidenhaft und ohne Sinn" in "Die Fahrt nach der Irrenanstalt I" ("Journey to the Insane-Asylum I"), 166.

38 For an analysis of this tendency towards dehumanization and "denaturization," see Jost Hermand, "Expressionismus als Revolution," *Von Mainz nach Weimar* (Stuttgart: Luchterhand 1969), 342–343.

## Forms of counter-discourse: the avant-garde poetics of representation as re-writing

The new discursive orders which the expressionists create should not necessarily be thought of merely as a means of creating a new orderliness and fixity to replace the old. For their function is not the banishment of chaos. Chaos is often valorized by these writers for its apparent resistance to being instrumentalized by ideology and is even embraced by the strong-willed of the expressionist generation for its radical and anti-systematic character. As Huelsenbeck suggests, writing on the expressionist theme of the "New Man," this figure "recognizes no system for the living, he welcomes chaos as a friend, since he bears order in his soul."[39] Rather than the establishment of a new dominant order we may assume then that it is the destruction of inherited cosmologies and illusions of meaning that assumes the greater importance. Again, the practice of revolution itself – as a provocative and life-enhancing activity in its own right – becomes the aim, rather than the pragmatic goal of the establishment through revolution of a new social order.

In an article published in June 1915 in a journal affiliated with the expressionists, *Die weißen Blätter*, Rudolf Leonhard addresses this notion of a continuous revolutionary momentum, describing the poet as bound to a perpetual oppositional activity with a permanently rebellious and anti-ideological function: although capable of becoming happily intoxicated with the ideals of the revolution he is still quite likely to turn towards his comrades on the barricade and stick out his tongue at them, "for he is the revolutionary in every camp, the one who is dissatisfied with every situation . . ."[40] Far from being expelled from the Platonic state for this destabilizing and subversive political stance, Leonhard argues that the poet should be retained precisely on account of his function as an ideological "gadfly." His role is to oppose the perennial danger of stasis: "This is where the poet can have a counter-effect. The state cannot get by without him. It needs the

---

[39] "er kennt kein System für Lebendes, Chaos ist ihm willkommen als Freund, weil er die Ordnung in seiner Seele trägt." Richard Huelsenbeck, "Der neue Mensch," *Neue Jugend* 1 (May 23, 1917), 2–3. Rpt. *Manifeste und Dokumente*, 132.
[40] "Denn er ist der Revolutionär in allen Lagern, der Unzufriedene mit allen Zuständen . . ." R. Leonhard, "Die Politik der Dichter," *Die weißen Blätter* 2, 6 (June 1915), 814–816. Rpt. *Manifeste und Dokumente* 364.

stimulation of agitation in its machinery. It should hire revolutionaries, the ambiguous ones, who rebel despairingly against all sides."[41]

It is clear that through this constant revolutionary agitation and subversion a particular form of epistemological and ideological critique emerges which is characteristic of expressionism as an avant-garde movement. It produces a form of insight both into alterity – the possibility of alternative ideologies – and consequently into the discursive status of reality. As a result an ideologically informed awareness is produced that opposes dogma and fixity of the kind which might pose the danger of becoming the "center" of any new order. It is for this reason that the expressionists attempt to inscribe this chaos and openness into their texts – in ways that extend far beyond the principle of montage as analyzed by Bürger – in order to acknowledge the provisional and fictional status of the heterocosms they create.

Now it is precisely the insistence upon this unavailability to closure and fixity of the discursive reality and upon the necessarily "inorganic" and "unnatural" status of all ideological universes which constitutes a key element of the way that the poetics of expressionism functions as an avant-garde. This is evident in the attitude to mimesis. The expressionists' immediate literary-historical predecessors – the writers of the naturalist movement – typically believed that their modes of formulating and representing reality bore a necessary correspondence to the phenomenal world. Clearly this position can no longer be upheld against the historical breakdown in discursive fictions of order, and such uncomplicated attitudes towards representation in the previous generation give way to a profound skepticism with regard to mimesis amongst the expressionists. They, by contrast, reject any naive mimetic stance which would re-present its object by attempting to make the literary discourse mediating it disappear. That is, they are opposed to the kind of text which, like the organic work of art or "classic realist text," erases the marks of the enunciation and, by thus effacing the indications of its own fic-

---

[41] "Hier kann der Dichter gegenwirken; der Staat kann ohne ihn nicht auskommen. Er braucht die treibende Unruhe im Getriebe, er sollte Revolutionäre anstellen, zweideutige, die verzweifelt gegen alle Seiten sich empören." Leonhard, "Die Politik der Dichter." *Manifeste und Dokumente*, 365.

tionality attempts to become a transparent window on the world.

Instead, as we have seen, the new generation of expressionist writers around 1910 adopts certain practices – for example the re-coding of nature and of the body, the subversion of traditional topoi, or the reversal of conventional hierarchies of value (such as placing the sublime over the marginal, the natural over the artificial) – which "re-write" the world as a construction of human consciousness, thereby liberating it from inherited values and perceptions. By emphasizing the artificial and constructed nature of their texts and the contingency of its images *vis-à-vis* the notional object of representation they foreground the inherent fictionality and perspectivism in any form of representation. Thus they draw attention away from the referential object as such and redirect it towards the materiality and mediated nature of the text and of its signs. In this way the balance in the representational relationship is shifted: rather than emphasizing the referent, the text is itself foregrounded first and foremost as a signifier.

This autonomy of the signifier and its liberation from the realm of the referential is linked to the purely "expressive" function of these texts. As we shall see in chapter 4 (on expressionist melodrama), the hysteria and the hyperbole characteristic of the movement underline this expressivity. Rather than striving like aestheticism for purity of the aesthetic image, or like classic realism for transparency of the representation (with the aim of forming the image as an authentic reflection of the referential object), expressionism concentrates only on developing an explosive force which will tear away surface appearances. As Pinthus says,

Art for art's sake and the aesthetic were never so disrespected as in that poetry referred to as the "new" or as "expressionist," which is all eruption, explosion, intensity – and which has to be so in order to break open the malignant crust [around reality]. That is why it avoids the naturalistic description of reality as a descriptive means . . .[42]

The emphasis is now on the medium itself as "Ausdruckskunst." Yet not in the sense of producing the refined and self-sufficient

[42] "Niemals war das Ästhetische und das l'art pour l'art so mißachtet wie in dieser Dichtung, die man die 'jüngste' oder 'expressionistische' nennt, weil sie ganz Eruption, Explosion, Intensität ist – sein muß um jene feindliche Krüste zu sprengen. Deshalb meidet sie die naturalistische Schilderung der Realität als Darstellungsmittel . . ." Pinthus, "Zuvor," Preface to *MHD* (1920). Rpt. *Manifeste und Dokumente*, 58.

formal consciousness characteristic of aestheticism. The "aesthetic" criteria have changed in this de-aestheticized art:

> For this reason one should not ask about the quality of this art, but about its intensity. The intensity is what constitutes its value. For it is not a matter of artistic accomplishment, but of the will . . . This art will blow apart the aesthetic, if one conceives of the aesthetic as the pleasurable formation of the given . . . [43]

In expressionism it is now the directness and "intensity" of expression offered in the image which count, not the sublations of form or the "artistic accomplishment" ("Kunstfertigkeit"). And this "intensity" frequently comes to mean that the signifiers free themselves from a prior, denotative relationship to the referent and its details in order to become the "unmediated" reflex of the "will" or of a more essential personal vision or realm of consciousness.

We can observe this connection between the intensity of the vision and the growing autonomy of the signifier in the pointedly arbitrary and idiosyncratic uses of metaphor in expressionist poetry. In examining the discursive re-coding of nature and the body we have already seen that this strategy often targets existing thematic conventions, for example the language and imagery through which the world is articulated and perceived within a certain tradition. An important aspect of this poetic re-orientation involved an assault upon traditional modes of perception and experience, and hence an attack upon dominant codes of representation. As an iconoclastic gesture such onslaughts foreground the fact that the perception of phenomena rests on a fiction, a metaphor imposed upon the world. Now this same foregrounding of fictionality through the violence of an imposed image may be seen again in the rather contorted and daring comparisons of which the expressionist poets were fond. To take some brief examples from the poetry of Lichtenstein: "The sky is grey wrapping paper / Onto which the sun is glued – a butter stain"[44]; or

---

[43] "Deshalb frage man nicht nach der Qualität dieser Kunst, sondern nach ihrer Intensität. Die Intensität macht ihren Wert aus. Denn es geht nicht um die Kunstfertigkeit, sondern um den Willen . . . Diese Kunst wird allenthalben das Ästhetische zersprengen, wenn man das Ästhetische als wohlgefällige Formung des Gegebenen auffaßt." Kurt Pinthus, "Rede für die Zukunft" *Die Erhebung* (1919), 420. Rpt. W. Rothe (ed.), *Der Aktivismus 1915–20*, 132.

[44] "Der Himmel ist ein graues Packpapier / Auf dem die Sonne klebt – ein Butterfleck." Lichtenstein, "Landschaft," *Lyrik des Expressionismus*, 209.

"The sun, a buttercup, balances / On a smokestack, its thin stalk."[45]

Clearly such images work by producing a clash between very different contexts which thereby creates a profoundly bathetic effect. More specifically however, it is the strategy of de-aestheticization common to the avant-garde and its "cynical sublation" of art and life which is responsible for this provocative effect. For by calling up a conventional romantic or sublime topos (the heavens, the sun) only to thrust it down into the context of the all too mundane and earthly is to produce an anti-aesthetics: a reversal of conventional aesthetic values which "shocks the bourgeois," frustrates his or her institutionally nurtured expectations and offends his or her sense of cultural propriety.

Such de-aestheticized images and idiosyncratic comparisons have their roots in the fundamental expressionist aesthetic which dictates that the images need not be "realistic," but rather should derive their validity from other criteria, such as the "power" they display, or from the assertion of "Wille" – sheer willpower. In this they are related to the painter Franz Marc's famous blue horses,[46] or to the personal color coding in Trakl's poems where the very contingency of the choice of epithet is in the forefront.[47]

The apparent arbitrariness of the epithet is crucial. Not only does it underline the rebellion against conventional modes of seeing and representing, but in emphasizing the necessarily fictional nature of the constructed image, it presents its message as merely one possible mode of perception among many. In the case of Trakl's poetry the choice of color or metaphor may be either completely contingent, or – as in the case of an important predecessor in the development of expressionist aesthetics, namely van Gogh – highly personal.[48] But in either case the function is the same, as we shall see.

Firstly, to take the example of Marc's blue horses, the painted body of the horse is turned into a mere function of its color, and

---

[45] "Die Sonne, eine Butterblume, wiegt sich / Auf einem Schornstein, ihrem schlanken Stiele." Lichtenstein, "Nachmittag, Felder und Fabrik," *Lyrik des Expressionismus*, 73.    [46] Franz Marc, *Turm der blauen Pferde*, 1914.

[47] See especially Trakl's "Elis" and "An den Knaben Elis," *MHD*, 100, 101.

[48] In a letter to his brother Theo of August 1888, Vincent van Gogh writes, "instead of trying to produce exactly what I have before my eyes, I use color more arbitrarily so as to express myself more forcefully." *The Letters of Vincent van Gogh* (New York, 1963), 276. John Willett also describes the influence of van Gogh's aesthetics in *Expressionism* (London: Weidenfeld, 1970), *passim*.

with its shocking lack of "authenticity," the color is now by far the more striking component. In a similar way, with the examples from Lichtenstein above, the referent of the poem becomes a mere vehicle for the metaphor, so that the traditional rhetorical hierarchy between the two elements is overturned. Secondly, the subversion of the referent and of its naturalistic detail re-directs the recipient away from a distracting concern with the mere particulars of the appearance towards a more essential or conceptual level of the phenomenon.

Thirdly, and perhaps most importantly, besides allowing the presented image to be understood thus as one of the many "manifestations of the concept 'horse',"[49] it is as if the deliberate "distortion," the contingency of the choice of color or epithet, serves as the attempt to place this particular manifestation "under erasure" (Derrida), or as if the artist were both using and then crossing through a term which could only be employed with caution. By invoking but simultaneously suspending the signifier the artist appears in other words only to gesture towards an entity which is either unrepresentable as such or which would only be falsified by succumbing to a concrete and "representable" form. Thus the violent discrepancy created by the shocking color or epithet emphasizes the provisional nature of the particular concretization of "das Wesen" which has emerged, insisting on the impossibility of final closure.

Furthermore, to the extent that the image is used under erasure it is also freed from any direct subservience to a referent, and can emerge as a liberated signifier.[50] Like all such terms used under erasure these signifiers can only be thought of as being grasped or comprehended in a very provisional sense, since, as their foregrounding as fictions or metaphors makes clear, they are involved in a permanent process of slippage and displacement by other

49 Hamann and Hermand, *Expressionismus*, 133.
50 Further evidence of the growing autonomy of the signifier may be seen for example in such diverse forms as the "Lautgedicht" or "sound poem" of Stramm and Ball, where the "materiality" of the medium itself is emphasized. It may also be traced, as we have seen in chapter one, in the many Expressionist narratives and dramas whose figures become increasingly free of the representational concerns of identity, plot and causality, and who tend instead to become free-floating symbols or "objective correlatives" (Sokel) rather than "realistic" characters. This independence is also related – as in the montage-structure – to a growing sense of autonomy of the various parts *within* the work, as for example in the conceptions of the "epic" in Brecht and Döblin.

possible metaphors. It is in this vital sense that the expressionist text must be understood as aiming at a permanent revolution: where the signifiers of the text are inscribed in a differential chain of signification they are constantly being effaced and so are resistant to any attempt to reduce them to a fixable meaning. This permanent denial of stability and fixity to fictions (whether aesthetic or epistemological), the constant overturning of reified or "naturalized" ideological codes and unquestioned epistemological premises defines expressionism's participation in the historical avant-garde and constitutes precisely the sense of the "expressionist revolution."

## Functional and stylistic transformations

In conclusion we can now draw together certain perspectives developed in the foregoing analyses regarding the nature of this revolution. It should now be clear that the frequent reluctance shown by many expressionists to pin themselves down to particular ideological tendencies or to state their goals in precise political terms does not mean that one must write off their revolutionary intentions as the vague rebellious aspirations of a band of adolescent literati who were either unwilling to abandon the protection offered by a conventionalized form of aesthetic autonomy, or who were unable to give this aesthetic autonomy a purposefully ideological edge.[51] Rather one must place these aims in a different category, on an ideological and epistemological level rather than in the realm of genuine social praxis.[52]

As we have seen, it is not through concrete social plans that the

---

[51] For a commentary and extensive bibliography on the political commitment and active participation of many expressionists in revolutionary activity such as the November revolution. See *Manifeste und Dokumente*, 326–332.

[52] The question of political engagement is often parried in the programmatic statements, frequently in a manner which does not so much sidestep a clear ideological commitment, as refuse to acknowledge the dichotomy between art and reality implied by such questions. Typically the dichotomy is itself subverted by the introduction of a third term, notably "Geist" ("spirit," or "soul"): "art is not a flight from reality, – but rather a flight into the reality of the spirit. It is not a form of balm, but rather of agitation . . ." ("Die Kunst ist nicht Flucht aus der Wirklichkeit, – sondern Flucht in die Wirklichkeit des Geistes. Sie ist nicht Beruhigung, sondern Erregung . . .") writes Kurt Pinthus in "Rede für die Zukunft," *Die Erhebung* (1919) 415. Similarly Kurt Hiller sees the task of activism as "politicizing the spirit" ("den Geist zu politisieren"). In *Das Ziel* Jb. III, 1. Halbband, (Leipzig: Wolff, 1919). Quoted in *Manifeste und Dokumente*, 326.

expressionists present their revolutionary agenda but through a vision which, in its extremism, in its pointed artificiality or subjectivism, may even appear at first glance quite unrelated to the concrete conditions prevailing in the social world.[53] Correspondingly, it is not through an accurate mimetic representation of the status quo that their critical standpoint is achieved. Rather, as with Peter Bürger's category of the montage or non-organic work, it is paradoxically through the distortions, through the pointed constructedness and artificiality of the image that this impulse towards change comes to the fore.

The comparison with the strategies of the naturalist movement is again instructive in this respect. From a socio-historical perspective one might advance the general proposition that new literary movements are frequently subject to a kind of "cultural lag" (Ogburn) in their response to a changed social and ideological situation.[54] They often display a discrepancy between the "functional transformation" ('Funktionswandel'), that is, the new critical functions accruing to their texts as they negotiate their response to the changed set of conditions and problematics pertaining to a new historical period, and the "stylistic transformations" ("Stilwandel") or stylistic means developed to mediate the innovation and so account formally for this socio-historical change. Now it appears to be just such a cultural lag which frequently produces within the naturalist text the kind of contradiction between progressive "tendency" and conservative "technique" which Benjamin ascribes to a failure to comprehend the institutionalized cultural codes. For although the discourse of naturalist drama for example is progressive, encouraging social change and rebellion against the constraints of determinism and milieu, its dramatic form, even down to the very props it employs on stage, are so solid, and its verisimilitude so precise and uncompromising, that against its own intentions it overwhelms us with an impression of the unchangeable fixity and immovable determinacy of the world and its appearance.[55]

---

[53] See Sokel, *The Writer in Extremis*, 161.

[54] According to Ogburn's famous thesis, a "cultural lag occurs when one of two parts of culture which are correlated changes before or in greater degree than the other part does ..." See William F. Ogburn, "Cultural Lag as Theory" (1957) *On Culture and Social Change* (Chicago: University of Chicago Press, 1964), 86.

[55] In his *Literary Theory* (Oxford: Blackwell, 1983) Terry Eagleton makes this point in a discussion of Raymond Williams' theory of drama (187).

The importance of expressionism's revolutionary iconoclasm and avant-garde innovations in this regard is that they resolve many of the literary-historical deficits and contradictions bequeathed by its main predecessor, naturalism. For example by contrast with the solidity of naturalist verisimilitude, what the expressionist text attempts to do is to undermine appearances in order firstly to shock the audience and undermine both the inherent conservatism and the sense of reassurance it derives from recognizing the familiar, and secondly to destroy the audience's comforting illusion of having conceptually mastered or "fixed" reality.

But there is a further important dimension to this avant-garde assault on aesthetic convention. If the "real" in art is an effect produced by the use of certain culturally-privileged codes of representation, then through the forceful re-writing of old codes expressionism militates against this semiotic hegemony. It is in breaking decisively with these old ways of seeing, that it rebels against the real. For by constructing its images through forms which are tentative or "under erasure," by foregrounding their fictionality and by presenting them as pure constructions it succeeds in inscribing a revolutionary openness and resistance to closure into the texts. In this it fulfills a primary goal of the avant-garde: it loosens the grip of dominant cultural codes (and thus of the institution of art) upon the construction of the real by holding open the possibility of alternative constructions, and by demonstrating the infinite re-writability of the real. Through this two-fold openness expressionism's message of dissent is made to correspond to its means.

Finally, if expressionism is to be seen primarily as a conceptual art full of anthropomorphosed concepts and concretized ideas – in Jost Hermand's words, as a "poetic formulation of definitions" of a "purely epistemological kind" ("definitorische Dichtung," "rein erkenntnismäßiger Natur")[56] – then it must be conceded that its revolutionary function is of the same order: it operates on the theoretical level of an ideological and epistemological re-thinking, in other words as a form of "Ideologie-" and "Erkenntniskritik" which challenges not only conventional views of the world but also the orienting concepts which support them, in

---

[56] Hermand, "Expressionismus als Revolution," 337.

order to reveal their fictionality, their arbitrary nature, and thus their fundamental susceptibility to change.

A talk given in 1917 by Robert Müller describes this attack on conventional "Weltbilder" (or "images of the world") in terms of a revolutionary displacement of old regimes and systems of meaning, and as an assault precisely on the fixity and closure which they prescribe:

We are going over to the elastic systems. The rigid classical systems are a *cas limite* and are only occasionally satisfying . . .
The picture of the new painter is independent of those moments of rigidity through which we reify our daily visual impressions . . . The picture of the new painter rocks the boat. Rock with it, give up your own rigidity – that is expressionism.[57]

From this it is clear that the task of the expressionist artist is to displace the fixity of the old systems with a new "elasticity" – a quality directly comparable, in terms of our discussion above, to the "openness" always inscribed into the texts of the expressionist avant-garde.[58] Through this new "elasticity" a picture is created which unsettles and "rocks" ("schaukelt") the recipient's every-day fixed images and rigid systems. Thus rather than confirming the reader's positioning within the inherited cosmology, as an avant-garde movement expressionism breaks up the stiff ideologies and fixed images on which the individual relies. This is a widespread practice within the movement, even embracing the sober poetics of Franz Kafka and his view that the text should serve as an axe "for the frozen sea within us" provoking and forcing the reader out of conventional attitudes and modes of behaviour.[59]

More than simply shocking the burgher ("épater le bourgeois"), such strategies as this "schaukeln" destabilize the social and discursive conventions by which he is protected. By thus revealing their own fictional nature the effect of such avant-garde texts is to

[57] "Wir gehen zu den elastischen Systemen über. Die klassischen starren Systeme sind Grenzfall und befriedigen nur fallweise . . . Das Bild des neuen Malers ist unabhängig von jenen Starrheitsmomenten, auf die hin wir unsere täglichen optischen Eindrücke versteifen . . . Das Bild des Malers schaukelt. Schaukeln Sie mit, geben Sie Ihre eigene Starre auf – das ist Expressionismus." Robert Müller, "Die Zeitrasse." In *Der Anbruch* 1 (1917/18). Rpt. *Manifeste und Dokumente*, 137.

[58] As we shall see in the chapter on the poetics of expressionism, this openness is precisely what distinguishes the work of the avant-garde writers from the "monological" texts of the "naive" expressionists.

[59] Franz Kafka, *Briefe 1902–1924*, ed. Max Brod (Frankfurt: Fischer, 1975), 28.

*decenter* the reader, that is, to force the subject out of any habitual positioning by these systems and to offer not simply an alternative (and consequently equally fixed) ideological position, but rather a multiplicity of alternatives – even if these appear only tentative and "under erasure."[60]

In 1910 at the outset of the movement, in the first edition of one of the most influential expressionist journals, *Der Sturm*, Rudolf Kurtz offers a warning to the audience about this revolutionary and decentering function of expressionism: "We don't want to entertain them. We want to demolish their comfortable, serious and noble view of life artfully."[61] Given the ongoing nature of the revolution prescribed by Expressionism and the shockwaves which it has sent out in the intervening years throughout the modern and postmodern world, it is a warning which must still be taken seriously.[62]

---

[60] Thus expressionism's mode of liberation may occasionally take the paradoxical form of making the reader aware that the real world which he or she inhabits is a fiction which simultaneously serves as a prison or labyrinth preventing him from gaining access to "genuine" experience. The work of Franz Kafka with his thematization of the labyrinthine nature of truth ("Gesetz") and his sceptical attitude towards interpretation as a mere "expression of despair" must be seen in this expressionist context.

[61] "Wir wollen sie nicht unterhalten. Wir wollen ihr bequemes ernst-erhabenes Weltbild tückisch demolieren." Rudolf Kurtz, "Programmatisches," *Der Sturm* 1 (3 March 1910), 2–3. Rpt. *Manifeste und Dokumente*, 515.

[62] An anonymous reviewer of an earlier version of this chapter (published as an article in *German Quarterly*) quite rightly pointed to the seemingly conservative features in what I describe as the "revolutionary" make-up of expressionism, and in particular to the "religious and prophetic" tendencies which respond to the death of God by "resurrecting such essentials as 'Geist'." I would account for this apparently conciliatory moment however by maintaining firstly that an important feature of the expressionists' proclamation of these "essentials" is that such values remain, like "Geist" or the "new Man" ("neuer Mensch"), amorphous and provocatively obscure, as if the goal were the iconoclastic act of proclaiming an impossible new order, rather than the more difficult and pedestrian task (more characteristic of the earlier utopian and "idealist" avant-garde) of defining its "center," and so fixing the new order to a single position. Secondly, it should be observed that there is a self-critical tendency within expressionism – embodied precisely by its genuinely avant-garde wing rather than its idealist faction – which comes to the fore especially in the later period of its "recoil" from such prophetic excesses (Sokel), and which eschews even such vague proclamations and subjects them to parody. This recoil has its counterpart in dada's later onslaughts on the expressionists' prophetic excesses, where the very name of the group "dada" itself becomes an empty signifier parodying the often repeated watchword of the idealists within expressionism: "Geist" (i.e. "spirit," "mind" or "soul"). This central term, like the name "dada" itself, could be thought of as a hollow vessel, and one which is receptive for any new contents one cares to fill it with.

# 3

❖❖❖❖❖❖❖❖❖❖❖❖❖❖❖❖❖❖❖❖❖❖❖❖❖❖❖❖❖❖❖❖❖❖❖❖❖❖❖❖❖❖❖❖

# Counter-discourses of the avant-garde: Jameson, Bakhtin and the problem of realism

❖❖❖❖❖❖❖❖❖❖❖❖❖❖❖❖❖❖❖❖❖❖❖❖❖❖❖❖❖❖❖❖❖❖❖❖❖❖❖❖❖❖❖❖

## Döblin and the avant-garde poetics of expressionist prose

In an essay on expressionism published towards the end of the "expressionist decade" in June 1918, Alfred Döblin reflects upon the nature of such movements and how they affect the aesthetic choices and directions pursued by the writers of the time:

People are the vehicles of the movement, its creators, its movers; others enter these waters consciously or unconsciously, and go along with it. Some individuals are hardly touched by the wave, some wade in knee deep, others swim in it in fits and starts according to their own impulses, some are washed away, and after high tide are left lying flat on the beach. Many experience a purification from such a movement, many a strengthening, many a sense of direction.[1]

Döblin himself is clearly indebted to the "purifying" and "strengthening" effects of his association with the movement of

---

[1] "Personen sind die Träger der Bewegung, ihre Macher, sind die Beweger, andere geraten in das Fahrwasser, ahnungslos oder bewußt, treiben mit ihm. Von dieser Welle werden einzelne kaum bespült, andere waten knietief hinein, andere schwimmen darin stoßweise nach eigenem Antrieb, andere werden weggeschwemmt, liegen nach Abflauen der Flut platt auf dem Strand. Von solcher Bewegung erfahren viele eine Reinigung, viele eine Stärkung, viele eine Richtung." Alfred Döblin, "Von der Freiheit eines Dichtermenschen," *Aufsätze zur Literatur*, ed. Walter Muschg (Freiburg: Walter, 1963), 24–25. Hereafter cited in the text as *AzL*.

expressionism, and at another point in the essay he acknowledges its importance for him, saying that "the breakthrough, the expansion, the finding of one's feet . . . the emergence into the public is first made possible in this decade"(*AzL*, 24).[2] As is the case also with Franz Kafka and Gottfried Benn, it can similarly be argued of Döblin that the most significant stage of his development as a writer – his "breakthrough" – occurred during the expressionist period.[3] It was during this decade that all three discovered and experimented with the central elements of their personal poetics and developed a defining style – a mode of writing which in its essential features was heavily indebted to expressionism for its critical or avant-garde impact.

Besides acknowledging in his essay the positive effects of the movement, Döblin is also conscious of its dangers, and is already wary of the fate that a few years later was to overcome many of expressionism's less established adherents: "Those who have dedicated body and soul to the movement will become its martyrs. They will be used up by the movement, and will remain lying there after, crippled, invalid" (*AzL*, 26.)[4] For Döblin it is clear that this danger of martyrdom is linked specifically to the movement's function as an "avant-garde" in the conventional sense of the word, as the means by which new artistic directions are explored. For although initially significant in terms of experiment and innovation, according to Döblin the works of many of the more progressive artists may in themselves be of merely fleeting value, important precisely as a mode of innovation and transition but with little lasting impact. The writers of such works

accompanied the day as its priest or perhaps as its advance guard, in order to be discharged at one particular stretch of the path. What they achieved: usually a soon-forgotten work which was highly significant for the good of the cause, sharply illuminating the way ahead for several years, but in which, on inspection, one later recognizes quickly the thin

[2] "der Durchbruch, die Ausbreitung, das Bodenfinden . . . das Hervortreten an die Öffentlichkeit ist erst in diesem Jahrzehnt ermöglicht."
[3] The notion that the expressionist movement facilitated the major "breakthrough" for many writers has also been widely adopted with regard to the work of Kafka. Walter Sokel for example places great importance upon this period of Kafka's development as a writer. See W. H. Sokel, *Franz Kafka. Tragik und Ironie* (Frankfurt-on-Main: Fischer, 1976), 46–67.
[4] "Die der Bewegung mit Leib und Seele verschrieben sind, werden ihre Märtyrer. Sie werden von der Bewegung aufgebraucht und bleiben nachher liegen, krüppelhaft, invalide."

homunculus, devoid of essence which is hanging from it and suffocating on account of his momentary talents. (*AzL*, 26)[5]

Given this awareness of the dangers awaiting these "avant-garde" artists in their role as the advance-guard or "Vorreiter," the question which then arises is the extent to which expressionist writers such as Döblin and Benn managed to contribute to the creation of a progressive poetics of expressionism yet avoid the fate of ending up as mere transitional phenomena pure and simple. Furthermore, if we want to understand the relationship between their expressionistic strategies and the general goals of the historical avant-garde as we have described them we must discover in what ways the innovations of these most prominent expressionists succeeded not only in confronting the inherited literary tradition, but in posing a challenge to the institution of art as a whole.

## Expressionist montage, "counter-discourse" and the model of the classic realist text

For Döblin this attempt to mark a distance to inherited tradition, in particular to the work of the preceding generation of naturalists, is characterized by deep ambiguity. Despite his clear admiration for the naturalists he is very skeptical regarding the unquestioned premises of their practice, especially with respect to their ideological baggage of positivism. In his theoretical writings (collected in the *Aufsätze zur Literatur* ["Essays on Literature"]) Döblin often acknowledges his debts to the naturalist movement, and he clearly considers it the most significant of the conventions within which he is working. From his earliest writing on his goal is always to produce a form of "systematic naturalism" which would refine the practice of his predecessors through an ever more rigorous attention to the power of observation, and through the exclusion of all superfluous stylistic flourishes. His response to Marinetti ("Futuristische Worttechnik" ["Futurist verbal technique"]) focuses its more positive observations precisely upon those aspects

---

[5] " . . . begleiteten den Tag als seine Priester oder vielleicht als Vorreiter, um an einer bestimmten Wegstrecke abgedankt zu werden. Was sie leisteten: ein meist bald verschollenes Werk, das höchst signifikant für die Sache war, scharf ein paar Jahre vorwärts leuchtete, bei dessen Betrachtung man später rasch das dünne wesenlose Menschlein erkennt, das daran zappelt, aufgehängt erstickt an seiner Momentbegabung." (*AzL*, 26).

of futurism which are closest to his own goals of producing a progressive form of naturalism: "We want no prettification, no decoration, no style, nothing external, but rather hardness, coldness and fire . . . without wrapping paper . . . That which is not direct, not immediate, not saturated with objectivity, we collectively refuse . . . naturalism, naturalism; we are not naturalist enough by a long chalk" (*AzL*, 9).[6] Yet despite his generally naturalistic aim of shifting the balance towards the referent and the object world – "we must get up against life more closely" ("dichter heran müssen wir an das Leben" [*AzL*, 11]) – Döblin is careful to avoid proposing any form of realism which smacks of mere reflectionism. His admiration for the naturalists for example is always tempered by his wariness of appearing to reduce writing to a merely documentary function, and of reproducing an "absolute" reality, "which we would have to take down respectfully in our report" ("der wir uns ehrfürchtig als Protokollführer zu nähern hätten" [*AzL*, 10]) even though this function might in many respects represent the logical extension of the naturalists' project – not the least important of whose goals was that of "objectivity" and of reducing the narrator's presence.

This relationship between the narrator's presence and the narrated "reality" becomes all-important in Döblin's attempts to re-work the inherited realist conventions of naturalism in a manner which will both systematically extend this tradition (a tradition he considered crucial), while at the same time integrating it within the expressionist practices and the very different ideological positions common to the avant-garde. The narratological subject–object relationship (between narrator and narrated reality) is equally decisive for the expressionist movement too, although for a different reason, since it is precisely the projection of the subject's emotions and impressions onto the environment, and the dialectical interaction between the two which now constitutes the central characteristic of all genres of the expressionist movement. It also marks the key difference between the two movements. For whereas naturalism's positivist premise is to assume the existence of an undeniably objective, discrete and observable "reality," in

---

6 "wir wollen keine Verschönerung, keinen Schmuck, keinen Stil, nichts Äußerliches, sondern Härte, Kälte und Feuer . . . ohne Packpapier . . . Was nicht direkt, nicht unmittelbar, nicht gesättigt von Sachlichkeit ist, lehnen wir gemeinsam ab . . . Naturalismus, Naturalismus; wir sind noch lange nicht genug Naturalisten."

expressionism the position is precisely the opposite: instead, there is an emphasis on a dialectical movement, a merging and mutual displacement of subject and object which serves to problematize the existence of such categories, to question their status as discrete entities, and to expose their (primary) function as mere hypotheses or "useful fictions."

Furthermore through this process of interrogation, the expressionist text begins also to institute certain critical changes in the relationship between the reader and the text. This relationship, as we shall see, is radically affected by what I will call the expressionist avant-garde's "counter-discursive" methods, and is characterized by the reader's growing autonomy both to discern the issues at the stake and to formulate a perspective on them independently, rather than being steered towards them unambiguously by the text (as is frequently the case for example with the more deterministic case-histories represented in naturalist texts). In order to understand the "progressive" quality of the changes in this reader-text relationship (which such expressionist writers as Döblin begin to work out early on in the movement's development), it is important to relate them to the more general innovations produced by the avant-garde as a whole. Of particular importance are those oppositional strategies described by Peter Bürger's *Theorie der Avant-Garde*.

As we have seen, according to Bürger, the historical avant-garde of the early twentieth century – comprising individual movements such as cubism, dada, surrealism, futurism, and expressionism – develops not only in response to the need to mark a break with the artistic tradition as a whole, but more specifically in response to the need to distinguish its emergent artistic credo from those conventionally aestheticist principles (for example the notion of aesthetic autonomy) which had taken on an overwhelmingly quietist and apologetic function as part of the general "institutionalization of art" in bourgeois society. It is important to stress in this regard that Bürger's argument, deriving as it does from Marcuse's theory of "affirmative culture," takes issue primarily with the *consolatory* functions of such art.[7] That is, it highlights the extent to which both the idealizing and the critical forms of art alike may fulfill the affirmative function of reconciling their

---

[7] Herbert Marcuse, "The Affirmative Character of Culture," *Negations*, trans. Jeremy Shapiro (Boston: Beacon, 1968), 88–133.

audiences to an imperfect reality by means of illusion: the former offer consolation by presenting beautiful and idealized images of a reconciled world, while the latter exercise their critique only within the abstract world of the text, thereby limiting the critical potential of the text solely to the relatively ineffectual realm of the aesthetic.

Against such false consolations of form, the avant-garde proposes an alternative set of literary categories linked by the central notion of non-organic form, foremost among which are the montage, the fragment, and the "ready-made." Such non-organic forms not only question the very notion of the "work" as an aesthetic totality. Through their provocation and problematization of the institutionalized criteria of aesthetic production they radically alter the relationship between art and its audience. For example, in emphasizing the fragmentary and incomplete quality of the work they expose its constructed and artificial nature. The audience no longer finds consolation either in a sense of formal harmony and totality, or in the illusion that the work contains a complete and self-sufficient meaning. Instead, the initial sense of alienation and shock at the disappointment of its conventionalized expectations pushes the audience towards a more active stance in which it must take responsibility itself for piecing together the disparate components of the work, and most significantly, for producing its meaning.

Examples of non-organic forms such as montage are common in expressionist literature. For example in the "Reihungsstil" constructions in the early expressionist poetry of van Hoddis and Lichtenstein the poem consists of a disjointed collection of one-line images.[8] Only through a heightened imaginative effort on the part of the reader can the links between these images be forged so that they can be assimilated into an aggregate picture (such as the "apocalypse," or the "city in the evening," etc.). As with the "epic" structures promoted by Döblin and Brecht (to which these poetic forms of montage are clearly related) the non-organic forms of the expressionist avant-garde offer little sense of an overall harmony or semantic wholeness to draw the individual components together. Consequently none of the individual images proves indispensable to the whole, since they relate to each other

---

[8] On the "one-line style" or "Reihungsstil" in early expressionist poetry see Vietta and Kemper, *Expressionismus*, 30–40.

not directly but only indirectly via the loosely organized, aggregate image they form through this process of accumulation.[9]

The expressionist "Ich-Drama" ("drama of the self") and "Stationendrama" ("stations [of the cross]") also takes on a fragmentary shape similar to a montage in both form and function. It is largely devoid of tension and linear "plot" (in the conventional sense of the term) and is frequently constructed instead according to spatial considerations: it commonly consists of a vaguely picaresque series of encounters, with a central figure wandering amongst reflections of his own persona on the path towards an undefined goal of redemption or enlightenment. As with the one-line method of the Reihungstil-poem (or the "epic" structures created by Brecht and Döblin) individual components, scenes and encounters may be left out without detriment to the overall effect of the play, since this effect depends less upon their direct interrelation – as it would by contrast in a conventional linear plot – than on the aggregate image which the audience is able to construct from the "raw material" which the play provides.

Although the avant-garde principle of non-organic form is readily recognizable in expressionist poetry and drama, the question arises as to whether it is possible to discover analogous fragmentary structures, montage forms, and counter-discourses in the field of expressionist prose. Now if we bear in mind that the crucial aspect of the non-organic as a progressive element is not necessarily the *form per se*, but rather its overall *function* – its effect with regard to the relationship between the reader and the text – then, as we shall see, it becomes possible to discover precisely the same oppositional characteristics in expressionist prose, even though their modes of operation and manner of achieving these similar effects are very different. In this regard Colin MacCabe's description of the "classic realist text" (the convention against which the "subversive" text constitutes itself) provides a means of understanding the specifically avant-garde aspects of the work of

---

[9] This structural dynamic is clearly related for example to that which Döblin demands of the "epic," namely that one should be able to cut it into separate sections, which, as with a worm, should be able to move independently. As Zmegac points out in his excellent article "Alfred Döblins Poetik des Romans" this is almost identical to Brecht's observation that one should be able to cut the epic "into separate pieces which nevertheless remain viable" (Brecht, *Schriften zum Theater*, 3, 53). See *Deutsche Romantheorien*, ed. R. Grimm (Fischer: Frankfurt-on-Main: 1968), 341–364. Here 349.

such expressionist prose writers as Döblin.[10] According to Mac-
Cabe, the nineteenth-century realist novel is typified by a very
particular hierarchical relationship between the discourses of the
characters and the surrounding discourse of the narrator. The
narrator frequently functions via a "metalanguage" which comments on the text's other discourses or "object-languages," judging their truthfulness and so effectively dominating them from its
role as the representative of a higher form of truth. This textual
hierarchy has a unifying effect upon the work, drawing together
the strands of plot and character and "homogenizing" its various
object-languages.[11] Inevitably this textual structure tends to align
the reader closely with the dominant discourse, offering reassurance of its correctness by means of its unquestionably secure and
"transparent" perspective, with the result that the reader's participation in the production of the text's meaning is streamlined.
Like the traditional "Aristotelian" drama whose illusionism
Brecht sought to undermine with his avant-garde conceptions of
"epic" theater, such classic realist texts attempt to efface the traces
of their own construction and perspective, so as to appear as a
neutral and transparent "window" upon the world, offering a
complete and impartial view of events. This neutral stance allows
the discourse narrating events to masquerade as a kind of objective "history," monumental and unalterable. In this way it dis-
arms the reader and, in contrast to the montage or "epic" form[12],
renders superfluous the pursuit of contradictory perspectives or
alternative versions of events.

It should be noted that MacCabe sees the "classic realist text"
mainly as a theoretical model, stressing that in concrete cases the
explanatory function of its realism is never absolute, and he

[10] MacCabe describes the classic realist text and develops the model of its "domi-
nant discourse" in the articles "Realism and the Cinema: Notes on Some
Brechtian Theses," *Screen* 15.2 (1974), and "Theory and Film: Principles of
Realism and Pleasure," *Screen* 17.3 (1976), 7–27. Both articles are reprinted in
*Tracking the Signifier. Theoretical Essays: Film, Linguistics, Literature* (Minneapolis:
Minnesota University Press, 1985), 33–57, 58–81 and I quote here from this
edition. This model is further explored in MacCabe's *James Joyce and the Revol-
ution of the Word*.

[11] MacCabe, "Theory and Film," *Tracking the Signifier*, 63.

[12] This role of the reader also stands in sharp contrast to that envisaged by Döblin
in his much later conception of the epic "Der Bau des epischen Werks" (1929), in
which, as he says, *"the reader participates in the process of production alongside the
author"* (*"Der Leser macht also den Produktionsprozeß mit dem Autor mit"*) *AzL*, 123.
Emphasis in original. See *AzL*, 103–132.

allows for significant breaches in the power of the dominant discourse and in its ability to account for everything.[13] Nevertheless, it is worth observing that however schematic such a model might appear, its essential features are precisely those valorized by Georg Lukacs during the "expressionism debates" of 1930s as a normative model of realism and as an example to the avant-garde of what it was lacking. For example Lukacs' model envisages a similar textual structure, characterized by the author's task of comprehending and abstracting the "essence" ("Wesen") of the objective reality he intends to represent. This process of "opening up" ("Aufdecken") which uncovers the objective relationship and laws underlying social reality is complemented by the artistic procedure of "covering over" ("Zudecken"), through which these abstractions are brought together and given an artificially harmonious appearance – and with it the illusion of reality. This illusionism produces "a constructed surface of life, which although it allows the essence to *shine through* clearly at every moment (which is not the case in the immediacy of life itself) nevertheless appears as immediacy" (Lukacs' emphasis).[14]

The model of realism which Lukacs envisages matches Mac-Cabe's notion of the "classic realist text" at several points. Firstly, it proceeds from the assumption that at a certain level the text possesses the "truth" about the reality it represents. Secondly, the text presents this reality illusionistically, so that both the arbitrariness of its perspective and the constructed nature of the reality it describes are obscured. Thirdly, both models disenfranchise the reader in a similar manner, effectively discouraging the discovery of alternative or contradictory meanings and consequently hindering the autonomous use of the subject's critical capacity in favor of a more passive acceptance of the single and all-exclusive legitimacy of the meanings proposed by the text.

Interestingly Lukacs explicitly rejects the work of expressionism and the avant-garde – specifically targeting its deployment of the montage technique – precisely because such works

---

[13] As MacCabe observes, "[c]lassic realism can never be absolute; the materiality of language ensures there will always be fissures which will disturb the even surface of the text." *James Joyce*, 27.

[14] "eine gestaltete Oberfläche des Lebens, die obwohl sie in jedem Moment das Wesen klar *durchscheinen* läßt (was in der Unmittelbarkeit des Lebens selbst nicht der Fall ist) doch als Unmittelbarkeit, als Oberfläche des Lebens erscheint." Lukacs, "Es geht um den Realismus," *Expressionismusdebatte*, 205.

fail to "form" reality into a "totality," and so end up merely reproducing the "chaos" of the times.[15] In other words, Lukacs faults the avant-garde for its failure to produce traditional, organic works of art which offer a clearly delineated sense of closure with regard to the "objective" truth beneath the surface of the real.

Against this model of the classic realist text and in stark contrast to Lukacs' version of "realism" it is possible to describe a set of divergent characteristics shared by the more progressive or avant-garde prose writers within the expressionist movement. Most important among these characteristics is the refusal to privilege any single textual discourse as the discourse of "truth." By extension, this means refusing to reduce the reader's activity to that of identifying comfortably with the transcendental position of truth underwritten by the text's dominant discourse. Through the principle of non-organic composition, such avant-garde texts refuse to evoke the illusion of having produced a comprehensive vision of social totality, while their open-endedness subverts any consolatory sense of having resolved the problems raised by the narrative – an effect frequently produced in the classic realist text for example through the convention of a final act of closure. Instead of the reader being maneuvered by the text into that privileged position from which its narrative is most readily mastered,[16] the reader is thrown back upon his or her own devices, and is forced to discover independently not only the text's contradictions but also the possible means of resolving them.

## Döblin's poetics and the avant-garde: the "naive" vs. the "sophisticated" expressionists

The counter-discursive strategies of the avant-garde can best be understood in relation to this goal of subverting classical representation and the classic realist text. Döblin's theoretical writings during the expressionist period show that these essential principles of the avant-garde "counter-text"[17] are central to his own

---

[15] Lukacs, "Es geht um den Realismus," *Expressionismusdebatte*, 210.
[16] Catherine Belsey describes this function of maneuvering the reader as the process by which the text produces "a single position from which the scene is intelligible." See *Critical Practice* (London: Methuen, 1980), 76.
[17] MacCabe, *James Joyce*, 100.

"program" of writing and, with certain modifications, to what he later conceived of as the "epic" work. Translated into MacCabe's terms, it is clear that Döblin's primary target here is the "dominant discourse" of the narrator. Döblin insists for example on the eradication of every aspect of this domination: "The hegemony of the author must be broken; the fanaticism of self-denial cannot be carried far enough. Or the fanaticism for renunciation: I am not me, but rather the street, the lights, this or that event, nothing more. This is what I call the stone-style" (*AzL*, 18).[18] This assault on the conventional narratological hierarchy extends even to the removal of those narrative interventions to be found in the text's stylistic and rhetorical flourishes: "The art of writing must display itself negatively through what it avoids, with an absence of decoration: in the absence of intention, in the absence of the mere flourish or the verbally beautiful, in the holding back of affectation. Images are dangerous and only to be employed on occasion"(*AzL*, 17–18).[19] Döblin is not interested here in eliminating merely the *traces* of the narrator – which are foregrounded for instance in what he sees as the stylistic accomplishments or aestheticist flourishes of the text – in order to promote the illusion of an unmediated and perfectly "transparent" representation, as might occur for example in the classic realist text. On the contrary his goal is the "elimination of the self, renunciation of the author, de-personalization" (*AzL*, 18),[20] in other words the complete removal of the narrator as a source of the text's "truth," and as the representative of those analytical and explanatory functions typical of the dominant discourse in classic realism. Consequently he attacks that form of causal explanation or "novelistic psychology" ("Romanpsychologie") which attempts to analyze and explain

18 "Die Hegemonie des Autors ist zu brechen; nicht weit genug kann der Fanatismus der Selbstverleugnung getrieben werden. Oder der Fanatismus der Entäußerung: ich bin nicht ich, sondern die Straße, die Laternen, dies und dies Ereignis, weiter nichts. Das ist es, was ich den steinernen Stil nenne." This statement is particularly relevant to Döblin's theoretical position at the time of completing the short story "Die Ermordung einer Butterblume." It appears in his famous essay "An Romanautoren und ihre Kritiker. Berliner Programm" which appeared in the expressionist journal *Der Sturm* in May 1913, three years after the publication there of "Die Ermordung einer Butterblume."
19 "Die Wortkunst muß sich negativ zeigen in dem, was sie vermeidet, ein fehlender Schmuck: im Fehlen der Absicht, im Fehlen des bloß sprachlich Schönen oder Schwunghaften, im Fernhalten der Manieriertheit. Bilder sind gefährlich und nur gelegentlich anzuwenden . . ." (*AzL*, 17–18).
20 "Entselbstung, Entäußerung des Autors, Depersonation."

the thoughts and motivations of characters. In its place Döblin proposes a form of counter-discursive writing which will shift the focus towards observation and away from explanation:

> One must learn from psychiatry, the only science dealing with the whole person: it has long acknowledged the naiveté of psychology, limiting itself instead to the notation of processes, movements, – shaking the head and shrugging the shoulders regarding the further details and regarding the "why's" and "how's." (*AzL*, 16)[21]

Invoking to this end a venerable rhetorical distinction, Döblin maintains that rather than merely "telling" the reader through a denotative and explanatory narration, the text is to insist upon the ability of the reader to judge events independently, and is to provoke interpretive activity by "showing" the reader these events in a concrete manner: they should "not appear as if spoken, but rather as if present" (*AzL*, 17).[22] Furthermore, through a technique very similar to that described by the Russian formalists as "defamiliarization,"[23] Döblin intends to circumvent the automatizing effects upon language of its merely denotative or communicative functions, in favor of a more concrete method relying upon a sharpened visual sensibility:

> Verbal formulations only help in practical interactions. "Anger," "love," "contempt" designate a certain complex of appearances entering the sensorium, but beyond this these primitive and hackneyed clusters of letters give us nothing . . . The novelist must penetrate beyond "love" and "anger" and get back to the concrete. (*AzL*, 17)[24]

By these means the reader is to be *directly* confronted with the text's central problematic and is forced to take responsibility for

---

[21] "Man lerne von der Psychiatrie, der einzigen Wissenschaft, die sich mit dem seelischen ganzen Menschen befaßt: sie hat das Naive der Psychologie längst erkannt, beschränkt sich auf die Notierung der Abläufe, Bewegungen, – mit einem Kopfschütteln, Achselzucken für das Weitere und das 'Warum' und 'Wie'" (*AzL*, 16).

[22] "Das Ganze darf nicht erscheinen wie gesprochen, sondern wie vorhanden."

[23] See for example Victor Shklovsky, "Art as Technique," *Russian Formalist Criticism. Four Essays*, trans. L. Lemon and M. Reis (Lincoln: Nebraska University Press, 1965), 12–13.

[24] "Die sprachlichen Formeln dienen nur dem praktischen Verkehr. 'Zorn,' 'Liebe,' 'Verachtung' bezeichnen in die Sinne fallende Erscheinungskomplexe, darüber hinaus geben diese primitiven und abgeschmackten Buchstabenverbindungen nichts . . . Genau wie der Wortkünstler jeden Augenblick das Wort auf seinen ersten Sinn zurück 'sehen' muß, muß der Romanautor von 'Zorn' und 'Liebe' auf das Konkrete zurückdringen" (*AzL*, 17).

its resolution: "completely independently the reader [will] be confronted with a fully fashioned and completed sequence of events ; he should be the one to judge, not the author" (*AzL*, 17).[25]

This de-emphasizing of the author, the breaking of his "hegemony," is an important axiom of a large group of expressionist writers, of which Döblin is one of the most prominent. Indeed, the issue of the author's personality and the narrator's presence is one which divides the prose writers of the expressionist movement into two quite distinct groups. On the one hand there are what Sokel calls the "naïve," "primitive" or "rhetorical" Expressionists, who consistently throw caution to the wind and unself-consciously inflate their personality, broadcasting their emotional excesses or their most private beliefs in a fully unrestrained manner.[26] And on the other hand there are those expressionist writers who are more attuned to the general spirit of modernism and who hold fast to its central aesthetic principles of "impersonality,"[27] couching even the most subjective states and ideas in an external or "dramatized" form, in the attempt to keep the personality reined in.[28]

Let us recall Döblin's comments quoted earlier regarding the dangers for those artists whose innovative contributions to the movement enjoy a brief moment of success, but who are subsequently left behind. In many respects it seems that the achievements of the "naive" or "primitive" expressionists are precisely of this order. They unleash their most private emotions in their texts and open up their personality to the point of excess. Yet although initially shocking and arresting, the full force of these powerful effects cannot be sustained for long. The novelty-value rapidly fades, and any attempt to repeat this effect necessarily involves trying to raise the emotional voltage still further in order to repeat the shock. This ends inevitably in hollow rhetoric and mere artifice.

Even among those in this group who do not lapse into the

---

[25] "Der Leser [wird] in voller Unabhängigkeit einem gestalteten, gewordenen Ablauf gegenübergestellt; er mag urteilen, nicht der Autor."

[26] See Sokel, *The Writer in Extremis*, 18–20.

[27] On the relationship between expressionism and the modernist aesthetic of "impersonality" in modernism see Sokel, *The Writer in Extremis*, 106–108.

[28] David Lodge describes this aesthetic of "impersonality" in terms of the typically "modernistic" narrative devices in *After Bakhtin. Essays on Fiction and Criticism* (London: Routledge, 1990), 38–39.

rhetorical or declamatory excesses of the "primitive" expressionists, many are nevertheless frequently limited by their tendency to place their subjectivity and their intensely personal beliefs so prominently in the foreground, that their texts become
"monological," in Bakhtin's sense. Bakhtin describes this "monological" attitude as follows:

> Monologism, at its extreme, denies the existence outside itself of another
> consciousness with equal rights and equal responsibilities, another *I* with
> equal rights (thou). With a monologic approach (in its extreme or pure
> form) *another person* remains wholly and merely an *object* of conscious-
> ness, and not another consciousness . . . Monologue manages without the
> other . . . Monologue pretends to be the *ultimate word*.[29]

In other words, such texts appear to present merely a single voice
and perspective, resulting in a rather unitary or totalized world-
view. The effect is to shut out any genuine "dialogue" with other
discourses which might disclose contradictions or the possibility
of alternative ideological positions.[30] With the "primitive" expressionists there is a lack of equilibrium between, on the one
hand the high emotional charge powering the authorial personality, and on the other the discipline needed to deploy those artistic
strategies capable of harnessing this passion and presenting it in
the "externalized" form characteristic of the more "sophisticated" writers of Expressionism.

Leonhard Frank's cycle of short prose texts *Der Mensch ist gut*
(*Man/Humanity is Good*) is an example of the monological ap-
proach typical of the "naïve" or "primitive" expressionists.[31]
Published in 1918 it presents a series of scenes depicting the

---

[29] Mikhail Bakhtin, *Problems of Dostoevsky's Poetics*, trans. and ed. Caryl Emerson
(Minneapolis: Minnesota University Press, 1984), 292–293. Emphasis by Bakhtin.

[30] In this respect the unitary world view of the rhetorical expressionists appears to
function by holding in check the inherently dialogical character of language.
Bakhtin offers the following image of this dialogicity: "[A]ny concrete discourse
(utterance) finds the object at which it was directed already as it were overlain
with qualifications, open to dispute, charged with value, already enveloped in
an obscuring mist – or, on the contrary, by the 'light' of alien words that have
already been spoken about it. It is entangled, shot through with shared
thoughts, points of view, alien value judgements and accents. The word, directed toward its object, enters a dialogically agitated and tension-filled environment of alien words, value judgements and accents." *The Dialogic Imagination*, trans. Caryl Emerson and Michael Holquist, ed. Michael Holquist (Austin:
Texas University Press, 1981), 276.

[31] Leonhard Frank, *Der Mensch ist gut* (Zurich: Max Rascher, 1918).

response of ordinary people to the war and to the loss of their sons and husbands. In particular it targets the hollowness of the patriotic rhetoric which had accompanied the young soldiers as they went off to die "on the field of honor" (9) and "on the altar of the fatherland" (22), and it exposes the hypocrisy of the similar linguistic deceptions intended to comfort the bereaved afterwards. In this respect the text thematizes a dialogical interaction, in as far as it sets itself up in opposition to the dominant social discourses which underwrite both the war and the jingoism of the times.[32] The bereaved characters, for example, are shown gaining insight into the empty ideological rhetoric of war and countering the "official" sanitized version of events with their own hard-won truths.

Yet against its own intentions Frank's text also becomes a kind of "propaganda" in as far as it scarcely acknowledges the free subjectivity of the reader, leaving him or her with no ideological or discursive contradictions to resolve, few textual problems in need of interpretation and little to discover independently of the perspective provided already by the narrator. Typically the central figure of each of the stories is reduced to a direct mouthpiece for Frank's own opposition to the war. The protagonist of the first story for example is depicted as leading a spontaneous demonstration, speaking out against the war: "We may no longer deceive ourselves and say: only the Czar, the Kaiser, the Englishman is at fault... Accept the guilt yourselves, so that you may take part in love once again, because only those who feel guilt can be absolved of sin and can love once again" (17).[33]

As we can see from this quotation, the issues are depicted very directly and in a manner offering little possibility for contradiction, while at the same time the speech is so utopian and idealized that it even risks turning the intelligent reader *against* it, in his or her desperate search for an alternative perspective to its constricting monologicity. Consequently, despite the number of characters

---

[32] I use the term "dominant social discourse" in analogy to Raymond Williams' much broader concept of "hegemony," discussed in detail below, 98–99. See Williams' *Marxism and Literature* (Oxford: Oxford University Press, 1977), 108–120.

[33] "'Wir dürfen uns nicht länger belügen und sagen: nur der Zar, der Kaiser, der Engländer ist schuld... Nehmt die Schuld auf euch, damit ihr der Liebe wieder teilhaft werden könnt. Denn nur wer hier sich schuldig fühlt, kann entsündigt werden und wieder lieben'" (17).

whose speech is quoted, there is not a true variety of discourses present in the text and the potential for alternative perspectives or for the "dialogical" effects Bakhtin describes is suppressed since each discourse is immediately subordinated to a restrictive and dominating narrative discourse.

## Abstraction and the "aesthetics of the impersonal"

The primitive and rhetorical expressionists stand in sharp contrast to those writers of the movement who are constrained by the aesthetic of "impersonality." As we have seen the pure, unadulterated and often formless expressiveness of the primitive writers of the movement gives way in the more sophisticated and "dialogical" expressionists (such as Benn, Kafka, and Döblin) to an alternative form of expressiveness, which channels the subject's excesses through an indirect and externalizing structure, producing what is in certain respects a more restrained form. Such externalizing structures serve, as Walter Sokel observes, "to objectify an intensely subjective content without losing its subjectivism, but, on the contrary, deepening and clarifying it."[34]

Although both groups clearly maintain their overall allegiance to the expressionist movement – not least on account of the forceful expression of subjectivity which always constitutes the essential and defining power behind their work – in the case of the more sophisticated expressionists, this expressiveness is transformed by the use of these powerful externalizing forms. For they have the effect of harnessing precisely those unselfconscious and narcissistic outpourings of the soul which, in the unrestrained works of the primitive expressionists, produce the purely monological textual structures and their correspondingly single-minded world views. This important process of "externalization" or "objectification" is tied to what may be considered the axiomatic feature of the most sophisticated forms of expressionist representation: the writer's concentration upon an intensely personal meaning, an expressive "vision" or "essence," which is then uprooted from its context and projected onto an outer landscape, without either the personal and rhetorical ballast of the undialogical and "naive" expressionists, or the stabilizing effect produced either by the

[34] Sokel, *The Writer in Extremis*, 50.

"objectivity" of an overall realist framework or by the realistic details forming its everyday context in the world.[35]

Walter Sokel has described this axiomatic technique of externalization in terms of a principle of "abstraction" which works by leaving behind all that is "purely incidental and extraneous" and packing the remaining essence into a metaphor.[36] Sokel cites the example of Trakl who

> substitutes everywhere for the lyrical and personal "I" metaphoric disguises such as "the stranger," "a thing putrified," "a dead thing," "the murderer" . . . Then inwardly dead, the poet becomes "a dead thing." He rejects the word "I" because it contains aspects purely incidental and extraneous to the dead self. Similarly stressing the violent and cruel passion in himself, he calls himself not "I" but "the murderer." The metaphor abstracts the person from the feelings . . . (50)

Similarly in Kafka's *The Metamorphosis*, Sokel observes that Gregor Samsa "has become identical with his wish" (46) and so is "transformed into a metaphor that states his essential self, and this metaphor in turn is treated like an actual fact" (47). The expressionists' reductive identification of the figure with a single attribute of character – typical also of the dehumanizing and defamiliarizing technique of synecdoche frequently employed in expressionist poetry – constitutes a central component of their poetics of representation.[37] The "expressive" quality of expressionism lies in the ability firstly to produce a "vision," but secondly to create what Sokel calls an "aesthetic attribute" as a metaphor or "objective correlative" of that expressive vision. This expressive quality then takes priority over all other realistic conventions or representational considerations. As a result, with many expressionist works a seemingly minor characteristic or even a character's phantasy –

---

[35] In some cases this strategy of externalization involves a dramatization of subjectivity or consciousness, in which aspects of the self emerge as seemingly separate and autonomous figures, while individual thoughts and emotions turn into concrete actions and events. The "Ich-Drama" is the most obvious example of this projective structure, for example, Sorge's *Der Bettler* or Becker's *Das letzte Gericht*. However it is also present, albeit in embryonic form, in expressionist prose, such as Kafka's early fragmentary piece "Description of a Struggle" ("Beschreibung eines Kampfes") in which the individual characters figure largely as aspects of a single consciousness. See also my description of the character "Cesare" (in chapter 6 on *Caligari*) as an example of an emotional "correlative."

[36] Sokel, *The Writer in Extremis*, 50.

[37] See for example Silvio Vietta's analysis of synecdoche in the poetry of Gottfried Benn. Vietta and Kemper, *Expressionismus*, 61–68.

may be "realized" as the metaphorical "vehicle" providing the framework for the entire text, thereby taking the place of the conventional realistic "Bezugswelt," or referential world.

Consequently the expressionist vision is characterized not only by the processes of reduction and abstraction but also by a loosening of the text's relationship to a recognizable and realistic context. This combination of effects is itself responsible for much of the harshness, distortion and exaggeration associated with expressionism. At the same time however its strategies of defamiliarization and alienation are responsible for the text's significant power to direct the audience's attention to its central issues. This is not to say however that the expressionist text typically explains or clarifies its vision. For this process of abstraction frequently produces enigmatic metaphors and dream-like images which *point towards* meaning without necessarily *disclosing* it.[38] As Sokel says, such images are like a dream image which "disguises as much as it expresses . . . " (47).

The paradox of expressionism then, as the work of Kafka demonstrates,[39] is that it reserves its most "realistic" and concrete forms of representation for its dreams and abstractions. In treating the metaphorical, the hallucinatory and the dreamlike with the same degree of "realism" that such conventions of representation as the classic realist text would reserve for the factual, the movement's "expressive" principle comes into its own as a critical and "deconstructive" moment of the historical avant-garde: it effaces those boundaries between the external and the internal, the real and the imaginary, which are still crucial not only to naturalism but even to many of the more sophisticated modernist texts.

## Fredric Jameson's "ideology of modernism" and the expressionist avant-garde

Seen from the broad perspective of the development of the mimetic tradition at large the "canonical" technical achievements of modernism, such as the stream-of-consciousness technique (perfected by Joyce, Faulkner and Woolf) might appear to mark the

[38] See the concluding chapter, where I discuss Kafka's poetics of the sublime in terms of a tension between the promise of meaningfulness and the representation of meaninglessness.

[39] See the later section on Kafka's *The Metamorphosis*.

major milestones in the continuing progress of realism as a means of recording and registering the details of life. In other words, they constitute a further refinement of realism as an epistemological instrument offering a more complete sense of control and mastery over reality. However, as the example of the stream-of-consciousness technique makes clear, many innovative modernist strategies streamline and update classic realism but leave its underlying conventions, value systems and epistemological principles – such as its distinction between subject and object – fully intact. By contrast I would argue that this is precisely *not* the case with the historical avant-garde, nor, I would maintain, is it true of the most progressive writers in the expressionist movement.[40]

The defining paradox of expressionism is that although it appears at times to move in a similarly realist direction – Döblin's logical "extension" of naturalism being a prime example – it is actually deeply opposed to this attempt by representationalism to master – and thus in a sense to "overcome" – the real by mimetic means. For expressionism not only questions the discrete existence of the subject and object, the division on which such realism is based, but similarly takes to task the very notion that an "objective" reality exists which can be observed impartially and then recorded as an isolated external phenomenon. Instead, it constantly raises the specter of epistemological uncertainty, attacking the credibility of those bourgeois subjects who place their faith in the creation of cast-iron objectivity, and exposing the arbitrary nature of the "real."

In an article on the "Ideology of Modernism," Fredric Jameson has discussed the problem of realism in the modernist text from a similar perspective.[41] He describes the genesis of realism and modernism in terms of social and cultural history, that is, in relation to the rise of the pragmatically oriented bourgeoisie, and in relation to the ongoing movement of the Enlightenment. The latter is important for the mimetic tradition since it brought about

[40] As MacCabe's book on Joyce makes clear, these progressive or "counter-discursive" functions are not the exclusive prerogative of the works of the avant-garde. It is clearly not my intention here to treat this progressive and critical effect of modernist writing reductively – let alone to deny its existence – but rather to point to its very different status among the goals and aspirations within the cultural formations of modernism and the avant-garde.

[41] Fredric Jameson "Beyond the Cave: Demystifying the Ideology of Modernism," *The Ideologies of Theory. Essays 1971–86*, Vol. 2 (Minneapolis: Minnesota University Press, 1988), 115–32.

a process of "demystification" and "decoding," with the "explicit task of destroying religion and superstition, of extirpating the sacred in all of its forms . . . " (127). The Enlightenment's explanatory model eventually developed into that form of realism characterized by "historical thinking," that is, by the emphasis on the dominant social values of causality and quantification. These were the primary explanatory modes of the nineteenth century and – for MacCabe too – they constitute the central epistemological values underlying the classic realist text.

Jameson links the emergence of modernism firstly with a sense of the irreconcilability between the need to grasp the enormity of the historical situation on the one hand, and the inadequacies of aesthetic language and private expression as a means of articulating it on the other (131). Secondly he associates modernism with a sense of "fatigue with the whole process of demystification and decoding" (129), an experience that brings about the attempt to reverse this process and to "recode" the world through modernistic works which possess their own "symbolic meanings" and "their own mythic or sacred immediacy" (129).

As a consequence of this *re*mystification through "recoding," according to Jameson "all modernistic works are essentially simply cancelled realistic ones," so that they tend to be read not in terms of their own symbolic meanings (that is, the meanings produced by the "recoding") but rather, "indirectly only, by way of the relay of an imaginary realistic narrative . . . " (129). The process of reading such modernist texts thus involves transforming the text's symbolic, stylized and mystified narrative into a realistic narrative, and then interpreting this secondary narrative as one would "the older, realistic novel" (130).

Accordingly Jameson maintains that the modernist text initially exasperates our beliefs in causality and chronology, but then, far from shaking them, actually succeeds through its very disorder in *intensifying* our need for, and obsession with them and with the order they provide. Thus, paradoxically modernism reinforces the basic suppositions of nineteenth-century bourgeois reality, but "in a world so thoroughly subjectivized that they have been driven underground, beneath the surface of the work, forcing us to reconfirm the concept of a secular reality at the very moment when we imagine ourselves to be demolishing it" (131).

Now although it is doubtless true that, like the reader of modernism postulated by Jameson, the reader of the expressionist text is similarly frustrated by the ubiquitous disorder or by the lack of causal explanation (the kind of explanation which Döblin for example so vehemently disavows), there is a significant difference between this model of modernism's ideological mechanism (as Jameson describes it) and the functioning of the texts typical of the expressionist avant-garde. For whereas the kind of modernist text which Jameson is describing produces a strengthened longing for causality and a corresponding renewal of the belief in the legitimacy of causal and chronological explanations as well as in the power of the "realist" reading to make sense of the text's obscurities, the expressionist text by contrast is characterized by the tendency to confront its readers head-on with their own desire for such realistic ordering. In doing so it not only pushes them still further into the contradictions underlying such a rationalistic approach but abandons them to these contradictions, without offering the possibility of the kind of recuperative re-reading which, according to Jameson's definition, the modernist text always makes available.

It is precisely in this sense that the expressionist text must be considered as avant-garde: not only does it cast off the conventions of organic form, as Bürger maintains, but it also consistently refutes and subverts the imposition upon it of any reading which would transform it into the equivalent of an "organic" work providing a sense of order, harmony and totality. The "meaningless" artifact of the historical avant-garde (such as Duchamp's "found-object") prods the audience into supplying what is missing, confronts it primarily with its own automatized expectations (by frustrating them), and thereby provokes the audience's realization that its own horizon of expectations has been thoroughly conditioned by the "institution of art." As we shall see, the prose-text of the expressionist avant-garde functions in a similarly enigmatic fashion. Although initially it launches a direct appeal to the reader's realist orientation and mobilizes the reader's powers of realistic "recoding," it inevitably refuses finally to accommodate the imposition upon it of realism's rationalist categories, thereby denying the validity of realistic "solutions" as the basis of an explanatory or interpretative model.

This enigmatic, counter-realist quality of the expressionist avant-garde, its characteristic resistance to a realist reading is again linked to the axiomatic strategies of what Sokel calls expressionism's "abstractionism."[42] The "dream-like" metaphors and images in Kafka's early works for example extend the *promise* of meaning yet do so only in a typically "duplicitous" manner: even where the text appears to be revealing its truth, the strategy of simultaneous revelation and concealment which marks these "expressive" oneiric images[43] has the effect of refusing to validate any single interpretation, let alone supporting a sense of closure. The modernist texts which Jameson describes may well provoke a "realist reading" in order to reinforce the causal and scientific world-view to which their realism corresponds. The same cannot be said of the enigmatic texts of the expressionist avant-garde. For example, as I will show in the chapters on *Caligari* and *The Metamorphosis*, their central allegiance is not to the nineteenth century's tradition of realism as a whole, but more specifically to its subversive, counter-tradition of the fantastic. In texts such as E. T. A. Hoffmann's "The Sand Man" for instance, the conquering scientific modes – frequently personified in these texts by a scientist or by an Enlightenment figure of rational clarity ("Clara") – are confronted by inexplicable events or characters which cannot be made to conform to the laws of causality and logic. Such moments emerge within these nineteenth-century texts as marginalized elements which remain unspeakable within the overall realist world-view in which the texts are framed. They are rendered within the texts' realism only in their significant fissures, as that which fails to signify within classically realist discourse and the interpretative system of rationalist thought which underpins it. Yet whereas in the fantastic these "non-conforming" elements constitute a kind of "demonic" aspect which breaks in from outside upon a fundamentally ordered world of realism, in expressionism the situation is precisely the reverse: far from inhabiting an outside or marginal space the demonic or irrational takes up the *central* position here, forming an essential element of the text's representational structure (as in the central tale told by the "madman" in *Caligari*); or it becomes the pivotal metaphor on which the narrative is based (as is the case with *The Metamorphosis*). As in Gregor Samsa's strange transformation, the real-life status of this unspeakable element is never explained. Conse-

42 Sokel, *The Writer in Extremis*, 49–51.
43 Sokel, *The Writer in Extremis*, 47.

quently that which in nineteenth-century fiction was a mere aberration – an unrealistic and irrational outburst within a largely believable and realistic world – frequently becomes the central principle underlying the reality of the expressionist narrative.

The enigmatic text of expressionism may initially invite the kind of realistic reading described by Jameson. But in contrast to the modernism he describes it does so only in a probing, provocative and highly self-reflexive manner, since its ultimate function is to investigate the limits of the knowable, interrogate the rational and question the scientific mode as a viable epistemology. As in the works of Gottfried Benn, Carl Einstein or Kafka, the Expressionist text frequently thematizes precisely the explanatory power of the dominant bourgeois modes of science and logic orienting its readers. And rather than reinforcing its readers' longings for order by encouraging them to make good its own deficits and produce a realist reading (as in Jameson's model of modernism), it confronts them with the inadequacy of such rationalist systems of order and explanation. Thus by exposing the contradictions in the reader's own seemingly logical and ordered approach, the avant-garde text once more takes up the Enlightenment tradition of demystification – although this time with a fundamental difference: its attack on the fragile bourgeois norms of order and rationality turns this model against itself, demonstrating that demystification in its traditionally rationalistic sense must *itself* now be demystified and interpretation re-interpreted.

For example, many expressionist prose texts critique the burgher for his narrow-mindedness, his philistinism and his monomaniacal yearning for rationality and order. In this regard the paradox of these texts is that having presented the characteristically insoluble dilemmas at the heart of their central figures' bourgeois existences (one thinks of Döblin's "Fischer," Kafka's "Gregor Samsa" and "Josef K.," or Benn's "Rönne"), and having demonstrated furthermore the absurdity of these characters' attempts to carry on living their regular ordered bourgeois lives in the face of the massive existential crises which overcome them, the texts turn the situation around so that it is now the *reader* who finds him or herself in a position very similar to that of the characters. For in attempting to discover meaning and order in the text, the reader finds himself turning ineluctably to the same norms of rational explanation, and craving the same forms of meaning and order which the text's account of its bourgeois protagonist has already exposed as absurd and contradictory.

Clearly then Jameson's description of modernism stands in need of adjustment by adding a further distinction in order to account for the place of the avant-garde within the broader context of modernism: if the modernist text elicits a realist reading which serves paradoxically to confirm the explanatory modes of realism, then the work of the expressionist avant-garde is defined by its *resistance* to any such realist recoding and recuperation: it short-circuits the attempt at superimposing upon the text any harmonious and orderly reading that might serve to valorize the rationalist-scientific discourse with which such "affirmative" readings are associated.

In this, the enigmatic text of expressionism shares precisely those features cited by Peter Bürger as essential to the avant-garde. Firstly, like avant-garde montage it lacks an obvious meaning or implicit final order or arrangement, and so provokes its audience into an attempt to produce the kind of semantic organization which is lacking in the text. Secondly, like the everyday, "found-objects" which Marcel Duchamp signed and offered for exhibition (a paradigmatically avant-garde gesture, according to Bürger, since it provokes the question of what constitutes the category of "art"), the enigmatic expressionist text frustrates the reader in such a way that it highlights his or her institutionalized criteria of interpretation and interrogates the value systems which underpin them. For the expressionist text entices its readers to interpret it at the same time as it confronts them with a vacuum of meaning. In doing so it forces them to apply their aesthetic expectations and interpretative criteria to an object which patently refuses to be interpreted, and – unlike Jameson's model modernist text – refuses to be recoded in terms of the conventional criteria of realism.

It is in this sense that the expressionist text takes up what Jameson sees as the Enlightenment project of realistic "demystification" but turns it against the very principle of conquering rationality on which such analysis is based, demystifying the very attempt to demystify. By reflecting back to its readers the institutionalized expectations and conventions of interpretation which they have taken on and made "second nature," it succeeds in demonstrating the extent to which they are already implicated in the very ideology of scientific rationality and conventional epistemology which the text is deconstructing. As with the texts of Franz Kafka, the endless attempts to interpret – and so gain admittance to the inner sanctum of meaning, be it the law, the castle, or the trial – lead to these interpretations being thrown back upon themselves, and exposed as a set of inappropriate and merely institutionalized responses. Through Kafka's textual enigmas and semantic vacuums – paradigmatic avant-garde structures, in this respect – the reader is made to experience not only the limits of the knowable, but the limits of the dominant social discourses (in this case, the discourses of conventional rationality and science) as the institutionally privileged modes by which the modern subject comes to know and organize the real.

## Benn: modernity and the double bind of rationality

### Dominant social discourse and "hegemony" (Williams)

With their intensely personal and "visionary" narratives which flout the logic and law of the real, the expressionists not only project a realm of alterity but dismantle "reality" as an ideological construction made up of "dominant social discourses." We can understand these dominant discourses in terms of a determining set of social practices and ideological forms of representation which are instrumental in the social construction of reality and subjectivity – and hence in the process of socialization and "interpellation" (Althusser) – on account of their ideological shaping of the social "imaginary." The "world-making" function of this "dominant social discourse" is similar to what Raymond Williams defines as "hegemony," in other words "a complex interlocking of political, social, and cultural forces." This discursive hegemony affects "our senses and assignments of energy, our shaping perceptions of ourselves and our world. It is a lived system of meanings and values – constitutive and constituting – which as they are experienced as practices appear as reciprocally confirming."[44] This understanding of the notion of ideology and ideological discourses in terms of hegemony adds a further dimension to what may be considered the specifically oppositional functions pertaining to the expressionist literature of the avant-

[44] Raymond Williams, *Marxism and Literature*, 108, 110.

garde. For the critiques of the burgher, of bourgeois culture and of contemporary civilization which expressionism produced are aspects of an overall strategy of what we might call "counter-discourse." By this I mean the attempt to make visible the unquestioned values and ideological practices by which a dominant world-view is both represented and held in place, and to adopt alternative voices, rhetorics and idioms which consciously depart from those stylistic forms and discursive strategies reinforcing an existing social and ideological configuration.

What is characteristic of the historical avant-garde's strategies in deconstructing the dominant social discourses is most obviously the reaction of its counter-discourse to specific elements in classical representation and the classic realist text. The counter-discourse responds to these conventions not only through an avowedly *formal* opposition but more importantly by undermining their foremost claim: that of possessing a coherent, non-contradictory and final knowledge of reality. As a consequence the more progressive expressionists tend to avoid the evocation of a "representative" and generalizable image of the real, for the most part eschewing "reality-effects" or the creation of an illusory sense of totality (such as that proposed by Lukacs with the term "Zudecken" ["covering over" or "closure"]). Although the reader of such expressionist texts may long for them to reveal their relationship to the broader world beyond their narrowly subjective confines, and may miss the reassuring support of an explanatory narration or "dominant discourse," these texts set out to show that in the decentered and "godless" world of modernity such epistemological certainties and points of orientation no longer exist – either for the protagonist or for the reader. For to cling fixedly to the outmoded forms of such cosmological fictions is tantamount to longing once more for an "affirmative" form of culture and for the textual illusion of aesthetic harmony and order with which it is associated: it is to be guilty also of a form of "bad faith" which attempts to cope with the multifarious and chaotic reality of modernity through a nostalgic return to outdated forms of order and fixity.

Since the expressionist poetic involves both abstracting the "essence" of this modern reality and leaving aside the superfluous "realistic" details, it consequently does not attempt to present "truths" or finalized forms. Rather it offers a *vision* – simulta-

neously an expression of subjectivity – which in its very arbitrariness, idiosyncrasy or incompleteness emphasizes its nature as a
mythical creation, and leaves open the possibility of alternative
constructions of the real.

## Modernism, order and myth: Benn and the expressionist avant-garde

The critical function of expressionist counter-discourse can be
defined in two specific ways: firstly in terms of the text's resistance to a realist reading (in Jameson's sense) and secondly in
terms of the attempt to interrogate bourgeois society's prevailing
forms of *rationality* (and not least that scientific-positivist principle
with which the classic realist text is intimately connected). Consequently it is no coincidence that those themes which define the
limits of rationality and the real – alienation, madness and the
irrational – are extraordinarily prominent in expressionist literature.[45] The madman or "irrationalist" is frequently treated explicitly as the bearer of a liberating and subversive logic, and as
the representative of an alternative mode of rationality.[46] Alternatively the madman's idiosyncratic vision is made the basis for a
"carnivalistic" effect[47] – which becomes an important means of
defamiliarization, breaking up the stiff and reified forms associated with the rational world of the burgher.[48]

[45] See Thomas Anz, *Die Literatur der Existenz. Literarische Psychopathographie und ihre soziale Bedeutung im Frühexpressionismus* Germanistische Abhandlungen. 46 (Stuttgart: Metzler, 1977). Also Edith Ihekweazu, "Wandlung und Wahnsinn. Zu expressionistischen Erzählungen von Döblin, Sternheim, Benn, und Heym," *Orbis Litterarum* 37 (1982): 327–344. See also the postscript by Thomas Anz to his collection *Phantasien über den Wahnsinn. Expressionistische Texte* (Munich: Hanser, 1980), 148–153.

[46] An example of this lionization of the madman as the only bearer of truth in a war-hungry society may be found in Leonhard Frank's story "Der Irre." Rpt. Anz, *Phantasien über den Wahnsinn*, 121–125.

[47] I use the term "carnivalization" in the sense employed by Bakhtin, namely as the special means shared by the aesthetic sphere and the carnival for providing an alternative vision of the (rational) everyday world, and for relativizing such oppositional concepts as the "rational" and the "mad." See the collection of Bakhtin's writings on carnival in the German edition: Mikhail Bachtin, *Literatur und Karneval: Zur Romantheorie und Lachkultur*, trans. Alexander Kaempfe (Munich: Hanser, 1969).

[48] An example of this defamiliarizing function may be seen in Georg Heym's story "Der Irre." Here the narrative is focalized through the madman, who looks upon such everyday phenomena as an elevator with complete bewilderment, seeing it in terms of its individual parts rather than recognizing its overall

Gottfried Benn's writing of the expressionist period offers an example of this counter-discursive critique of rationality. At the beginning of Benn's novella-cycle *Gehirne* the young doctor Rönne is in a strange psychological and existential state. He is suffering from a "peculiar and inexplicable" exhaustion (3) – characterized by his extreme alienation from his patients, his medical duties, his colleagues, his surroundings, and even from his own body. The text is notable for its evocation of this psychological state, which it never attempts to explain or analyze, even though in the very opening lines it intimates to the reader a (too-simple) causal connection: Rönne is suffering a kind of "shell-shock" brought about by the experience of having 2,000 corpses pass through his hands *"ohne Besinnen"* (3) – literally that is, "without consciousness." This is a curious and highly significant formulation that – characteristically for Benn's text – effaces the distinction between subject and object by invoking in one phrase both the corpses' and the doctor's insensate state, thereby equating their form of lifelessness with his own.

The text is notable secondly for the paradoxical nature of the strategies through which Rönne attempts to overcome this state: he uses the rational in order to exorcise rationality. For the familiar expressionist notion of cold and cerebral rationality – emblematized by the theme of "Gehirne" ("Brains") – becomes both the dominant principle behind the harsh and dehumanizing routine of the hospital in which Rönne works, but also the founding norm of order and meaningfulness which he finds difficult to do without.

The title "Gehirne" itself points to the paradoxical nature of this central problematic of rationality. For one of the key images of the Rönne-Novellas is the doctor's mysterious and repeated mime-like gesture of appearing to open up an imagined object like the two halves of an orange, a gesture which – as we later discover – is really meant by Rönne to signify the opening up of the two halves of the brain. The repetition of this strange gesture functions as a mime which dramatizes Rönne's unsuccessful search for the

function. This defamiliarizing vision also introduces an alternative, spiritual dimension into the story where, with his metaphorical vision, the madman can only make sense of the department store he enters by seeing it in terms of a church. See Heym, "Der Irre," repr. *Prosa des Expressionismus*, ed. Fritz Martini (Stuttgart: Reclam, 1970), 140–155.

source of rationality. Simultaneously it mirrors his frustration with the positivist and analytical approach of science – its probing and murderous mode of dissection – which masquerades first as a mere means of discovery but then later reveals itself as an end in its own right (demonstrated here perhaps by the circularity and repetitiveness associated both with Rönne's compulsive gesture and with his analytical probing of the center of rationality itself by rationalist means). Secondly the gesture seems to be a response by Rönne to the alienating experience of death at the medical institute and to the "two thousand corpses" he has been obliged to examine. The gesture appears in this regard to articulate Rönne's desperate need to discover an alternative to the "senselessness" not only of life and death but of his scientific inquiries, and to show his frustration that rational inquiry is not the means by which a renewed sense of redemption or of a meaningful order can be conjured up. The disorientation and meaninglessness which Rönne suffers result then precisely from a characteristic double bind: the paradoxical inability to continue living either *with* these alienating and inhumane rational principles, or *without* the sense of structure and predictability they confer.[49]

As with many other expressionist texts on this theme, in Benn's *Gehirne* the rejection of the central techno-scientific logic behind bourgeois civilization's irrational authority is followed by a rather desperate search for an alternative to this constricting and brutal form of rationality. This search frequently finds respite in a return to a mythological past.[50] In returning to the mythical, Benn's text seems not only to free itself from the topoi of conventional realism

[49] The particular form of paradox known as the "double bind" was first developed productively as an analytical concept in the realm of psychoanalysis and communicative theory by Gregory Bateson et al. in the paper "Toward a Theory of Schizophrenia," (1956) to describe the conflict produced by a subject's inability to fulfill two mutually exclusive injunctions from an authority figure. See Bateson, *Steps to an Ecology of Mind* (New York: Ballantine, 1972), 201–227. It was elaborated upon as a paradoxical communicative structure by Watzlawick, Beavin and Jackson in their book *Pragmatics of Human Communication* (New York: Norton, 1967).

[50] In his famous essay "Ulysses, Order, and Myth" T. S. Eliot defines the importance of myth in modernism as a means of "ordering" the chaos of the contemporary world. See *Selected Prose of T. S. Eliot*, ed. Frank Kermode (New York: Harcourt Brace Jovanovich, 1975), 177. However, with many of the expressionists – particularly the less "naive" among them, such as Benn – this longing for a mythical order is already clearly problematized as a regressive and nostalgic turning-away from modernity – as if the imposition of a myth were merely another act of bad faith or an attempt to fill the cosmological vacuum left after the "death of God."

but at the level of the narrative it is able to invoke the dream of an archaic and pre-rational age freed from the constraints of the dominating cerebrality of the present, from quotidian logic and syntax, and from the conceptual divisions associated with them:

It was necessary to complete the philosophy of life which the work of the past century had created. It seemed necessary as a matter of honesty to exclude the Thou-character of grammar, for the familiar form of address had become mythical. He felt bound to this path . . . (26).[51]

Following the corollary we derived from Jameson's "Ideology of Modernism" we can observe that the text's character as "counter-discourse" is demonstrated in such cases by its refusal to be "recoded," that is, by its resistance to being read and reconfigured according to realist criteria. For mirroring Rönne's own linguistic-epistemological revolution here, the narrative has the tendency frequently to slip out of a conventional narration into a mode which suppresses or undermines those conventional realist signposts by which the reader normally finds his or her bearings within a text.[52] These include the deictics of "here" and "there"; the marks distinguishing between different discourses, for example between spoken and unspoken thoughts, and between the narrator, protagonist and subsidiary figures; or the indications of a change of time or place, etc.. A typical effacement of these "signposts" occurs in the following passage:

Shattered he sat before his breakfast table one morning; he felt so deeply: the senior doctor would be away on business, a substitute would come, get out of this bed at this time and eat his toast: one thinks, one eats, and breakfast does its work inside one. Nevertheless he continued to deal with whatever questions and orders needed to be dealt with . . . went up to beds: good morning, how's your body? (5).[53]

51 "Die Weltanschauung, die die Arbeit des vergangenen Jahrhunderts erschaffen hatte, sie galt es zu vollenden. Den Du-Charakter des Grammatischen auszuschalten, schien ihm ehrlicherweise notwendig, denn die Anrede war mythisch geworden. Er fühlte sich seiner Entwicklung verpflichtet und ging auf die Jahrhunderte zurück." Gottfried Benn, *Gehirne* (Stuttgart: Reclam, 1974), 26.

52 Hohendahl makes a similar point in his brief but very substantial discussion of the text and the problem of rationality (to which the present section of this chapter is in part a response). See Hohendahl, "The Loss of Reality: Gottfried Benn's Early Prose," 85–86.

53 "Erschüttert saß er eines Morgens vor seinem Frühstückstisch; er fühlte so tief: der Chefarzt würde verreisen, ein Vertreter würde kommen, in dieser Stunde aus diesem Bette steigen und das Brötchen nehmen: man denkt, man ißt, und das Frühstück arbeitet an einem herum. Trotzdem verrichtete er weiter, was an Fragen und Befehlen zu verrichten war . . . trat an Betten: guten Morgen, was macht Ihr Leib?"

Rönne "feels" a series of distant and imagined events so closely, that they appear indistinguishable from the here and now ("at *this* hour and out of *this* bed"). The action then suddenly appears to shift unaccountably from the breakfast table to the hospital. Here a doctor appears to be asking how the patient is doing. Yet it is unclear whether it is Rönne or the substitute-doctor, since typically the previous identificatory reverie has effaced all the features distinguishing the figural subject from the figural object. However in making this inquiry he employs a reductive and alienating turn of phrase ("How's your body?") which is so unlikely to be used by a professional medical practitioner that, given the absence too of any quotation marks, it is possibly best understood as merely imaginary – as a thought rather than an actual spoken question.

Besides effacing these "signposts" it is significant that the text has also suppressed what MacCabe calls the "dominant discourse" of the narrator, which – as in the classic realist text for example – might otherwise guide the reader towards a more "objective" or "external" point of view. These strategies of dislocation are important for two reasons. Firstly the reader begins through them to dismantle conventional representations of the real. As Hohendahl argues with respect to the text's "blurring" of the categories of time and space: "This narrative strategy indeed decomposes traditional reality; it brings into the foreground the fact that the mode of reality underlying nineteenth-century fiction is a *construct* that was grounded in institutionalized narrative conventions" (86). But secondly through these effects of dislocation the reader's experience is made directly analogous to that of the protagonist: he or she experiences at first hand a sense of disorientation and meaninglessness (similar to that attributable to the character in the text), as well as a sense of frustration at confronting the limitations of rational explanation – an experience which is most evident for example in any attempt to apply conventionally realist criteria in interpreting Benn's text.

For example, just as Rönne has great difficulty in putting together the fragments of reality which he perceives, so the reader too is constantly confronted with the problem of how to construct the world of the text and so make it meaningful. This task is made all the more difficult on account of the fact that, even if the narrator intervenes occasionally, the narration is still focalized mainly from the shifting and alienated standpoints of the character, so that the "reality" of the text emerges largely as the mere correlative of Rönne's consciousness: in a sense it *exists* only as that consciousness and cannot, in Jameson's sense, be re-read, re-coded or reduced to a more fundamental "realist" substratum:

> He looked around: a man was submerging his softness in a girl . . . The lower jaw of a cretin was mastering a cup with the help of two crippled hands. On all the tables there stood implements, some for hunger, some for thirst. A man was making an offer; loyalty entered in his eyes . . . Someone was impartially assessing a discussion. Someone was chewing up a landscape, the walls' ornamentation.(9)[54]

It is the alienated and alienating character of this synecdochic vision – its "expressive" quality – which is significant, and it is this that helps to distinguish the avant-garde qualities of this text from many of its modernist counterparts. Central for example to Jameson's postulation of a process of realist reading or "recoding" common to modernist texts is the notion that a discrete "object-reality" exists within the narrative, over and beyond the world of the figure's consciousness, which can then be reconstructed by the reader from the fragments of "mystifying" information which filter through the figure's reflections. As the quotation makes clear, in this case such a reality clearly cannot be meaningfully recovered or extrapolated from the "expressive" vision which powers the text.

Its mimetic stance also distinguishes this as an avant-garde rather than a modernist text. It would be a fallacy to see this fragmentary flux of consciousness in *Gehirne* simply in terms of a more accurate or more up-to-date version of the realism of Flaubert – as might be argued by contrast of some modernist innovations with the stream-of-consciousness technique – in other words as an innovation within the tradition of realism which has simply refined those functions of processing and mastering the phenomenal world previously attributed to the classic realist text. In this regard Benn's Rönne-Novellas demonstrate not merely a

---

[54] "Er sah sich um: Ein Mann versenkte sein Weiches in ein Mädchen . . . Der Unterkiefer eines Zurückgebliebenen meisterte mit Hilfe von zwei verwachsenen Händen eine Tasse . . . Auf allen Tischen standen Geräte, welche für den Hunger, welche für den Durst. Ein Herr Machte ein Angebot; Treue trat in seine Auge . . . Einer bewertete sachlich ein Gespräch. Einer kaute eine Landschaft an, der Wände Schmuck."

decisive break with the conventions of realism, but illustrate more importantly the radical epistemological reorientation, the function of interrogating art's institutionalizing structures associated with expressionism and the historical avant-garde. And although the radical modernist texts of Joyce and Woolf, for example, clearly share this progressive function, the expressionist avant-garde makes this critical concern its central issue or *starting point*. While the historical avant-garde may no longer hold to the Romantics' utopian vision of an idealist sublation of art and life, or to the activists' allegiance to what Charles Russell calls the traditional avant-garde "belief in the progressive union of writer and society acting within history," even as an insoluble aporia this sublation still remains a guiding principle for the historical avant-garde, the central problem or point of reference for even the least "political" of its artists. Thus although "they are little more able than the modernists, their contemporaries, to find in modern, bourgeois society hope for either art or humanity,"[55] it is nevertheless this principle of sublation – albeit sublation in its more "cynical" form (for example as a de-aestheticized "anti-art" or an "aesthetics of the ugly") – that continues to distinguish the avant-garde from the modernists.

In this respect my argument here for distinguishing modernism from the avant-garde is again related to Peter Bürger's crucial thesis that the avant-garde does not merely criticize previous *individual* movements within art – in this case the convention of nineteenth-century realism – but rather the *entire* institution of art itself. For I would argue analogously to Bürger that although the critical and progressive *functions* of the avant-garde may overlap with those of other cultural formations within modernism, the dominant concerns which produce these critical effects – such as the concern to expose the broader historical, institutional and discursive framework responsible for administering signifying practices in a particular culture – are simply not of such central importance outside of the historical avant-garde.[56]

Let us pursue this question in more detail with regard to

[55] Charles Russell, *Poets, Prophets, and Revolutionaries: The Literary Avant-Garde from Rimbaud through Postmodernism* (New York: Oxford University Press, 1985), 7.
[56] Again, as MacCabe's book on Joyce makes clear, these progressive or "counter-discursive" functions belong not only to the avant-garde, but share in broader, subversive aspect of modernist writing generally.

*Gehirne.* At first glance Benn's text appears to align itself fully with modernism. It clearly shares some of the central characteristics of modernist prose fiction, such as its "progressive" or "experimental" structure, its fragmented appearance, and its tendency to investigate in the minutest detail both the intricate movements of consciousness and the emotional or unconscious reflexes of the central figure. Benn's text also emulates modernism in marking a distance to the realist tradition by rejecting the classic realist text's reliance on the kind of central narrator who provides a set of references to a coherent and recognizable external reality.

What is it then that distinguishes Benn's text from modernism? To play devil's advocate for a moment we could view modernism as a vast extension of the aestheticist credo of "art for art's sake" – a position which had already been decisively rejected by the avant-garde. From this perspective the "classic" modernist innovations, such as the stream-of-consciousness technique and the liberation and radical manipulation of the categories of time and space, then appear merely as an updating of realism's technical virtuosity. They represent a new stage in the ongoing development of the formal means of registering, reflecting and mastering the real, marked as "progress" by their ability now to penetrate the soul, and to record in detail the intricate movements and associative faculties of consciousness.

Although this aspect of modernism represents a vast technical and formal refinement one could argue that it has no other goal than the perfection of the art itself. It represents the continuation of the same principles which guide the classic realist text, but a continuation by other means. Indeed, one could argue that many of the radical innovations in modernism lie largely on a purely *formal* level: although they break up the appearance of reality and its "classical" mode of representation, they frequently leave untouched the more fundamental inherited belief in the realist form as a privileged means knowing the world. Jameson's proposal that the (seemingly) unrealistic texts of modernism demand a reading which resurrects and reconstructs them as realist narratives implies that such a reading works by re-instituting the text's "missing" realist categories, such as the division of subject and object (that is, the belief in the opposition between a discrete Cartesian subject, and a separate and external world), and by re-inserting the categories of time and space. But if it is true that

modernism has the tendency to resurrect such traditional organizing categories, then this links it to precisely that "affirmative"
quality – associated with aestheticist and organic works of art –
against which the avant-garde by contrast protests. For although
such works initially profess a radical content which appears to be
subversive of the bourgeois construction of the real, they risk
merely reinforcing the principles which support the general ideological construction of social reality, just as the affirmative work
may take as its subject a radical theme but end up satisfying a
desire for change only at an abstract level and within the sanitized
confines of the aesthetic sphere. Such an outwardly critical approach ends up being recuperated as affirmative culture not
merely because its radical character is limited to the level of form,
but – as Benjamin argues in the article "The Author as Producer"
– because it does not take into account the overall conditions of
production and reception, in other words, the *institutionalized*
uses to which art is put. By contrast the work of the expressionist
avant-garde is not only radical and progressive in its *appearance*,
but in its very substance as a system of representation it also has
inscribed within it the means of *resisting* any ideological recuperation as merely the illusory expression of a (past) ideal of
harmony.

The expressionist avant-garde – in this case Benn's *Gehirne* – is
characterized then not only by a negation of the *formal* traits of the
realist tradition, but additionally by a thoroughgoing negation of
the underlying *epistemological* structures of such art. In particular
it attacks the ideological presuppositions of a knowable, shared
reality as well as the idea that reality can mastered by the rationalist principle embodied in realism's narrative structures. Consequently, whereas modernism is always in danger of merely defamiliarizing the *surface* of the world, Benn's text instead targets
reality's underlying, unquestioned premises: the social construction of reality and of the subject according to rationalist principles.

## Bad Faith: rationality and the social imaginary

What does it mean to say that the defining function of the expressionist avant-garde is the creation of a form of "counter-discourse"? In this case it implies the goal of interrogating the institu-

tionalized and unquestioned dominance of certain social or discursive values, such as the scientific-rationalist "reality-principle" and the epistemological model it underpins. Benn's text for
example presents a world which is not only heterogeneous, discontinuous and fundamentally contradictory, but which resists
synthesis and ordering to the point of deconstructing the very
principles of logical association and correlation on which such
interpretive synthesis is conventionally grounded. That is to say,
the counter-discourse of the avant-garde text not only dismantles
the real as a construct then, but also takes apart even those
rationalistic interpretative strategies and values (legitimized by
the institution of art) which would otherwise offer the reader the
means for re-constructing the text as a "meaningful" whole.

These socially condoned modes of making order are an explicit
target throughout the narratives of the Rönne-Novellas. Firstly, in
a typically expressionistic critical diatribe against civilization's
inherent barbarism, rationality is associated with the clinical-
scientific principle which dominates the practice of medicine at
Dr. Rönne's hospital. As in Benn's earliest expressionist poetry (in
the *Morgue* collection) the patient is reduced to a mere synecdoche, to the reified parts of the body that the doctor treats: "an
ear," "a back," an "injured finger."[57] The dehumanizing and
alienating character of this clinical rationality affects the entire
moral system under which the hospital – as a supposedly benevolent social institution – tends to operate. Incurable patients for
example are not treated at all but, after being re-categorized by the
clinic's reductive principle of scientific rationalization and effi-
ciency as mere administrative problems, are sent home "because
of the paperwork and the filth that death brings with it" (4).[58]

This cold and clinical principle of rationalism also affects the
doctor, whose work becomes merely a set of mechanical responses ("broken down into a series of manipulations by the
hands" [3–4]),[59] and whose own person appears just as fragmented as the patients he treats: as we have already noted, he
seems completely alienated from his own body ("Then he himself
took his hands, ran them across the x-ray tubes . . . " [4]). Faced
with the meaninglessness produced by the cold logic of this

---

[57] *Gehirne*, 4.
[58] "wegen der Schreibereien und des Schmutzes, den der Tod mit sich bringt."
[59] "in eine Reihe von Handgriffen aufgelöst."

purely rationalistic and clinical system Rönne is constantly overcome by nihilism of a very specific kind: a lack of faith in the
analytical categories underpinning the act of interpretation:
"What is there to say about an event? Either it happens this way,
or it happens a little differently" (6).[60] Nevertheless, the paradox
that the narrative pursues is that a complete lack of faith is better
than no faith at all: Rönne's lack of faith itself becomes his religion,
albeit an inauthentic and merely consolatory belief system, a form
of "mauvaise foi."

Like many other expressionist protagonists, Rönne is caught in
a curious paradox: he can only find meaning through precisely
that discredited principle of rationality and civilization which has
already alienated and decentered him. He feels repulsed by the
world of concrete entities, but longs for the abstract sense of order
associated with the object-world, since even the most mechanical
aspects of cognition and the most rationalistic conventions of
perception and mental association serve to orient him by constructing a logical space-time continuum. The world of cognitive
objects itself then becomes completely secondary to his delight in
these logical structures: "Rönne enjoyed the ordered nature of a
velvet mantilla, the utterly successful subordination of materiality
under the concept of clothing; a triumph of determined, causally-
directed action was imminent" (20).[61] Rönne finds ontological and
existential consolation in these cognitive and epistemological pur-
suits. With the hope that it will envelope him with a comforting
sense of meaning and order Rönne forces himself to go through
the mechanics of constructing a logical and synthetic associative
process of thought: "One must simply be able to associate something with everything one sees, bringing it into accord with earlier
experiences and placing it under general points of view. That is
the way reason works, as I recall" (12).[62]

These peculiar existential strategies are always exposed in the

---

[60] "Was solle man denn zu einem Geschehen sagen? Geschähe es nicht so, geschähe es ein wenig anders."

[61] "Rönne labte sich an dem Geordneten einer Samtmantille, an der restlos gelun-
genen Unterordnung des Stofflichen unter den Begriff der Verhüllung; ein
Triumph trat ihm entgegen zielstrebigen, kausal geleiteten Handelns."

[62] "Man muß nur an alles, was man sieht, etwas anzuknüpfen vermögen, es mit
früheren Erfahrungen in Einklang bringen und es unter allgemeine Gesichts-
punkte stellen, das ist die Wirkungsweise der Vernunft, dessen entsinne ich
mich."

narrative finally as a sham, an inauthentic form of role-playing which provides at best the temporary illusion of order. Nevertheless the narrative mechanism by which these ploys are exposed makes the text especially interesting, since it rests on a form of rhetorical "duplicity" employing a subtle use of ironic exaggeration. The contradictions produced in Rönne by this rationalistic-scientific principle reflect the paradoxical quality of the "double bind" itself,[63] emerging in the "duplicitous" manner typical of the expressionist poetics: revealing and disguising his feelings at the same moment. For example, when Rönne sees an abattoir it sparks a series of associations:

Now he had to articulate himself thoroughly regarding the slaughterhouse. The Dresden slaughterhouse for example, built at the beginning of the seventies by the chief builder Köhler, equipped with the most up-to-date hygenic-sanitary devices ... He spoke drawing on such a wealth of the factual; this is the way he articulated himself, this is the way he engaged in answers and talk, explaining things, clarifying misapprehensions, he served the cause and was bound in service to the general public, which thanked him. (12) [64]

At the very moment Rönne begins to bask in the glow of his achievement – the rationalistic bolstering of the self through his command of the realm of knowable and indisputable facts – the cracks and fissures in this positivist cogito become apparent to the reader precisely through the ironic *excesses* of the description. Rather than covering over or repressing his fundamental cognitive insecurity the very wealth of factual details that he pours out serves instead to mark all the more clearly the site of this unresolved problem for Rönne.

Similar rationalist self-deceptions ensue when Rönne makes a rare attempt to bridge the gap which separates him from others and to strike up a conversation: "Then a man came up to him, and ha ha, and nice weather it went, back and forth, past and present

---

[63] On the paradoxical structure of the double-bind see Watzlawick et al., *Pragmatics of Human Communication*, 187–211.

[64] "Nun mußte er sich eingehend über Schlachthof äußern. Der Dresdener Schlachthof vergleichsweise, erbaut Anfang der siebziger Jahre von Baurat Köhler, versehen mit den hygienisch-sanitären Vorrichtungen modernsten Systems ... Heraus aus einer solchen Fülle des Tatsächlichen sprach er; so äußerte er sich, so stand er Antwort und Rede, klärte manches auf, half über Irrtümer hinweg, diente der Sache und unterstand der Allgemeinheit, die ihm dankte."

for a while in categorial space. When he was gone, Rönne tottered" (21).[65] The emphatically mechanical quality of these communicative strategies – revealed here by the terse synopsis of the conversation and its reduction to the empty and abstract categories of time and space – make it apparent that such attempts at a rationalist reconsolidation of the self serve only to alienate the subject still further.

In a similarly mechanical manner Rönne attempts to create stability by instantly registering the world he perceives, in order to fix his perceptions through the instrumental categories provided by language: "I want to buy myself a book and a pen; I want to write down as much as possible, so that things don't trickle away so" (3); "house, he said to the next building; house to the one thereafter; tree to all the lime-trees on his path" (19).[66] Once again the description of Rönne's characteristically simplistic ploys here frequently verges on pure caricature. Yet in its very excess, it also contains a darker and more cynical side, since Rönne's naive recourse to these abstract categories of language exposes the real mechanism by which all discourse assembles the world as a social and ideological "imaginary" from such building-blocks, a process associated primarily with the dominant rationalist and scientific discourses.

This broader critique of the "world-making" function of dominant social discourse emerges in the text not only through language and its ability to pin down the real with *linguistic* labels, but also through Rönne's use of *mathematical* systems of order:

There was even a picture on the wall: a cow in a meadow. A cow in a meadow, he thought . . . There she stands with four legs, with one, two, three, four legs, this simply cannot be denied; she stands there with four legs on a field of grass and looks at three sheep, one, two, three, sheep – oh numbers, how I love numbers, they are so solid, they are simply so all round unimpeachable, they stiffen with unassailability, they are completely unambiguous, it would be ridiculous to want to find fault with

---

65 "Da trat ein Herr auf ihn zu, und ha ha, und schön Wetter ging es hin und her, Vergangenheit und Zukunft eine Weile im kategorialen Raum. Als er fort war, taumelte Rönne."

66 "Ich will mir ein Buch kaufen und einen Stift; ich will mir jetzt möglichst vieles aufschreiben, damit nicht alles so herunterfließt" (3); "Haus, sagte er zum nächsten Gebäude; Haus zum übernächsten; Baum zu allen Linden seines Wegs" (19).

them; now whenever I am sad, I will always say numbers to myself; he laughed happily and left. (10)[67]

Such absurd attempts to constitute meaning and order link Benn's Rönne to those other figures in expressionist literature whose attempts to organize a sense of self often end up embroiled in a similar double bind: they stave off the threatening sense of discontinuity in the world by pursuing rationalist (or pseudo-rationalist) projects, even though it is this same rationalism in bourgeois civilization which is responsible for their alienation in the first place.[68]

The rationalist double bind constitutes a central structural feature of many expressionist narratives, and is frequently linked to the theme of "Ichdissoziation," the experience of dissociation within the self, and of the self from society.[69] For in renewing his efforts to integrate himself into the community (or at least to follow more closely the discursive principles on which such social groups are founded), the bourgeois protagonist is often unaware of (or unperturbed by) the fact that in doing so he is merely submitting himself to those dominant social principles which alienate him in the first place. At best he thereby succeeds only in entrenching himself ever more firmly in the contradictions inherent in the process of socialization.

[67] "Nun hing sogar ein Bild an der Wand: eine Kuh auf einer Weide. Eine Kuh auf einer Weide, dachte er . . . Da steht sie nun mit vier Beinen, mit eins, zwei, drei, vier Beinen, das läßt sich gar nicht leugnen; sie steht mit vier Beinen auf einer Wiese aus Gras und sieht drei Schafe an, eins, zwei, drei, Schafe, – o die Zahl, wie liebe ich die Zahl, sie sind so hart, sie sind rundherum gleich unantastbar, sie starren von Unangreifbarkeit, ganz unzweideutig sind sie, es wäre lächerlich, irgend etwas an ihnen aussetzen zu wollen; wenn ich noch jemals traurig bin, will ich immer Zahlen vor mich her sagen; er lachte froh und ging (10).

[68] These absurdly rationalist projects of "bad faith" in expressionism clearly prefigure the existential games of "divertissement" played by the protagonists in the works of Beckett as well as in many postmodern narratives. Beckett's figures are particularly creative in inventing fictions and games to distract themselves while they "wait" for meaning and order to arrive, frequently giving these projects an explicitly rationalist or mathematical character – such as the precise permutations for alternating the "sucking stones," or the detailed observation and mathematical calculation of the frequency of the protagonist's bouts of flatulence. All of these games of permutation and calculation serve a similar function, namely to preempt the sense of meaninglessness by grasping at the straws of an outmoded and absurdly ineffectual rationalist tradition.

[69] On the notion of "Ichdissoziation," see Vietta and Kemper, *Expressionismus*, 30–40.

## Bakhtin and double-voiced discourse: Döblin's "The Murder of a Buttercup" and the double bind

Further instances of the double bind scenario may be seen not only in the case of Rönne and many of Kafka's protagonists,[70] but also most notably in the bourgeois figure Herr Michael Fischer in Döblin's early expressionist story "The Murder of a Buttercup" (1910) ("Die Ermordung einer Butterblume").[71] The story concerns an archetypal "burgher" who sets off for a walk in a forest swinging his cane as he goes. As the cane appears to get stuck in the undergrowth, Fischer suddenly and unaccountably explodes with rage, lashing out at the vegetation with his stick. This event is quickly followed by an even more peculiar occurrence: Fischer appears to see before him a re-enactment of the scene, with his own double lashing out at the undergrowth and decapitating a buttercup. Alternating between bouts of anger and fear, of remorse and malevolent satisfaction for his deed, Fischer develops a full-blown fixation upon the flower. He attempts at first to make good for his murderous outburst by searching out the injured flower in order to "save" it, but quickly reneges on his obligations. The narrative continues in this mode with Fischer oscillating between malevolence and remorse, until a chance incident allows Fischer to believe himself relieved of guilt, at which point he returns to the forest vowing violent retribution.

The text is remarkable less for this "plot," than for its discursive organization, particularly the manner in which it moves between various levels of narrational and figural discourse, and the way in which it manages – although focalized almost exclusively from Fischer's very idiosyncratic perspective – to take account of a broad variety of those organizing forms or dominant social dis-

---

[70] On the problem of the double bind in Kafka, see Gerhard Neumann's pathbreaking study *Franz Kafka. Das Urteil. Text, Materialien, Kommentar* (Metzler: Munich, 1981).

[71] Döblin, "Die Ermordung einer Butterblume," rpt. *Prosa des Expressionismus*, ed. Fritz Martini (Stuttgart: Reclam, 1970), 102–115. Matthias Prangel believes that the earliest drafts of this story may be dated to 1904–1905, to Döblin's early period in Freiburg. See his *Alfred Döblin* (Stuttgart: Metzler, 1987) 25–26. Similarly, Joris Duytschaever's insightful analysis of the story as a "pioneering achievement" of expressionism is based on Robert Minder's unpublished conversation with Döblin, in which it also emerged that the first draft of the story was begun around 1905. See Joris Duytschaever, "Eine Pionierleistung des Expressionismus: Alfred Döblins Erzählung *Die Ermordung einer Butterblume,*" *Amsterdamer Beiträge zur neueren Germanistik* 2 (1973): 27–43.

courses by which Wilhelminian culture constructs and represents itself. Although these discourses impinge upon, constrain and thoroughly condition Fischer, he nevertheless draws upon them for ontological sustenance, and thereby subjects his fragile sense of self to a destructive process of simultaneous centering and decentering.

We have already observed that Döblin's theoretical writings of this period explicitly exclude the traditional function of the narrator as a means of explaining the underlying order or causality behind the events of the story. However, as we have also noted, it is important to realize that in eliminating the narrative commentary, Döblin's "logical extension" of naturalism should not be thought of simply as producing a purer, more "objective" form of the classic realist text in which all traces of the narrator are finally removed while leaving intact other conventional functions of narratological domination. In fact, "The Murder of a Buttercup" is unusual firstly for its resistance to those narrative "dominant discourses" associated with classic realism (whose function is normally to simplify the reader's tasks), and secondly for the degree to which it makes it difficult even to isolate the different discourses at play within it – both of which are integral to the oppositional or "counter-discursive" stance characterizing the historical avant-garde.

## Mimesis vs. diegesis: counter-discourse and the classic realist text

In order to understand the significance of the radicalized narratological structure instituted by Döblin's expressionist poetics, it is useful to refer to the Platonic distinction between "diegesis," the representation of the events in the "author's" voice, and "mimesis," the representation of events through the voices (or impersonated voices) of the characters.[72] According to David Lodge, the development of prose fiction is characterized in the late realist and early modernist period by a general tendency

---

[72] For a discussion of this distinction and its ramifications for narratological theory, see David Lodge, *After Bakhtin: Essays on Fiction and Criticism* (London: Routledge, 1990), 28; also Brian McHale, "Free Indirect Discourse: A Survey of Recent Accounts," *PTL: A Journal for Descriptive Poetics and Theory of Literature* 3 (1978): 258.

towards "mimetic" (or "figural") narration, with the actual or reported speech of characters tending to dominate, while "diegesis," (that is, authorial comment or the narrator's interpretation of events) is kept to a minimum.[73]

This thesis accords with our previous observation of a poetics of "impersonality" in the modernist period generally.[74] More particularly it is borne out by the narrative structure of "Die Ermordung einer Butterblume," which can be characterized by Döblin's theoretical maxim that "one does not narrate, one builds" ("man erzählt nicht, sondern baut"). In other words, the author should attempt to present a sequence of uninterpreted images or events which must be confronted autonomously by the reader since, as we have already noted, Döblin believes that "*he* should be the one to judge, not the author" ("*er* mag urteilen, nicht der Autor") (*AzL*, 17, my emphasis). The diegetic (or in MacCabe's terminology, "metalinguistic") construction still typical for example in the classic realist text is clearly rejected by the expressionist avant-garde in general, and by Döblin in particular, on account of its implied claim to a perspective associated with an Olympian overview and sovereign mastery of events. In the chaotic and decentered world of modernity the pretense of providing such an interpretive framework and an explanation of causalities could only be maintained by those bourgeois writers for whom the real was to be perceived as an objective entity (rather than as a mere construction), and for whom the recording of social reality was still an unquestioned and relatively unproblematic undertaking.[75] For the expressionists by contrast, it is the process of *deconstructing* precisely such unquestioned ideological premises which forms the critical perspective defining their work as both "counter-discursive" and avant-garde. This distinguishes them clearly from those heirs to aestheticism within the modernist period, for whom the goal of perfecting the formal means of the work frequently overrides any quietist or affirmative ideological functions which it may take on in the process.

[73] Lodge, *After Bakhtin*, 32–33.
[74] See also Sokel, *Writer in Extremis*, 107.
[75] In this context one should recall Ernst Bloch's defense of expressionism against Georg Lukacs: the expressionists allowed that reality might exist as a "discontinuity," rather than in the form of that "closed and ordered reality" created by Lukacs' favored authors. See Bloch, "Diskussionen über Expressionismus," *Expressionismusdebatte*, 186.

This critical position is most obvious in the narrational structure of Döblin's "Butterblume." By contrast to the classic realist structure, Döblin's text has no diegetic meta-language ordering the mimetic discourses of the character, nor a dominant discourse through which events and issues can be organized and presented with the air of neutrality. Instead, Döblin's text superimposes the axis of the mimetic upon the diegetic, and makes the narrational merge with the figural to such an extent that the narrative voice becomes virtually indistinguishable from Fischer's own voice.

The first sentence of the story demonstrates the almost imperceptible means by which this superimposition is achieved: "The man dressed in black had first counted his steps, one, two, three, up to one hundred and backwards, as he walked up the broad path through the pine-trees to St. Ottilien . . . " (102).[76] Although the text begins with a narrative *description* of Fischer counting his steps, it is followed by what amounts to an *act* of counting ("one, two, three") – an act which would logically derive from the character, rather than from the narrator. At the earliest stage of the narrative then, we have an indication of the degree to which the discursive chaos it describes has entered into the text's *own* discursive organization: the diegetic is already completely contaminated by the mimetic.

Frequently the narration is also subtly focalized through the figure, to reflect his visual perspective, as in the sentence, "the light brown eyes which protruded amiably, stared at the ground which moved on under his feet . . . " (102).[77] This reflects Fischer's confusion by projecting the movement (i.e. his walking) from the cognitive subject onto the object. More ominously however such forms of focalization occasionally smuggle in Fischer's psychological and moral perspective, as in the sentence "the thin walking-stick swished in his right hand over the grass and flowers on the edge of the path and amused itself with the blossoms" (102).[78] This sentence contains not only the narrator's external description of the action but more importantly, in the figural phrase "amused

---

[76] "Der schwarzgekleidete Herr hatte erst seine Schritte gezählt, eins, zwei, drei, bis hundert und rückwärts, als er den breiten Fichtenweg nach St. Ottilien hinanstieg . . ."
[77] "die hellbraunen Augen, die freundlich hervorquollen, starrten auf den Erdboden, der unter den Füßen fortzog . . ."
[78] "das dünne Spazierstöckchen wippte in der Rechten über Gräser und Blumen am Wegrand und vergnügte sich mit den Blüten . . ."

itself" ("vergnügte sich") it presents an internal, mimetic voice –
the phrase being marked as deriving from Fischer's idiosyncratic
perspective by the accent of *desire*, the distorting personification
(or "eroticization") of the cane.[79] Thus on closer inspection the
narrative again reveals that it contains an element which cannot
logically belong to the narrator. Instead it must derive from the
figure's point of view and in particular from his highly ambivalent attitude regarding nature and the world of the senses: an
ambivalence marked by prudery and latent desire.[80]

## Cinematic prose: "Kinostil"

In his "Berliner Programm" of May 1913 Döblin proposed a
non-interpretative and "external" mode of narration under the
term "Kinostil": "Given the enormous mass of already formed
material a cinematic style is needed for representation. The 'full-
ness of appearances' should march past us with optimal terseness
and precision. One must wring out of language the utmost plasticity and liveliness . . . one does not narrate, one builds" (*AzL*, 17).[81]
    Something of this "Kinostil" can be seen in the description of
Fischer's attack on the undergrowth. It records the event with the
literary equivalent of a cinematic close-up, focusing metonymi-
cally upon the synecdochic details of the action itself, rather than

---

[79] Many commentators have seen the narrative in terms of an erotic encounter. See
for example, K. Müller-Salget, *Alfred Döblin. Werk und Entwicklung* (Bonn, 1972),
75; Thomas Anz, *Literatur der Existenz* 121–129. Further individual commentaries on the story: Ernst Ribbat, *Die Wahrheit des Lebens im frühen Werk Döblins*
(Münster: Aschendorff, 1970), 56; Leo Kreuzer, *Alfred Döblin. Sein Werk bis 1933*
(Stuttgart, 1970), 31–35; Roland Links, *Alfred Döblin. Leben und Werk* (Berlin-Ost,
1965), 18–20; Roland Links, *Alfred Döblin* (Munich: Beck, 1981), 22–26. 74–79;
Werner Zimmermann, *Deutsche Prosadichtungen unseres Jahrhunderts*, Vol. 1
(Düsseldorf, 1966), 167–178. On the relation of Döblin's early work to the
development of expressionist prose, see Klaus Kanzog, "Alfred Döblin und die
Anfänge des expressionistischen Prosastils," *Jahrbuch der deutschen Schillergesell-
schaft* 17 (1973): 63–83.

[80] Similarly the negative description of the forest wildflowers as "deformed,"
("*verwachsenen* Blumen") is most readily comprehensible not as an objective
observation on the part of the narrator regarding the outward appearance of the
vegetation but rather as an otherwise unsubstantiated criticism deriving from
Fischer's point of view, and more particularly, from his somewhat problematic
relationship to nature.

[81] "Die Darstellung erfordert bei der ungeheueren Menge des Geformten einen
Kinostil. In höchster Gedrängtheit und Präzision hat 'die Fülle der Gesichte'
vorbeizuziehen. Der Sprache das Äusserste der Plastik und Lebendigkeit ab-
zuringen . . . Man erzählt nicht, sondern baut."

viewing the subject as a whole or describing the underlying causes of the action: "The blows whistled right and left. Stems and leaves flew across the path" (103).[82] Yet this emphasis on the external and observable aspects of the story, which in the classic realist text might tend to efface the traces of the narrator's presence, leads in Döblin's text to the production of significant contradictions in the narrative perspective.

In the following sentence for example a seemingly "objective" and incontrovertible narrative description of Fischer's outward appearance at the attack is directly and seamlessly followed by another – equally innocent at first glance – which conceals a complicated mixture of narrational and figural viewpoints: "Puffing out air loudly, the man went on with flashing eyes. The trees marched quickly past him; the man paid no attention to anything" (103).[83] The clause beginning "the trees" reverses subject and object, projecting the movement outwards and attributing it to the object-world in a manner typical of the cognitive confusions and altered (or "overloaded") conditions of perception in modernity, a reversal which also characterizes for example the disjointed perspective in much early expressionist poetry.[84] Yet the tone in which this observation is stated is as matter-of-fact and seemingly "objective" as the purely external description of Fischer's appearance in the preceding sentence. Furthermore, the following clause "the man paid no attention to anything" (which registers the fact that Fischer "ignores" the trees rushing past) offers a paradoxical "confirmation" of the fact that this reversal is to be attributed not to the narrator but to Fischer's perspective, since it clearly arises from *his* perceptual confusion and – as the narrative later insinuates – from his incipient madness. In this the text remains true to the Expressionist poetics of "duplicity," that is, the tendency for the act of "representation" simultaneously to reveal and paradoxically to *conceal* its object – a poetics that Sokel rightly equates with the logic of the unconscious and the "dream image." For the very syntax

---

[82] "Die Hiebe sausten rechts und links. Über den Weg flogen Stiele und Blätter"

[83] "Die Luft laut von sich blasend, mit blitzenden Augen ging der Herr weiter. Die Bäume schritten rasch an ihm vorbei; der Herr achtete auf nichts"

[84] On the notion of the "cognitive overload" in modernity, see Silvio Vietta, "Großstadtwahrnehmung und ihre literarische Darstellung. Expressionistischer Reihungsstil und Collage," *DVjs* 48 (1974): 354–373; also Vietta and Kemper, *Expressionismus*, 30–40.

here has the effect of denying and affirming at one and the same moment.

In order to understand this mechanism in terms of the important relationship between Döblin's poetics and the expressionist avant-garde it is necessary to examine Döblin's attitude regarding narrative "objectivity" and in particular the term "cinema style" ("Kinostil"), paying special attention to the extent to which they might harbor a lingering reliance on objectivism. For the "Kinostil" is employed in the story in a fully expressionist manner, very much against the grain of its realist connotations: it is applied not just to objective or "photographable" phenomena, but equally to hallucination and to purely internal events. As a result, rather than reinforcing through mimetic faithfulness the sense of the objective world's immovable solidity – as is frequently the case, for example, even with the most radical and revolutionary works of naturalism – it undermines the conventional representational categories, in particular by effacing the boundaries between subject and object.

The most prominent example of this "Kinostil" is the central passage of the story in which Fischer sees played out before him the scene of his double reenacting the murder of the buttercup. The narrator here remains true to Döblin's dictum of preserving a purely external observation of events, without psychological explanation. This foregrounding of the concreteness of the action is emphasized by a series of "cinematic" techniques: firstly a "slow-motion," which retards the action in order to describe in detail the head of the flower spinning through the air; and secondly by a form of microscopic "close-up" which follows the flower's descent and observes at close range the "blood" gushing out of its "neck":

His arm went up, the cane whistled, whoosh, off flew the head. The head spun around in the air, disappeared in the grass . . . Plop, the severed head of the plant sank, burying itself in the grass . . . And from above, out of the rump of the body, it dripped, white blood welling up out of the neck, first a little, like saliva running out of the corner of the mouth of someone paralyzed, then it ran in a thick stream, ran slimily with yellow foam towards Mr. Michael . . . (104)[85]

---

[85] Sein Arm hob sich, das Stöckchen sauste, wupp, flog der Kopf ab. Der Kopf überstürzte sich in der Luft, verschwand im Gras . . . Plump sank jetzt der gelöste Pflanzenkopf und wühlte sich in das Gras . . . Und von oben, aus dem

This virtuoso performance of "Kinostil" combines a range of astonishingly detailed and concrete observations with a breathless passage of short staccato phrases, emphasizing the excitement and terror of the situation. Yet impressive as this bravura performance may appear as a piece of "realism," its technical virtuosity has the paradoxical effect of obscuring the single most important fact about the situation, namely that the whole scene is entirely subjective and hallucinatory, and cannot occur in the concrete and factual manner produced by the "Kinostil." Far from "watching" a transparent and objective "cinematic" record of the event, the reader at this point is instead made doubly conscious of the process of mediation – the circuitous route which the narration of the scene is made to undergo – on account of the *mise-en-abyme* effect: the narrator is watching Fischer, who in turn is watching himself (i.e. his "Double") committing the "murder." Consequently the objective and "logical naturalism" of the technique of "Kinostil" is in a sense turned against itself, making the reader wary of accepting as certainty that which appears to be described in that reassuringly factual manner conventionally associated with the dominant discourse of the classic realist text.

## Bakhtin: "Hybrid" discourse

A similar duplicity occurs at those moments in which the narrative appears to lapse into the narrative form of "free indirect discourse," or into that omniscient and external mode referred to by Dorrit Cohn as "psycho-narration."[86] Such narrative forms are conventionally used to describe the thoughts, emotions and inner life of the character. But in contrast to the more directly mimetic forms of figural self-articulation (such as the internal monologue or stream-of-consciousness) they possess the important difference that they reproduce the thoughts of the character by imposing upon them an external diegetic framework. Both free indirect discourse and "psycho-narration" tend to introduce their own perspective, order and logic into the description, frequently pro-

---

Körperstumpf, tropfte es, quoll aus dem Halse weißes Blut, nach in das Loch, erst wenig, wie einem Gelähmten, dem der Speichel aus dem Mundwinkel läuft, dann in dickem Strom, rann schleimig, mit gelbem Schaum auf Herr Michael zu . . ." (104).

86 Dorrit Cohn, *Transparent Minds. Narrative Modes for Presenting Consciousness in Fiction* (Princeton: Princeton University Press, 1978), 11.

jecting their own causal explanations and rational associations upon the chaotic and fragmented movements of the figure's consciousness. Indeed, in the case of the "psycho-narration," Cohn maintains that it can "effectively articulate a psychic life that remains unverbalized, penumbral or obscure."[87] Consequently this process of diegetic ordering frequently takes on a narrative function of organization analogous to that of the "meta-language" associated with the classic realist text.

Now this is where Döblin's text distinguishes itself sharply from the conventional use of such narratological forms. For wherever the narrative presents itself as a form of "psycho-narration," offering the reader what appears to be a reliable and external overview of the situation from the narrator's uncontested position of authority, the apparent objectivity of the narration inevitably reveals itself to be deeply "infected" not only by the figure's linguistic idiom, but by what, in a Bakhtinian sense, we can think of as the characteristic set of attitudes and ideological viewpoints corresponding to his vocabulary.

Döblin's text frequently balances itself delicately on the boundary line between the mimetic and the diegetic, the figural and the narrational. For example where Fischer is described as "the fat, correctly attired businessman" (115) there occurs within the space of this single line a distinct clash of different discourses.[88] The sentence places the narrator's own rather derisory, schoolboy-ish jab at the childlike Fischer as "chubby" or "fat" ("dick") next to the kind of inflated self-description ("correctly attired") more reminiscent of Fischer's own vocabulary and social aspirations, amongst which "correctness" – with its connotations of social acceptability and of the burgher's adherence to the group-identity and norm – would certainly figure prominently. The strongly defined sense of what constitutes social "correctness" here clearly does not belong so much to the narrator as to Fischer himself. Juxtaposed to the mocking term "chubby" the correctness aspired to by Fischer is ironically deflated and – by contrast to his self-estimation – we are reminded of what a pathetic figure he actually makes.[89]

---

[87] Cohn, *Transparent Minds*, 46.
[88] "der dicke, korrekt gekleidete Kaufmann..."
[89] Bakhtin offers a very similar example of a social norm embedded in the narrator's discourse, taken from Turgenev's *Fathers and Sons*: "'The fez and the

According to Bakhtin such an embedded or "concealed" frag-ment of discourse seems "to belong to the author, i.e., he is formally at one with it; but in actual fact, the motivation lies within the subjective belief system of his characters, or of general opinion" (305). Just as the comic novels described by Bakhtin take this "general opinion" as the target of their criticism, so Döblin makes the butt of his satirical humor the bourgeois prejudices and opin-ions which, taken together, form the common world view and prevalent mode of constructing reality in the Wilhelmine period: in other words, its dominant social discourse.

In this case, what Bakhtin would call the "common language" is that associated with the dominant values and ideological dis-courses of the burgher-class, consisting amongst other things of the typical phrases and associated norms of behavior to which Fischer clings in vain in his schizophrenic dialogues and his talk of law and authority. But it is significant that this "common language" regu-larly finds its way subtly into the narrator's discourse too – with a similar satirical effect. For example, after his massacre in the forest, Fischer appears completely disheveled. Yet the protagonist's typi-cally bourgeois values of propriety and rational order emerge as his automatic response to the madness of his situation. He is as concerned as ever for appearances, fearing that someone might observe him in this condition. Consequently despite his desperate state, when he begins to run from the scene he is absurdly self-conscious: "He began to go faster, to forget his deportment, to run" (107).[90] Although the phrase "He began . . . to forget his deport-ment" appears within the narrator's discourse (or "voice"), the idea of proper deportment clearly belongs not so much to the narrator as to the vocabulary of the "correct" burgher. Conse-quently the effect of this technique of the narrational "double voice" is that it makes it appear as if the narrator is standing at a slight distance from the embedded figural-mimetic phrase, allow-ing the absurdity of the attitude it implies to become apparent, isolated as it is within the diegetic discourse of the narrator.

carelessly knotted cravat carried a suggestion of the more free life in the country but the stiff collar of his shirt – not white, it is true, but striped *as is correct for morning wear* – stood up as inexorably as ever against his well-shaven chin'" (Bakhtin's emphasis). Bakhtin notes that the highlighted phrase is not a simple authorial statement "but rather the norm of the [protagonist's] gentlemanly circle, conveyed ironically." See Bakhtin, *The Dialogic Imagination*, 317.

[90] "Er fing an schneller zu gehen, seine Haltung zu vergessen, zu rennen . . ."

Bakhtin describes this satirical narrative technique in these terms:

> To one degree or another, the author distances himself from this common language, he steps back and objectifies it, forcing his own intentions to refract and diffuse themselves through the medium of this common view that has become embodied in language (a view that is always superficial and frequently hypocritical). (302)

In these "hybrid" forms of discourse the axes of the diegetic and the mimetic are completely conflated, since the external description of the event is colored or "contaminated" by the idiom and the outlook of the character to such an extent that the two poles become indistinguishable.[91]

The "verbal-ideological belief systems" (311) which are fore-grounded through such "double-voiced" or "hybrid" narrative structures emerge both in the form of these "common languages" and "character zones" but also in the guise of other, *non-verbal* semiotic and gestural codes satirized throughout the text. In many of the descriptions of Fischer's physical gestures for example this satirical strategy works to similar effect by exposing the mechanical quality of the burgher's conventions and automatic responses. For example although alone in the forest he adopts the façade of a "cool, hostile countenance" (105) as a defense against the inscrutable forces of nature which he fears are confronting him. Similarly automatic is the way in which "(he) turned on his heel, as if inadvertently" (107), unable to avoid this stiff, Prussian gesture even when alone in the midst of the forest.[92] Like Fischer's verbal clichés such gestures are marked as belonging to the standard repertoire of the burgher, to be trotted out in all their absurdity regardless of the appropriateness of the circumstances.

This analysis of "double-voiced" or "hybrid" discourse can be extended a good deal further, for even *within* Fischer's discourse, there is a clear conflict of different discourses and perspectives. The most obvious example of the clash of two perspectives can be seen in the following:

[91] Brian McHale describes in detail the various categories which critics have used in order to pinpoint this phenomenon of narrative "contamination." He also relates this idea productively to the distinction between mimesis and diegesis. See "Free Indirect Discourse," 261.

[92] "kühle, ablehnende Miene" (105); "(er) drehte sich wie versehentlich auf den Hacken um" (107).

He walked along quietly. Why was he panting? He smiled in embarrass-ment. He had jumped out at the flowers and had butchered them with his cane, yes, he had employed those same powerful yet well-aimed strokes with which he was accustomed to box his apprentices' ears when they were not deft enough in catching the flies in the office and in showing them to him sorted according to size. (103)[93]

The phrase "those same powerful yet well-aimed strokes with which he was accustomed to box his apprentices' ears" occurs in the midst of a passage of internal observation, in which Fischer's thoughts are framed by the narrator. Regardless of whether we interpret this passage as "psycho-narration" or as free indirect discourse its clear purpose is to explain from a more sober view-point the reasons for Fischer's "embarrassed smile." Since clearly the narrator himself can have no interest in praising the accuracy with which Fischer cuffs his apprentices with "well-aimed strokes," we must assume that this observation belongs primarily to Fischer's perspective and vocabulary, and that it corresponds to a set of values he shares with others belonging to his class and ideological background. Yet occurring in the midst of Fischer's attempt to explain to himself in rational terms what has just happened, the voice – against its own conscious intentions, so to speak – begins to take a rather defiant pride in the skill and accuracy with which the blows were inflicted. The objective and logical tone which is lent to the "well-aimed strokes" then con-trasts with the completely absurd and illogical rationale for the punishment itself, so that Fischer's actions and his manic desire for order appear all the more ridiculous, treated as they are with disproportionate seriousness. As with the double-voiced narra-tive then, this duplicitous structure gives Fischer's discourse a distinct and ironic "echo," reminding us both of its hollowness and of its internal contradictions. Thus the double-voice drama-tizes the familiar double bind: it reveals the inextricable link between on the one hand Fischer's longing for order through authoritarianism, and on the other, the latent aggression and the disorder which this destructive authoritarianism inevitably brings about.

[93] "Er ging ruhig. Warum keuchte er? Er lächelte verschämt. Vor die Blumen war er gesprungen und hatte mit dem Spazierstöckchen gemetzelt, ja, mit jenen heftigen aber wohlgezielten Handbewegungen geschlagen, mit denen er seine Lehrlinge zu ohrfeigen gewohnt war, wenn sie nicht gewandt genug die Fliegen im Kontor fingen und nach der Größe sortiert ihm vorzeigten" (103).

Through these peculiarly "hybrid" forms the text succeeds in presenting simultaneously two mutually contradictory view-points, while all the time operating nominally through a single voice.[94] Consequently these duplicitous forms of narration may be said in such cases to produce a kind of textual "parapraxis": typical of the progressive expressionist representational strategies which we described as a poetics of "duplicity" and "enigma," and similar in structure to a dream, they reveal and conceal, assert and deny at the same time.

## Irrational authority and the bourgeois imaginary: narration as counter-discourse and critique of ideology

From these examples, it is clear that Döblin's text represents the absolute antithesis to the ideal model decribed by the term "classic realist text." For instance the transitions between the figural and the narrational are so fluid here that not only are these discourses not easily distinguishable, but given the dialogical relationship between them no discursive hierarchy can possibly establish itself: no sense emerges that any of them function as a "meta-language" which could dominate or order the others. The clear differences in narrative structure between Döblin's avant-garde text and the classic realist text may be gauged for instance from MacCabe's description of the latter's typically realist division between what we have referred to as "mimesis" (the quoted discourse of figures) and "diegesis" (the narrator's commentary):

While those sections in the text which are contained in inverted commas may cause a certain difficulty for the reader – a certain confusion vis-à-vis what really is the case – this difficulty is abolished by the unspoken (or more accurately the unwritten) prose that surrounds them.[95]

In Döblin's text by contrast, even on those occasions where the direct discourse of the figure *is* clearly separated and enclosed within quotation marks in the manner of the classic realist text, this punctuation quickly reveals itself to be completely arbitrary. Thus rather than offering a form of discursive "signpost" to the

---

[94] On the notion of the "hybrid" forms of language, see Bakhtin *The Dialogic Imagination*, 359–61; also Tzvetan Todorov, *Mikhail Bakhtin: The Dialogical Principle*, trans. Wlad Godzich (Minneapolis: Minnesota University Press, 1984), 73.

[95] MacCabe, "Realism and the Cinema," *Tracking the Signifier*, 34–35.

reader it becomes instead a mere deception. Paradoxically it serves then not to clarify differences but rather to *call into question* the narratological status of those previous, seemingly secure sections of the text which appear to derive from the figure, but which nevertheless remain *without* quotation marks: the very distinction which MacCabe sees here as crucial to classic realism – the difference between what we have called the mimetic and the diegetic – is thus completely undermined.

To be sure, the narration does frequently break into direct, quoted discourse and thus into a correspondingly clear and ordered syntax, as if to mirror Fischer's emergence back into consciousness: "'What has happened?' he asked after a while. 'I'm not intoxicated'" (104).[96] But again this apparent narrational clarity merely reflects a deeper, underlying deception, since the more carefully delineated discourse here only serves as a rationalistic and orderly "cover" for Fischer's more fundamental acts of denial, as for example when he is quoted exclaiming, "'I do not remember this flower, I am aware of absolutely nothing'" (104).[97]

In this way the text's own deceptive clarity and seemingly cinematic "objectivity" merely illustrates the fundamental contradictions and self-deceptions which underlie all of Fischer's attempts to reconstruct his subjectivity and his world by mechanically imposing upon it an order aligned with rationalistic consciousness. It supports the idea that the "dominant discourse" of rationalism in society merely enables Fischer to put on the pose of sanity and rationality – just as he can muster a logical and linear syntax when needed – simply in order to deny his dilemma all the more convincingly.

Like many other expressionist figures, such as Benn's Rönne, Fischer clearly longs for such consolations of order and mastery. In this regard it is significant that the text is organized – both in its depiction of the figure's absurdly rationalist behavior, and in its own narrative structure – according to precisely the kind of progressive or counter-discursive structures typical of the avant-garde which resist and subvert such "addiction to order." It is worth observing for example that while depicting in Fischer the frustration of his longings for single, unambiguous, and authoritative meanings, the text itself also frustrates in its reader any

[96] "'Was ist geschehen?' fragte er nach einer Weile. 'Ich bin nicht berauscht.'"
[97] "'Ich erinnere mich dieser Blume nicht, ich bin mir absolut nichts bewußt.'"

similar longings at the hermeneutical level: the desire, for example, for the kind of unassailable truth offered by conventional forms of narrative authority and by its dominant discourse. A close analysis reveals that this avant-gardist orientation is inscribed into the very narrational structure of the text, as a means of countering those conventional modes of imposing order and epistemological authority which produce the kind of traditional "affirmative" functions (such as an artificial sense of closure for example) which are associated with the classic realist text. This can be seen most clearly in the depiction of Fischer's discursive role-switching. For instance, since Fischer himself needs a principle of order – the equivalent of a dominant discourse – to organize his unruly thoughts and put his emotions in their place, when he begins to panic, his phantasies take on a predominantly *ideological* form of role-playing. To enact these roles he borrows certain stereotypes of dominant social discourse – bourgeois models of rationalistic and authoritarian language, such as that of a doctor, a lawyer, or businessman – through which he imagines himself to be taking back control of his fragmented and radically decentered world:

He wanted to subjugate these willful thoughts: self-control. He, the boss, would vigorously take charge of this lack of obedience. One must take decisive steps against these people. 'What can I do for you? In my firm such behavior is not customary. Servant, throw the man out.' (104–5)[98]

It is important to note that the linguistic role Fischer adopts here is not depicted as belonging to any other *specific* figure. It represents rather a bourgeois "imaginary," that is to say, the generalized discourse, the verbal gestures and corresponding attitudes – in short the ideology – of the average burgher in the Wilhelmine period. And through this kind of linguistic role and its correspondingly authoritarian verbal ballast, Fischer is lent a vicarious identity, an artificial sense of authority and power with which to shore up the fragments of his own fragile personality.

The passage reveals the extent to which a progressive form of narratological subversion is inscribed into the very narrational

---

[98] "Die eigenwilligen Gedanken wollte er schon unterkriegen: Selbstbeherrschung. Diesem Mangel an Gehorsam würde er, der Chef, energisch steuern. Man muß diesem Volk bestimmt entgegentreten: 'Was steht zu Diensten? In meiner Firma ist solch Benehmen nicht üblich. Hausdiener, raus mit dem Kerl'' (104–105).

structure of the text. This progressive organization opposes the conventional hierarchy of sub-discourses and the affirmative sense of closure and control characteristic for example of the narrator's meta-language in classic realism. The passage begins with a description of Fischer's inner turmoil, mediated through the narrator via free indirect discourse. This culminates in the phrase "self-control," an associative link to a realm of discourse which cannot derive from the diegesis but which, paradoxically, does not belong directly to Fischer himself either. For as we have seen, rather than imitating a particular character, it "quotes" from an abstract set of "superior" attitudes and behavioral norms – the dominant social discourse – embodied by a general class of bourgeois figures of authority, an ideological realm to which Fischer clearly aspires.

As we have seen, Bakhtin views such doubly-oriented narrative as a "hybrid construction" since it produces

an utterance that belongs, by its grammatical (syntactic) and compositional markers, to a single speaker, but that actually contains mixed within it two utterances, two speech manners, two styles, two 'languages,' two semantic and axiological belief systems. (304)

Fischer's discourse here clearly falls into this category of the "hybrid" since the various linguistic roles he adopts are taken over wholesale as an existing set of ideologies and systems of belief. In crucial respects these ideologies represent authoritative discourses in which he has been only partially initiated. In this regard the textual irony is all the more effective since those authoritarian discourses with which he identifies so fully emerge through his voice only in the form of a "hybrid": they are at once part of his discourse and yet always foreign to it.

In contrast to the conventional realist technique of "containing" the character's speech through quotation marks – and so demarcating clearly the mimetic/diegetic boundaries – the quotation marks in the passage ("'What can I do for you?'") are again positioned in a rather arbitrary manner. In fact, when we analyze carefully Fischer's gradual adoption of this particular linguistic role, it is clear that his "hybrid" voice of authority actually begins in the previous sentence – well before the appearance of the quotation marks – when Fischer first takes on the mantle of the "boss." This arbitrary positioning of the quotation marks serves once more to highlight the fact that, given the complete overlapping between the poles of diegesis and mimesis, any hope that the reader might rely on clear and fixed boundaries between different realms of discourse has long since evaporated. The undermining of the boundaries between discourses, and between the mimetic and diegetic axes indicates at the same time that other such conventional markers and signposts between discourses – the textual signs which orient the reader within the reality of the text – have also disappeared, as the text takes on the characteristic structure of a "counter-discourse."

## Dominant social discourse and the double bind

The particular form of double bind from which Fischer suffers links him to many other expressionist characters who are also confronted by a massive existential crisis, a dissociation and disorientation of the self, and who long for a sense of fixity. Kafka's protagonists seek stability in precisely those mindless quotidian habits and absurdly rationalist responses which have alienated them in the first place. For even after his metamorphosis, Gregor Samsa still operates within the logic of the quotidian, endeavoring to catch the next train to work, and hoping that he can explain away his absence from work to his boss as well as the massive problem of his metamorphosis as if it were something of the order of a mere headcold.

Fischer too is confronted with a similar experience of alienation and responds in an analogous fashion to Gregor: with the automatic responses of the bourgeois rationalist. The initial signs of his crisis firstly take the form of an "Ichdissoziation" (or internal alienation)[99] – an experience linking him also to Benn's protagonist – in which the various parts of his body appear to function autonomously: "The feet began to infuriate him. They too wanted to take over as the boss . . . " (106).[100] Secondly there emerges within him a set of deep internal contradictions: on the one hand there is the combination of his stiff, bourgeois external appearance – dressed as he is in his black suit and his "stiff" hat (although he

---

[99] See Vietta and Kemper, *Expressionismus*, 30–49. See also Thomas Anz, *Literatur der Existenz passim.*
[100] "Die Füße begannen ihn zu grimmen. Auch sie wollten sich zum Herrn aufwerfen . . ."

is only out for a walk in the forest) – with his corresponding need always to remain in control; and on the other hand a latent desire to let slip his desperate grasp upon his social identity, and to lapse into the natural environment (as seems to be suggested initially by the playfulness of his gait, the swinging of his hips etc.).

Like many of Kafka's characters Fischer reacts to this abstract and intangible crisis by producing automatically a set of absurdly rationalist and mechanical responses which merely give him a *fictional* sense of control over his existential predicament. For example, he plays out his relationship to the injured flower by taking up another linguistically-mediated role, that of a lawyer citing legal procedure and attempting to take control of the situation through the sheer weight of his legalistic terminology: "Hand her over. Conditions must be arranged. Preliminary talks. The doctor has rights with regard to the patient. Laws must be upheld" (108).[101] Like Fischer's mania for counting his steps as he walks, these fantasies of the self invariably cater to the burgher's need for a sense of order and control, asserting his authority over the other, as well as over his own identity. The series of voices he adopts share a set of attitudes associated with an "imaginary" of bourgeois power and authoritarianism: that of a businessman ("'I refuse most decisively to initiate any relationship with your firm'" (106); a doctor ("'She is wounded, on the head, slightly below the head . . . I want to help her, I am a doctor, Samaritan'" (108); and the brief role of a common street ruffian, encapsulated in one telling sentence ("'Watch it you, I'm telling you, watch it idiot, damned idiot'"(106).[102] In each of these short scenarios – some of which may consist only of a single line (as in the latter example) – not just a role but a whole world of attitudes and norms is briefly enacted before being displaced by the next discourse or idiom and by its corresponding "supplementary" self.

These roles are all linked by the desire to control and to dominate, whereby this need for mastery is directed, ironically, towards his own errant self. He is annoyed for example by the "willfulness" of his own feet, as we have seen: "their willful

---

[101] "Herausgeben. Es müssen Bedingungen gestellt werden. Präliminarien. Der Arzt hat ein Recht auf den Kranken. Gesetze müssen eingebracht werden."
[102] "'Ich weigere mich auf das entschiedenste, mit Ihrer Firma irgendwelche Beziehung anzuknüpfen'" (106); "'Sie ist verwundet, am Kopf, etwas unterhalb des Kopfes . . . Ich will ihr helfen; ich bin Arzt, Samariter'" (108); "'Paß auf, du, ich sag dir's, paß auf, Lump, verfluchter'" (106).

hurrying forward annoyed him. He wanted to bring these little horses to heel soon. They would feel it. One sharp jab in the flank would soon tame them" (106).[103] But since this role-playing – here the role of a horseman – is directed against the emergent sense of a failure of discipline and order within his own self, the attempt to adopt these social stereotypes and so to draw upon the larger authority of dominant social discourse must ultimately serve only to divide and alienate still further his already decentered self. Thus Fischer's strategy fails on two counts: firstly in as far as it represents the attempt by a schizophrenic to stabilize the self by adding further roles to his already destabilizing repertoire; but secondly in as far as the roles he adopts embody the very principles of rationality and order, which – according to many Expressionists – were the major forces responsible for tyrannizing the subject in the first place.[104]

Thus the problem of "Ichdissoziation" – the alienation of the subject from both the world and from the body – forms merely one aspect of the broader crisis of rationalism in modernity which is articulated through the emergence in the text of these fictional roles. For over and beyond this a far more fundamental form of alienation is at work here – one which may be seen to underwrite the effects of the other two forms. It is registered by the text not just at the fictional level of the narrative, in the peculiar behavior of its central figure, but even at the level of its narratological structure and rhetoric. For the forces of fragmentation and displacement against which Fischer struggles in order to maintain his identity are always associated in the text with the *ideological power of discourse itself*. It is discourse which always exists prior to the individual and beyond his control, occupying with its own semantic determinations the world of objects he inhabits and confronting him at every turn with its own autonomous meanings. It is for this reason that Fischer's attempt to overcome the

---

[103] "ihn empörte ihr eigenwilliges Vorwärtsdrängen. Diese Pferdchen wollte er bald kirren. Sie sollten es spüren. Ein scharfer Stich in die Flanken würde sie schon zähmen."

[104] This critique of rationalism took many forms and became one of the central targets of the expressionists' "Zivilisationskritik." In this respect it is clearly the most important historical and philosophical context in which the text should be read. Among many possible examples of this expressionist genre of cultural criticism that one might cite, the most well-known and influential is probably Paul Kornfeld's expressionist manifesto "Der beseelte und der psychologische Mensch." Rpt. *Manifeste und Dokumente*, 222–238.

experience of dissociation and discursive decentering merely en-
snares him still further in a familiar double bind: the attempt to
seek a kind of ontological shelter by identifying with the dominant idioms and authoritative discourses of bourgeois ideology
proves useless as a defense against the experience of decentering,
since this experience is itself fundamental to the ideological and
discursive process by which the individual is socialized – the
brutal but seemingly perennial condition of civilized life against
which such Expressionist writers as Otto Gross and Paul Kornfeld
for example never ceased to aim their polemical "Zivilisationskritik" ("critique of civilization").

According to the models of subject-construction described for
instance by Lacan and (with certain differences) by Althusser, the
inherent condition of subjectivity in civilization involves the individual being socialized and constituted by language, but at the
same time also being decentered and divided by these same
means. The individual does not appear *ab ovo* as a unified self,
with an inherent character and fixed "significance," but emerges
rather in relation to a collection of linguistic roles, constantly
subject to a differential displacement between these various positions and metaphors of self. As the "subject" of language then, the
individual is simultaneously its object, for according to Lacan's
well-known observation: "it is not only man who speaks, but that
in man and through man *it* speaks [ça parle] . . . his nature is
woven by effects in which is to be found the structure of language,
of which he becomes the material, and . . . there therefore re-
sounds in him . . . the relation of speech."[105] The individual is
consequently the object of a process of decentering or differential
slippage between roles which are continually displacing and
overturning each other. In the essay "Aggressivity in
Psychoanalysis," Lacan sees in this multiplicity of roles an ontological ambivalence leading to the *decentering* of the subject. It is
through such identification with other roles – especially that involving the assimilation of the authority-figure and the victim –
that "the human individual fixes upon himself an image that
alienates him from himself."[106] And as a result this constant

[105] Jacques Lacan, "The Signification of the Phallus," *Ecrits* (London: Tavistock, 1977), 284.
[106] Lacan, "Aggressivity in Psychoanalysis," *Ecrits*, 19. See also Louis Althusser, "Ideology and Ideological State Apparatuses," *Lenin and Philosophy and Other*

process of mutual reconstruction pre-empts all attempts to "fix" meaning and identity absolutely.

## Conclusion.

## The critique of modernity and dominant social discourse: the "critique of civilization" and the counter-text

It is here that one might point to the beginnings of a critique of civilization in Döblin's text that is far more subtle and theoretically refined than the simple "Bürgerfeindlichkeit" (or animosity towards the bourgeois) with which such expressionist texts are commonly associated by their commentators. It is true that in its critique of the power of discourse Döblin's text displays two paradigmatically expressionistic attributes: firstly it functions as a satirical reflection on modernity, a "critique of civilization," exposing the destructive aspects of contemporary existence[107]; and secondly, in its ironic treatment of the burgher-figure Fischer it functions as a one of the expressionists' most familiar polemical forms, the "satire on the philistine" or "Spießersatire," the central feature of which is to expose to criticism and ridicule the self-satisfied attitude and authoritarian norms of behavior of the Wilhelminian burgher-class – that social and ideological grouping which rose to power as the generation of founding fathers of the Reich (the "Reichsgründer") in turn-of-the-century Germany. As we have seen however, the text emphasizes the *social* aspect of its critique primarily by focusing on the problem of the ideological function of language, for instance by satirizing Fischer's unthinking reliance on the clichéd phrases and prefabricated discourse of the burgher-class.[108] The bourgeois is in this respect not *merely* an

Essays, trans. Ben Brewster (London: New Left Books, 1977). A useful discussion of this notion of linguistic socialization (including a commentary on its significance in the thought of Benveniste, Lacan and Althusser) may be found in Catherine Belsey's *Critical Practice* (London: Methuen, 1980), 56–67.

107 On the theme of "Zivilisationskritik" see Vietta and Kemper, *Expressionismus*, 83–110.

108 To read the story merely as a kind of psychoanalytic case-history of a madman – a response which Döblin, judging by his stated theoretical position at the time was clearly trying to preclude – would amount to reducing it to the terms of Fischer's private idiosyncrasies, that is, to a series of extreme personal reactions (rather than as a *generally* felt experience of alienation, as a *social* fact). The "psychological" view risks reducing considerably the scope of the story as a critique of the burgher since it makes it difficult to generalize Fischer's experi-

object of satire for the expressionists, a pathetic philistine and abhorrent symbol of the Wilhelminian society rejected by the young artists. Over and beyond this, and especially within the more sophisticated and "duplicitous" poetics of the expressionist avant-garde, he is also the primary representative of the general civilizing process in modernity, and a victim – albeit a seemingly willing victim – of the rationalistic value-system and of the dominant social discourses by which reality and self are constructed.

Despite the obviously humorous elements of hyperbole and caricature in "The Murder of a Buttercup" its ideology-critique and its analytical dismantling of the underlying process of socialization demand to be taken in absolute earnestness. For the patent excesses and existential absurdities of Fischer (like those of Rönne and Gregor Samsa) reflect the double-bind structure or rationalist paradox on which the narrative is patterned: that is, the attempt to overcome the effects of a constricting form of rationality and a compulsion for order through further appeals to rationality and order. The absurd paradoxes in which Fischer is constantly trapped (his attempts to master his psychological destabilization through further schizophrenic role-playing) reflect in only slightly more extreme form a similar double bind structure which is made to appear central to the entire process of socialization and to the (discursive) construction of the subject in civilization.

This illustrates again the paradoxical character of the movement's problematic and problematizing relationship to realism: the expressionist text succeeds in locating a real-life site or referential social world ("Bezugsrealität") as the target of its criticism, not despite, but precisely *by means of* its "unrealistic" distortions, abstractions and representational excesses. Clearly the text lacks that conventional form of "realism" which would offer a more complete picture of the world of its protagonist. It scarcely presents for example any details of the individual's life, his work, or his family relations, nor does it show the broader picture of the social world in which he lives. Yet it does succeed in giving an

ence of alienation and to see his peculiar behavior and eccentric attitudes as representative of the norms of his class. This point again clarifies the reasons for Döblin's resistance to "psychoanalytic" explanation. It also shows once more the links between Doblin's and Brecht's conceptions of the "epic" structure: both encourage the audience to move away from a myopic consideration of a single individual or case and towards a broader social and historical perspective.

important insight into that broader social and historical reality *indirectly* through the expressionistic method of "abstraction." For by excluding all conventional "reality-effects" as well as the extraneous details of the character, and by abstracting the "essence" of the figure *as a bourgeois* it pinpoints precisely the constitutive *discursive* elements of society which are responsible for producing such extreme character-types.

Furthermore the text's "dialogical" forms of counter-discourse, such as its "hybrid" or "double-voiced" constructions (involving, as we have seen, a variety of narratological contradictions and parapraxes) produce a polyphony of voices representative of bourgeois society's "general opinion" and idiom. Consequently despite the typically expressionistic manner of exaggeration and excess which presents a world distorted by a subjective vision and restricted by the seemingly narrow scope of the narration's focus on a single character, there emerges here (as with other "sophisticated" expressionist works by Kafka or Benn), a broader, more "objective" or "externalized" form. This introduces an alternative perspective on Fischer's monomania which both ironizes it, revealing its hollowness, and which presents it "dialogically" as an echo of the social formation at large.

The function of the counter-text is not for example to confront the "monological" discourses of authoritarianism (in which Fischer for instance seeks refuge and re-fashions himself) with any alternative, more enlightened discourses or set of values, or with any alternative means of fulfilling the ideological task of identity-formation. Instead, the subversive and avant-garde effects of the text take the form of what Bakhtin calls "heteroglossia." This involves forming a discursive pluralism "aimed sharply and polemically against the official languages of its time." It becomes the means by which the "unifying, centralizing, centripetal forces of verbal-ideological life"[109] may be exposed and subjected to a dialog with their alternatives. Like the process of "abstraction" at the center of expressionist poetics, heteroglossia distances Fischer's authoritarian discourses from the individual figure, as well as from the generic or professional context of the kinds of characters who might articulate them. In doing so heteroglossia forces these discourses out of their otherwise inconspicuous and trans-

---

[109] Bakhtin, *The Dialogic Imagination*, 272–273.

parent state as the accepted, "official" language of "verbal-ideological life" and into a visible form in which they become legible as discursive constructs and are thus opened to interrogation as ideology. Typical of the avant-garde's critique of social institutions and the administration of cultural and discursive formations in society this counter-discursive strategy demonstrates both the arbitrariness with which particular discourses are elevated ideologically to a position of dominance, while at the same time it illustrates the purely ideological functioning of the "official" system of social discourses – a system which the text links with the process of socialization responsible for producing the burgher's one-dimensional world-view.

It is again characteristic of the avant-garde's poetics that in exposing the means by which such dominant social discourses become the vehicle of social ideology, Döblin's text itself refuses the narrational form of dominant discourse, in other words the kind of authoritative narrative organization associated with classic realism. Instead, the proliferation of different idioms to which Fischer gives voice then produces a plurality of discourses in the text at complete odds with the classic realist hierarchy (in which a metalanguage organizes and homogenizes the text's discourses). And through this heteroglossia the text takes on a form analogous to the non-organic work and to the montage, confronting the reader with an unresolved, dialogical interaction of voices, attitudes and values. As a consequence the image of reality which emerges from this "heteroglossia" is particularly appropriate as a reponse to modernity: corresponding to the new and vastly more complex experience of the real – the world of modernity which Ernst Bloch conceives of in terms of "discontinuity" and "interruption," and in which no neutral or Olympian position can exist – it is highly appropriate that, like a montage, the avant-garde text emerges as a multifarious and fundamentally contradictory entity.[110]

## Expressionist poetics and Brecht: anti-illusionism, the "epic" and the decentered reader

It is from this perspective that we can return finally to a reconsideration of the complexity of Döblin's important notion of "Kinostil" ("cinema-style"). My analysis of "The Murder of a Butter-

[110] See Bloch, "Diskussionen über Expressionismus," *Expressionismusdebatte*, 86.

cup" has shown that although the concept appears at first glance to imply the possibility of a neutral narrative position from which events might be observed "objectively," it turns out instead to harbor a very different function. For since the narrator's voice is always contaminated by other idioms, it can never recede quietly into the background in the manner of the transparent narration characterizing the classic realist text. The function of Döblin's pursuit of the extremes of "logical naturalism" ("konsequenter Naturalismus") then is to deconstruct the very concept of naturalism. By exposing its "logical consequences" Döblin shows that its supposedly neutral viewpoints are merely the effects of artifice, and that all narration is necessarily implicated – whether by its particular perspective, or conversely by its attempt to appear to do without one – in the production of specific meanings and ideologies. The supposed purity and (feigned) diegetic neutrality of Döblin's "cinematic style" of narration for example is constantly made to conflict with the intensely *subjective* nature of the mimetic realm in which the narrated events take place: the diegetic axis of narration is contaminated by the interaction with the mimetic axis. Consequently, the very "stylization" of the narration in terms of a camera and its "neutral" mode of observation turns out to be an avant-garde mechanism, a strategy of intentional paradox, by which the text provokes and critiques the very conditions of conventional art and the institutionalized, mimetically-oriented system of classical representation: the narrative device is "laid bare," so that the limits and the illusionistic foundations of such narrative "neutrality" are dismantled.

Expressionism's strategy of laying bare the representational device – both formally and ideologically – is a defining feature of its poetics as an avant-garde phenomenon. It also allows us to see the links to those later avant-garde styles which eventually developed out of it, and most importantly to Brecht's aesthetics. For at the most obvious level the characteristic excesses and distortions associated with all genres of expressionist art have an anti-illusionistic function similar to the Brechtian alienation device or "V-effect": they push its style obtrusively into the foreground and so make the audience intensely conscious of the text's artifice. As I have shown above, even where at the manifest level the text purports – by using the "Kinostil" – to present events and actions in the "transparent" or "illusionistic" manner associated with the classic realist text, at the latent level the narrative still succeeds by indirect means – namely through its paradoxical mode of simultaneously revealing and concealing – in achieving one of the avant-garde's key objectives: the interrogation of the unspoken premises of art as an institutionalized cultural phenomenon, and the disclosure of its socially affirmative functions. For the apparent clarity of the "Kinostil" as a mode of revelation is undermined by an opposing principle: the multiplicity of voices in the text and the manner in which they color the diegesis illustrates that a pure "histoire," in other words the kind of narrative which appears to be "objective" and unnarrated, is now a patent impossibility. Furthermore it demonstrates that such a transparent window upon events is inappropriate to the chaotic world of modernity and is in fact only *ever* an illusion, since – like the organic work – the "histoire" merely creates an *effect* of completeness and irrefutability by hiding the marks of its own construction and by effacing the traces of the "discours" from which it is created.[111] But finally, almost against Döblin's own naturalistic inclinations, it shows that reality does not necessarily exist in the kind of concrete form (as Döblin phrases it, "saturated with objectivity" ["gesättigt von Sachlichkeit"] *AzL*, 9) which is accessible to "naturalistic" or "cinematic" representationalism. For in pushing the mimetic principle to its logical extreme, Döblin's "filmic" imagination takes the text far beyond the limits of such concrete representationalism: it shows that the mimetic tradition is now deprived of its customary object and can only gesture towards the more powerful presence of an abstract "verbal reality"[112] which must remain unrepresentable to it – this is the significance of

---

[111] Benveniste's distinction between "histoire" and "discours" has gained wide currency, not least via the work of Christian Metz. See Christian Metz, "Story/Discourse. (A Note on Two Kinds of Voyeurism)," *The Imaginary Signifier: Psychoanalysis and Cinema*, trans. Celia Britton, Annwyl Williams, Ben Brewster and Alfred Guzzetti (London: Macmillan, 1982), 91–98.

[112] "sprachliche Realität" *AzL*, 13. Erich Kleinschmidt observes similarly that the "filmic" quality of Döblin's narrative position emerges from the insight that the "concreteness" of reality can no longer be reconciled with language. I am grateful to Professor Kleinschmidt for his 1979 Freiburg seminar on Döblin and for drawing my attention to this general problematic. See Kleinschmidt, "Roman im 'Kinostil.' Ein unbekannter 'Roman'-Entwurf Alfred Döblins" *DVjs* 63. 3 (1989): 582.

reality's emergence as an intangible *discursive* entity.

Far from concealing the evidence of its fabrication the non-organic or montage text of the avant-garde by contrast thrusts its constructedness into the foreground, very much in the manner prescribed by Brecht with his anti-illusionistic epic theater.[113] The consequence is that like the Brechtian "epic" the avant-garde work refuses to allow its audience to identify simplistically with the kind of privileged and authoritative perspective through which it would vicariously achieve a sense of unquestioned mastery over its content.[114] Both progressive aesthetic models are characterized by a relationship between the audience and the work of art based on the disavowal of any simple audience identification – either with the characters[115] or with narratorial or other set interpretative positions.[116] Instead of being invited to identify with the authority of the narrative's meta-discourse and so to share in that "position from which the text is most 'obviously' intelligible,"[117] the reader of the expressionist avant-garde's "counter-texts" is *decentered*, deprived of the conventional unitary position of pseudo-mastery, and forced to confront a set of contradictory ideas and discontinuous perspectives which can no longer be synthesized by reference to a static and transcendent set of truths.

It is significant in this regard that the texts of both Brecht and the expressionist avant-garde tend to be open-ended, refusing the kind of closure which subordinates individual events to the overriding concerns of the plot and its resolution.[118] Similarly, where

---

[113] Viktor Zmegac has described the similarities between Döblin and Brecht's treatment of this point in their progressive conceptions of the "epic" in the article cited above, "Alfred Döblins Poetik des Romans," 341–364.

[114] Döblin criticizes such traditional practices as responsible for producing something of an "increasing, subtly-cultivated inability of the public to read" ("(einer) zunehmenden, raffiniert gezüchteten Leseunfähigkeit des Publikums") *AzL*, 20.

[115] Döblin's position is to oppose such "psychological prose" ("psychologische Prosa") with the evocation instead of a "reality devoid of the soul" ("entseelte Realität"). See *AzL*, 17.

[116] It is worth noting that Döblin explicitly links his new poetics of the "impersonal" and "depersonalized" ("Entselbstung, Entäußerung . . . Depersonation") to a call for a new "epic" form of prose: "The novel must experience its rebirth as a work of art and a modern epic" ("Der Roman muß seine Widergeburt erleben als Kunstwerk und modernes Epos"). *AzL*, 18–19.

[117] Belsey, *Critical Practice*, 57.

[118] In his "Observations on the Novel" ("Bemerkungen zum Roman"), Döblin for example rails against the traditional values of plot and tension, complaining

the classic realist text sets the reader before problems that it will itself also inevitably resolve, in the avant-garde text the reader is implicated much more directly and obviously in the ongoing production of the text's meaning: the reader is made to question the way in which meaning is produced, and by extension question the institutionalized signifying practices of art in general. In attempting to resolve the multifarious montage of discourses and viewpoints characterizing Döblin's text for example, the reader is invariably forced into a situation similar to that confronting the audience of those "meaningless" works of the avant-garde described by Bürger: in being cast back upon his or her own devices by the text the reader is made aware of the extent he or she inevitably resorts to precisely those interpretative conventions supported by the institution of art – an experience reinforced not least through the frustration of encountering the limits of such an interpretative approach.

As we have seen, in the case of the expressionist texts by Benn and Döblin for example, the reader will automatically find him- or herself in a position curiously analogous to that of the texts' protagonists: the text encourages the search for meaning but frustrates the attempt to find a unitary interpretation, a rationalistic and consistent construction for the diverse and contradictory perspectives it embodies. In other words, the expressionist avant-garde leads to a provocation which draws out of the reader those petrified and rationalistic constructions of meaning which the institution of art has made conventional.

that 'the thickening and resolution of the conflict" ("Konfliktschürzung und -lösung") as well as "tension ruins the novel . . . " ("Spannung ruiniert den Roman . . ."). *AzL*, 19.

# 4

❖❖❖❖❖❖❖❖❖❖❖❖❖❖❖❖❖❖❖❖❖❖❖❖❖❖❖❖❖❖❖❖❖❖❖❖❖❖❖❖❖❖❖❖

# The poetics of hysteria:
# expressionist drama and the
# melodramatic imagination

❖❖❖❖❖❖❖❖❖❖❖❖❖❖❖❖❖❖❖❖❖❖❖❖❖❖❖❖❖❖❖❖❖❖❖❖❖❖❖❖❖❖❖❖

> . . . one should not ask about the quality of this art, but
> about its intensity. The intensity is what constitutes
> its value. For it is not a matter of artistic accomplish-
> ment, but of the will . . . This art will blow apart the
> aesthetic . . ."
>
> Kurt Pinthus.[1]

## Melodrama as counter-discourse

Kafka's reported reaction on first reading a volume of poetry by a
particularly strident expressionist writer – "It is screaming. That
is all" – has frequently been taken more broadly as expressing his
general attitude of skepticism towards the expressionist movement as a whole.[2] Brief as it is, Kafka's response nevertheless
constitutes a troubling criticism, pointing to an inherent danger
within expressionism where the seemingly liberating impulse
towards expression turns into mere excess, into an hysterical
"sound and fury" which exhausts itself at the level of its extravagant and desperate gestures and fails to carry any further meaning with it.

---

[1] "[man] frage nicht nach der Qualität dieser Kunst, sondern nach ihrer Intensität .
. . Diese Kunst wird also allenthalben das Ästhetische zersprengen . . . ." See my
commentary on this passage in chapter two above. Kurt Pinthus, "Rede für die
Zukunft," *Die Erhebung* (1919), 420. Rpt. W. Rothe, ed., *Der Aktivismus 1915–20*,
132. Parts of the present chapter were originally published in *GRM* 6.6 (1990):
339–49.

[2] "Es ist ein Schreien. Das ist alles." This comment reported by Janouch was in
response to an edition of poetry by J. R. Becher. See Gustav Janouch, *Gespräche
mit Kafka* (Frankfurt: Fischer, 1951), 53.

In this chapter however I would like to propose that it is precisely this hysterical aspect of expressionism which aligns it with another literary mode, namely melodrama, whose method is similarly excessive, yet whose deeper significance lies in the fact that it resorts to such "screaming" only in order to reach beyond dominant representational systems, codes and conventions, and beyond the epistemological and discursive restrictions associated with them.[3] Far from "signifying nothing" the typical forms of excess in expressionism – its characteristic bombast, its unashamed opening of the soul, its "sentimental" claims to privileged insight into a transcendent world beyond – share with the mode of melodrama the urge to create a means of signification which employs these wild, formless and often paradoxically "mute" forms of expression in order to point to a meaning which lies in the realm of the unspeakable and beyond the epistemological grasp of conventional representation.

The use of a term such as melodrama may not appear to offer much of a defense against the kind of criticism represented by Kafka's comment. For melodrama is traditionally burdened with pejorative connotations on account of its tendency to eschew the more sophisticated means of "managing" underlying fears and desires through formal organization and aesthetic "sublimation." Furthermore, it is associated instead with more "primitive" means, since it works by employing polarized and manichaeistic schemes, preferring to use "types" as stock-characters (rather than closely-observed individuals with their own psychological complexity) and to unleash raw or overblown rhetoric (rather than the more intricate or "controlled" forms of expression). Although it deals primarily with psychological and rhetorical extremes, and engages its issues by using inflated and radically

---

[3] Many previous attempts to apply the notion of melodrama to German theater have tended, rather restrictively, to focus upon it simply as a "musikalisch-dramatischen Mischform" (a "musical-dramatic hybrid") as in W. Schrimpf, *"Faust* als Melodrama? Überlegungen zu einer Bühnenfassung von 1815," *Euphorion* 81 (1987): 347–352; or as a purely sensational popular-entertainment as in J. Hüttner "Sensationsstücke und Alt-Wiener Volkstheater. Zum Melodrama in der ersten Hälfte des 19. Jahrhunderts," *Maske und Kothurn* 21 (1975): 263–281. By contrast, Christoph Eyckman's chapter "Das Pantomimische als Strukturelement im expressionistischen Drama" develops a more refined concept of "mime" through which certain of the more obscure plays of the movement (by Einstein, Kandinsky, Goll, Stramm and Hasenclever) are illuminated. See *Denk- und Stilformen des Expressionismus* (Munich: Fink, 1974), 144–66.

polarized terms, I hope nevertheless to show that within expressionism melodrama may be viewed as an important mode of literary response to the historical and social crises of the period. For however desperate in appearance, even the very excesses of its form function in the expressionist period as a mode of counter-discourse making visible those meanings and values which remain repressed and unarticulable by the socially legitimized discourses and by conventional modes of representation such as realism.

For if the fundamental claim of realism is to explain the world and make it comprehensible, and if this leads to a second, related claim, namely that "grasping" reality conceptually means possessing and controlling it also, then when melodrama functions as a form of *counter-discourse* it sets about undermining precisely these assumptions. For as a progressive, countervalent mode it suggests a range of social and psychological fears and desires that the dominant epistemology and its social discourses of explanation simply cannot account for. It protests for example against the reality principle which underpins the dominant social discourses, against what Christine Gledhill calls the "codes of social behavior, conventions of language and the structure of the psyche."[4] In doing so it demands "acknowledgment of all that cannot be contained within the dominant order – anti-social desire, the 'numinous,' the struggle of good and evil" (30). Melodrama thus exerts an oppositional power upon the "conventional and repressive discourses of the post-Enlightenment order" (30) forcing them to yield up their limitations and to reveal the sites of their repressions. The result, as Peter Brooks observes, is that "melodramatic rhetoric, and the whole expressive enterprise of the genre, represents a victory over repression . . . The melodramatic utterance breaks through everything that constitutes the 'reality principle,' all its censorships, accommodations, tonings-down."[5]

If, as Gledhill maintains, "melodrama feeds a demand for significances unavailable within the constraints of socially legitimate discourse for which there is no other language . . . " (37), then the nature of the melodramatic response as a kind of literary "hys-

[4] Christine Gledhill, "The Melodramatic Field: An Investigation," *Home Is Where The Heart Is* (London: BFI, 1987), 30.
[5] Peter Brooks, *The Melodramatic Imagination. Balzac, Henry James, Melodrama and the Mode of Excess* (New Haven: Yale University Press, 1976), 41.

teria" is particularly important in its function as a counter-discourse. For even as a seemingly primitive or "uncivilized" form it figures as a cultural "constant" associated with the anthropological roots of theatricality and dramatization – in other words as a signifying practice and as an aesthetic mode of cognition whose value lies in its ability to use the aesthetic sphere as a vehicle for transgressing the limits of the real and the constraints of the reality-principle.

The point at which realist representation is unable to accommodate such problematic and unspeakable issues is frequently the moment at which – at least in the more progressive narrative structures common to the avant-garde – this transgressive option is set in motion. As with the fantastic and the gothic one could argue of melodrama that the switch into an alternative representational mode fulfills the function of accommodating that which would otherwise fail to signify under conventional realistic codes and rational discourses. Melodrama in this respect need not be conceived of as an entirely separate genre which informs and differentiates every aspect of a work *as* exclusively "melodramatic," but rather as a variation on realism, predicated primarily on a response to the deficits of realism and the classical system of representation.

Geoffrey Nowell-Smith conceives of melodrama similarly in relation to realism, namely as a form which responds "hysterically" to the limitations and deficits of realism's conventions:

Often the 'hysterical' moment of the text can be identified as the point at which the realist convention breaks down ... The breakdown of the stable convention of representation allows such questions to be temporarily suspended in favor of what is, at one level, simple narrative confusion, but on another level can be seen as an enactment of a fantasy ...[6]

In expressionist melodrama the "fantasy" which is enacted corresponds to any content which would otherwise fail to find expression in the dominant social discourses and their corresponding modes of representation. As with the modes of the fantastic and the gothic, melodrama represents a radical alternative to realism: it is at once a reaction against rationality and against the processes of demystification and desacralization – albeit a reaction which

[6] Geoffrey Nowell-Smith, "Minelli and Melodrama," *Screen* 18.2 (Summer 1977): 117–118.

ultimately acknowledges that the "reassertion of spiritual forces and occult issues hidden in the phenomenal world cannot lead to the resacralization of experience"[7]; but it is also a form of counter-discourse offering an alternative and relatively unrestrained method of communication, and able to resurrect certain marginalized modes of consciousness so as to place them at the center of society's conscious, waking life. As such, it offers a space for the working-out of a psychological or moral response to situations which, left to more conventional or refined modes of representation, might otherwise remain unarticulated and bound by precisely that repression characterizing the reality-principle and the dominant social discourses, as well as their related conventions of signification.

Described in these terms it becomes possible to show that even the work of one so wary of expressionism's excesses as Kafka may share with the movement many of the fundamentally progressive features of what has been called the melodramatic "vision"[8] or "imagination."

## "The melodramatic imagination": revolution, the family drama, and its social consequences

Of the many recent attempts to re-evaluate melodrama as a valid literary form, not just in the theater but in prose fiction, Peter Brooks' *The Melodramatic Imagination* provides one of the most insightful and comprehensive approaches, and it is the framework established by Brooks that I would like to follow here.[9]

While open to the possibility that melodrama might also turn

---

[7] Brooks, *The Melodramatic Imagination*, 17.
[8] See Eric Bentley, *The Life of the Drama* (London: Methuen, 1965), 195–218.
[9] See also Patrice Petro, *Joyless Streets. Women and Melodramatic Representation in Weimar Germany* (Princeton: Princeton University Press, 1989). Other works of theoretical interest in this context are Eric Bentley, *The Life of the Drama* (New York: Atheneum, 1964), esp. 195–218, which sets up a notion of melodrama in opposition to tragedy on account of their differing relations to external action and internal experience; Robert Heilman, *Tragedy and Melodrama: Versions of Experience* (Seattle: University of Washington Press, 1968) pursues this idea of an opposition further. Both Frank Cahill, *The World of Melodrama* (University Park: Pennsylvania State University Press, 1967) and David Grimstead, *Melodrama Unveiled: American Theater and Culture, 1800–1850* (Chicago: University of Chicago Press, 1968) offer more detailed historical descriptions of the various theatrical modes of melodrama. A brief overview of the topic is offered by James L. Smith, *Melodrama*, The Critical Idiom, no. 28 (London: Methuen, 1973).

out eventually to constitute a kind of anthropological "constant of the imagination" (14), Brooks nevertheless deals with it primarily as an historically-conditioned phenomenon. Very similar to Jameson's analysis of the historical roots of modernism in the process of "demystification," Brooks sees melodrama as a response to a specifically modern crisis, namely the general process of "desacralization" (16) which has been operating since the Enlightenment and which has eroded the sacred myths of Western thought and belief, affecting in particular their explanatory and cohesive power. He sees this process of disintegration as coming to a head through the great revolution in France which lead to a general sense of moral and spiritual discontinuity. In Brooks' opinion,

Melodrama starts from and expresses the anxiety brought by a frightening new world in which the traditional patterns of moral order no longer provide the necessary social glue. It plays out the force of that anxiety with the apparent triumph of villainy, and it dissipates it with the eventual victory of virtue. (20)

Melodrama emerges in the post-revolutionary cultural sphere in response to the need for a new cosmology and a renewed sense of moral and epistemological significance. It figures as a means of recuperating a new sense of the "sacred," and as an attempt "to find, to articulate, to demonstrate, to 'prove' the existence of a moral universe" (20).

The revolutionary destruction of social institutions, and the corresponding erosion of conventional values and ideological tropes, meant that the cultural forms and signifying practices dependent upon them also began to be questioned. Rather than producing any of the more subtle and considered cultural reactions one might envisage as arising in response to this historical crisis, melodrama emerges instead as a spontaneous if rather desperate medium both for communicating the anxiety associated both with this breakdown of moral and ideological systems, and for expressing the desires (to which this revolution lends support) for the creation of a new order. Thus those more sophisticated and traditional cultural forms such as tragedy which previously served to articulate a sublimated response to social and historical experience give way to the seemingly less refined and direct cultural expressions such as melodrama. For melodrama returns

147

to a primary impulse behind all theatricality: it stages fundamental human conflicts and gives vent to unleashed desires in an open transgression of social restraints and psychological repressions.[10]

Given the prevalence of these crises of belief in the dominant cultural myths and institutions, it is understandable, as Brooks observes, that the process of desacralization should shift the focus to the *psyche* as the sole remaining repository of untainted spiritual and ethical impulses.[11] Consequently in its attempt to respond to the decline of the sacred, the melodramatic imagination frequently resorts, as we shall see, to a dramatization of subjectivity and of the psyche which stages the broader, metaphysical or social conflicts of ideas and beliefs in starkly down-to-earth terms. Citing Brooks, Christine Gledhill points out that the family is a particularly important psychological factor in this regard:

The family, with its ties of duty, love and conflict, the site where the individual is formed, and the center of bourgeois social arrangements, provides a repertoire of such identities and the space for melodramatic enactments. Characters in melodrama "assume primary psychic roles, father, mother, child, and express basic psychic conditions."[12]

Thus, through a focus upon family conflict, such as the rivalry in expressionist melodrama between the father and son (as burgher vs. revolutionary), the more ambitious melodramatic forms succeed in invoking the wider social and psychological issues over and beyond a restrictive concern with individual characters (which in melodrama consequently tend to be cast as "types" rather than as "believable" individuals with their own interiority) and also beyond the schematic polarization of the manichaeistic forces operating within the family.

Consequently the dramatization of subjectivity, that is, the acting out of pent-up psychological conflicts in melodrama, should

---

[10] See Bentley, *The Life of the Drama*, 216–218, and Brooks, *The Melodramatic Imagination*, 12, 35.

[11] As Brooks maintains, with the irremediable loss of the traditionally sacred, "[m]ythmaking could now only be individual, personal; and the promulgation of ethical imperatives had to depend on an individual act of self-understanding that would then – by an imaginative or even terroristic leap – be offered as the foundation of a general ethics." See *The Melodramatic Imagination*, 16. This turn to the self characterizes very precisely the reaction of many expressionists in the face of the epistemological and moral crises which troubled Wilhelmine Germany.

[12] Gledhill, "The Melodramatic Field: An Investigation," 31, citing Brooks, *The Melodramatic Imagination*, 4.

then be read (as Gledhill insists) as "working less towards the release of individual repression than towards the public enactment of socially unacknowledged states," for in melodrama "the family is a means, not an end" (31). It is in this sense that even where expressionist melodrama appears to burst out uncontrollably without any clear purpose, or where it favors sheer "intensity" beyond all other, more intellectual qualities, it still harbors a serious and progressive critical function: that of "making the world morally legible"[13] and demonstrating the existence of "repressed 'ethical and psychic" forces"[14] in order to expose the discursive mechanisms of repression. It thus functions as a form of counter-discourse which not only signifies the demonstrative act of breaking through repression, but in doing so also lays bare the repressive practices of dominant social discourses themselves.

With its concern for the disappearance of spiritual values and hence for what becomes the unarticulated or marginalized side of experience, melodramatic representation thus insists primarily upon an unspeakable and repressed realm, upon a moral universe which exists – analogous to the position of desire or the unconscious within the individual – as a kind of "occult" inhabiting the edges of the unstable visible world. And it is towards this marginalized realm that melodrama constantly gestures as its secret theme.

This concern with the "sacred," with the recuperation of a moral and spiritual world beyond appearances, is associated with the hysterical character of melodrama's poetics of representation. For the elusive and ineffable nature of the meanings to which the melodramatic text is desperately reaching out corresponds to a kind of "blockage" of fear, anxiety and desire. This unaccommodated excess of energy is responsible for the frenzied and exaggerated quality of the expressive gestures with which the "sacred" and the "unspeakable" is evoked. Consequently the tendency to invest the everyday with higher significance, to look further than the details of the real for the traces of a more essential realm beyond the constraints of the quotidian results (as Brooks notes) in a comparable "pressure" at the level of the sign. He observes that in melodrama "the represented world won't bear

13 Brooks, *The Melodramatic Imagination*, 42.
14 Gledhill, "The Melodramatic Field: An Investigation," 30.

the weight of the significances placed upon it" and that "the more elusive the tenor of the metaphor becomes . . . the more strained with pressure to suggest a meaning beyond" becomes the vehicle (11). For the intensification of the ordinary and everyday exerts a strain upon the signifier and upon the power of the representation to embody the unspeakable, producing a symbolic heightening or "overdetermination" of the signifier. And this frequently leads – especially in the more sophisticated melodramatic modes – to the displacement of attention onto the broader metaphysical issues beyond the range of the human dramas of the real.

It is precisely this desperate need to respond to the sense of conflict or crisis on the one hand, coupled with the frustration experienced at the impossibility of articulating the unspeakable on the other, which links this representational practice to hysteria, producing on the one hand the characteristically exaggerated mannerisms and emphatic codes of melodrama, and on the other its equally paradigmatic tendency towards voicelessness. For as we shall see later, as with certain types of clinical hysteria, this strain and crisis in communication is frequently associated paradoxically with various forms of muteness. And at critical moments the expressive mode of melodrama may lapse into other non-verbal forms, such as gesture, mise-en-scène and tableau, which offer a visual or symbolic image of its unspoken and unspeakable meaning, and which encourage the pursuit of meanings over and beyond the range indicated by the narrative and its dramatization.

## Desacralization, hysteria and the "body of the text"

> [Melodrama's] method of exploiting thoughts
> is by means of the human body.
>
> Bram Stoker

In exploring melodrama and its relations to expressionism it is important to note that expressionism, like the melodramatic mode which (according to Brooks) typically arises in the historical context of post-revolutionary turmoil and anomie, also emerges as a response to a situation characterized by a special crisis in the inherited patterns of morality and belief. Those outbursts of spirituality and brotherliness which characterize many expressionist texts may thus be read similarly to what Brooks calls the re-establishment of the "sacred" in a post-sacred era: the resurrection of a moral universe. And indeed a survey of the expressionist journals published during the "expressionist decade" (1910–1920) reveals that the dissolution of the moral world was a constantly repeated theme in the manifestos and programmatic statements of the movement.[15] Hugo Ball's lecture "Kandinsky"[16] (discussed in chapter 2) concerning the destruction of a millennial culture and the ensuing moral and epistemological chaos is just one of many contemporary documents that might be cited to demonstrate the omnipresent sense of crisis in the period.[17]

This experience of desacralization, of moral dissolution and epistemological discontinuity was doubtless linked to a combination of very unusual socio-historical factors in this particular epoch. As we have already observed, the turn of the century in Wilhelmine Germany was a period of unusually rapid expansion – of mass-industrialization and urbanization as well as technological advancements and innovations such as electricity, motorized transport, the beginnings of the "mass media" – all of which served to change the face of the environment and the texture of everyday life within an extremely short space of time.[18] In a period of such unparalleled technological acceleration and economic expansion the degree to which of moral and ideological attitudes (such as religion and the other traditional repositories of the sacred) were able to keep pace and adapt to these new social conditions was surely subject to a certain "cultural lag," to refer once again to W. F. Ogburn's term.[19] What results is a predica-

---

[15] See the section "Krisenbewußtsein in der veränderten Welt: Entfremdung, Orientierungsverlust und Ordnungssuche" in *Manifeste und Dokumente*, 115–127.

[16] Hugo Ball, "Kandinsky." Lecture held in Galerie Dada, Zürich April 7, 1917. Rpt. *Manifeste und Dokumente*, 124.

[17] For further commentary on this loss of orientation and the search for order see Silvio Vietta's introduction to his collection *Lyrik des Expressionismus* (Tübingen, 1975), as well as the introduction to the theme by Anz and Stark in *Manifeste und Dokumente* 115–117.

[18] See Vietta and Kemper, *Expressionismus*, 30–39, 110–117.

[19] To recap: Ogburn's thesis states that a "cultural lag occurs when one of two parts of culture which are correlated changes before or in greater degree than the other part does . . ." See William F. Ogburn, "Cultural Lag as Theory" (1957) *On Culture and Social Change* (Chicago: University of Chicago Press, 1964), 86. Thomas Anz introduces the concepts of "anomie" and the "cultural lag" to this context in his essay "Entfremdung und Angst," *Sozialer Wandel*, ed. H. Meixner and S. Vietta (Munich: Fink, 1982), 19–21.

ment with marked similarities to the chaotic post-revolutionary atmosphere which Brooks sees as crucial in calling forth the response of melodrama. It is the special crisis to which we have already referred, known in sociological terms as "anomie,"[20] in which the traditional orienting values and the ordering system lose their validity.[21] In other words it is a breakdown in those social constructions and institutions of order which would otherwise offer a shield against terror and chaos. For according to Berger and Luckmann in their book *The Social Construction of Reality*, "*All* social reality is precarious. *All* societies are constructions in the face of chaos," and if the "institutional order represents a shield against terror" then "to be anomic means to be deprived of this shield, and to be exposed, alone . . . "[22]

It is this anomic and post-sacred state – so similar to the post-revolutionary chaos creating the historical preconditions of nineteenth-century French melodrama – to which the melodramatic imagination of expressionism responds. And it does so precisely in the manner of its French counterpart: by casting around frenetically for a new moral order. Like the post-revolutionary French melodrama this search also expresses itself primarily in the demand for a revolution of the spirit, in the attempt to bind together the new republic with a new regime of morality.

There is however a crucial difference between the two models. For in the case of expressionist melodrama – and particularly the work of the more "sophisticated" or "counter-discursive" writers on the avant-garde wing of the movement – the excessive melodramatic forms are important not only as a means of uncovering that which in classic realism remains unrepresentable (for instance what Brooks calls the "moral occult"), but in bringing attention to these hidden contents *as* unrepresentable. For as I have argued, the wild outbursts characteristic of the movement's "expressiveness" are important precisely because they uncover not only the repressed but also the site of the "repression" itself:

[20] Robert K. Merton, "Social Structure and Anomie" and "Continuities in the Theory of Anomie" *Social Theory and Social Structure* (New York: Free Press, 1968), 216.

[21] For a brief history of the concept of "anomie" from its origins in the late Middle Ages to Durkheim's use of it in 1893, see Hans Peter Dreitzel, *Das gesellschaftliche Leiden und das Leiden an der Gesellschaft* (Stuttgart: Enke, 1968), 35.

[22] Peter Berger and Thomas Luckmann, *The Social Construction of Reality. A Treatise in the Sociology of Knowledge* (1966; Harmondsworth: Pelican, 1984), 121, 119.

they point both to the excluded material as well as to the limits of existing institutionalized modes of representation, and in doing so highlight the inability of these conventional systems to deal with particular psychological or ideological contents.

In this respect the melodramatic modes of expressionism differ markedly on the one hand from those of the post-revolutionary dramatists cited by Brooks, and on the other from the related "Romantic" or "idealist" avant-garde writers of the same period. For as we saw in chapter two, unlike the latter, the avant-garde wing of expressionism does not place its hopes in the attempt to elevate reality and reconcile it to an ideal realm prefigured by art. For since its Nietzschean premise is the "death of God" and the interrogation of all such a prioris, it can "offer no terminal reconciliation, for there is no longer a clear transcendent value to be reconciled to. There is rather a social order to be purged, a set of ethical imperatives to be made clear."[23] On the other hand it cannot make art *directly* instrumental in instituting a new, post-revolutionary morality and social organization either. Whereas Brooks observes of French melodrama's concrete political aspirations that "A new world, a new chronology, a new religion, a new morality lay within the grasp of the revolutionary legislator. . . . The Revolution attempts to sacralize the law itself, the Republic as the institution of morality" (15), this is clearly not the case in the more progressive forms of expressionist melodrama. For besides its abstract rhetoric and the heavily symbolic or overdetermined quality of its images and tableaux, it is characterized by a high degree of self-consciousness and by a clear rejection of the more "affirmative" melodramatic conventions (such as the happy-end, the final vindication of good, and the banishment of evil). In other words, with their self-consciousness, their disavowal of convention and their risky attempts to stage "a fundamental drama of the moral life," the more progressive expressionist melodramas share precisely the qualities Brooks associates with the ambitious, sophisticated or "higher" melodramatic forms at the top end of his hierarchical ordering of the genre.[24]

While intensifying its anti-illusionistic impact the more pro-

[23] Brooks, *The Melodramatic Imagination*,17.
[24] As Brooks observes "there is a range from high to low examples in any literary field, and the most successful melodrama belongs to a coherent mode that rewards attention . . . " (12).

gressive expressionist melodrama also sharpens its resistance to melodrama's organic convention of interpretative closure, even at the level of its rhetoric. For its hysterical and rather top-heavy discourse of proclamation produces a paradoxical or – in the sense I have outlined in the previous chapter – "duplicitous" counter-effect: in the moment of putting forward its abstract goals and principles it immediately takes them back again. Thus its unrealistic and excessive qualities not only always exert a "pressure" upon the sign (that is, upon the rhetorical forms for example) to reveal a semantic dimension far beyond their immediate meanings, but also have the effect simultaneously of "bracketing" them or placing them "under erasure."

Given this tendency towards excess, anti-illusionism and self-destabilization it is paradoxically only when we take the bombast too *seriously* and misread the central category of the enigmatic expressionist poetics of "abstraction" and "duplicity" for example in terms of an attempt to set out a concrete revolutionary program of radical social reform, or as an attempt at sublating life with an idealist form of art that it appears overblown, unjustifiably idealistic and thus – in the common, pejorative sense of the term – merely "melodramatic." For in judging it in this way we make the mistake of ignoring its acute self-consciousness and self-reflexivity, and of measuring it instead solely against the dominant social discourses of "realism": the mistake, that is, of judging it against the false criteria of political pragmatism and verisimilitude.

Instead, our understanding of this aspect of expressionism needs to take more fully into account the distinguishing central characteristic of progressive expressionist melodrama – that which it shares with the more avant-garde, non-organic forms, such as montage, or the "epic" structures of Brecht and Döblin: its open-endedness and its resistance to closure. For it is noticeable that the melodramas of expressionism typically end not with the release of tension through the happy resolution of problems and the overcoming of evil forces – as is conventionally the case with the lower melodramatic forms. Rather than simplifying complex social processes by assigning evil to particular issues and to particular conceptual straw-men (such as the burgher), the more ambitious melodramas use these caricatures and schematic figurations merely as starting points: consequently they tend to sharpen such conflicts and present them as contradictions which exist more broadly in society and so cannot be resolved simplistically.[25] Indeed by contrast to the works of the "naive" expressionists it is a distinguishing feature of the "sophisticated" expressionist melodramas that they articulate problems which they signally *fail* to resolve. Similar to Nowell-Smith's observation with regard to the relationship between cinematic melodrama and Hollywood's dominant realist discourses, the importance of melodrama as a form of counter-discourse lies precisely in this failure, for although "it cannot accommodate its problems either in a real present or in an ideal future, but lays them open in their shameless contradictoriness, it opens a space which most Hollywood forms have studiously closed off" (118).

On the other hand the most ambitious expressionist melodramas also do not end even with the kind of *formal* resolution common to tragedy, in which the conflict is "contained" and its conflicts and pains "sublimated"[26] within the overall "tragic vision" or within the necessity of aesthetic form.[27] The melodramatic mode of expressionism frequently climaxes instead merely in the achievement of *unconditional expressiveness* itself: in the protagonist's newly discovered freedom to formulate – however provisionally and "hysterically" – a new set of social, psychological, or moral demands, and to project these unresolved goals into the distant future: hence the unpolitical nature of the frequent clamor in these expressionist works for a rebellion against the narrow-mindedness of bourgeois society and against its outmoded patriarchal values, and hence too the abstractness of their calls for social and spiritual redemption through the diffusion of ideals of universal brotherhood.

[25] See Thomas Elsaesser, "Tales of Sound and Fury. Observations on the Family Melodrama" *Monogram* 4 (1972): 4.
[26] These "unrepressible" dramatizations of desire in expressionism are characterized by their obstruction of any attempt to recast them within the kind of sophisticated cultural form which Norman Holland has called the psychological "defense" – in other words, that which is generally understood in terms of "sublimation." As Brooks observes, the result is that the audience may be "attracted to" but simultaneously "repulsed by" such unrefined transgression of the boundaries of restrained behavior, and may erect its own defenses against this free flow of emotion (42). No doubt this goes some way towards explaining the critical resistance often expressed at the hysterical plays of both melodrama proper and expressionism. See Holland, *The Dynamics of Literary Response* (New York: Oxford University Press, 1968).
[27] See Herbert Marcuse's formulation in *An Essay on Liberation*, 42–45.

Far from implicating art here as a formal prototype of an harmonious and ideal sphere with which life ought to be sublated (as the Romantic avant-garde tends to do), and far from defusing the criticisms and canceling the indictments of art in advance by depicting their illusory realization within the aesthetic realm (as occurs in affirmative culture) expressionist melodrama insists instead upon the act of expression itself, the externalized "working-through" and acting out of the repression in the most direct, raw and *unsublimated* manner. In dealing with this excess of what are normally "unspeakable" demands the expressionist text does not simply displace and repress them in the manner of classic realism. Rather it takes up one of two "enigmatic" forms of expression: either the problematic contents are acted out directly in the emphatic, unsublimated mode – an approach which constitutes as much an attempt to point to those limitations and forms of repression inherent in dominant discourse still to be overcome, as it does a mode of articulating the repressed contents themselves; or alternatively the melodramatic mode succeeds by switching to an other discursive form – a discourse of otherness – which, although it appears "paralyzed" or "muted" at the level of conventional means of communication, in fact turns these muted forms to its own advantage by making them "speak" – and speak not only of the repressed but of the act of repression itself.

As in Freud's "conversion hysteria"[28] – the model to which Geoffrey Nowell-Smith's theory of melodrama refers – the energy attaching to that which is repressed (or which at least is not accommodated) by the representation is transformed or re-routed by the melodramatic mode. It is "somatized" or displaced onto the "body of the text" in analogy to the conversion of an "undischarged emotion" which returns in a patient as a bodily symptom, for example in the form of an hysterical paralysis.[29] In other words that material which cannot be accommodated in more conventional "realistic" textual discourses either bursts out uncontrollably in expressionist melodrama's expansive gestures and bombastic rhetoric, or it becomes a potent, explosive and undis-

---

[28] Laplanche and Pontalis observe of the "conversion-hysteria" that "the psychic conflict represents itself symbolically in various symptoms occurring at its climax (e.g. an emotional crisis with theatrical gestures) . . ." J. Laplanche and J.-B. Pontalis, *Vocabulaire de la Psychanalyse* (Paris: PUF, 1967), 178. My translation.    [29] Nowell-Smith, "Minelli and Melodrama," 117.

charged excess which is re-routed (hysterically) into its "mute" forms, such as dumb show, mime and symbolic tableaux. As Helene Cixous remarks with regard to this paradoxical character of hysteria, "silence is the mark of hysteria. The great hysterics have lost speech, they are aphonic . . ."[30] In the hysterical scenarios of expressionist melodrama then, bombast and muteness are two sides of the same coin.

## Melodramatic counter-discourse: desublimation, abstraction and the rhetoric of revolution

If we now turn to an examination of some of the most prominent dramas of the expressionist movement, we can see that in the areas of rhetoric, characterization, plot-structure and the poetics of representation, the melodramatic mode and the model of hysteria I have described are of singular importance in the response of its writers to the cosmological and epistemological crisis of the Wilhelmine period.

The revolutionary spirit which underpins melodrama frequently takes up expressionism's highly-charged rhetoric in order to call for a form of spiritual and moral revolution through messianic redemption and the creation of a "New Man." The melodramatic nature of these demands for renewal lies not only in the emphatic tone and high-flown language with which they are uttered but also in the contrast with the down-to-earth and everyday context in which this urge is so openly and frankly declared.

In the second scene of Johannes Sorge's *The Beggar* for example, after witnessing an everyday scene in a cafe where a group of figures read aloud a series of banal and sensational newspaper stories, we see a group of drama critics discussing a play. The debate ascends rapidly from the quotidian to the metaphysical, from a cursory argument regarding the play's formal characteristics to the demand for a new kind of writer – again the familiar expressionist figure of the messiah or the "New Man" – who will bring about a full-scale spiritual regeneration: "We are waiting for one who will re-interpret our fate for us . . . one person must ruminate for all of us"[31] A few scenes later the central figure of the

---

[30] Helene Cixous, "Castration or Decapitation?" *Signs: Journal of Women in Culture and Society* 7.1 (1981): 41–55. Here 49.

[31] "Wir warten auf einen, der uns unser Schicksal neu deutet . . . einer muß für uns alle nachsinnen." J. Sorge, *Der Bettler, Werke in Drei Bänden*, ed. Hans Gerd

play (here "the Poet"), lapsing at the drop of a hat into the same high-flown messianic rhetoric of redemption, discusses a form of art which will miraculously transform the world:

... Masses of workers / Carried away in great waves / by the anticipation of a higher life / For there, out of the smoke / And the towering scaffolds, out of / The screaming wheels of machinery / They see their souls rise up / Beautiful and completely purified. . . . (33)[32]

What is most noticeable regarding the melodramatic qualities of this scene is the speed and unseemly ease with which the emotional and metaphysical voltage of the play are raised by several notches within such a short space of time and without any clear "motivating" cause. This typifies what Elsaesser sees as the melodramatic, namely the

exaggerated rise-and-fall pattern in human actions and emotional responses, . . . a foreshortening of lived time in favour of intensity – all of which produces a graph of much greater fluctuation, a quicker swing from one extreme to another than is considered natural, realistic or in conformity with literary standards of verisimilitude. . . .[33]

At the same time the excessive claims which are voiced (in this case for a miraculous spiritual renewal) arise fully unmotivated by the everyday context in which they are uttered, and clearly unsupported by its evident possibilities. Thus they take on that familiar tone of melodramatic "sentimentality": what Brooks calls an "'excess' of claim in relation to what has been demonstrated."[34] Similarly "sentimental" are the immoderate proclamations and the self-assured attitude of many of expressionism's messianic protagonists as they take up the burdens of mankind: "In deepest purity my goals burn: / I want to take the world upon my shoulders / And carry it with songs of praise to the sun" (80).[35]

Rötzer (Nürnberg, 1962–67), 23.
[32] " ... Massen der Arbeiter / Schwemmt an die Ahnung ihres höheren Lebens / In großen Wogen, denn sie sehen dort / Aus Rauch und Ragen der Gerüste, aus / Sausenden Fährnissen der Räder ihre / Seelen aufsteigen, schön und ganz geläutert. . . ."
[33] Thomas Elsaesser, "Tales of Sound and Fury. Observations on the Family Melodrama" 7.
[34] Brooks takes up this definition of "sentimentality" (104) in line with T. S. Eliot's notion as developed in "Hamlet and His Problems," *Selected Essays, 1917–1932* (New York: Harcourt Brace, 1932), 124–25.
[35] "Aus tiefster Reinheit brennen meine Ziele: / Ich will die Welt auf meine Schultern nehmen / Und sie mit Lobgesang zur Sonne tragen."

The expansive rhetoric in which these claims are couched demonstrates the tendency to inflate the individual soul until it becomes a new repository for the sacred. This is a clear variation on the old melodramatic technique (observed by Elsaesser) under which "complex social processes were simplified either by blaming the evil disposition of individuals or by manipulating the plots and engineering coincidences and other *dei ex machina*, such as the instant conversion of the villain . . . " (4). In this case the individual is made the vehicle and mouthpiece for a vast range of social and psychological hopes and revolutionary aspirations. As in Brooks' model it is "Man" – here the expressionists' hopelessly idealistic construction of the messiah and the "neuer Mensch" ("New Man") – in whom the hopes for the "sacred" and for a new spirituality come to rest, and in whose subjectivity the broader social fears and anxieties are played out.

In expressionist melodrama all states of the soul – pathos and ecstasy alike – are openly and unashamedly declared. Whether it is the desperate cry of the soul seeking redemption, or the strained proclamation of universal love, all is uninhibited by any thought of self-censorship. But it is significant that in articulating these ecstatic states, instead of presenting the kind of idealization of the real which sublimates and defuses the tension created by real social fears and desires, expressionist melodrama brings the sublime sharply down to earth (in the "de-aestheticizing" or "desublimating" mode characteristic of the historical avant-garde), adding only a minimal aesthetic gloss to its raw and immediate expressiveness. The language of expressionist melodrama is reduced to a wild outpouring of existential questions and ecstatic stammerings: "Will it soon be day? Oh what torture! / Redemption! Higher! From out of the necessity of the body / The soul reaches out towards its work . . ." (81).[36] As is the case here, the melodramatic rhetoric of expressionism is often simple and transparent. The raw and unmodified exclamations "Oh what torture! / Redemption! Higher!" are associated with the stirrings of a primitive stage of selfhood, or with an hysteric's frenzied urge to expression: the kind of rhetoric typified by the "cry" of pain or ecstasy – the famous expressionist "Schrei" – or by the impas-

---

[36] "Wird's nicht bald Tag? O Qual! / Erlösung! Höher! Aus des Leibes Not / Reckt sich die Seele frei zu ihrem Werk. . . ."

sioned and unrestrained appeals to one's fellow man in the so-called "O Mensch!"-texts.

Nevertheless, in reproducing the avant-garde's characteristic effect of "desublimation" or "de-aestheticization," that is, in undermining the sublime, "unrealistic" and affirmative aspects of the language of melodrama, this excess should not be thought of as merely switching the focus to an absorbing interest in the mundane and the banal. On the contrary, it destabilizes not only the ideal but also the realm of the real, so that the audience's attention is no longer directed towards a purely mimetic reading of the drama and thus cannot be concerned primarily with the *realism* of the play or its lifelike details. Instead, we are drawn to a level of reflection at which we can detach ourselves both from an exclusive interest in the events and actions of the narrative as well as from a false sense of harmonious reconciliation within the sphere of the ideal, and can instead fix upon a more fundamental level of concern.

This shifting of the focus away from the merely "realistic" is linked once more to the expressionist poetics of "abstraction" discussed in the previous chapter.[37] For in the case of the more ambitious expressionist melodramas, a familiar and defining aesthetic paradox comes into play whereby "an intensely subjective content" is "objectified" so that "the expressive element swallows the representational" (51). It is precisely this ability to "objectify through abstraction" which distinguishes these more sophisticated writers "from the naive or rhetorical Expressionists who simply shriek out their feelings" (50). Thus although this simple "shrieking out" of feelings seems at first glance to define *all* expressionist melodrama, as Sokel's careful distinction makes clear, it is only in the more "sophisticated" writers that "the expressive gesture or movement possesses the figure to such a degree that the figure becomes the carrier of the expression, a means for making an emotional state visible" (51). And it is through this "emotional state" that in turn a broader social and psychological horizon is also made visible.

This undermining of the mimetic in favor of a set of broader concerns is borne out not only at the level of rhetoric but also at the level of *characterization*. Melodrama's convention-bound lack of

---

[37] Sokel *The Writer in Extremis*, 50–51.

interest in the figures as individuals is extended still further by expressionism's characteristic mode of "abstraction." The characters in expressionist melodrama tend very frequently to be at best mere symbolic representatives or types. This is often emphasized by the nomenclature employed: figures are referred to merely via their function as "the Poet," or "the Son." In *The Beggar* for example, the name of the central figure changes according to the context in which he is found. Alternatively, characters may merely be given a number instead of a name, as in *The Beggar*, Goering's *Battle at Sea*, or Toller's *The Transformation* and *Mass Man*.

Where the nineteenth-century popular melodrama reverts constantly to the stock characters of the dark and "swarthy" villain,[38] or to the suffering and saintly heroine, expressionist drama too has its interchangeable and unnaturalistic set-figures, such as the spiritual pilgrim of the "Station-dramas" or the messiah-figure of the "proclamation plays" ("Verkündigungsdramen"). As regards the villain of the piece the perennial expressionist figures of the "burgher," the "Philister" (philistine) and the authoritarian father function as the omnipresent "bad guys" in the more manichaeistic expressionist works. The degree to which this villain-figure becomes a recognizable "type" rather than an individual character may be seen in its frequent reduction to the level of a virtual caricature. As a stock figure the philistine burgher is frequently codified throughout expressionism by a collection of easily recognizable signifiers: for example the "hat" and the "pointed head" of the burgher in Jakob van Hoddis' poem "End of the World," or the overly stiff and formal "man dressed in black" with his watch chain strapped proudly across his chest in Döblin's short story "The Murder of a Buttercup." Even where the figure of the bourgeois is presented in less extreme, less villainous form, as for example in Carl Sternheim's satirical plays *From the Heroic Life of the Bourgeoisie* (*Aus dem bürgerlichen Heldenleben*), it is still as a *type* rather than as an individual that the figure interests us: as the representative of a certain category of human beings.[39]

These starkly contrasting good and bad figures play out the fundamental "manichaeism" underlying melodrama, the eternal

---

[38] Brooks, *The Melodramatic Imagination*, 17.
[39] H. F. Garten sees Sternheim as a forerunner to the "classical" expressionists in his *Modern German Drama* (1959; London: Methuen, 1964), 96–101. On this point see especially 96.

conflict between the forces of good and evil.[40] As a consequence
the characterization and plot of the expressionist drama frequently follows a starkly defined structure of polar opposites. Through
this it turns its storyline into an interplay of mere signs connoting
the conflict between powerful elemental forces over and beyond
the mere "individuals" – who are thus reduced in status merely to
the inconsequential representational vehicles of this scheme.

One example of this manichaeism is Kokoschka's *Mörder, Hoffnung der Frauen* (1910) (*Murderer Hope of Womankind*), in which the
conflict between elemental forces is fought out as a bestial and
primal battle of the sexes resembling an orgiastic and Dionysian
rite. There are no "characters" as such, and while the figures
clearly embody certain fundamental principles and have a powerful symbolic weight, they are scarcely even capable of "real"
speech beyond the utterance of a primitive dream language full of
aphasic stammerings devoid of complete syntax:

> The Man *powerfully*:
> Stars and moon! Woman! A singing being, bright shining, in
> dream or waking state I saw. Breathing, dark things are
> unraveled before me. Who nourishes me?
> Woman *lying on him completely; separated by the grille . . .*
> The Man:
> Who nurses me with blood? I fed on your blood, I devour
> your dripping body.
> Woman:
> I do not want to let you live, you vampire, feeding on my
> blood, you weaken me, woe betide you, I'll kill you – you
> shackle me – I captured you – and you hold me – let me go,
> bloody one, your love embraces me – as if with iron chains –
> strangled – away – Help.[41]

[40] Brooks, *The Melodramatic Imagination*, 12–13.
[41] "Der Mann *kraftvoll*: Sterne und Mond, fressende Lichter, Frau! Versehrtes
Leben, im Traum oder Wachen sah ich ein singendes Wesen. Atmend entwirrt
sich mir Dunkles. Wer nährt mich?
*Frau liegt ganz auf ihm; getrennt durch das Gitter, auf dem sie sich wie eine Aeffin hoch
in der Luft ankrallt.*
Wer saugt mich mit Blut? Ich fraß Dein Blut, ich verzehre Deinen tropfenden
Leib.
Frau: Ich will Dich nicht leben lassen, Du Vampyr, frißt an meinem Blut, Du
schwächst mich, wehe Dir, ich töte Dich – Du fesselst mich – – Dich fing ich ein –
und Du hältst mich – – laß los von mir, Blutender, Deiner Liebe umklammert
mich – – wie mit eisernen Ketten – erdrosselt – los – Hilfe.''

This strategy of dreamlike symbolism was described in terms similar to the notion of aesthetic "abstractionism" by a contemporary commentator on expressionism, Max Picard, in a lecture published in the expressionist journal *Die Erhebung* in 1919. He begins by describing it as the attempt "by means of polar oppositions to get a fix on a constellation of the imagination," and he continues in a manner which seems particularly pertinent to Kokoschka's play:

In the opposition between the sexes the individual experience is problematized no longer as the arbitrary one between *one* man and many women and from *one* woman to many men, but rather as a singular case between this one man and this one woman. It should appear as if there were no longer chaos, but only these two, this one man and this one woman. And since chaos should no longer exist, so the two must hate each other in the extreme or love each other in the extreme, as if all the hate and all the love from the chaos now banished rested with them.

The expressionist wants nothing but this opposition . . . ; this one here, the other there, each getting a fix on each other, a marker, after the chaos. This is how fathers and sons, burghers and spiritual seers relate.[42]

As in melodrama Picard sees the strategy of polarization as an essential characteristic of expressionism: "for the expressionist this possibility has almost become a *formula* which allows the experience from the start to be fashioned through oppositions" (570).[43] For the setting up of a scheme of extremes or opposites – reminiscent of melodrama's manichaeism – has the effect firstly of

---

Oskar Kokoschka, *Mörder, Hoffnung der Frauen, Einakter und kleine Dramen des Expressionismus*, ed. Horst Denkler (Stuttgart: Reclam, 1968), 52.

[42] "durch polare Gegenüberstellung auch die Vorstellungsgebilde zu fixieren"; "Im Gegensatz der Geschlechter problematisiert sich das Erlebnis nicht mehr als Zufälliges von *einem* Mann hin zu *vielen* Frauen und von einer Frau hin zu *vielen* Männern, sondern als einmaliges ganz allein zwischen dem einen Mann und der einen Frau. Es soll scheinen, als ob es das Chaos nicht mehr gäbe, sondern nur diese beiden, diesen einen Mann, diese eine Frau. Und da es das Chaos nicht mehr geben soll, so müssen sich die beiden ungeheuer hassen oder auch ungeheuer lieben, als ob aller Haß und alle Liebe aus dem vertriebenen Chaos nun bei ihnen sei.
Der Expressionist will nichts sehen als dieses Entgegensetzte, das sich nur selber ansieht; das eine hier, das andere dort, beides einander aus dem Chaos heraus sich fixierend, markierend. So markieren, fixieren sich ihm noch Vater und Sohn, Geistige und Bürger." Max Picard, "Expressionismus. Ein Vortrag," *Die Erhebung* (1919). Rpt. *Manifeste und Dokumente*, 569.

[43] "diese Möglichkeit ist dem Expressionisten schon beinahe eine *Formel* geworden, die das Erleben von vornherein in Gegensätzen gestaltet."

imposing upon the surrounding "chaos" a powerful semiotic structure which exorcises the spirit of uncertainty by mapping out the field through extremes and by imposing a sense of unavoidable necessity upon it. But secondly while providing a sense of the concrete it nevertheless moves in the opposite direction and away from any latent realism by simultaneously "abstracting" from the real ("that is associated with the clear rejection of psychology in Expressionism" 570).[44] That is, it functions by displacing attention from the individual ("this one man, this one woman"), and shifting it towards the more generalized sets of social or epistemological opposites, the "possibility of reducing the chaos, by extrapolating the thing and isolating it, fixing it in its oppositional relationship . . . " (569).[45]

Like Kokoschka's play the expressionist "Stationen-" and "Verkündigungsdramen" ("proclamation" or "prophesy plays") are similarly structured on the basis of opposing forces in as far as they invariably represent the conflict fought out by a messianic figure bearing dreams of a new order of mankind against the old, fallen world which must be transcended. The stations on the path of the hero, the spiritual pilgrim, may be understood in similarly stark, manichaeistic terms as representing the forces of evil which tempt him from the road of redemption.

In the romantic melodrama of post-revolutionary France, the dichotomy between good and evil is fought out by those on the one hand who would defend the old regime with its decrepit values, and those on the other hand who attempt to institute a new republic of ideals and virtues. In expressionist writing we discover a very similar moral polarization. Many of the plays of the expressionist movement respond similarly to the historical disorder of the times, taking up pronounced melodramatic gestures and attitudes which express analogous longings for a new *revolutionary* order, yet – typical of the nature of the "expressionist revolution" as a permanent and ongoing process rather than as a teleological scheme of terminal reconciliation with fixed goals and ideals – which couch this idealism in such tentative and "unrealistic" terms that its full force can only be felt as a general

---

[44] "das bedingt die scharfe Ablehnung der Psychologie im Expressionismus."
[45] "Diese Möglichkeit, das Chaos zu verkleinern, indem man das Ding herausnimmt und es in seiner Gegensätzlichkeit fixiert, isoliert. . . ."

expression of the repressed "ethical and psychic forces" in society. The melodramatic rhetoric of excess in which this idealism is couched has a deeply ironic or "duplicitous" effect: at the very moment of articulating its objectives its grandiloquence is operating at another level to undermine the message by displacing it into an ethereal and unreal world. For example, Ernst Toller's *The Transformation* (*Die Wandlung*) closes with the players joining hands and crying out ecstatically for a new fraternal and revolutionary state: "Brothers, extend your tortured hands, / Aflame with a joyful sound / March through our free land / Revolution! Revolution!"[46] Similarly in Hasenclever's *The Son* (*Der Sohn*) this same spirit of reformation is prominent, and the Marseillaise is even played as all the sons join together in vowing to carry out a revolution against the dictatorship of their authoritarian fathers.

Yet rather than functioning "affirmatively" as a symbolic resolution – and thus as a further mystification – of real social antagonisms, such scenes are staged in such an extreme and unlikely manner that they should be read not as the representation of a *private* set of family repressions but rather as the *public* enactment of their disavowal, an act whose significance lies correspondingly at a more generalized social and historical level.

The constant polemics aimed by the expressionists at the previous generation – the authority-figures of burgher and father – and the pervasive, almost hysterical sense of persecution and alienation of the "good" by those they perceive as the villains is fought out in expressionism's confrontational narratives in precisely these terms. Besides that primary topos of the expressionist movement, the oedipal conflict between the son (who is frequently depicted as an isolated intellectual) and his overbearing father (often a burgher-figure), there are several other family scenarios where it is similarly the alienated, the oppressed and the marginalized who are in conflict with the inherited social structure and its representatives. Thus in Hasenclever's *The Son* the new generation rises up in rebellion against the old; in Toller's *Mass Man* (*Masse Mensch*) and in Kaiser's *Gas* the masses are engaged in a struggle against the factory-owners, and the workers against the purveyors of technology; while in Kaiser's *The Burghers of Calais*

---

[46] "Brüder, recket zermarterte Hand, / Flammender freudiger Ton! / Schreite durch unser freies Land / Revolution! Revolution! " Ernst Toller, *Die Wandlung* in: *Prosa, Briefe, Dramen, Gedichte* (Reinbek: Rowohlt, 1979), 123.

(*Die Bürger von Calais*) a new "community of the spirit" is threatened by the old conservative hegemony.[47]

In all of these examples what is at stake is more than a revolutionary struggle for power. This is almost a by-product for many expressionists, for as Pinthus says, "to go up against the insanity of politics and a degenerate social order was the obvious thing to do."[48] Instead the narrative is always pushed further, made to signify more than what it would appear most obviously to describe, more than an individual oedipal conflict, more even than the generational conflict between the sons and the fathers as the representatives of the new and the old orders. What counts here – even beyond the pragmatic goal of attempting to change the existing power-relations in society – is a *discursive* confrontation between two opposing epistemologies, two versions of rationality and truth.

### Semiotic overloading and the semantic vacuum: voicelessness, symbolic gesture, tableau

So far we have examined the extent to which expressionist theater follows melodrama in reducing plot and characterization to a simple dichotomy between good and evil, between progressive and conservative forces, and the way that this schematization is embodied by stock figures functioning largely as mere signs. What still needs to be examined is the way in which such strategies lead to a specifically *countervalent* poetics of melodramatic representation, to the creation of a set of counter-discursive strategies which transcend the constraints of verisimilitude in order to evoke a level of meaning lying beyond the scope of conventional realism and its epistemology.

One approach to discovering the agonistic relationship between the two modes of the melodramatic and the realistic in expressionist poetics is to use the framework we have established in order

---

47 Similar antagonistic structures may be found throughout the movement, most notably where the madman for example is locked in combat with his warders, as in Walser's story "Ein Traum," Friedrich W. Wagner's "Irrenhaus" poems, Heym's poems "Die Irren."

48 "gegen realpolitischen Irrsinn und eine entartete Gesellschaftsordnung anzurennen, war nur ein selbstverständliches und kleines Verdienst." Kurt Pinthus, "Zuvor," *Menschheitsdämmerung. Symphonie jüngster Dichtung*, ed. Pinthus (Berlin: Rowohlt, 1920). Rpt. *Manifeste und Dokumente*, 58.

to re-read the central programmatic statements of expressionism. For example, in his essay "Zuvor" ("Before") which introduced the famous *Menschheitsdämmerung* collection of expressionist poetry, Kurt Pinthus maintains that rather than merely reproducing reality naturalistically, Expressionism employs all the disruptive power at its disposal ("because it is constituted entirely as eruption, explosion, intensity") in order to "break through the malignant crust" of convention and to create instead its own sphere of significance.[49] The terms of the representation are not important for what they correspond to in the real world of referents. As with melodrama, they serve instead merely as metaphors for an emerging abstract realm beyond: "Thus social realm is not represented in the form of realistic details, or objectively conveyed as the painting of wretchedness (as in the art of around 1890), but rather it is always raised to the level of the general, to the great ideas of humanity" (58).[50] As a form of counter-discourse melodrama too abstracts from the level of "realistic detail" to a more "general" level, confronting the particular epistemology of conventional verisimilitude with one corresponding to an alternative discourse of representation in which the "real" is displaced by its "occult" other. Given this disjuncture between the two the melodramatic heightening of the quotidian serves not to stabilize the status quo by acknowledging mimetically its immovable fixity (as occurs in naturalism, for example), but rather to emphasize the anomic and fragmentary state of the quotidian world while insisting simultaneously upon the necessity of a search for those alternative, "higher" forces normally obscured by the real.

The attempt to gesture towards this uncertain and elusive realm through the representation of the very reality which normally obscures it clearly creates a tension within the representational medium, and it is this tension which results in the melodramatic or hysterical quality – the "powerful energy" (58) associated with the movement's means of expression – to which Pinthus refers. For when the plane of realist representation is put under excessive pressure to suggest an abstract or ideal dimension beyond, it

---

[49] "weil sie ganz Eruption, Explosion, Intensität ist"; "jene feindliche Krüste zu sprengen." Pinthus, "Zuvor," rpt. *Manifeste und Dokumente* 58.

[50] "So wird auch das Soziale nicht als realistisches Detail, objektiv etwa als Elendsmalerei dargestellt (wie von der Kunst um 1890), sondern es wird stets ganz ins Allgemeine, in die großen Menschheitsideen hingeführt."

inevitably resorts to exaggeration, hyperbole and – to use a key world in the expressionist programs – "intensity."[51] The similarity of this intensity to the kind of effect achieved by melodramatic means is brought out clearly in Pinthus' description of expressionism:

[expressionism] produces its means of expression with forcefulness and violence through the power of the spirit [Geist] (and does not bother itself about avoiding their misuse). It hurls forth its world . . . with ecstatic paroxysms, with tortured sadness, with the sweetest song, with the simultaneity of criss-crossing emotions, with the chaotic smashing of language, with the most gruesome derision of failed human existence, in flagellating, shrieking, enraptured longing for God and the good, for love and fraternity. (58)[52]

The desperate expressiveness that Pinthus describes here resembles that of melodrama and in particular its way of putting pressure upon the signifier in order to push beyond the limits of the real and to gesture towards an elusive or ideal set of significations (such as "longing for God and the good, for love and fraternity"). The conventional discourses fail to account for such "occult" meanings – whether they be the conventions of realism ("'(expressionism) avoids naturalistic descriptions of reality as a means of representation, however plastic this ruined reality was")[53] or "the aestheticist principle of l'art pour l'art " – since they all fail to penetrate the "crust" of habitualization. Expressionism resorts instead to excessive means of expression, frequently taking on a frenzied or hysterical attitude ("flagellating, shrieking, enraptured longing ").

As a counter-discourse the expressionist-melodramatic mode transgresses the common taboos and repressions, adopting alternative voices in order to give vent to the powerful build-up of

[51] For a discussion of the central expressionist notion of "intensity," see Rene Schickele's piece in *Die weißen Blätter* 3 (1916), 1. Quartal, 135–136. Rpt. *Manifeste und Dokumente*, 38.
[52] " . . . erzeugt sich mit gewaltiger und gewaltsamer Energie ihre Ausdrucksmittel aus der Bewegungskraft des Geistes (und bemüht sich keineswegs, deren Mißbrauch zu meiden). Sie entschleudert ihre Welt . . . in ekstatischem Paroxismus, in quälender Traurigkeit, in süßestem musikalischen Gesang, in der Simultanität durcheinanderstürzender Gefühle, in chaotischer Zerschmetterung der Sprache, grausigster Verhöhnung menschlichen Mißlebens, in flagellantisch schreiender, verzückter Sehnsuch nach Gott und dem Guten, nach Liebe und Brüderlichkeit" *Manifeste und Dokumente*, 58.
[53] "[Der Expressionismus] meidet die naturalistische Schilderung der Realität als Darstellungsmittel, so handgreiflich auch diese verkommene Realität war . . . " (58).

desire and the unconscious – as in the model of hysteria discussed above. Like the hysteric too, this alternative mode of speech may take the paradoxical form of an "ecstatic paroxysm," such as a paralysis or a kind of *muteness*: "And pathos, ecstasy, great gestures not only pour forth, but often fall apart in seizures, because they cannot find their essential form" (59).[54] Thus where words also become inadequate for the expression of ineffable meanings, then the inability to say the unspeakable leads to a kind of hyperbole or semiotic overloading, and to a lapse into mute gesture, tableau and other forms of meaningful but voiceless signification analogous to a "semantic vacuum."

Let me indicate briefly some of the common variations on the theme of voicelessness and mute gesture which are prevalent throughout the expressionist movement.

A pronounced example is the turbulent and emotionally-charged penultimate scene in Hasenclever's *Der Sohn*, where the severe and authoritarian father-figure threatens to call the police in order to restrain his wayward and rebellious son. The son responds by pulling out a revolver and pointing it at him:

THE SON:   Another word and you die.

THE FATHER:   (makes an involuntary movement to defend himself. He lifts his arm, drops the telephone. He lets his raised arm fall. They look into each others' eyes. The barrel of the weapon stays pointed at the father's chest – he breaks down, a spasm goes through his body. His eyes roll back and he becomes stiff. He rears up briefly, then his full weight falls slowly from the chair to the floor. A seizure . . . )[55]

We are presented here with the most intense of climaxes bearing a multitude of symbolic resonances: firstly a patricide – magically

---

54 "Und Pathos, Ekstase, große Gebärde brechen nicht nur hervor und empor, sondern stürzen oftmals zusammen in Krampf, weil sie zur Form sich nicht verwesentlichen können" (59).

55 "Der Sohn: Noch ein Wort – und du lebst nicht mehr. Der Vater: (macht unwillkürlich eine Bewegung, sich zu schützen. Er hebt den Arm, das Telephon entfällt ihm. Er läßt den gehoben Arm sinken. Sie sehen sich in die Augen. Die Mündung der Waffe bleibt unbeweglich auf die Brust des Vaters gerichtet – da löst sich der Zusammengesunkene, ein Zucken geht durch seinen Körper. Die Augen verdrehen sich und er wird starr. Er bäumt sich kurz auf, dann stürzt das Gewicht langsam über den Stühl zu Boden. Der Schlag hat ihn gerührt . . .)" Walter Hasenclever, *Der Sohn* in: *Geschichten, Dramen, Prosa*, ed. K.Pinthus (Reinbek: Rowohlt, 1963), 155.

bloodless since it is brought about by the massive expansion of the son's primary narcissism, and the deadly realization of his oedipal desires as a form of "omnipotence of thought"[56]; this in turn signifies secondly not only an individual's oedipal rebellion against a particularly overbearing father but also the need for a rethinking of the repressive structures dominating the bourgeois family structure in general; thirdly, the start of a mass conflict between the generations aimed at overturning the irrational authority of the father/burgher and the patriarchal structures dominating bourgeois Wilhelminian society.

If the almost dreamlike manner in which the "murder" occurs is a form of "wish-fulfillment" which satisfies but displaces the antagonistic oedipal desire of the subject, leaving him without any sense of real guilt for the deed, then this is matched by the lapse from realism into the magical or "fantastic" mode – that is, a mode disavowing realistic and rational explanation. But as we have observed before of melodrama, it is highly significant that at precisely such "overdetermined" emotional crescendos the text not only switches completely from a realistic and believable logic into a fantastic mode, but also that (at another representational level) it simultaneously lapses into muteness, into an alternative *voiceless* discourse expressing desires which normally remain unspoken. In this respect the "melodramatic" quality of the scene lies precisely in its ability to function as a psychological dramatization or "playing-out" of subjectivity. The melodrama in effect stages the unconscious itself, disclosing and articulating those repressed and marginalized desires which normally lie beneath appearances in the conscious world.[57]

The nature of gesture in expressionism is not conceived mimeti-

---

[56] On the notions of "primary narcissism" and the "omnipotence of thought," see Sigmund Freud's work of 1913, *Totem und Tabu* (Frankfurt: Fischer, 1956), 97. For an oedipal reading of the 1914 play see also Otto Rank's contemporary review of *Der Sohn* in *Imago* 5.1 (1917): 43–48. Rpt. *Manifeste und Dokumente*, 154–158.

[57] A further example of such voicelessness is the central figure of the "Bettler," who exclaims towards the end of the Sorge's play: "I must become a sculptor of symbols . . . let me think . . . think . . . symbols . . . (rapid upward movement, with his hands stretched up) Oh the comfort of light . . . enlightenment . . . . " ("Ich muß Bildner werden der Symbole . . . laß sinnen . . . sinnen . . . Symbole . . . (Jäh empor, mit Händen aufwärts) Oh Trost des Blitzes . . . Erleuchtung . . . " 88). Here the melodramatic possibilities for an excessive gesture of striving in this scene are played out to the full, heightening its already intense expressive quality.

cally as a realistic *accompaniment* to the word – a means of lending weight to what is said – but rather as an autonomous and entirely self-conscious sign in its own right. As Paul Kornfeld writes a propos of *Die Verführung* (*The Seduction*, 1916) in his prescriptive "Nachwort an den Schauspieler":

> The actor should be bold enough to spread his arms out wide, and in a soaring passage, to speak as he never would in real life; thus he is not an imitator . . . he is not ashamed that he is acting, he doesn't deny the theater and should not seek to simulate a world . . .
>
> Thus he abstracts from the attributes of reality and is nothing but the representative of thought, feeling or fate! [58]

The demonstrative forms which are prescribed here, far from enhancing the illusionism – and thus effacing the act of enunciation, as they might for example in a naturalist performance – serve instead to emphasize the text's self-consciousness and to underline the very act of representation itself. As a consequence they demand a different attitude from the audience than would otherwise be required in the realist and naturalist tradition. For by displacing the discourse of the real with a discourse of "abstraction" they succeed in drawing attention away from the world of referents, and towards the signifier and the interplay of gestures and signs.

The melodramatic counter-discourse does not encourage a mimetic reading, in other words a reading that looks to the details or to the strict correspondence between the signifier and its referent. As is the case with the "iconographic" mode of characterization (that is, the creation of stock-characters without psychological depth or interiority),[59] it does not encourage an approach which is tightly bound into the narrative with a concern for the fate of the figures as individuals or with the outcome of the plot and the conventional resolution of its dramatic tension. As Brecht's later development of this melodramatic quality in expressionism dem-

---

[58] "[Der Schauspieler] wage es, groß die Arme auszubreiten und an einer sich aufschwingenden Stelle so zu sprechen, wie er es niemals im Leben täte; er sei also nicht Imitator . . . er schäme sich nicht, daß er spielt, er verleugne das Theater nicht und soll nicht eine Wirklichkeit vorzutäuschen suchen . . . Er abstrahiere also von den Attributen der Realität und sei nichts als Vertreter des Gedankens, Gefühls oder Schicksals!" Paul Kornfeld, *Die Verführung* (1916), 202. Rpt. Paul Pörtner, *Literaturrevolution 1910–1925*, vol. 1, 350–351.

[59] See Petro's use of this notion of stereotyping and iconographic representation in *Joyless Streets*, 31, 134.

onstrates, the self-conscious aspect of melodrama's excess means that the audience is drawn instead into a more contemplative attitude. Where the access to easy meaning is refused, then rather than demanding the kind of goal-oriented manner of interpretation associated with solving the problems of the plot and resolving its tension, the text insists instead upon moving on to a new level of response, one which pays more attention to the moral, psychological and epistemological conditions operating in society's discourses in general rather than to the fate of particular families and individuals.

This is especially true of those dramatic episodes which are arranged compositionally, either as tableaux or as a mises-enscene. Here the conflict is dramatized in metonymic form, creating a psychological projection, externalization or symbolic correlative of the issues at stake. An example of this compositional or symbolic technique is found in Julius Maria Becker's Stationendrama *Das letzte Gericht* (*The Last Judgment*). In the "fifth station" the messianic protagonist, constantly distracted from the path of redemption by a series of worldly temptations, is now sidetracked by a love affair. He attempts to flee the world, abandon the responsibilities of selfhood and give up the search for redemption, and seeks instead to merge his identity fully with that of his lover. Rather than culminating in a conventional denouement which resolves all the issues and restores order, the problematic is laid bare in a highly symbolic *mise-en-scène*. And rather than clarifying the dilemma this emphasizes instead the effacement of all signs of difference: it takes place in the oceanic, white-on-white infinity of a "snowy landscape" at dusk, and features the protagonist offering up his self with an expressive gesture to the heroine, whose angelic standing is now melodramatically intensified even further by her symbolic schematization as an image of absolute and unimpeachable purity:

Ossip: Your still whiteness yearns to draw all my blazing colors into yourself . . . (He kisses her and falls, gliding down her, to his knees, as if he were praying to her. In the meantime it is dark and the sky is clear. The stars come out and create a circle in the form of glittering halo around the head of his beloved).[60]

---

[60] "Ossip: Dein gestilltes Weiß ist begierig, alle meine lodernde Farben in sich einzusaugen . . . (Er küßt sie und gleitet an ihr hinab, fällt auf die Knie, als ob er sie anbete. Es ist mittlerweile dunkel und sternklar geworden. Die Sterne

The extravagant compositional arrangement here does more than merely represent the problematic in stark visual signs. The massive semiotic overloading of the image makes demands upon the audience's attention over and beyond any easily graspable meaning. For like the "exaggerated gestures and expressions" which Patrice Petro finds typical not only of the melodramatic conventions of expressionist theater but also of the Weimar cinema which grew out of it, such voiceless tableau cannot be read concretely or "realistically" in terms of their contribution to the plot, but "must be read for how they charge the narrative with an intensified significance, with meaning in excess of what the narrative depicts."[61] For on the one hand the heavily-laden religious symbolism compels the audience to look towards some essential spiritual significance in the scene, while on the other hand the melodramatic exaggeration and the willful obscurity of the composition encourage a reading which rejects any simple and conventional religious solutions and – in this respect reflecting precisely the tortuous path chosen by the protagonist – forces the *audience* too into taking up the continuing search for alternative meanings.

A more extreme example of this effect comes from the related form of the *tableau*: at a moment of climax and crisis the action is halted completely and frozen for a moment in a static and symbolic arrangement. Brooks analyzes such melodramatic tableaux as the "visual summary of an emotional situation" (48). However, in expressionist melodrama the functions of the tableau are extended much further, and given a distinctly progressive and critical edge. For as Petro argues (from an evidently Brechtian perspective) with regard to the poetics of expressionist and Weimar cinema, the compositional arrangement of the tableau "may allow the spectator to concentrate on the *manner* in which conflicts are acted out" (32; my emphasis). In other words, as with Brecht's dramaturgical strategies, the interruption encourages the audience to perceive the plot's development as merely *one* of many possible lines of development, and to envisage alternative outcomes and resolutions of its dilemmas beyond those it actually depicts.

treten hervor und reihen sich in Form eines flimmernden Heiligenscheins um das Haupt der Geliebten)." J. M. Becker, *Das letzte Gericht* (Berlin: Fischer, 1919), 63.

[61] Petro, *Joyless Streets*, 31.

Alternatively the tableau may have the effect of suspending the action, forcing the audience's attention away from a simple realistic-mimetic reading of the events in terms of their contributions to the plot and its eventual outcome, and redirecting it towards the multiple, overdetermined meanings connoted (rather than denoted) by the self-consciously symbolic construction of the scene. The tenth station of Becker's play for instance takes place in a castle before an image on the wall depicting St. George killing the dragon. The pacifist protagonist Ossip is compelled by his twin brother (and alter-ego), the war-hero Leonid, to enact a dream the latter has had the previous night in which Ossip had driven his spear into a winged monster. In the dreamlike atmosphere prescribed in the stage directions, Leonid now clothes his pacifist brother as a warrior while himself putting on a crocodile skin, and together they re-enact the mythical scene of the saint slaying the monster.

The suggestive power of this symbolic tableau is heightened initially by the numerous clues for a possible interpretation of the image offered by the figures in the scene: it is implied for example that the dramatization of Ossip's subjectivity reflects a ritual "killing" of his old pacifist self and his adoption of the new role of a warrior. Above all the evocative power of the tableau is supported by its static quality: the suspending of the play's linear progression is compounded by a kind of "vertical" *mise-en-abyme* effect which repeats simultaneously and on various levels of representation the image of the warrior and the monster. For example, besides the play-within-the-play and Leonid's verbal narration of his dream (i.e. the re-enactment of the dream), the scene is reflected on a further level by the image of St. George and the dragon which figures prominently on the wall behind them.

The suspension of the play's linear progression and its projection into a timeless vertical dimension by the tableau structure ultimately encourages the construction of a *meta-critical* perspective. This point of view does not so much reflect the down-to-earth questions of the "plot" and its outcome, as rather meditate self-reflexively on those questions of the play's *own* ontology, the conditions of it possibility, which spring directly from its thematization of multiple selfhood. For at one juncture, for example, Ossip reminds the audience – in a moment representing an extreme point of textual anti-illusionism and self-reflexivity (prefiguring those similar moments occurring for example much later in Pirandello's work) – that all the characters are figments of an "unknown person's" (i.e. writer's) imagination, and "von irgendeiner unbekannten Intelligenz geträumt" (96).

## Conclusion. Melodrama, abstraction and the avant-garde

In conclusion I want firstly to re-examine some of the central reasons for expressionism's turn to melodrama in its development of a poetics of excess, as well as for its implementation of melodrama as a form of counter-discourse. Secondly, I want to underscore the relation of this melodramatic counter-discourse to the general project of the historical avant-garde.

The melodramatic tableau and its mute symbolism clearly has a progressive and critical effect on the structuring of character and plot according to the dominant conventions of the organic – effects which converge precisely with those produced by the avant-garde's "montage" and "epic" forms. Firstly, in halting the "horizontal" and action-oriented progression of the plot, and in interspersing instead a series of purposefully "vertical" or anti-linear images expressionist melodrama undermines the plot's suspense and illusionism. It encourages the audience to concentrate not on the resolution of the plot's linear tensions, but rather on the play's challenging sense of semantic "overdetermination" and on the multiple layers of meaning embodied by the semiotically intensified tableau.

Secondly, the effects of overdetermination on the tableau all underscore the self-conscious quality of the image as pure symbol, unbound by any direct allegorical connotation or absolute fixity of reference. As Jost Hermand notes of such conceptualized signs in expressionism, "what these concepts correspond to in nature, that is, beyond the concept itself, is completely irrelevant to many expressionists." Instead they are interested only in the "metaphysical connections" and semantic "wealth" which this "conceptually constructed world" is able to yield up.[62]

Curiously then, in the hands of the more progressive or avant-garde writers of expressionism the common notion of melodrama

---

[62] "Was diesen Begriffen als Natur, also jenseits der Begriffe entspricht, ist vielen Expressionisten völlig gleichgültig." See Hermand, "Expressionismus als Revolution," 337.

as a primitive or libidinal art of hysterical gestures and ecstatic emotions is transformed into a more conscious and abstract instrument. Its task is no longer to represent a human reality and the mythical (and still mystical) powers of good and evil operating upon it, but to construct a conceptual world of personified ideas, stylized rhetoric and overdetermined signs which point beyond the real, and which demand, not audience-identification and empathy, but rather, conscious reflection and critique.

For example where the unambiguous social and psychological characterization given to the expressionist figures as stock characters – as bourgeoises and revolutionaries, heroines and messiahs – becomes a kind of "iconographic" or "conceptual" mode of representation it denies them the illusion of psychological individuality. Where these figures become instantly recognizable "types" (rather than individuals with their own psychological complexity) then instead of arresting the attention and enlisting the empathy of the audience, they serve instead merely as conceptual vehicles or "correlatives" pointing beyond themselves and embodying a conflict or an idea. The exaggeration involved in this typically melodramatic mode of characterization emphasizes the purely formal nature of the figures as vehicles for the expression of a meaning *in excess* of any individual significance. And since they are readily identifiable as types, the audience need not be held up by a consideration of their "realism." Instead it can thus move off from the level of the real, away from a limiting interest in the individual conflicts, and towards the contemplation of a more essential level: the metaphysical, psychological or epistemological forces operating beyond the material stratum of the plot.

This is fully in keeping with the counter-discursive strategies even of those expressionist writers who do not adopt the melodramatic mode. Typically, expressionism shows little direct concern for "realistic" social factors such as milieu, history, and the social and moral conventions which traditionally determine the individual coloring of a figure. Similarly any interest in the private and the intimate, or in psychological close-ups is lost beneath the overriding strategy of iconographic representation. If this turns the characters into constructions for the illumination of ideas, it also makes them into pure signs freed from constraint to offer direct reference. And it produces the kind of critical, epistemological and abstract art of expressionism that Jost Hermand, as we have seen, calls a "poetic formulation of definitions" of a "purely epistemological kind" ("definitorische Dichtung," "rein erkenntnismäßiger Natur")[63] It is the kind of art in other words that deflects attention away from a restrictive interest in the real and shifts it towards that "essential" cognitive or conceptual realm which is always the central concern of the more challenging expressionist writers.

What links many of the melodramatic expressionist writers with the progressive goals of the avant-garde in general then, is firstly their attempt to avoid a mode of dealing with the real which allows itself to be defined (and thus distracted) by the object it criticizes, that is, by a limiting and all-consuming oppositional concentration on the realistic details of the quotidian at the expense of the more fundamental ethical and epistemological issues underlying the construction of the real. It is secondly the expressionists' insistence on a correspondingly metaphorical and metaphysical "vision" which will keep the focus on precisely those alternatives normally excluded by the discourses of the real – such as the undefinable realm of "Geist" or the world of "essences" ("das Wesen") towards which the "New Man" of expressionism constantly strives.

Thus the role of melodrama is as a form of counter-discourse, a mode of abstraction which transcends the real in favor of an "excessive" meaning. This function is absolutely crucial for the kind of expressionist poetics propounded for example by Kasimir Edschmid:

No-one doubts that the genuine thing cannot be that which appears as external reality. Reality must be created by us. The meaning of an object must be rooted out. One must not be satisfied with facts which are believed, imagined or noted down . . .

Thus for the expressionist artist all space becomes vision . . . He does not reproduce, he fashions . . . Facts have significance only in as far as through them the hand of the artist grasps what is behind them. He sees the human in the whore, the godlike in the factory. He works the individual item into the broader picture, which is what the world consists of. He gives us the deeper image of the object.[64]

---

[63] Hermand, "Expressionismus als Revolution," 337.
[64] "Niemand zweifelt, daß das Echte nicht sein kann, was als äußere Realität erscheint. Die Realität muß von uns geschaffen werden. Der Sinn des Gegenstands muß erwühlt sein. Begnügt darf sich nicht werden mit der geglaubten, gewähnten, notierten Tatsache . . .

As with melodrama this mode of abstraction reveals that the "outer world" of the "factual" is actually only a world of appearances, and that it can justifiably be replaced by the purely conceptual and "constructed" world of the "expressionist artist's vision." This abstract and "visionary" approach to the real embodies the counter-discursive function shared by the "melodramatic imagination": it makes the world "morally legible"[65] and lays bare an occult universe usually obscured by those "rational" and "demystifying" practices of signification dominating the desacralized and anomic world of modernity. In doing so it "accesses the underside of official rationales for reigning moral orders – that which social convention, psychic repression, political dogma cannot articulate."[66] It is for this reason that expressionism in general shares with melodrama a disregard for any privileging of lifelike detail or the depiction of the fallen world of facticity, and instead pressurizes the real into evoking the essential moral world beyond: as Edschmid says, "Everything takes on a connection to eternity. The sick person is not the cripple who is suffering. He becomes the sickness itself" (46).[67]

While keeping open this abstract and visionary standpoint, only the most "naive," dogmatic and regressive expressionists fall into the trap of imagining they can "resacralize" the fallen world of modernity by restoring to it an equivalent set of universal or transcendental values. For even the idealist, "visionary" expressionists (to whom Edschmid refers) write from a post-Enlightenment perspective, with the tacit acknowledgment – shared by Brooks' melodramatists – that if "the Sacred is no longer viable, the rediscovery of the ethical imperatives that traditionally depended on it is vital" (19).

At the same time the emphatic lack of formal or interpretative

So wird der ganze Raum des expressionistischen Künstlers Vision . . . Er gibt nicht wieder, er gestaltet. . . . Die Tatsachen haben Bedeutung nur soweit, als durch sie hindurchgreifend die Hand des Künstlers nach dem greift, was hinter ihnen steht. Er sieht das Menschliche in den Huren, das Göttliche in den Fabriken. Er wirkt die einzelne Erscheinung in das Große ein, das die Welt ausmacht. Er gibt das tiefere Bild des Gegenstands . . ." Kasimir Edschmid, "Expressionismus in der Dichtung," *Die neue Rundschau* 29 (1918), Bd. 1 (Märzheft), 359–374. Rpt. *Manifeste und Dokumente*, 46.

[65] Brooks, *The Melodramatic Imagination*, 42.
[66] Gledhill, "The Melodramatic Field: An Investigation," 33.
[67] "Alles bekommt Beziehung zur Ewigkeit. Der Kranke ist nicht der Krüppel, der leidet. Er wird die Krankheit selbst . . . ."

closure associated with melodrama's non-organic forms means that – as with the paradigm of the historical avant-garde – it avoids the pitfalls of quietism associated with the aestheticizing effects of affirmative culture and with the sublimations of the Romantic or idealist avant-garde. The counter-discursive strategies of expressionist melodrama – the openness of endings, its highly self-conscious and stylized manner, the hopelessly idealistic nature of the complaints and demands it voices, the conceptual status of its characters, and the constructed quality of its realities – mean that it avoids the tendency to postpone or sublimate the most pressing claims of the real either by re-containing them within the sanitized realm of the abstract and the ideal, or by resolving them only within the aesthetic sphere via the text's formal harmonies. At the same time the tentative and constructed nature of its representations acknowledges that, given the anomic state of modernity, it is at best "constructed on, and over, the void" and can only postulate "meanings and symbolic systems which have no certain justification because they are backed by no theology and no universally accepted social code."[68]

Thus in the hands of the most progressive and ambitious expressionists, even the most direct or primitive versions of melodrama – those whose effects may appear at first glance merely mundane, sentimental or overflowing with pathos – are transformed into a mode of counter-discourse with forms and functions directly analogous to those of the historical avant-garde. And as a consequence, it is from this incessant "screaming" – its poetics of hysteria – that expressionism is able to create a vision of alterity and a language of excess with which it can begin to speak of the unspeakable.

[68] Brooks, *The Melodramatic Imagination*, 21.

# 5

❖❖❖❖❖❖❖❖❖❖❖❖❖❖❖❖❖❖❖❖❖❖❖❖❖❖❖❖❖❖❖❖❖❖❖❖❖❖❖❖❖❖❖❖❖❖

# Kafka's photograph of the imaginary. Dialogical interplay between realism and the fantastic. *(The Metamorphosis)*

❖❖❖❖❖❖❖❖❖❖❖❖❖❖❖❖❖❖❖❖❖❖❖❖❖❖❖❖❖❖❖❖❖❖❖❖❖❖❖❖❖❖❖❖❖❖

Nature hath no outline
but Imagination has.
William Blake, 1822

## Semiotic excess, semantic vacuity

True to the peculiar hermeneutics associated with his literary works Kafka's poetological utterances are both very infrequent and usually terse and indirect, taking on that familiar paradoxical form which characterizes the articulation of anything resembling a "statement" in his writing. Approached with the necessary caution however, certain of these utterances provide an interesting perspective firstly on the difficult problem of determining Kafka's poetics of representation and secondly on the complex relationship of his literary works to the tradition of realism, to the fantastic and to the historical avant-garde.

In a conversation with Gustav Janouch for example, Kafka allegedly played down the apparent plasticity of certain of his characters as a mere by-product, emphasizing that "he was not depicting people" but was involved only in "telling a story," the characters being merely "images, only images." Typically he went on to undermine even this modest claim by denying that the production of such images implies or encourages their visual perception (i.e. as part of the mimetic process of representation), and he added the anti-statement, "one photographs things in order to chase them out of one's mind. My stories are a kind of closing of the eyes."[1] This opposition to any premature closure afforded by a conventional photographic approach may be seen again in Kafka's reaction upon hearing that the published version of *The Metamorphosis* was to include a drawing of that central figure which is referred to obscurely there merely by the general term "Ungeziefer," that is, "insect" or, even more broadly, "vermin":

The insect cannot itself be drawn. It cannot even be shown in the distance . . . If I might be allowed to make suggestions as regards an illustration I would choose scenes such as: the parents and the chief clerk before the closed door, or even better, the parents and the sister in a lighted room, while the door to the unlit neighboring room stands open.[2]

As we shall see later, it is of the utmost significance that Kafka seems to be attempting here to protect the integrity and anonymity of his central image by suspending any impulse towards a mimetic or naturalistic mode of depicting it and redirecting this mimetic tendency towards the kind of object which by its very nature resists and defers fixity and representation: the unknown and the imaginary. For by displacing attention onto the door of Gregor Samsa's darkened room, Kafka is inscribing openness into the corresponding act of interpretation, so that however detailed and "photographically" perfect the finished product of representation may be, its ultimate determination is at best that of semantic vacuity.

It is this paradoxical image of a realistic representation of a door opened onto an impenetrable darkness which may serve as a way of understanding the complex nature of Kafka's version of realism as a mode which is in constant interaction with the fantastic. Before we examine this dialogical relationship in more detail, let us first consider two paradigms for these modes, as presented in

[1] "er zeichnete keine Menschen"; "Bilder nur Bilder"; "Man photographiert Dinge, um sie aus dem Sinn zu verscheuchen. Meine Geschichten sind eine Art von Augenschließen." Gustav Janouch, *Gespräche mit Kafka* (Frankfurt: Fischer, 1951), 25.
[2] "Das Insekt selbst kann nicht gezeichnet werden. Es kann aber nicht einmal von der Ferne aus gezeigt werden . . . Wenn ich für eine Illustration selbst Vorschläge machen dürfte, würde ich Szenen wählen, wie: die Eltern und der Prokurist vor der geschlossenen Tür oder noch besser die Eltern und die Schwester im beleuchteten Zimmer, während die Tür zum ganz finstreren Nebenzimmer offen steht." Letter to K. Wolff, October 25, 1915, in Kafka, *Briefe 1902–24*, ed. Max Brod (Frankfurt: Fischer, 1958), 136.

the first case by Georg Lukacs,[3] and in the second by Tzvetan Todorov.[4]

## The "debates on expressionism": Lukacs' theory of realism

Lukacs' model of realism is a particularly appropriate one to take up in order to explore Kafka's peculiar approach to realism via the fantastic. Firstly, Lukacs himself explicitly criticizes the ways in which Kafka's texts conflict with his conception. And secondly, the very rigidity of Lukacs' model serves to highlight the "unorthodox" nature of Kafka's texts and their link with the progressive goals of the historical avant-garde[5]: the manner in which they depend upon such realism only in order to produce a counter-discourse which transgresses its strictures and deconstructs its drive towards mimetic closure.

Despite those limitations to which we will be referring presently, Georg Lukacs' conception of realism is anything but a merely mechanical, reflectionist model.[6] Indeed in the three major essays in which he outlines his model, namely "Erzählen oder Beschreiben?" ("To Narrate or to Describe?"), "Es geht um den Realismus" ("A Matter of Realism") and "Franz Kafka oder Thomas Mann. Die Gegenwartsbedeutung des kritischen Realismus" ("The Contemporary Significance of Critical Realism") he polemicizes against that simplistic, reflectionist kind of approach (as it is manifested for him for example in the naturalist movement) where no attempt is made to go beyond a mere reflection of the surface of phenomenal reality. For Lukacs this version of realism lacks the overall ideological conception and analytical apparatus which would provide the criteria by which firstly the elemental forces of history may be perceived, and by which secondly the selection of material for the representation may be determined. Where an author lacks the insight provided by an

---

[3] Georg Lukacs, "Essays über den Realismus," *Werke IV* (Neuwied: Luchterhand, 1971).

[4] Tzvetan Todorov, *Introduction à la littérature fantastique* (Paris: Editions du Seuil, 1970).

[5] Lukacs himself acknowledges Kafka's position as the "greatest artistic figure" of "contemporary avant-garde literarature." See Lukacs, "Die weltanschaulichen Grundlagen des Avantgardeismus," *Werke IV*, 496.

[6] In fairness it should also be noted that in these essays Lukacs is presenting in extremely condensed and possibly somewhat simplified form a model of realism which was to be developed and refined over the entire course of his work.

overview of reality (that is, by a sense of the "totality" ("Totalität") he has no means of deciding which aspects should be selected as important for his description and which can be omitted. The consequence of this is a version of realism as a mere superficial form of "describing" ("Beschreiben"), reflecting an anxious and stupefied response of simply "standing still" ("Stehenbleiben")[7] before the surface of reality. Into this category Lukacs places the work of Franz Kafka.

However in this it is clear that Lukacs' claims for what he sees as the superior art of analytical "narration" ("Erzählen") rests upon a thoroughly Platonic conception. For he implies that his superior realism reflects reality not as it appears but as it "really" is. Lukacs' conception of realism consequently relies as we have seen on the operation of "opening up" ("Aufdecken"), whereby the realist author penetrates the surface phenomena of reality to a more "essential" underlying reality. As we have already seen, the starting-point for any work of realism according to Lukacs is the perception of "objective reality." As he famously observes, "as always it's a matter here of a *content which is correctly* perceived."[8] The task of the writer is "not to look upon reality any longer as chaos, but to recognize its regularities, the directions in which it develops, the role of man within it."[9] And in this, Lukacs would seem to have no qualms in deciding what is a "correct" and what is "incorrect" perception, for he appears to operate from the premise that "objective reality" is readily accessible, and that chaos only arises from "the lack of a social, that is to say an omni-human [gesamtmenschlichen] perspective ..."[10]

Complementary to this act of "opening up" of essences, is "the artistic covering over of the abstractly-produced connections – the sublation of the work of abstraction" (205).[11] The goal here, as we

---

7   See Lukacs, "Franz Kafka oder Thomas Mann?" (in section II, "Die Gegenwartsbedeutung des kritischen Realismus") *Werke IV*, 534.
8   "es kommt also hier, wie überall, auf den *richtig erkannten Inhalt* an." See Lukacs, "Es geht um den Realismus," *Expressionismusdebatte*, 225 (emphasis by Lukacs).
9   "die Wirklichkeit nicht mehr als Chaos zu betrachten, sondern ihre Gesetzmäßigkeiten, ihre Entwicklungsrichtungen, die Rolle des Menschen in ihnen zu erkennen." Lukacs, "Franz Kafka oder Thomas Mann?" ("Die Gegenwartsbedeutung des kritischen Realismus"), 525–526.
10  "das Fehlen einer gesellschaftlichen, also gesamtmenschlichen Perspektive ..." Lukacs, "Franz Kafka oder Thomas Mann?" 529.
11  "das künstlerische Zudecken der abstrahiert erarbeiteten Zusammenhänge – das Aufheben des Abstrahierens."

have seen, is the "fashioning of the surface of life, which, although at every moment it allows the essence to *shine though* (which is not the case in the immediacy of life) nonethess appears as immediacy, as the surface of life."[12] Lukacs demands in other words the creation of a "realistic gloss" which would tie the fictional world together as an illusionary unity.

Responding to this conception during the so-called "Debates on Expressionism" (in *Das Wort*, 1937–38) Ernst Bloch effects a simple critique or deconstruction of Lukacs' position by pointing to the unreflected "a prioris" in his system, and to his reliance on a notion of "objective totality" which is really only at best a "useful fiction." Where Lukacs suggests unproblematically that the writer needs only to step back and recognize the underlying order in the chaos, Bloch as we have seen proposes instead the radical notion that reality itself might exist as "discontinuity" or "interruption."[13]

If the foundation upon which Lukacs' entire system of realism depends is the idea that there is an objective level of reality, a "totality" which can be apprehended and represented by the author, by calling its objectivity into question, and by posing the possibility that reality exists in a fragmentary state as "interruption" ("Unterbrechung"), Bloch implies that the notion of "objective reality" is merely a fictional construct which is imposed *a posteriori* upon the discontinuous world in order to provide a sense of order. Thus Lukacs' critique of expressionism and the historical avant-garde in general, and of Kafka in particular, must be relativized by this pespective: if in fact there is no such thing as an "objective reality" outside of a system of fictions then it is clear that there can be no code of realism which is not in one way or another a "deformation" and thus Kafka's version of realism is no more a deformation than "objective" realism of "Erzählen" proposed by Lukacs.

Thus where Lukacs criticizes Kafka and the avant-garde for their lack of social perspective or insight into the "totality," and

12 "gestaltete Oberfläche des Lebens, die, obwohl sie in jedem Moment das Wesen klar *durchscheinen* läßt (was in der Unmittelbarkeit des Lebens selbst nicht der Fall ist) doch als Unmittelbarkeit, als Oberfläche des Lebens erscheint." Lukacs, "Es geht um den Realismus," *Expressionismusdebatte*, 205.
13 Bloch argues, "aber vielleicht ist Lukacs' Realität, die des unendlich vermittelten Totalitätszusammenhangs, gar nicht so – objektiv . . . vielleicht ist die echte Wirklichkeit auch Unterbrechung." See Ernst Bloch, "Diskussionen über Expressionismus," *Expressionismusdebatte*, 186.

where he belittles their subsequent "anxiety" at experiencing the world as chaotic, he is in fact denying one of the essential functions of his own model of realism.[14] For just as the texts valorized within his tradition of realism allow an insight into that which might otherwise remain hidden beneath appearances, so in the same way, the particular perspective of Kafka's "subjective" system of realism fulfills a similar function in providing the possibility of discovering that which might be excluded by dominant social discourse and so remain hidden by other more dominant and conventional "images of the world" (or "Weltbilder") and epistemological systems.

If there is a difference between the two representational and epistemological systems in this regard, it lies in the constant disruption of the realistic trajectory in Kafka's texts by alternative modes such as the fantastic. For in undercutting the claims to objectivity of such "Weltbilder" (or "constructions of the world") the "deforming" realisms of the avant-garde distinguish themselves from the more ideological versions proposed by Lukacs. In sharp contrast to the texts valorized by his conception of realism, they do not claim to represent the objective truth as "reality" *per se*, but – to use Christian Metz' distinction – through this moment of deformation they foreground themselves not as "history" but as "discourse," as mere constructions or models of reality at best, the means for evoking merely the *structure* of experience.[15]

It is in this respect that Kafka's fantastic texts may be seen as constituting a form of "counter-discourse" fully consonant with the goals of the expressionist avant-garde. They share a disregard for the novelistic conventions of the organic, since like the fantastic, their preoccupation with identities, categories and limits is oriented negatively towards the "projected dissolution" of such organizational terms. For as Rosemary Jackson observes, the fantastic "establishes, or dis-covers, an absence of separating distinctions, violating a 'normal,' or commonplace perspective . . ." (48) Similar to the historical avant-garde the fantastic raises fundamental questions concerning the "nature of the real" (37) and

---

[14] Lukacs, "Franz Kafka oder Thomas Mann?" ("Die Gegenwartsbedeutung des kritischen Realismus"), 529.

[15] See Metz "Story/Discourse. (A Note on Two Kinds of Voyeurism)," *The Imaginary Signifier*, 91–98.

undermines its hegemonic status by opposing it to an alternative or "unreal." Thus as a counter-discourse the fantastic does not target realism for its own sake – as an outmoded or unfashionable form, for example – but rather aims more broadly at the dominant social discourses associated with it. As Jackson notes, "It subverts dominant philosophical assumptions which uphold as 'reality' a coherent, single-viewed entity, that narrow vision which Bakhtin termed 'monological'" (48).

Like the fantastic Kafka's texts function as "dialogical" counter-discourses which radically question such unitary perspectives. Lukacs' harsh criticism that Kafka is a "classic when it comes to being petrified before reality by panic and a blinding fear" is thus countered by this characteristic function of the fantastic, namely of transgressing the boundaries of more conventional notions of reality, and so undermining thereby their claim to the status of "objectivity" per se.[16] Rather than a mere "petrification" or "standing still" ("Stehenbleiben") before the surface of phenomena, such transgressive discourses as Kafka's therefore represent a deconstruction of fixed concepts of reality. Thus a more telling difference between Lukacs' notion of literary discourse as "dis-covery" and Kafka's is, as we shall see, that whereas it may be conceivable for the particular insights into the underlying and invisible social forces (which Lukacs claims for his realist discourse) to be conveyed in much the same manner by a non-literary discourse such as a sociological or historical medium, that undiscovered realm which Kafka's texts make visible is revealed by a function which pertains exclusively to literary discourse and the aesthetic sphere: as a means of experiential access to what otherwise constitutes an "impenetrable" level of reality.

A further criticism which Lukacs directs at the avant-garde (and by implication at Kafka) is that the subjectivist standpoint has the effect of limiting the possible entrances to the text, that is, of closing down the text's general accessibility by a broad audience. Lukacs contrasts the avant-garde's inaccessibility with the tradition of "critical" realism which he valorizes as giving "to the reader among the broad masses of the people access to his own

---

[16] "der Klassiker dieses Stehenbleibens bei der blinden und panischen Angst vor der Wirklichkeit." Lukacs, "Franz Kafka oder Thomas Mann?" ("Die Gegenwartsbedeutung des kritischen Realismus"), 534.

life-experience from the widest variety of angles."[17] Implicit in this position is the requirement that literature provide a means or position through which to identify – an "Identifikationsangebot" – which, together with the effect of the realist gloss (the process of "covering over"), will effect an illusionism and thus encourage the reader to experience the world of the text as real. The demand for accessibility and identification will obviously not be fulfilled in quite the same manner nor to quite the same extent by the avantgarde as it is by Lukacs' realist paradigm. For the illusionism which is the condition for the fulfillment of these demands takes a very different form in each of these modes, and in the case of Kafka it becomes very difficult to talk about an illusionism at all, since the realist code through which it might be erected is constantly being undermined by the fantastic element. As we shall see later however, the notions of accessibility and the potentialization of the reader's own life-experiences are nevertheless of the greatest importance in the reception of Kafka's texts, despite the latter's complete disdain for that "illusionism" which Lukacs demands.

## Todorov: fantasy as realism's uncanny other

Before turning to *The Metamorphosis* I want to give a brief outline of Todorov's model of the fantastic and to describe its function as a mode which exists *primarily* as a form of counter-discourse, existing "only against a background to which it offers reversal."[18] The fantastic is not only subversive of realism but relates to realism in a "symbiotic" manner: as Jackson points out, it is inextricably linked to realism as its repressed, excluded or occult Other: "The fantastic exists as the inside, or underside, of realism, opposing the novel's closed, monological forms with open, dialogical structures, as if the novel had given rise to its own opposite, its unrecognisable reflection" (25). The thoroughly subversive and marginal nature of the fantastic – what the German translators of Todorov's book aptly term as the "Grenzcharakter" – is underlined by the "differential" definition which Todorov

---

[17] "aus den breiten Massen des Volkes von den verschiedensten Seiten seiner eigenen Lebenserfahrung her Zugang." Lukacs, "Es geht um den Realismus," *Expressionismusdebatte*, 227.

[18] Eric Rabkin, *The Fantastic in Literature* (Princeton: Princeton University Press, 1976), 216, cited in *Fantasy: The Literature of Subversion* (London: Methuen, 1981), 21.

attributes to it.[19] He situates it between two realms. On the one side there is the realm of the marvelous ("le merveilleux"), an area in which supernatural events may occur and can be accepted as such through the literary convention of the "once-upon-a-time" contract, whereby all "reality-testing" by the reader and figure alike is suspended. On the other side there is the realm of "l'étrange" or the uncanny (similar to Freud's "Unheimliche") in which the function of reality-testing is preserved, so that the apparently supernatural events which occur in the narrative may be rationally explained as deriving for example from the unconscious.[20] Since the realm of the fantastic falls immediately between the two, it is characterized by an extended hesitation on the part of the reader and an inability to decide whether the unusual events are real or illusionary, naturally or unnaturally caused:

either he is the victim of an illusion of the senses, of a product of the imagination – and the laws of the world then remain what they are; or else the event has indeed taken place, it is an integral part of reality – but then this reality is controlled by laws unknown to us . . . The fantastic occupies the duration of this uncertainty. Once we choose one answer or the other, we leave the fantastic for a neighboring genre, the uncanny or the marvellous.[21]

This hesitation, which in the fantastic is often reflected and foregrounded in the behaviour of a fictional character, is symptomatic of the confrontation of a "normal" person with the inexplicable: "The fantastic is that hesitation experienced by a person who knows only the laws of nature, confronting an apparently supernatural event" (25).[22] Consequently it accompanies a subversive process whereby the existing systems of order and reason by which that person was anchored and oriented undergo a radical

---

[19] The original is "le caractère différentiel du fantastique," 31. "Grenzcharakter" is the term used in the German translation *Einführung in die fantastische Literatur*, trans. K. Kersten, S. Metz and C. Neubaur (München: Hanser, 1972), 27.

[20] Freud's essay "Das Unheimliche" was first published in *Imago* 5 (1919).

[21] Tzvetan Todorov, *The Fantastic. A Structural Approach to a Literary Genre*, trans. R. Howard (Ithaca: Cornell, 1973), 25. *Introduction à la littérature fantastique*: "ou bien il s'agit d'une illusion des sens, d'un produit de l'imagination et les lois du monde restent alors ce qu'elles sont; ou bien l'événement a véritablement eu lieu, il est partie intégrante de la réalité, mais alors cette réalité est régie par lois inconnues de nous . . . Le fantastique occupe le temps de cette incertitude; dès qu'on choisit l'une ou l'autre réponse, on quitte le fantastique pour entrer dans un genre voisin, l'étrange ou le merveilleux . . . " (29).

[22] "Le fantastique, c'est cette hésitation éprouvée par un être qui ne connaît que les lois naturelles, face à un événement en apparence surnaturel" (29).

interrogation. In this context Todorov quotes an observation by Roger Caillois, which simultaneously serves as an apt description regarding the function of the fantastic in Kafka's *The Metamorphosis* and in its interaction with the mode of realism: "The fantastic is always a break in the acknowledged order, an irruption of an inadmissible within the changeless everyday legality."[23] The fantastic is thus reliant upon the code of realism and upon a corresponding realistic attitude.[24] For in order to subvert and transgress the "laws" of reality, it must first call up and legitimize them, or the situation will simply slide into the category of the marvelous, where all is accepted as "believable." In the case of Kafka's texts this dependence is very extreme, for here the partial reliance on the real by the transgressive element of the fantastic develops into a full mutual interaction of the modes of realism and the fantastic. Let us now examine this process by close reference to Kafka's *The Metamorphosis*, and to the ways in which it deviates from the paradigm of the fantastic.

## Metamorphosis and transgression

The course of the fantastic narrative, according to Todorov's description, usually moves from an everyday world of the rational, towards a realm of the supernatural. Kafka's *The Metamorphosis*, however, effectively reverses the direction of this conventional trajectory. For, as Todorov observes, after an initial "twist" the narrative moves into a rational and realistic mode. In other words, in the case of *The Metamorphosis* although the factual statement of Gregor's transformation in the first lines of the text serves to set the event within the realm of the fantastic-marvelous, this literary convention is broken almost immediately and soon abandoned completely as the text moves into a realist vein. Thus that hesitation (which we have seen to be the characteristic of the fantastic) in deciding whether the events are naturally or supernaturally caused, hardly arises in the case of the miraculous metamorpho-

---

[23] Caillois, *Au Coeur du Fantastique*, quoted in Todorov, *Introduction*, 26. "Tout le fantastique est rupture de l'ordre reconnu, irruption de l'inadmissable au sein de l'inaltérable légalité quotidienne" (31).

[24] Georges Jacquemin provides a useful discussion of the dependence of the fantastic upon a realistic mode in "Über das Phantastische in der Literatur" *Phaicon* 2. Almanach der phantastischen Literatur, ed. R.A.Zondergeld, (Frankfurt: Suhrkamp, 1975), esp. 46–50.

sis. For although it is true that the narrative begins with Gregor in his bed, waking up after uneasy dreams, and that, as in the fantastic, the real status of narrated events might thus initially be questioned as a continuation of the dream, these doubts are firstly undermined by the narrative statement "it was no dream," and are surely dispelled at the very latest, when the Prokurist hears Gregor's voice inside the room and exclaims "'that was the voice of an animal'."[25] If indeed the metamorphosis *is* a "nightmare," it is one from which Gregor (and the skeptical reader) fail to wake up.

In the fantastic it is this hesitation which signals a transgression with regard to the distinction between dream and reality, thereby serving to question and undermine our notion of reality and thus to destabilize our conventional means of representing it. In Kafka's texts by contrast this function is fulfilled by the interaction between the fantastic-marvelous event, and the ensuing realistic attitude towards it, as conveyed by the realistic mode. For example, if the reader remains hesitant in his or her attitude towards the causality of narrated events, then this hesitancy is certainly not shared by the central figure, who attempts by and large to act as if nothing had happened: the change in his voice he puts down to a "chill," and he is confident that the metamorphosis will "clear itself up like a dream" (60). Similarly, throughout the first section of the story, despite the momentous event which has occurred, Gregor's thoughts continue to revolve around his dislike of his duties in general while much of the first section of the text is devoted to the immediate problem of Gregor's attempts at getting up from his bed in order to face the workaday world. In this manner, the immediacy of the everyday attitude towards the real, the tendency of this rationalistic mode to exclude even the most pressing existential concerns is shown as being absurd and laughably inappropriate – a theme which runs throughout Kafka's works.

Another difference with Kafka's texts is that whereas in the general convention of the fantastic there is usually a foil (frequently embodied in a secondary figure and representing a contrasting scientific and rational approach to the questionable and the fantastic phenomena) whose logic is invariably proven later to be

[25] "'das war eine Tierstimme'." Kafka, *Die Verwandlung, Gesammelte Werke*, ed. M. Brod (Frankfurt: Fischer, 1983), 66.

erroneous in the face of the surrounding mysterious forces,[26] in Kafka's texts this realistic attitude and overwhelming rationality is questioned not in the contrast-figure of a scientist, a rationalist or any other representative of Enlightenment thinking and "de-mystification," but in an average human being, the "everyman" – frequently the narrative's central figure – whom the reader is able to view and, to a large degree, identify with, in an unproblematical manner. Consequently it is patently *not* the case as Todorov suggests, that Kafka's world is "completely bizarre and just as abnormal as the metamorphosis itself" or that it "obeys a logic which has nothing to do with the real world."[27] For with the exception of that original "twist" of the marvelous, the ensuing events in *The Metamorphosis* are frequently rather mundane and are treated absolutely realistically. In all this, as Adorno says, "it is not the monstrous but rather its self-evident quality which is shocking."[28] Thus we can accept the monstrous change in Gregor under the reading conventions of the mode of the fantastic, but are nevertheless shocked – not by the peculiar event itself but by the realism, and by the ease with which the characters adapt to the uncanny and unreal metamorphosis.

We have seen that the fantastic fulfills its function of allowing a transgression of boundaries by introducing that which is beyond our everyday norms and systems of perception. In the case of *The Metamorphosis* however, through its interaction with the realist mode, the fantastic allows realistic attitudes and patterns of behaviour which the reader recognizes as his or her own to be provoked, questioned and ironized. Let us examine how this receptive process of self-ironization is brought about.

Gregor's transgression of the boundary of the normal, and his existence in the realm of the Other is associated with his abhorrence of his quotidian existence and his many everyday anxieties.

[26] Rolf Günter Renner offers an interesting commentary on this figure of the rationalist in "Kafka als phantastischer Erzähler" *Phaicon* 3. Almanach der phantastischen Literatur, ed. R. A. Zondergeld (Frankfurt: Suhrkamp, 1978), 149.

[27] "Chez Kafka . . . le monde décrit est tout entier bizarre, aussi anormal que l'événement même [la métamorphose] à quoi il fait fond"; " . . . son monde tout entier obéit à une logique onirique, sinon cauchemardesque, qui n'a plus rien à voir avec le réel." See Todorov, *Introduction*, 181.

[28] "nicht das Ungeheuerliche schockiert, sondern dessen Selbstverständlichkeit." Quoted in Lukacs, "Franz Kafka oder Thomas Mann?" ("Die Gegenwarts-bedeutung des kritischen Realismus"), 534–535.

It is primarily his sense of responsibility towards the family which appears to be preventing him from breaking free of his quotidian existence and into the realm of Desire: "If I didn't have to hold myself back for my parents' sake, I would have resigned long ago, I would have gone to the boss and would have told him from the bottom of my heart what I felt. That would have thrown him for a loop!" (58)[29] As a consequence, in the place of a genuine liberation Gregor consoles himself through such fantasies. The most powerful of these is displaced onto his sister Grete, who, in her relatively carefree existence becomes a figure representing above all the possibility for "Entgrenzung," for a realizable transgression of the quotidian reality which has imprisoned Gregor. In her role as a de-limited and fictional projection of Gregor's subjectivity, she represents a "supplementary" self harboring the possibility of escape through the aesthetic sphere: "it was his secret plan to send her, who by contrast to Gregor loved music and could play the violin movingly, to a music conservatory next year" (79).[30] As a transgression of the everyday world's demands of duty and responsibility, these expressions of desire take on the character of an excluded realm – an occult or a taboo. Consequently although Gregor retains his plan, it figures however "only ever as a beautiful dream, whose realization could not be pondered, the parents being unwilling to hear even the most innocent mention of it" (79).[31] Thus Gregor's escape from the quotidian demands of duty, work and the family are given a negative twist by the metamorphosis. For while it still represents a "core-fantasy," or "experiential structure" on the theme of liberation it is also connected not only with the loss of his functional identity within the family as the breadwinner, but with his subsequent exclusion from the family circle. In other words it is an image which becomes instrumental both in Gregor's escape and simultaneously in his incarceration at the very heart of the family. In terms of the text's dramatization of subjectivity, the metamorphosis may similarly

---

[29] "Wenn ich mich nicht wegen meiner Eltern zurückhielte, ich hätte längst gekündigt, ich wäre vor den Chef hingetreten und hätte ihm meine Meinung von Grund des Herzens aus gesagt. Vom Pult hätte er fallen müssen!"

[30] " es war sein geheimer Plan, sie, die zum Unterschied von Gregor Musik sehr liebte und rührend Violine zu spielen verstand, nächstes Jahr . . . auf das Konservatorium zu schicken" (79).

[31] "immer nur als schöner Traum, an dessen Verwirklichung nicht zu denken war, und die Eltern hörten nicht einmal diese unschuldigen Erwähnungen gern ..."

be seen as a form of "Entgrenzung" or "de-limitation" through which occult desire is allowed to come to the surface and exert its own influence upon that territory from which it is otherwise excluded, namely the real. This textual structure may thus be experienced by the recipient as a dramatization of his or her own fears and longings for a similar lapse into desire, as a dramatization for example of similar fantasies of an escape from everyday responsibilities and from the social group. Thus far from denying access ("Zugang") as Lukacs would maintain, the text in fact encourages an identificatory response – albeit a highly ambiguous one – by the reader, who can fill the open framework of this core-fantasy with his or her own experience and fantasies.

## Bakhtin: *The Metamorphosis* as a dialogical or "hybrid text"

By creating a tension between the two discursive systems of representation, and thus establishing an oppositional relationship between their corresponding epistemologies and signifying systems, the text dramatizes two sets of mutually exclusive systems of meaning. This produces a dialogical relationship between the dominant discourse of realism and its fantastic counter-discourse with the effect firstly of clarifying what Bakhtin calls the "semantic positions" or "language worldviews"[32] corresponding to each discursive system. In Kafka's text for example the central image of the insect is a key element in this regard, for as a dreamlike abstraction the everyday, waking self (and its reality-principle) are brought into a form of co-presence with the occult Other of the real, in other words with that which reality excludes. In the process the "realist" notion of identity for example is not so much *extended* as rather completely *undermined* by being made to incorporate a fantastic (and completely non-realist) double, namely Gregor's fantasy-self.

In as far as the abstract image of the "Ungeziefer" embodies the "internal" or subjective elements of desire and anxiety in "objective" or externalized form, it also fulfills what Sokel sees as the typically expressionist function of providing an expressive "correlative" or Kantian "aesthetic attribute" serving the "rational

[32] Bakhtin, *Problems of Dostoevsky's Poetics*, 184

idea as a substitute for logical presentation."[33] Yet characteristically this "expressive element swallows the representational; the aesthetic attribute becomes the aesthetic substance" (51). Consequently as Kafka's text demonstrates, the abstract image leaves far behind it the kind of representational considerations that it might take on in realist discourse and instead begins to embrace completely this fantastic and abstract quality in its own right – not as a realist signifier with a clear denotative function but as a semantic vacuum whose very essence is to undermine realism's credo that the world is fundamentally accessible to rational explanation and representation.

Thus the dialogical structure of the text involving the interaction between the mode of realism and the mode of the fantastic allows a confrontation between two opposing epistemologies and two mutually exclusive systems of meaning: that pertaining to a dominant version of reality and that pertaining to what it excludes. As a result of this confrontation for example, any systematized and unitary notion of reality as "objective" in Lukacs' sense loses its fixity. Furthermore through the subversive and relativizing effect of this oppositional relationship, concepts such as the "objective" are revealed to be merely ideological constructs, held in place at best by an economy of power. This dialogical interaction between the two discursive systems consequently has a deconstructive effect. For as with the "useful fiction" of objectivity, it calls up and interrogates other such dominant notions, realistic attitudes, rationalist norms and models of reality which are the unreflected premises of the reader's orientation in the world.

If we view the discourse of realism and its fantastic counter-discourse as two separate "verbal-ideological systems"[34] which are nonetheless engaged in a dialog with one another, then the interactive text-structure in Kafka's work may be thought of in Bakhtin's terms as a kind of dialogical "novelistic hybrid." For as Bakhtin observes, the "novelistic hybrid is *an artistically organized system for bringing different languages in contact with one another*, a system having as its goal the illumination of one language by another . . ." (361). Such an interactive structure therefore con-

[33] Sokel, *Writer in Extremis*, 11. Sokel is citing Kant, *Critique of Aesthetic Judgment*, trans. J. C. Meredith (Oxford: Oxford University Press, 1982) Part II ("The Analytic of the Sublime"), §49: 177–178.

[34] Bakhtin, *The Dialogic Imagination*, 371.

trasts sharply with the system of realism implied by Lukacs' concept of "totality," under which a single unified system of meaning is held rigidly in place. For in Kafka's text the dialogical interaction becomes the condition whereby that which is excluded by one discursive system is resurrected by a second system. The consequences of this structure of dialogicity are of the utmost significance for an avant-garde poetics of representation and reception oriented towards the creating of a counter-discourse.

The effects of the dialogical structure may be observed for example in the frustration with which the recipient responds to the mass of seemingly superfluous realistic details in the text – the semiotic excess – and their failure to crystallize into the conventional kind of "organic" and unified fictional heterocosm (envisaged for example by Lukacs) which conventionally both organizes the world coherently and positions the subject within it.[35] Lukacs himself concedes that these realistic details take on a paradoxical function in the avant-garde. For if in the "logical anti-realism" ("konsequenten Antirealismus") of the avant-garde the "omnipresence of realism persists above all in the details" then in such writers as Kafka, the function that Barthes would later call their "reality-effect" is paradoxically turned against the very realism that produces it, so that "the most improbable, the most unreal aspects appear real on account of the suggestive power of truthfulness in the details."[36] The peculiarly "allegorical" character of Kafka's texts – an allegorical structure which remains completely open and indeterminate at the level of the signified – is rooted in the suggestive power of precisely this semiotic excess. For as Lukacs notes, "the magnificently expressive power of the details relates to a transcendent reality beyond them . . ." And as a consequence the determinate details of the signifier remain undetermined at the level of the signified, "mere ciphers of an ungraspable world beyond" (535).[37]

[35] Lukacs invokes Thomas Mann as a contrast to Kafka, reducing the latter to "diesem faszinierenden Irrlicht auf dem Wege einer Literatur, die das Spezifische unserer Zeit vom bürgerlichen Standpunkt ausdrücken will . . ."
[36] "diese Allgegenwart des Realismus bewährt sich natürlich vor allem in den Details"; "das Unwahrscheinlichste, das Irreellste wegen der suggestiven Wahrheitskraft der Details als real erscheint." See Lukacs, "Franz Kafka oder Thomas Mann" ("Die Gegenwartsbedeutung des kritischen Realismus") *Werke IV*, 501.
[37] "Denn die großartig ausdrucksvollen Details beziehen sich ununterbrochen auf eine ihm gegenüber transzendente Wirklichkeit . . ."; "bloße Chiffrezeichen eines unfaßbaren Jenseits." Lukacs, "Franz Kafka oder Thomas Mann," 535.

Judged according to the criteria of Lukacs' realist paradigm, this failure of Kafka's text to form a realist heterocosm would indicate a deficiency in the representational process of "covering over" responsible for creating an illusionary unity. For example in Lukacs' judgement it results in the tendency for avant-garde art to be oriented towards "objectlessness" and "nothingness."[38] In the works of Lukacs' paradigmatically realist writer, Thomas Mann by contrast, "his time and his place, with all their details, always crystallize in the socio-historical essence of a socio-historical situation."[39]

However given the nature of the dialogical interaction in Kafka's text, we can see that this characteristic lack of heterocosmic coherence is by no means to be considered a "deficiency." For although the realist illusion of unity fails to materialize, the multiplication of details creates an interrelated set of "Realitätsbezüge" without a "Bezugsrealität," that is, "references to the world" without a real-life "referential world." In other words, the very *structure* of reality is presented, but minus its relation to any specific *instance* of reality. And it is through this laying bare of structures, as we have seen, that the text fulfills its deconstructive function of making visible the fictional bases of conventional models of reality.

This is the reason why the recipient's experience of frustration, when faced with the familiar "Rätselhaftigkeit" or puzzling quality of Kafka's texts, must be seen as symptomatic for the confrontation not only with the dialogical text-structure but with the historical avant-garde *per se*. As a counter-discursive strategy this dialogicity presupposes an attitude towards semantic acts which is very different from the position implied by realism, as Lukacs for example, understands it. For through the co-presence of opposing systems, a semantic openness – characteristic of the historical avant-garde – is inscribed into the processes of production and reception, and this openness endlessly resists precisely such fundamentally "organic" concepts as "totality" or "covering over."

---

[38] "Die künstlerisch auf Gegenstandlosigkeit, auf das Nichts orientierte avantgardeistische Kunst . . ." Lukacs, "Franz Kafka oder Thomas Mann," 539.

[39] "sein Ort und seine Zeit, mit allen ihren Details, konzentrieren in sich immer das gesellschaftlich-geschichtlich Wesentliche einer konkreten gesellschaftlich-geschichtlichen Situation." Lukacs, "Franz Kafka oder Thomas Mann," 536.

Conclusion. Semiotic excess, semantic vacuity: the fantastic
as counter-discourse

If one concedes that indeterminacy is an elementary condition for the
functioning of literary effects, one must ask what the significance is of its
expansion, above all in modern literature. Without doubt it changes the
relationship between reader and text.... At this point the question arises
as to what insights into the human condition literature is capable of
opening up.

Wolfgang Iser[40]

This dialogical interaction has important consequences for any
progressive attempt to counter the restrictions and conventions of
the dominant realist systems of representation. We have seen for
example, that it is the function of this interaction between the two
signifying systems of discourse to question the solidity of the real
by presenting that marginalized realm of the Other which the real
would deny. In its central preoccupation with a change of identity
and with the ensuing problematization of the boundaries of the
real, Kafka's text necessarily moves towards an interrogation not
just of particular representations but of conventional notions of
representation and signifying systems per se. This is reflected in
the way in which the fantastic image of the "Ungeziefer" ("insect") is elaborated.

It is significant, for example, that Gregor not only loses his
former identity and position but, as Jackson points out, that his
powers of perception and communication suffer: with his "animal voice" ("Tierstimme") he loses his ability to speak; furthermore he is gradually becoming blind.[41] In this respect, what is
being challenged on a thematic level is the very idea of identity
and differentiation itself, and – to extend this argument to the
level of epistemology – the ability to isolate and to "represent." It
is possible for example to claim that the theme of Kafka's text is a
meaning which would be excluded by a system of representation

---

[40] "Unterstellt man, daß Unbestimmtheit eine elementare Wirkungsbedingung
verkörpert, so fragt es sich, was ihre Expansion – vor allem in moderner
Literatur – besagt. Sie verändert ohne Zweifel das Verhältnis von Text und
Leser . . . An diesem Punkt ergibt sich dann die Frage, welche Einsichten die
Literatur in die menschlichen Situation zu eröffnen vermag." Wolfgang Iser,
"Die Appellstruktur der Texte" (Konstanz: Konstanzer Universitätsreden,
1974), 230–231.
[41] See Rosemary Jackson, *Fantasy: the Literature of Subversion* (London: Methuen,
1981), 160–161.

such as the one that Lukacs proposes, and that as a result it would remain "non-representable" under such a system. For to a large degree, Gregor's loss of social identity, his withdrawal from the "Symbolic Order" and his retreat from self to Other come across as a failure to signify, a retreat into semantic absence.[42] This is thematized firstly by the emptying of Gregor's room of all the symbols of "homeliness" (his furniture and belongings – such as the framed picture on the wall to which he clings as a last reminder of this lost identity).[43] Secondly it is thematized through the process whereby his room is re-categorized as a "junk room" ("Rumpelkammer") and filled with junk and filth ("Unrat") – from which Gregor, covered in dust, ultimately becomes indistinguishable or "undifferentiated." The story of Gregor's exclusion from the family is described in terms of his treatment as an absence: to a large extent the family tries to go on living as if he did not exist, that is, as if he did not fit into their notion of the "real."

Now it is significant that although the realistic attitude of the family and its mechanisms of exclusion are conveyed within the text in terms of realism, no attempt is made to fix precisely or otherwise determine Gregor's ontological status. In as far as his behavior falls within the scope of conventional realist discourse, Gregor is "represented." For example his quotidian anxieties, his concern to exercise "consideration" as regards his family, even the urgency he feels to catch the next train to work – all are precisely delineated. But the *meaning* of the central image of the text – his transformation – remains undetermined precisely because any fixity of outline which would attempt to define the openness of his new "identity" within the imaginary realm, that is, by imposing realist categories upon the fantastic, would necessarily falsify it. Consequently Kafka sketches around this

---

[42] For this perspective on the notion of identity and signification (and also for the formulation "semiotic excess and semantic vacuity" which I have taken out of its original context in this article) I am indebted to Rosemary Jackson. See *Fantasy*, 41.

[43] "Did he really want his room, warm and comfortably fitted with inherited furniture to be turned into a den, albeit one in which he could crawl about unhindered in all directions, but at the cost of leaving behind completely his human past?" ("Hatte er wirklich Lust, das warme, mit ererbten Möbeln gemütlich ausgestattete Zimmer in eine Höhle verwandeln zu lassen, in der er dann freilich nach allen Richtungen ungestört würde kriechen können, jedoch auch unter gleichzeitigem schnellen, gänzlichen Vergessen seiner menschlichen Vergangenheit?") *Die Verwandlung*, 85.

semantic vacuity, describes in detail the family's various responses and Gregor's own reactions to this event but – typical of the expressionist avant-garde's poetics of duplicity – ultimately does no more than offer us a photograph of the imaginary: an image of an open door and a darkened room.

From the perspective of an aesthetics of reception this interaction of antagonistic signifying discourses and verbal-ideological systems in Kafka's text is particularly important. For although that which remains hidden from us in our everyday reality or which is excluded from our normal worldview may resist representation, it can nevertheless become the object of experience via the exploratory medium of literary fictionality. And it is an important counter-discursive function of the fantastic, and in particular the strategy of semantic vacuity, to facilitate the attempt to account for the unrepresentable. For via the dramatization of subjectivity, that dialogical attitude towards representation and interpretation which is subversive of conventionally realist notions of identity similarly takes on the deconstructive function similar to "epistemological criticism" ("Erkenntniskritik"), of undermining even our most private and concealed notions of selfhood. As a "core-fantasy," the narrative structure of Gregor's boundary-crossing or "Entgrenzung" encourages the audience to invest some of their own fantasies and experiences in it, and thereby encourages them to experience ironically and from a distance that which would ordinarily remain invisible to them in their everyday life: their own everyday norms, conventions and those "realistic attitudes" which, as in Gregor Samsa's case, are made to appear capable of precipitating similar existential dilemmas and falsehoods.

Through its thematization of the transformed self as Other, the text puts fictional brackets around subjectivity itself, so that it may be experienced in various forms (which in "reality" would otherwise remain inaccessible) and so that the conventional and closed concept of subjectivity may be opened to further reflection. And typical of the expressionist avant-garde's duplicitous poetics – that is, the dreamlike mode of representation which reveals and conceals at the same moment – in taking the form of a semantic vacuum or photograph of the Imaginary it then produces a curious effect: it resists closure but simultaneously attracts unending semantic determinations and interpretations by the reader.

In conclusion we can see that the arrival of Kafka's work at the end-point of conventional realist representation (in Lukacs' sense of the term) marks the beginning of an avant-garde poetics of counter-discourse. For where the limits of conventional realist representation and of the organic sense of totality are reached, it turns instead to the creation of structures such as the semantic vacuum. These progressive counter-discourses undermine the monological tendencies of realism to grasp the world as unproblematically comprehensible and to exclude as unreal whatever resists its dominant discourse, and instead they throw the recipients back upon themselves and their own interpretative devices. Similarly although in Kafka's work the realistic details may not add up to form a continuous and overall context or "world" – the traditional realistic heterocosm – they nevertheless reveal an interconnection and underlying structure – analogous to the structure of "reality" – through their relationship to the central semantic vacuum of the text (the "insect," "castle," "trial" etc.). These vacuums, although by no means "allegorical" in the sense of referring to a concrete signified nevertheless display an allegorical structure which provokes and encourages semantic closure. This open-ended structure is such however, that it both stimulates semantic acts but at the same time fails to valorize any single interpretation, so that the ensuing experience of hermeneutical helplessness (shared by reader and protagonist alike) contrasts radically with the typical demands for absolute meaning by those "average" human beings who are the protagonists in Kafka's texts. Their self-assured stance and realistic attitude are also made to appear uncomfortably close to the reader's own realistic norms and rationalistic expectations.[44] And it is precisely this function of bringing into co-presence these two mutually contradictory worldviews or "verbal-ideological systems"[45] – the approach typified by the rationalistic demand for absolute comprehensibility and a realistic "grasp" of the world on the one hand, and on the other a fantastic awareness of the limits of this realistic-rational principle – which characterizes both Kafka's writing and

---

[44] This effect of self-ironization which brings out the reader's own dispositions has been examined in detail by Wolfgang Iser. See especially chapter 6 of *Der Akt des Lesens* (Munich: Fink, 1976).

[45] Bakhtin, *The Dialogic Imagination*, 371.

his reader's self-dramatization through the medium of literary fictionality.

Thus it is through this impossible literary photograph of the Imaginary, the attempt to exert pressure upon the real in order to gesture towards that which resists representation, that a process of performative reception is initiated by which the excluded may be made the object of experience. Rather than photographing a representable object "in order to scare it out of one's consciousness" ("um sie aus dem Sinn zu verscheuchen") that is, in order to define, fix and close the object to further acts of interpretation, Kafka exercises the anti-mimetic art of "closing one's eyes." And it is by this method that the paradoxical is achieved: the projection of the reader into an unknown and imaginary realm, which is his own life.[46]

[46] My thanks go to Prof. Wolfgang Iser who offered invaluable criticisms regarding an earlier version of parts of this chapter (published in *DVjs* 65.2 (1991): 304–17), and to Prof. Walter H. Sokel who first suggested its theme.

❖❖❖❖❖❖❖❖❖❖❖❖❖❖❖❖❖❖❖❖❖❖❖❖❖❖❖❖❖❖❖❖❖❖❖❖❖❖❖❖❖❖❖❖❖

# 6

# Weimar silent film and expressionism: representational instability and oppositional discourse in *The Cabinet of Dr. Caligari*

❖❖❖❖❖❖❖❖❖❖❖❖❖❖❖❖❖❖❖❖❖❖❖❖❖❖❖❖❖❖❖❖❖❖❖❖❖❖❖❖❖❖❖❖❖

## Carnival desire: representation and discourse

In the preceding chapters I have described expressionism's avant-garde function in terms of its creation of a variety of oppositional discourses. As we saw in chapter 2, these radical discourses are characterized not so much by their adoption of a pragmatically "revolutionary" or political mode of criticism, as rather by the attempt to inscribe a "rebellious" openness into its forms which destabilizes the image and – in contrast to the conventional organic work – denies the reader any sense of cognitive fixity and conceptual closure. This turns out to be a highly appropriate response, given that the authority of the "classical" modes of representation correspondingly lies not so much in the *explicitly* ideological character of their depiction of events, objects and characters but rather in another dimension entirely. It is ingrained in the very structure of the representational system itself as a means of organizing the recipient's experience. For the almost imperceptible and unchallenged air of authority in classical representation derives from the peculiarly deceptive nature of its construction: it creates a unitary organization of narration, signification, and discourse, and prevails upon the reader or spectator to conform to its power-structure and to enjoy vicariously the sense of coherence, omniscience and mastery it engenders, while at the same time disguising itself as a transparent and "objective" window on the world.

Like the historical avant-garde, expressionism's oppositional discourses consequently set about dismantling this illusory authority by targeting this deception and deconstructing the conventions and values underlying classical representation's organization of experience. Instead of presenting reality in a form which can be coherently "grasped" expressionism's discursive organization is now characterized by its fundamental instability and by its problematization of conceptual mastery. If the Wilhelmine period is marked by anomie, by a deep sense of epistemological and cosmological crisis, then rather than attempting to produce an illusory sense of control and stability (for example either by conservatively reproducing the familiar external appearance of things with an exact and stabilizing verisimilitude, or conversely by asserting aesthetic control through escaping into utopianism and sublimation) the expressionist avant-garde "tears open still further" (as Bloch says) any ideological facade which would attempt to order experience by giving it an aura of organic wholeness or a lifelike gloss – the process Lukacs termed "covering over."

In this respect expressionism's discourses of protest also take account of the deficits of previous forms of progressive art. For example it avoids the naturalist movement's significant failure to balance its political tendency ("Tendenz") with its technique ("Technik") – to urge change at the level of content, while as a formal system of representation uncritically reproducing (and so substantiating) both the appearance of the status quo and the rationalist conceptions which underpin it. Consequently rather than merely targeting realism's various conventions and outward forms (for example by producing a set of anti-illusionist techniques in direct opposition to it), expressionism's oppositional discourses operate at a different level: they deconstruct the ideological dimension of the conventional system of representation itself, namely its central principle of rationalism and the unshakable positivism of its belief in empirical, knowable forms of truth. The expressionist counter-discourses embody instead an alternative logic of representation with a narrative composition and a mode of constructing reality in which the dominant discourses of time, space and causality, identity and difference are fundamentally destabilized in direct proportion to the anomic crisis of the period.

Rather than *representing* an unstable reality then these counter-discourses simulate the structure of experience as disjointed and ambiguous: their mode of representation does not merely *depict* a crisis concerning the integrity of cognition and of phenomena, but demonstrates that it is itself marked as a formal system by duplicity and ambiguity. In direct contrast to the classical system of realism the overwhelming sense of "indecidability" embodied in these oppositional discourses responds to a pronounced *lack* of epistemological authority in mastering phenomena and discerning identities. One can point to no clearer illustration of this anti-rationalist sentiment in expressionism than its fantastic films and in particular a "founding text" *The Cabinet of Dr. Caligari.*

## The indecidable and the uncanny: *Caligari*

Following in the steps of Siegfried Kracauer's analysis of *The Cabinet of Dr. Caligari* (Robert Wiene, 1919), recent discussions of the film have tended to focus on the vexed problem of its frame-structure.[1] For the main tale, concerning a mad doctor who uses his malevolent authority and hypnotic power over a somnambulist to disrupt the happiness of the young protagonist Francis and his "fiancée" Jane, is told explicitly as a narrative by Francis to a companion. With the close of this framed tale, there is a critical reversal of roles. Francis is revealed to have been telling the story as the inmate of an asylum, while its kindly director – whom Francis has accused of being the alter ego of Caligari (and who does indeed bear a striking physical resemblance to the evil doctor) – claims that he understands at last the aetiology of his patient's complaint and that he knows how to cure him.

The framing structure – dominated by the benevolent director – literally "incarcerates" both Francis and his story, and so constitutes for Kracauer an act of closure valorizing authority and imposing a conservative and optimistic meaning upon the anti-

---

[1] Siegfried Kracauer, *From Caligari to Hitler: A Psychological History of the German Film* (Princeton: Princeton University Press, 1947), 62–76; Marc Silberman, "Industry, Text and Ideology in Expressionist Film," *Passion and Rebellion. The Expressionist Heritage,* ed. Stephen Eric Bronner and Douglas Kellner (South Hadley, MA: J.F. Bergin, 1983), 374–383; Thomas Elsaesser, "Film History and Visual Pleasure: Weimar Cinema," *Cinema History/ Cinema Practices,* ed. Patricia Mellencamp and Philip Rosen, The American Film Institute Monograph Series, Vol. 4 (Frederick, MD: University Publications of America, 1984), 47–84 (esp. 59–65); Noel Carroll, "The Cabinet of Dr. Kracauer," *Millenium Film Journal* 1. 2 (1978): 77–85. Parts of the present section were originally published in *Germanic Review* LXVI.1 (1991): 48–56.

authoritarian nature of Francis' narrative. Kracauer sees this as a perversion of the non-conformist message of the original screenplay by Carl Meyer and Hans Janowitz.[2] The argument then is that the frame-structure has the effect of turning the main body of the story into the mere illusion of a madman and so takes on the reactionary function of interiorizing the events so that they appear to be taking place merely within an internal or psychological landscape without reference to a "real" world beyond.

Against Kracauer's position I would like to argue in this chapter that the psychological and representational structure in *Caligari* is characterized instead by a particular "logic" of perception which cloaks identities and phenomena in ambiguity, and by a corresponding tendency towards the creation of doubles, double-meaning and duplicity, which is subversive of precisely the kind of conventional rationality purporting to offer a clear-cut distinction between figures and between events. I will argue that it is this conventionally rationalistic understanding of the film's narrative and representational organization – which for example Kracauer relies upon when he speaks both of the transformation of the film's "revolutionary" message "into a conformist one" (67) and of the way in which the rational "framing" reality overlays and contains the world within the frame – which the film's counter-discursive organization sets out to deconstruct.

In his work on Weimar cinema Thomas Elsaesser has usefully invoked an interpretative framework with a direct bearing on the issues of doubling and repetition so common in early German silent cinema and particularly in *Caligari*: Samuel Weber's analysis of the "uncanny" in E. T. A. Hoffmann's "The Sand Man."[3]

[2] Interestingly, an early draft of the original screenplay, recently discovered and now housed in the Stiftung Deutsche Kinemathek in Berlin, reveals a frame of a rather less than "progressive" nature than that envisaged by Kracauer. It appears that Mayer and Janowitz had intended the story to be told by Francis as a man now happily married for some years to Jane. With the rather conventional happy-end situated thus at the very beginning of the narrative and so offering a reassuring foundation and stable resolution for the nightmarish tale, any claims for a progressive intention such as Kracauer imputes, would appear to evaporate. See S. S. Prawer, *Caligari's Children: The Film as Tale of Terror* (Oxford: Oxford University Press, 1980), esp. 168; also Michael Minden, "Politics and the Silent Cinema: *The Cabinet of Dr. Caligari* and *Battleship Potemkin*," *Visions and Blueprints: Avant-Garde Culture and Radical Politics in Early Twentieth-Century Europe*, ed. E. Timms and P. Collier (Manchester: Manchester University Press, 1988), 288–306 (esp. 288–289).

[3] See Samuel Weber, "The Sideshow, or: Remarks on a Canny Moment," *Modern Language Notes* 88 (1973): 1102–1133.

Weber explores the uncanny as an experiential structure marked by the persistent doubling of characters and by the repetition of occurrences, and linked to a "crisis of perception and phenomenality": the inability to distinguish clear and fixed identities and events. Weber maintains that "repetition, duplication, recurrence are inherently ambiguous, even ambivalent processes: they seem to confirm, even to *increase* the 'original' identity, and yet even more they *crease* it as its problematical and paradoxical precondition." Weber associates the peculiar doubling or "splitting" of figures and the duplication of similar events in the narrative with a "repressed or (half-) overcome narcissism" (1114). Consequently such doublings and repetitions are marked by a darker side. Like the figure of the double – which in Otto Rank's formulation (of 1914 and 1925) originally emerges as the narcissistic attempt to secure one's survival against a threat to selfhood by duplicating the self – these multiplications then come to betoken not life but rather the threat against it.[4] Thus rather than *confirming* the identity and unity of the figures and events through reiteration, the structure of recurrence and multiplication which marks the narrative organization takes on a duplicitous function: it reveals instead their non-identity, their split and doubled nature or "decenteredness." And since they now appear to belong to a seemingly infinite series of confusing alternatives and duplicates the structure of duplication comes to be linked furthermore to a characteristic "crisis of perception."

What is "uncanny" for Weber about such texts then is "a certain indecidability which affects and infects representations, motifs, themes and situations . . . " (1132), in other words precisely that form of representational duplicity which also characterizes expressionism's typically avant-garde deformation of clear-cut modes of perception and its subversion of authoritative forms of rationality. As a result a typically expressionist strategy emerges: the text produces a dreamlike psychological constellation of figures and a repetitious structure of representation in which the unique identity of figures and actions is replaced by their mutual displacement, permutation and infinite variability. And as is often

---

[4] Otto Rank, "Der Doppelgänger," *Imago* III (1914); *Der Doppelgänger, eine psychoanalytische Studie* (Leipzig, 1925), trans. as *The Double: A Psychoanalytic Study*, trans. and ed. H. Tucker, Jr. (Chapel Hill: University of North Carolina Press, 1971).

the case in expressionism this indecidability – as the principle around which the text is structured – becomes the means of dramatizing this fundamental state of epistemological crisis. Thus the "crisis of perception," of "corporeal unity" and of "phenomenality" associated with the experience of being unable to grasp identities becomes a means of destabilizing and questioning those authoritative and rationalist constructs at the center of dominant discourse and classic realism which have been disguised as "natural."

It is this sense of crisis and structural ambiguity which, at the level of narration, characterization and *mise-en-scène* shares that dreamlike form of "representational instability" (such as the duplication of figures and the repetition of important events) and which typifies the film *Caligari* as expressionist. Various acts of murder, seduction, voyeurism and incarceration recur as "primary fantasies" (frequently at the characters' bedside and in association with their dreams); while many of the figures, as we shall see, appear to be strangely linked to each other either as doubles or split-selves (such as the "good" and "bad" doctor-figures embodied by Caligari, or the two rivals for Jane's love, Francis and Alan). In fact it is almost as if the entire narrative were organized – as in a dream – according to a narcissistic associative structure.

It is this dreamlike recurrence of events and dis-placement of identities which characterizes *Caligari* – like Hoffmann's classic fantasy "The Sand Man" (which is Weber's starting point) – as belonging to the category of the uncanny, the duplicitous and the "indecidable." This kind of associative oneiric structure necessarily calls into question any conventionally rationalistic approach which, like Kracauer's, would attempt to view the various figures, events and different levels of narration in the text as separate entities. Instead, its fundamental instability and duplicity contaminates the film's representational structure and, typical of the expressionist avant-garde's purposeful disruptions and deconstructions interrogates the typically rationalistic conventions of classical narrative such as its clear distinctions between "inside" and "outside," "reality" and "hallucination," "consciousness" and "dream."

## Indecidability: sleep and the displacement of desire

Let us begin by examining the various means by which the representational structure is destabilized by this "indecidability" or "duplicity." The film's characteristic ambiguity is foregrounded even in its title. The obvious meaning of the "Kabinett" is a form of spectacle, the analogy being to a cabinet as a special room (in a museum for example) which houses a collection. Additionally, however, there are two important secondary connotations of the word. Although overlooked by most film-historians,[5] it is significant that the original title – as can also be seen in original prints of the film or of its posters – adopts the French or English spelling, "Cabinet," rather than "Kabinett."[6] With the alternative spelling a prior meaning of the word "cabinet" surfaces – still retained in French – as the practice or office of a professional person, in this case the "surgery" of a doctor. Simultaneously however, the term contains in both French and German the sense – especially interesting in the light of the medical connotation and the links to hypnotism and psychoanalysis – of a *side-room*, or adjacent space.

Given the dual identity of the Caligari figure the divergent connotations of the title are highly appropriate. For through the title the character is associated both with the role of the psychiatrist and his official "scientific" and rationalist practice (as the doctor at the asylum), but also with that of the shady huckster of the "sideshow." In this latter role his arts (such as hypnotism and the "tricks" performed by his assistant) belong to a field *adjacent* to the main area of science,[7] functioning in other words as a kind of "sideline."[8]

[5] An exception here is John D. Barlow, *German Expressionist Film* (Boston: Twayne, 1982).

[6] The original posters are shown in Minden, "Politics and the Silent Cinema" and Barlow, *German Expressionist Film*.

[7] As such the spectacular feats of Caligari and Cesare are doubly linked to psychoanalysis and the adjacent areas of its practice. Like the earliest forms and prefigurations of psychoanalysis as a marginal medical science, such as mesmerism or even the work of Freud's teacher Charcot, they are also associated with the suspicion of charlatanism.

[8] I employ the terms "sideshow" and "sideline" in conscious allusion to Samuel Weber's notion of the uncanny (as that which is "off-beat, off-side, and far-out, abseits . . .") and in association with the notion of "duplicity." Like the uncanny this is a marginalized phenomenon which achieves its results similarly by indirection and oblique means, since the regular and open modes of operation and communication remain closed to it. See "The Sideshow, or: Remarks on a Canny Moment," 1109.

At the same time these sideshow feats are similarly associated not only with a "sideline" of science, namely psychoanalysis, but also with its its prime area of investigation, the psychological "Nebenzimmer" (or "side-room") of sleep, desire and the unconscious. The various dark "practices" and strange goings-on which are linked in the film to the characters' nocturnal life, form a suggestive constellation of meanings around the theme of sleep and desire – the "nightlife" of the rational self – where sleep, like the uncanny and its associated crisis of perception, is instrumental both in concealing, and simultaneously *revealing* (albeit in a duplicitous and displaced form) the identity and the agency of desire. It becomes significant for example that the murder of the protagonist's best friend Alan is associated with sleep (and thus with an "indecidable" realm) since it occurs at his bedside as a dreamlike shadow-play, hinting at, but finally withholding the identity of the agent involved. Similarly although the perpetrator of Jane's abduction is clearly the sleep-walker Cesare, in a sense he is not really the one "in authority" and in control – as his name (Caesar) ironically suggests. Rather he is merely the agent of others' desires: firstly and most obviously he plays out the desires of Caligari, for whom he has already served as a lure to arouse Jane's specular/erotic interest; secondly, Cesare may also dramatize Jane's own desires and anxieties – or at least a male projection of passive female desire/anxiety – in response to that earlier scene, since the "seduction" occurs while she herself is asleep (and so may be seen as succumbing to it through her own dreams). The kidnap also involves a further disguise or displacement of identity since it occurs while those who are supposed to be keeping a "conscious" eye on the suspect are deceived by yet another false self: Cesare's effigy and double, which lies "sleeping" in his cabinet.

As in a dream there is thus always a displacement involved: either in the form of a transference (or shifting) of the origin or "subject" of desire between what appeared at first to be two separate and autonomous figures (Caligari–Cesare), or as a covering-up or camouflaging of intentions by indirection and the doubling of identity. In this way the themes of sleep and the unconscious are coded in the film as part of a dark and oblique power, an alternative to rational authority, through which transgressive desires are fulfilled by indirect means, and through which any clear rationalist notions of causality or identity are subverted. Sleep is then the central metaphor for this peculiar slippage between various characters and for the "crisis of perception" which afflicts the film with its chronic "indecidability": its inability to discern identities and events. Sleep thus becomes the thematic "correlative" of the abstract representational principle of epistemological instability which characterizes *Caligari* as a whole.

## The grotesque as counter-discourse: desublimation and the avant-garde

With the fantastic as its central element the text is clearly related not only to the expressionist avant-garde's deconstruction of dominant rationalist notions of identity, difference and causality, but is linked more generally to the similarly disjunctive mode of the "grotesque." As Wolfgang Kayser has shown, the grotesque is most readily understood as "one pole of a tension whose opposite pole is constituted by the sublime."[9] For whereas the sublime "guides our view towards a loftier, supernatural world, the ridiculously distorted and monstrously horrible ingredients of the grotesque point to an inhuman, nocturnal and abysmal realm" (58). The grotesque consequently becomes an important strategy of desublimation and de-aestheticization in expressionism. According to Kayser, the grotesque always occurs in conjunction with a state of anomie, responding to a perceived lack of meaning and order in the world. Like the expressionist avant-garde it responds to disorder not by pointing by means of an uplifting and ennobling form of art to an ideal realm of harmony beyond, but by laying bare the world's underlying madness and irrationality – for example through the use of excessive and de-aestheticizing forms such as caricature and exaggeration (61) which subject the familiar and recognizable world to further estrangement (184).

The grotesque not only shakes the reader's confidence in his or her own world view (60) but the very foundation of ordinary truths and values, so that the "categories which apply to our world view become inapplicable" (185). Thus true to the period of

---

[9] Wolfgang Kayser, *The Grotesque in Art and Literature*, trans. U. Weisstein (1963; New York: Columbia University Press, 1981), 58.

epistemological and cosmological crisis in which it emerges, the grotesque typically undermines the dominant modes of rational thought and discourse. For it

questions the validity of the anthropological and the relevance of the scientific concepts underlying the syntheses of the nineteenth century. The various forms of the grotesque are the most obvious and pronounced contradictions of any kind of rationalism and any systematic use of thought. (188)

As we shall see in *Caligari*, this interrogation of the norms of systematic and rationalist thought is so extreme that even when the grotesque actively encourages the reader "to seek an explanation within the limits of verisimilitude" (75) it inevitably frustrates the logical search for meaning within the parameters of that representational system.

In the case of the expressionist avant-garde's use of the grotesque this duplicitous strategy of simultaneous encouragement and frustration is even more pronounced. Indeed it is worth appending to Kayser's theory the observation that in expressionism – as can readily be seen in the case of Kafka's expressionist works for example – the dynamic of the grotesque text often rests upon a central contradiction in which it traps both its protagonist and its interpreter alike: at one level, in its own representational structure, it is organized according to a set of rationalist values and pragmatic-realist attitudes which it appears to put forward as a valid method of orientation and meaning, while at another level, as a form of dialogical counter-discourse it works at completely discrediting these same values. In other words the grotesque becomes an intrusive and disruptive element within the rationalist system, a source of irritation and unresolvable hermeneutical contradictions. For since the grotesque is inscribed into the very structure of the text as an alienating and anti-rationalist element it inevitably short-circuits the attempt to impose rationalist solutions and meanings upon it. Consequently by shifting them into strange and unfamiliar territory the text defamiliarizes not only prevailing conventions and norms, but also its own meaning, which remains suspended within this same realm of the alienated and the inexplicable.

In *Caligari* it is the theme of sleep by which this important sense of the grotesque and the abysmal enters into the text and defamiliarizes certain key elements of the narrative. Like the grotesque sleep becomes the metaphor for an alien and impersonal force opposed to rationalism, the means by which the dichotomy between orthodox science and its marginal and occult sidelines is foregrounded. This division between "good" and "bad" science, and between rationality and its Other which is established in this founding text of Weimar cinema runs not only through this film but, it may be argued, constitutes a defining feature in many Expressionist or Weimar silent films (such as *Metropolis, Nosferatu, The Golem, Dr. Mabuse* and *Waxworks*). And it is through this dichotomy that modernity's uneasy relationship to technology, science and "administrative reason" is explored and played out against earlier forms of rationality.

It is sleep which is instrumental in revealing the double nature of Caligari's sideshow activity as both dark science and cheap spectacle. For Caligari attempts to instrumentalize sleep, that is, to harness and manipulate the power of dreams and the unconscious directly in the cause of a marginally rationalist endeavor. For example, the dreamer Cesare is made a kind of *medium*, literally the mid-point between two worlds: in his trance he is made to interpret the future; at the same time he is also transformed into the occult medium by which the murderous or erotic desires of another are discerned and fulfilled. The pseudo-scientific rationale for Caligari's experiments with sleep and the somnambulist is the attempt to prove the "Caligari theory." This theory concerns the horrifying notion – "horrifying" again as an anxiety responding to the loss of *rational* control – that while asleep a person may be capable of committing acts which his waking self would shrink from. Yet although the premise of Caligari's experiment is supposed to be the scientist's manipulation of the *sleeper*, it is the doctor – very much in the vein of the "mad scientist" whose rationality has turned against him and taken him over – who has apparently become obsessed and who loses control.

Moreover alongside certain intended results, the experiment also produces more notably a series of indirect and unintended irrational "side-effects." For example, typical of the film's problematization of the notions of agency and cause as "indecidable" categories, there are a series of mysterious and unexplained murders (crimes for which the narrative later implicates Cesare).

These are perpetrated both on the town clerk and on Francis' friend Alan, and as such are obviously understood more readily as fulfilling by displacement the desires of other "dreamers": not only the showman Caligari's desire for revenge on the bureaucrat who insulted him, but also Francis' unspoken and unspeakable rivalry towards his friend Alan with regard to their competing love for Jane. In this respect, it is as if the dreams of various sleepers are not distinct, but are linked together through the text's peculiar logic of displacement, repetition and recurrence – just as the identities of the figures themselves appear intertwined.

Dream thus resists restriction to the identity of a single dreamer. It fails to adhere to the rationally definable parameters of the doctor's experiment, even turning against the one who attempts to control it. For example, the experiment with the sleeper leads firstly to Cesare's death and to Caligari's breakdown at the sight of the lifeless body. And secondly, the "true" identity of Caligari and the origins of his obsession with his dark art are discovered by the other doctors at the asylum – as in a psychoanalytic scene on the couch – as they sift through his "private materials" and "memoirs" while he sleeps. The rationalism of Caligari's attempt to instrumentalize sleep and bring it under rational control – the power which Caligari employs through Cesare in the cause of his "science" – thus itself returns to haunt Caligari in uncanny, indecidable and irrational form.

## The interaction between realism and the fantastic: Cesare and semantic vacuity

The dichotomy between conscious and scientific practice on the one hand, and unconscious and unspeakable forces of resistance on the other recalls the dichotomy which frequently occurs not only in the grotesque but also in the related mode of the fantastic, a tradition with which so much of the history of German silent cinema and especially *Caligari* is obviously linked.[10] For paradigmatically in the fantastic the attempt to control or to account logically for that which appears unmasterable or unspeakable frequently produces a counterreaction, an overpowering eruption

[10] Thomas Elsaesser describes the relation of the fantastic to Weimar cinema in his important essay "Social Mobility and the Fantastic: German Silent Cinema," *Wide Angle* 5. 2 (1982): 14–25.

of irrational and scientifically indeterminable forces. In a manner reminiscent of Bakhtin's description of the "carnival" as a site for the wild eruption of previously repressed and marginalized desires, this upsurge of the occult turns the world upside-down, inverting the hierarchy between the rational and the irrational, and eliciting a revolt against the realm of established authority.[11]

The same resistance to rational mastery and interpretative "framing" also emerges at the level of the narration. As Thomas Elsaesser has suggested, the fantastic or magical moments in such tales frequently arise at precisely the point where one would expect the beginnings of a rational investigation of the problematics described by the narrative.[12] Instead, any such logical investigation is interrupted or blocked by the intervention of the fantastic which recasts the whole train of events from its counter-rationalist perspective, disguising them or attributing them to the influence of supernatural forces.

The emergence of the fantastic as a means of interrupting rational explanation and deferring a logical investigation turns out to be the structure on which the whole narrative of *Caligari* is based. For example in the opening scene the specter of Jane in her trancelike state demands an explanation, which Francis' tale (the framed narrative) initially purports to provide. However this attempt at a rational explanation is itself displaced by a new problematic introduced in Francis' tale, namely the fantastic murders it describes. Although the framed narrative hints at an explanation (encouraging the conclusion that Cesare has perpetrated the crimes while under the hypnotic control of Caligari) this "explanation" is in turn displaced by the renewed intrusion of the fantastic – the revelation of Francis' "madness" – which shifts the narrative yet again to a new level, at which the resolution of the previous problematic of the murders now becomes moot. If this chain of deferred and displaced explanations produces any hard and fast result at all, it is that the very notion of "rational explanation" is itself called into question, so that the apparent stability that returns at the end of the film with the authority of the kindly doctor (and his promise to "cure" Francis) can only be regarded

---

[11] A useful collection of Bakhtin's writings on carnival is to be found in the German edition: Mikhail Bachtin, *Literatur und Karneval: Zur Romantheorie und Lachkultur*, trans. Alexander Kaempfe (Munich, 1969). See also Jackson, *Fantasy: The Literature of Subversion, passim.*    [12] Elsaesser, "Social Mobility," esp. 18.

with the greatest scepticism. As with the grotesque, the fantastic structure of the text thus ensures that rationality as a mode of investigation and interpretation is itself suspended and the attempt to impose meaning is derailed, with the result that the narrative remains within the sphere of the inexplicable.

A further example of the manner in which the fantastic destabilizes the very notion of "rational explanation" is Caligari's confrontation with the authoritarianism of the town-clerk. This marks a specific narrative problem to be negotiated: Caligari's failure to "signify" within the bourgeois world and retain an identity in the realm administered by the apparatus of officialdom. The ridiculing of Caligari's application for a permit for the fun-fair concession – which would "legitimize" both the sideshow as well as his marginal science, and which, metaphorically, would bring the realm of carnival and desire into the "official" public sphere – thus presents a conflict or crisis to be overcome in the narrative. However, after Caligari skulks away from the clerk's office this aspect of the plot is not pursued further, and the sideshow goes on without the problem being dealt with on a "rational" level. Instead, it is resolved magically – as in a wish-fulfillment – by the fantastic coincidence of the town-clerk's mysterious murder. In this way, the fantastic – as the embodiment of that which subverts the principle of science and rationality – intervenes to suspend any development of the narrative along logical lines, interposing instead the dark and irrational power centered on the mysterious Caligari. The power he embodies blocks a rational investigation. Thus his irrational authority resists the imposition of quotidian logic and administrative authority and so becomes the primary embodiment of the duplicitous force contaminating the entire text.

Like rationality the notions of reality and identity are also affected by the "crisis of phenomenality" and are subject to a similar destabilizing process which resists fixity and logical "framing." They too are made fantastic as if in explicit opposition to the conventional parameters of realist narrative. Most notable in this regard is the figure of Cesare, whose only clear identity-trait is that of absolute ambiguity: he is simultaneously passive and active, innocent and evil, and peculiarly androgynous; and in his coffin-like cabinet he appears neither clearly alive nor dead, awake nor asleep. Constantly framed like a picture by the black box he inhabits, it is his status as a mere image or representation which is foregrounded, rather than his existence as an autonomous character. But more than this, he is not so much an independent figure in his own right as a kind of neutral vehicle or representational medium for wish-fulfillment and fantasized desire, a semantic vacuum to be filled with meanings pertaining to other characters.

Cesare's peculiar semantic function is highlighted by the filmic organization of that scene in which we first encounter him – as a sideshow attraction, waking, according to Caligari's explanation, after twenty-five years of sleep. A series of shots heighten the effect of this unveiling. Positioned similarly to the sideshow audience, we are first shown the outside of Caligari's tent, which Caligari then opens with a flourish for the spectators. On the stage a curtain too is now pulled aside to reveal Cesare's upright cabinet. This in turn is opened dramatically to reveal the sleeping Cesare. The very theatricality of this performance and its filmic presentation already anticipate the abiding sense of Cesare as a mere spectacle and as the "empty" object of the spectator's voyeurism, in other words as a mere "semantic vacuum," permanently subjected to the projection of meanings by others yet without an innate "identity." Consequently, when the last covers are drawn aside and Cesare opens his eyes, this ultimate disclosure leads not to the revelation of any innate personality in the waking figure.[13] The series of unveilings does not produce the revelation of identity, but, true to the text's principle of "indecidability" ultimately withholds the sense of having grasped and fixed the character, as if the unveilings were instead a mark of the infinite process of deferral or displacement of identity along a chain of such empty theatrical roles and appearances.

Since Cesare "comes to life" as a kind of theatrical prop, his rebirth before the audience as a waking "subject" is clearly made subservient to the fact that he is simultaneously re-animated or re-created only as the *object* of the spectator's gaze. In this sense his new life becomes merely a continuation of his deathlike sleep and of his existence as a non-identity: he is the lifeless object of the

---

[13] Michael Minden in "Politics and the Silent Cinema" has described this scene along similar lines, yet with rather different conclusions. He sees it as a reenactment of the audience's "own hypnotised enslavement to the lure of the camera" (294).

viewing subject and a function of another's dreaming, a mere representation or "imaginary signifier"[14] without a real identity or presence. Thus the successive unveilings and acts of disclosure which the scenario rehearses reveal only the impossibility of a final revelation. He is caught in the eternal nightmare from which he cannot awaken: he fails to signify as an autonomous subject and is trapped in the role of a representational middle-man for the fantasy of the sideshow spectator.

Cesare's status as a semantic vacuum, as an empty vehicle for the imaginary is also mirrored by the characteristics of his "doubles," such as the lifeless effigy which serves as his substitute (and alibi) in the cabinet while he is off enacting the dreams and carrying out the desires of others; or the full-size, two-dimensional representation of the somnambulist which Caligari holds up and manipulates before the sideshow audience. Both are doubles which merely reproduce Cesare's status as a lifeless and empty signifier, which can come to life only vicariously as a function of the fantasy and of the gaze of others. His effigy for example only begins to take on meaning via the construction put upon it when Francis and the investigators spy on it voyeuristically through the window. Similarly the flattened, cut-out version of Cesare which the showman Caligari holds up and animates at the sideshow in order to stimulate the crowd's appetite for spectacle and visual gratification, and to arouse their curiosity to see the "real" thing is like a two-dimensional figure on a projection screen. And like the cinematic signifier it recalls, it emphasizes that it is only the *vehicle* for the imagination of the audience, which is responsible for filling it with life. In this way these doubles reinforce the idea that Cesare is simply an exhibited object, a mere semantic vacuum that is made to signify only as a consequence of the gaze of the other.

## Representational instability

Taken together, these forms of duplicity – the ambiguity of the figure of Cesare, the undermining of identity and events through various modes of doubling, displacement and repetition in the

---

[14] As a figure existing largely as a construct of the cinematic apparatus and within the imagination of the viewer, Cesare shares some of the essential features of Christian Metz' well-known film-theoretical model. See *The Imaginary Signifier*, 91–98.

narrative, as well as the numerous irrational interventions of fantastic or dreamlike coincidences – point to what, in conscious allusion to the narrative problematics connected by Weber to the crises of identity and phenomena, can be termed the general condition of "representational instability" within the film.[15] This instability appears to affect most aspects of its narration, its characterization, and its scenery as well as its codes of decor, costume, and make-up, all of which are marked – however unsystematically – by typically expressionist moments of excess: by the use of extreme forms, by distortion and by discontinuity.[16]

The opening shot of the framed sequence where Francis' tale begins to unfold – the curtain-raiser – anticipates the manner in which the film as a whole sustains this instability. With the initial iris-in, held for some seconds on the static and clearly two-dimensional painted image of the "Holstenwall" district in which the story is to take place, we are given anything other than the conventional opening "establishing shot" of classical film narrative (or its early cinematic equivalent). Rather than situating the scene, providing the context, and so creating the impression of a limitless and omniscient narration which will embrace the spectator in its illusion, the iris-in (here as throughout the film) serves as a kind of "dis-establishing shot": through the foregrounded restriction of the initial image to a limited visual space on the blacked-out screen – like the blinking of the cinematic "eye" which is responsible for organizing this image of the real – it makes the spectator aware of the act of representation itself, and thus of the conditions of mediation imposed upon his or her perception. As the iris opens, the effect of this act of unveiling – as in the case of Cesare's first unveiling – is again a paradoxical incarceration: rather than the sense of omniscience and visual control associated with classical narrative the spectator is made aware both of being enticed and "locked" into the narrative, and at the same time he or she perceives the representational constric-

---

[15] This notion of "representational instability" is developed productively by Patrice Petro in *Joyless Streets*, 21 and *passim*.

[16] An example of this stylistic inconsistency – itself a destabilizing factor – is that only certain of the characters (such as Caligari) are wearing outlandish costumes and exaggerated make-up – as if they represented the personified elements of the fantastic as opposed to the other, more realistic figures. Similarly as regards the set-design not all of the flats are distorted "expressionistically." The set for Jane's room for example is by contrast rather cozy and ordinary.

tions placed upon the viewing, foregrounded as they are by the obvious artificiality of the Holstenwall scene as a constructed and re-presented two-dimensional image.

Moreover this initial scene, as is the case with many others throughout the film, clearly lacks a precise and unambiguous "compositional center," an organizing principle by which the viewer can be directed to the obvious meaning, to a central figure or dominant narrative position which would enunciate the essential concerns of the tale. An example of this lack of center is that the film quite frequently resists the early cinematic equivalents of those conventions which position the spectator via the dominant male gaze. As Patrice Petro argues, the film displays a distinct "narrational instability" since it pointedly resists "the conventional logic of narrative editing [by which] we are . . . aligned with a masculine point of view." For example in the scene in which Cesare is "exposed" to Jane, her

originally active and investigating gaze is momentarily paralyzed by her look at the monster. On a narrative level, this freezing of Jane's look is meant to suggest that Cesare has mastered the woman through the sheer power of his gaze. Nevertheless what this scene also permits is a different structuring of point of view, since our perspective is no longer aligned with a single (male) character but is split between "the two objects of the cinema spectacle who encounter one another in this look – the woman and the monster.[17]

One might add to Petro's analysis the important point that Cesare's gaze, as we have seen, is by no means *consistently* active and dominating, and that given his androgyny and his peculiarly ambiguous ontological status, it is not even clearly "male." This heightens the effect of the film's unstable positioning of the viewer, since in the important scenes between these two marginalized figures – the woman and the monster – no central organizational position emerges. For the audience the cumulative effect of such scenes – with their disturbed identification and "split" positioning, their lack of narrative guides and their fantas-

[17] Patrice Petro, "The Woman, The Monster, and *The Cabinet of Dr. Caligari*," *"The Cabinet of Dr. Caligari": Texts, Contexts, Histories*, ed. Mike Budd (New Brunswick: Rutgers University Press, 1990), 212, citing Linda Williams, "When the Woman Looks," *Revision: Essays in Feminist Film Criticism*, ed. Doane, Mellencamp, Williams, (Frederick, MD: University Publications of America, 1984), 87.

tic deferral of rational explanation – is again to undermine the sense of stability and coherence usually required in order for the spectator to be able to lapse comfortably into the illusion of the film and into the reassuring embrace of its narrative structure.

## Expressionist poetics and *Caligari*: the visionary, the supplementary and Kant's "aesthetic idea"

The effect of this general condition of representational instability is perhaps most obvious with regard to the backdrops. The image of the Holstenwall district clearly sets up a disconcerting contradiction between the conventional intention of representing "reality" and the obvious artificiality of the image. Such irritations are frequently compounded in the film by the sense of the precariousness of the reality presented in the setting: the carousel of the fun-fair turns jerkily and perilously, while the acute angles of the "roofs" along which Cesare carries Jane are treacherous (if indeed these slopes represent roofs at all, since typically any emergent reality-effect that might provide a signpost or conceptual foothold for the audience too is always destabilized here in favor of a foregrounded sense of artifice). These discomforting aspects are then made even more disquieting by the extremity of the slanted perspectives of the backdrops and by the menacing and jagged painted patterns with which they are overlaid.[18]

This representational instability characteristic of the film's structuring of the real brings us back to its fundamental problematization of the notion of identity. For just as any firm sense of reality is undermined by the film's organization of the real in terms of a crisis of perception and phenomenality, so the corresponding notion of identity pertaining to the characterization of the figures is subject to the same strategy of destabilization. The identity of characters is not firmly anchored in a recognizable, mimetically re-presented world. Rather, the reality they inhabit is a visionary and preeminently psychological realm.

As a consequence Noel Carroll has even proposed that "Francis, Caligari and Cesare could be read respectively as the ego,

---

[18] Noel Carroll observes the "painted, knifelike shadows" and the "pointed angular shapes" throughout the film. See "The Cabinet of Dr. Kracauer" *Millenium Film Journal* 1.2 (1978): 77–85 (esp. 80–81).

super-ego and id . . ."[19] But however suggestive this reading may appear at first glance it does not fit the film's structure in as far as the proposal is based on the notion of a *centered* identity, in which these three figures would be the components that complete the psyche as a self-contained unity. Besides the incongruity of describing this aspect of the film in terms of an all too rationalist, clear-cut and "decidable" organization of subjectivity, the problem then arises as to how the other figures in the film would fit into this limited psychological structure.

Instead it would make for a more comprehensive interpretation to read the film's constellation of figures in terms of a "decentered" notion of subjectivity characterized by the slippage, multiplication or supplementation of the self. As we have seen Cesare for example exists less as an autonomous, realistic figure in his own right than as the external embodiment of the desires of others. His being thus takes on the functional or metaphorical quality typical of many expressionist characters. For he becomes what Walter Sokel terms an abstract or psychological "objective correlative" revealing those inner states in another character which would otherwise remain concealed (33). Now although this strategy of supplementation occurs in other literary movements and representational forms besides expressionism – Sokel develops his theory of the "correlative" for example from Flaubert – only in expressionism does it become the central structural principle underlying the entire composition, and only in expressionism is it developed to such a level of abstraction that the supplementary characters emerge, similar to dreamlike symbols, without any rational justification or "motivation" being provided for them by a pragmatic, realistic framework.

As we saw previously, this strategy of supplementation is intimately connected to what Sokel views as the center of the expressionist poetics: the development of a mode of artistic practice which pursues to an extreme Kant's notion of the "aesthetic idea." We should recall that Kant defines the latter as a "representation of the imagination which induces much thought, yet without the possibility of any definite thought whatever, i.e., *concept*, being adequate to it . . ." The aesthetic idea thus becomes a "substitute for logical presentation" which succeeds in "animating the mind"

[19] Carroll, "Dr. Kracauer," 78.

yet without being rendered "completely intelligible."[20] The dreamlike characters in many expressionist texts (particularly in *Caligari*) and their peculiarly "supplementary" relationships to one another share precisely this form of aesthetic (rather than rational) presentation: the structure of characterization reveals through its dreamlike and "indecidable" manner that which would remain concealed and inconceivable via conventional modes of rationality, and consequently also unrepresentable via realism's "logical presentation."

This preference for abstract forms and "aesthetic ideas" rather than "logical presentations" is not only at the center of expressionism's poetics but is also the key to its stance as an avant-garde and oppositional mode of discourse. Expressionism's characteristic sense of liberation from the need to render itself "completely intelligible" in logical modes lends itself to the creation of pointedly abstract and de-aestheticized forms. Thus rather than any isolatable critical "content," it is the very *form* of the expressionist work – in this case *Caligari's* structure of repetition, doubling and indecidability – which preempts the comforting sense of harmony, consolation or control still harbored for example by the conventional organic work.

At the same time, through these alternatives to conventional logic the expressionist avant-garde articulates its scepticism regarding the prevailing concepts of the rational and the scientific – the "dominant social discourses" at issue in the epistemological crises of the expressionist period – presenting them as part of the problem rather than the cure. As Sokel maintains, "expressionism, like dream, replaces intellectual analysis by direct visual presentation" (39). Consequently, expressionism does not resort to rationalism as the basis for a *critique* of rationalism nor does it make conventional representation account for a crisis concerning the inability to perceive and represent clear identities and phenomena. Instead it presents a dreamlike *vision*, which remains inscrutable, but which nevertheless embodies the "essence" of what is at stake, in this case the problem of rationality and identity. This is the sense in which *Caligari's* dreamlike structure of "indecidability" simulates (rather than representing or ana-

---

[20] Kant, *Critique of Aesthetic Judgment*, trans. J. C. Meredith (Oxford: Oxford University Press, 1982) Part II ("The Analytic of the Sublime"), §49: 175–178, cited by Sokel, *Writer in Extremis*, 10–11.

lyzing) the crisis of perception, phenomenality and identity which is its prime concern. For if this crisis is by nature beyond the reach of conceptual experience, then expressionism's visionary poetics accounts for it not by logical presentation or the depiction of its extraneous details and outward appearance. Instead, it presents a "vision" embodying the "essence" of the problematic or the "feel" of the situation.

In his celebrated essay of 1917, "Art as Technique," Victor Shklovsky observes that the purpose of art is to create "a special perception of the object – *it creates a "vision" of the object instead of serving as a means for knowing it.*"[21] As with its implementation of Kant's "aesthetic idea" expressionism's strategy of representation takes this principle to its logical extreme, and, to the exclusion of any realistic conventions or pragmatic representational consider-ations, creates a poetics of visionary abstraction. In 1917 Kasimir Edschmid's seminal talk on expressionism (to which we referred in chapter 4) describes the poetics of the movement in precisely these terms, emphasizing that the expressionist artist's "vision" overlooks the purely factual and representational in favor of the essential: "Now the chain of facts no longer exists: factories, houses, disease, whores, crying, hunger. Now there is just the vision of all this."[22] Consequently the determinate and individual qualities of characters recede while the "essence" they embody takes over: "The key component is transformed into the idea: not a thinking person, no: thought itself. Not two people embracing: no, the embrace itself" (49).[23]

This approach makes it clear that the relationship between expressionist poetics and the structuring principle behind *Caligari's* composition goes deeper than the mere attempt by the film merely to "quote expressionist decor and acting,"[24] to "in-strumentalize" expressionism,[25] or to employ it reductively as a representational code for simply conveying Francis' madness. Rather, the expressionist poetics of "vision" means that the text's

---

[21] Victor Shklovsky, "Art as Technique," *Russian Formalist Criticism*, 18. Emphasis in original

[22] "Nun gibt es nicht mehr die Kette der Tatsachen: Fabriken, Häuser, Krankheit, Huren, Geschrei und Hunger. Nun gibt es die Vision davon." Kasimir Ed-schmid, "Expressionismus in der Dichtung," *Die Neue Rundschau* 29. 1 (1918): 359–374. Rpt. *Dokumente und Manifeste*, 46.

[23] "Das Wichtigste gibt die Idee: nicht mehr ein Denkender, nein: das Denken. Nicht zwei Umschlungene: nein, die Umarmung selbst."

[24] Elsaesser, "Film History," 72.      [25] Budd, "Moments of *Caligari*," 26.

characters are determined by its logic as abstract "correlatives" or "supplementary" selves. According to this structure Cesare for example emerges as a concrete figure only in the most ambiguous and tenuous manner: his significance for the narrative remains highly indeterminate, since he appears only as a kind of "vision," as the embodiment or "objective correlative" of those desires and anxieties (notions linked to the "indecidable" themes of sleep, the irrational and the destabilization of identity) that remain unarticulated in others.[26]

Conventional notions of identity are destabilized by this radical – and typically expressionist – projection of subjectivity in terms of the mutual dependence and supplementation of separate figures. To take one central example of the way in which subjectivity is decentered by "correlative" figures we might re-examine Cesare's function as a medium for the dramatization of subjectivity and desire. As a "supplementary" self he dramatizes the most essential concerns of the characters to whom he is linked. In the case of Francis and his love for Jane, Cesare clearly acts out an Oedipal scenario on behalf of Francis: he both dispatches the rival Alan,[27] and with his indecision whether to obey the father and kill Jane, or pursue the "son's" own desire and keep her for himself, he dramatizes the son's Oedipal anxiety towards the father-figure's interventions or "prohibitions."[28]

As we have seen Cesare is equally important as a supplement *vis-à-vis* Caligari's identity, which, despite his menacing and seemingly omnipotent authority, is itself frequently presented in the film as being deeply unstable, strangely incomplete and in an

---

[26] This approach would go a long way towards describing the peculiar doubling which exists in the relationships between the other characters too. Francis and Alan might then be seen as two versions of a similar role, representing alternative ways in which the struggle for desire and the fight against an overbearing authority principle founder. Similarly the roles of Francis and Caligari are clearly interlocked ontologically and can scarcely be conceived of independently, as at the end of the film when their respective positions (as incarcerator and victim) are inverted. This identification of the two is also made clear cinematically by the doubling of identical set-ups, angles and decor where Francis is incarcerated.

[27] Elsaesser also views the figure of Alan in terms of an oedipal rivalry. See "Film History," 60.

[28] Like Hoffmann's Sand Man-figure, Caligari seems repeatedly to intervene in the "son's" love-affair, by reminding him (with the dominating stare of the patriarch) of his fears of not having completed the rebellion against the father's castrating gaze.

underlying state of crisis. For example, through the flashback motivated by his notebooks Caligari is initially portrayed as having experienced a "dark night of the soul" in which his obsession with an eleventh-century mountebank monk (who also kept a somnambulist) leads him in a state of Faustian desperation to adopt this powerful, alien image of the monk as a false self, displacing his own identity. In a typically expressionist scene, the extent of this internal crisis of Caligari's subjectivity is emphasized by being projected in words onto the very landscape through which he walks, with the phrase "You must become Caligari!" – the call to bolster his identity by adopting an even more powerful and authoritative persona – emerging as letters on the landscape as if in the form of an external injunction.[29] The advertising posters which were plastered around Berlin before *Caligari's* opening night bore the same injunction, encouraging its potential audience to "become" Caligari. Yet it is precisely the viewer's identification with Caligari and with the seductive sense of specular mastery embodied in his dominating male gaze – a spectator-position of illusory control central to the consumerist aesthetics of classical narrative film – which is precluded by the film's explicitly expressionist counter-discursive elements. For firstly the film delegates the gaze to Jane and Cesare so as to align the spectator with the "other" of the "masculine point of view." Secondly, Caligari as the bearer of the dominating gaze is himself later "framed" by being spied upon and so made the object of another's look, with the result that his hypnotic power to "frame" others and control their lives is in a sense turned back upon him. And as in many Weimar films this "specularization" of the underlying power relationships through the emphasis on vision and surveillance[30] becomes an oppositional cinematic code subtly articulating the familiar expressionist theme of oedipal rebellion and of resistance against the irrational authority of such overbearing patriarchal characters.[31]

---

[29] When Caligari, as head of the asylum, is then sent a patient (Cesare) suffering from sleeping sickness, he finally has the missing component with which to re-enact the mountebank's role in every detail, and so "complete" his identity.

[30] Elsaesser, "Film History," 70–75.

[31] One might also add a third point here, namely that Caligari is further destabilized as the film's compositional center where the text reveals the extent to which his identity is decentered and displaced onto "supplements" such as Cesare.

Cesare acts as a supplement to Caligari's identity for example by taking revenge when the doctor's calling card (a detail important enough to be emphasized by one of the film's few close-ups), his "passport" within the bourgeois world and a primary metonym of his identity, is flatly ignored by the town-clerk, and when Caligari's "professional" status is called into question by the rebuke against his "other" identity and occult "sideline": "Fakir!" If the flashback-scene with the notebooks throws doubt upon Caligari's mysterious (and borrowed) identity as well as the false origins of his irrational authority, this scene dramatizes the instability of his bourgeois identity and makes it clear that it is also in crisis, since Caligari fails to signify within the sanctioned reality of official authority (as inhabited and administered by the clerk). It is Cesare, the vehicle or "correlative" of narcissistic desire, who then compensates for this lack and who fulfills Caligari's dream of omnipotence, magically settling old scores and re-asserting Caligari's power against this institutional reality. Similarly, in the "seduction" scene where Caligari lures Jane into his sideshow and gives her a private showing of his "erect" somnambulist, it is as if he is once more employing Cesare narcissistically as an erotic supplement to gain the magical fulfillment of his own desires: he borrows a sexual identity in order to arouse Jane's attention vicariously by this displaced exhibitionism.[32]

This notion of a narcissistic supplementation of the self brings into sharper focus the question of representational instability and duplicity throughout the film. The supplementation of figures appears to be a response to the threat to the identity in as far as it offers instead a narcissistic experience of control. Like Otto Rank's concept of the double, however, such a defense is itself marked by duplicity. For the supplement serves not only to bolster the subject, but simultaneously through repetition and doubling, to defer and undermine any final sense of the fixity of the self. Consequently as a supplement to Caligari, Cesare embodies the doubling and splitting through which the self is re-iterated but also paradoxically decentered[33]; he is a token both

---

[32] Thomas Elsaesser observes a related erotic subtext in "Social Mobility," 23, as does Catherine Clement, who views it from the standpoint of Jane in her *Miroirs du Sujet* (Paris: Editions du Seuil, 1975), 185–205.

[33] The general instability of identities in the text – what Weber calls the "indecidability" – and the tendency for them to multiply profusely as doubles or split selves, displacing or overlapping one another, may be a token of the paradox

of the crisis of identity and of the narcissistic defense against it.[34]

## Visual displeasure: instability and the spectator

The representational instability which undermines notions of identity and causality in *Caligari* has a similarly subversive effect upon the way the spectator is positioned by the film. This can be demonstrated again by reference to the figure of Cesare. As a mesmerized figure dramatizing the desires of others he would appear to offer the perfect object of scopophilic fascination. Yet true to the duplicity which characterizes the management of fantasy in the film, he necessarily embodies not just a vehicle of desire but simultaneously an image of anxiety too. Recalling for a moment the first appearance of Cesare, it should be noted that the series of unveiling shots which aligns the spectator of the film with the diegetic audience of the sideshow builds up an appeal to the scopophilic pleasure of the viewer, drawing him or her into the tent by presenting the progressive revelation of the spectacle, only then to draw an abrupt halt to this trajectory: the gaze of the viewing subject which had appeared to be in control of the object is suddenly returned by Cesare's horrifying (and horrified) stare directly at the viewer.

With this the ambiguous situation of the viewer and the duplicity of Cesare's status come to the forefront. Up until this point the spectator's visual gratification had been linked to a pleasurable sense of seduction by the spectacle and of scopophilic mastery over the striptease-like process of unveiling, a visual pleasure guided and "managed" for example by the reassuringly smooth editing and purposeful sequence of shots it produces. In offering up to the viewer's gaze Cesare as the helpless object of this visual pleasure this process had provided the spectator with

that subjectivity here – as is frequently the case in expressionism (such as in Benn and Döblin) – is always destabilized and revealed as displaced and duplicitous through the very defenses (namely repetition and duplication) which are supposed to secure its fixity and unity.

[34] This duplicitous logic of the "uncanny" psychological defense is also developed (in the light of a reading of Samuel Weber's article) by Mary Ann Doane, who sees narcissism as "a *defensive* reaction to the possibility of castration" and who finds the denial of the "crisis" rearticulated through "the narrational structure of the Weimar films." Doane's unpublished essay "Narrative Strategies in Weimar Cinema" is quoted in Elsaesser, "Film History," 63.

a reassuring illusion of control over the spectacle, a sense of mastery prefigured and demonstrated within the text for the spectator by that similar control over Cesare displayed by Caligari, who orders the somnambulist to walk and wake up, and who manipulates his life-size image. When Cesare suddenly gazes back at the viewer, however, the confrontation momentarily questions his or her status: is the spectator the viewing-subject or rather the object of the gaze?

As with the sudden turning of tables brought about by the framing device at the end of the film where – in a gesture typical of expressionism's deconstruction of the institutional and conventional basis of such irrational authority – the hierarchy between patient and doctor, between the mad and the sane is unexpectedly inverted, the unveiling of Cesare here brings about the paradoxical "incarceration" or "framing" of the viewer in an indecidable (or uncanny) reorganization of the space of the real. It entangles him or her too in the film's problematization of those relations pertaining to the logic of the conventional space-time continuum such as those between subject and object, or as we shall see, between inside and outside. For by destabilizing these categories it makes it increasingly evident that there is no secure place outside the filmic text from which its events may be viewed "objectively" and impartially, or in which they remain unaffected and uninfected by its duplicitous structure. In the case of the similarly destabilizing frame-structure (described below), the unveiling of Cesare and his return of the gaze coincides with the spectator's sudden awareness of a critical reversal of perspectives. Not only is the spectator no longer clearly the viewing *subject*. More perniciously, as the *object* of Cesare's gaze he or she is caught by the gaze of an other who is not clearly "present"[35] and whose own status appears equally to hover between the terrifying and the terrified.

---

[35] Typical of expressionism's treatment of the realistic treatment of character, plot and causality, instead of providing a clearly defined reality and a set of correspondingly stable subject-selves the film subverts such fixity. Similar again to the image of the carnival described by Bakhtin in which the quotidian world is turned upside down and the institutional orders and concepts which underpin it are suspended, the film's carnivalesque circulation of dreams and unfixed identities subverts conventionally centered concepts of reality and self. See Mikhail Bachtin, *Literatur und Karneval: Zur Romantheorie und Lachkultur*.

In a similar act of reversal and carnivalistic rebelliousness the narrative willfully sets up and simultaneously undermines several strategies associated with an attempt to fix that which is duplicitous by seeking to trace and assert its origin or to master it by imposing an authoritative perspective upon it.[36] The progressive unveiling of Cesare is one example of the ways in which the narrative gestures towards the inclination to reveal (and so pin down) identity, only to withhold ultimately this possibility of providing knowledge and truth. The series of narrative embeddings or framings functions similarly. For example, at the point within Francis' narrative – already a tale-within-a-tale – at which we see Francis and the doctors reading through Caligari's notes in order to discover the secret of his identity there is a further narrative interpolation, namely the flashback-scene (dramatizing the notes) which centers on the way in which Caligari's false identity was assumed. The interpolated discourse both displaces the previous version of the "truth" of Caligari's identity and is itself in turn later displaced as an explanation by the framing narrative. Like the constant interventions of the fantastic which subvert rational explanation by deferring the investigation of each successive mystery, what seems to be happening here is that the telescoping of perspectives and framings sets up a series of authoritative perspectives or mutually competing discourses in which each in turn pretends to offer the final "truth" regarding the identity of the characters and simultaneously regarding the corresponding reality within which each figure is valorized. What still needs to be explored, however, is the extent to which the attempt to establish any such foundation and authority within the narrative is necessarily subject to the same principle of ambiguity and indecidability which governs the entire text. For just as the characters' identities are destabilized where they supplement each other and slide between alternative positions, so the authority and truth pertaining to each of the sub-narratives appears subject to the same doubling and decentering, and it is to this issue that we now turn.

---

[36] Mary Anne Doane makes a similar point when she writes that the framing devices "simply establish a false origin or authority for the text – the narrative as a whole remains unqualified." Quoted in Elsaesser, "Film History," 63.

## Framing the interpretation: The frame-narrative and the conflict of discourses

The frame-tale narration of *Caligari* juxtaposes two very different and contradictory perspectives on a linked series of events: the first perspective is associated with the outer, framing narrative and the second with the tale within the tale. As we have seen Siegfried Kracauer interprets the framing structure as an act of closure which imposes a reactionary meaning upon the revolutionary nature of Francis' tale of rebellion against authority, and upon the message of the original screenplay so that "a revolutionary film [is] thus turned into a conformist one."[37] However given the ambiguity and structural instability observed here, I would like to argue that the film does not exclusively enforce that point of view embodied by the final scenes of the framing-tale, and so need not lead automatically to the narrowly pessimistic conclusion drawn by Kracauer.

In order to propose an alternative analysis of the film's narrative structure I would like to return to Colin MacCabe's critical concepts of the "dominant discourse" (or "meta-language") and the "classic realist text," described in chapter 3.[38] Although MacCabe does not treat the problem of frame-narratives as such, his analytical model is highly appropriate since it investigates the way in which texts are often divided, like the frame-narrative, into separate and opposing perspectives representing competing versions of "reality."

### Colin MacCabe's model of "dominant discourse" and the "classic realist text"

According to MacCabe, literary and filmic texts alike build up their fictional worlds through the accumulation of a series of alternative perspectives or "discourses" – for instance the viewpoints pertaining to different characters or to narrator-figures – which represent various attitudes towards the world and thus differing constructions of reality. The most obvious examples of

---

[37] Kracauer, *From Caligari*, 67.
[38] See Colin MacCabe, "Realism and the Cinema: Notes on Some Brechtian Theses," and "Theory and Film: Principles of Realism and Pleasure" in *Tracking the Signifier*; also his book *James Joyce and the Revolution of the Word* (London: Macmillan, 1979).

such discourses are, in film, the "point-of-view shot," and in the literary text, the utterances of figures. Whether set within visible quotation marks or not, these are distinguished by being derived clearly from the subjective point of view of a particular individual. In this they differ from the surrounding narrative which consequently possesses a special status: the narrating discourse often appears to be objective and impersonal, as if belonging to a superior order of truthfulness offering a seemingly unbiased view of reality.

Like Benveniste's concept of "histoire," this dominant narrative discourse is a kind of "history" from which all traces of a speaking or "enunciating" subject have been removed.[39] Since its origin as discourse, as a mere perspective, has been effaced, the dominant discourse presents itself as a transparent window on reality. It consequently seems to present the recipient with direct access to knowledge and truth, by offering reality as given and self-evident, so that "the events" as Benveniste says "seem to narrate themselves."[40] In contrast to the subaltern discourses in which the traces of the speaking subject from whom they derive testify to their lack of any superior or transcendental viewpoint, the dominant discourse foregrounds itself as clear and impersonal. It consequently operates as a "meta-language" or framing discourse, commenting upon the degree of truthfulness embodied by the other discourses and criticizing their relative opaqueness while itself remaining invisible, "unwritten," and thus immune to criticism.

The paradigmatic form of this hierarchical discursive organization occurs as we have seen in what MacCabe calls the "classic realist text," and in a form typified by the nineteenth-century realist novel. It is defined precisely by this superiority of the commentating discourse, as well as by the manner in which it manipulates the reader or spectator into adopting a particular attitude *vis-à-vis* both the text and the reality depicted. For although each discourse offers a distinct perspective on the reality

---

[39] Emile Benveniste, *Problems in General Linguistics* (Miami: University of Miami Press, 1971), 206. MacCabe discusses Benveniste's crucial notion of "enunciation" in *James Joyce*, 86–87.

[40] Benveniste, *Problems in General Linguistics*, 208. Extensive and insightful commentary on MacCabe's model and its links to Benveniste's distinction between "histoire" and "discours(e)" may be found in Catherine Belsey's excellent *Critical Practice* (London: Methuen, 1980), 70–72.

of the fictional world, in the classic realist text it is only the master-discourse which is valorized both as the sole bearer of the truth, and as the recipient's central guide. As the "meta-language" it orients the reader or viewer among these competing perspectives, and judges the rival discourses and viewpoints. Consequently it positions the recipient by offering a comforting sense of mastery over the problems and enigmas posed by the text. However, since the dominant discourse denies that it is really a discourse at all, but claims instead that it is "objective reality" (or "histoire"), the recipient is invariably kept ignorant of the fact that the position or the view offered is actually merely the product of a *particular* system of representation, which has simply been privileged as the exclusive vehicle of truth by the hierarchical structure of the text.

Similar in their positioning of the recipient to the "lisible" or "readerly" work described by Roland Barthes, with their dominant discourse such texts offer the reader or spectator a position which is seemingly secure and free of contradictions, and in which the conflicts and problems created by the narrative are also resolved automatically.[41] Classic realist texts define themselves as "realistic" then not so much by sharing in a common code of realism or by representing a recognizable world. It is rather the positioning of the recipient, the nature of the relationship set up between the recipient and the fictional world of the text which determines the real since it also determines the way the meaning of the text is produced. The classic realist text – in this respect a paradigmatic form of "affirmative culture" – is consequently characterized by the attempt to manipulate its recipients into a particular attitude of naive compliance and illusory mastery. For in accepting the illusory sense of mastery which the text offers them they are also bound to accept the power-structure of the text, that is, the hierarchy of discourses it simultaneously implies. It is this compliance which subsequently makes them blind to the fact that what the text sets up as "histoire" is really only a mere articulation or "discours"; it is merely one of many possible perspectives on an event, rather than the definitive or "objective" perspective on it – let alone that event itself.

Of course endless permutations on this basic realist structure

---

[41] Roland Barthes, *S/Z*, trans. Richard Miller (London: Cape, 1975).

are possible, involving all manner of realities and modes of representation. Indeed it is possible for the conventional realist formula
to be varied considerably without the narration ceasing to operate
typically as a classic realist text. For example, some types of classic
realist narrative will deal with themes which are in other respects
entirely "unrealistic," such as fantasy and science fiction, in
which the most improbable events occur transgressing the laws of
time, space and causality. Yet these texts remain "realistic" in so
far as they reproduce precisely the basic structure of classic realism with its guiding meta-language and the characteristic sense of
trust and mastery it inspires in the recipient. Similarly, the most
conventional of nineteenth-century forms, the detective genre,
regularly gets away with suppressing – albeit temporarily – another central characteristic of this classic structure: it postpones
the claim of the dominant discourse to possess the truth, in order
to keep the reader guessing until the end. Clearly, this temporary
suppression of the truth does not undermine the "realist" text's
relationship towards the recipient. Indeed, by prolonging the
conflict between the competing perspectives it keeps the reader in
uncertainty and suspense, and so heightens this relationship of
dependency. Such deviations from the paradigm do not so much
question its validity as illustrate both its powerful scope and the
many permutations on its basic pattern which it is capable of
generating.

Like Peter Bürger's description of the organic work of art (to
which it is clearly related) MacCabe's model of classic realism is
also important as a way of understanding those progressive or
avant-garde texts which directly challenge the presumptions of
the paradigm. For example MacCabe describes certain alternative
categories to that of the classic realist text, such as the "subversive" text, in which either no explicit discursive hierarchy exists
(so that the various discourses compete without any one of them
being valorized or presented as the exclusive vehicle of an abiding truth),[42] or alternatively in which the very possibility of a
dominant discourse is problematized or exposed as pure artifice.
This would include for instance the more progressive anti-realist
narratives which reproduce the pattern of the classic realist text –
for example by adopting its hierarchical structuring around an

---

[42] MacCabe, "Realism and the Cinema," *Tracking the Signifier*, 48–50.

"histoire" – but only in order then to problematize or subvert its "meta-discourse," exposing its assumed objectivity as a groundless fiction. By thus "decentering" the narrative and opening it up to the rivalry between competing perspectives, the text also casts its interpreters adrift, by denying them any sense of mastery. Here they obviously remain without a "given" position from which to regard the story. They are left to their own interpretative devices, and are forced to weigh up the narrative's various discourses and perspectives against each other without the help of a guiding meta-discourse, and without the sense of closure and empowerment which it provides. It is this deviation from the paradigmatic structure of the classic realist text which is highly relevant for a reading of *Caligari*.

The distinctions introduced by MacCabe go a long way for example towards illustrating the interrelation between the two major parts of the film *Caligari* and its division by the framing device. For as we have seen, the film is structured by what appear to be various opposing "discourses," each of which is linked to a different perspective on events. If we read the film in terms of MacCabe's scheme it is apparent that where Francis' discourse and perspective prevail at the outset, this occurs largely in a manner analogous to that of a dominant discourse. Firstly, his narrative appears to legitimize itself as a transparent window on the truth: Francis' initially verbal narration (in the framing tale) is "objectified" and in a sense, substantiated as "reality" by being transformed very quickly into the concrete visual images of the inner tale. Secondly, Francis' discourse undercuts the other, subaltern perspectives as unreliable. For example, the inner tale describes how (from his position of implied superiority and truthfulness) Francis is able to overcome his opponent Caligari by imposing upon him his (Francis') own version of events, that is, by revealing the hidden "truth" he has unearthed about Caligari and the history of his madness. For, discovering that the doctor has a double and unstable identity (as both a pseudo-scientific sideshow huckster and as the director of an asylum) he exposes this duplicity and pins down the mysterious and protean figure by defining him within his (Francis') masterful narrator's discourse.[43] Through this re-definition he manages thus to overcome

---

[43] As we have seen this triumph itself comes about in a preeminently "discursive" fashion through Francis' discovery of the journal which Caligari has kept,

Caligari's own powerful and magical control over people and events, which itself threatens to refashion them as mere objects in his own private discursive world.[44]
Yet then comes the twist. In the same way that Francis' narrative "frames" Caligari (by re-defining his identity and linking together his contradictory roles of doctor and huckster) so Francis' identity and discourse ultimately succumb in turn to a further act of framing by a superior and still more "objective" perspective – that of the outer "framing-narration" dominated by the seemingly benevolent doctor and the scientific and rationalistic principle he embodies. This new perspective legitimizes itself (functioning precisely as a kind of "histoire") by exposing Francis' version of events as actually merely another "enunciated" or subaltern discourse, while it presents itself as the new "discourse of truth" – operating from a more authoritative level still – where there is no personal, enunciating narrator and where it can consequently take on the status of objective (and unenunciated) window on the truth.

This "framing" of Francis' narrative by the new dominant discourse and the struggle for power between the two is highlighted by the key scene in which Francis is incarcerated. This is shot from a set-up identical to a previous one in the inner tale which had shown the incarceration of Caligari. Yet whereas in Francis' version it was Caligari who was put screaming into a strait-jacket, it is now Francis himself who stages a wild outburst and has to be restrained – in what appears to be the same room and the same bed as in the previous scene of Caligari's capture in the framed tale.

---

describing the origins of his career. The emphasis here on writing and the power of the discursive world ("You must become Caligari") as well as the mise-en-abyme effect of the interlocking narratives, points to the same problematization of the differences between "histoire" and "discours" to which the film returns repeatedly.

[44] In the typical "expressionist" oedipal scenario (with which the film is linked) – such as Kafka's key story of the expressionist period "Das Urteil" ("The Judgement," 1912) – the "real" is decided by the struggle between those in authority (the father-figures) and those who are the victims of authority (the sons). As with *Caligari* this is a struggle which is obviously fought out in order to gain a position of power allowing the one to "frame" the other, to incarcerate him within a personal version of events, and so to legislate over which concept of reality and corresponding definition of rationality is to prevail: that valorizing the son or that valorizing the father-figure.

Precisely in the manner of MacCabe's model the final sequence of the film consequently serves as a dominant discourse to "explain" and "frame" Francis' version of events, as false: the framed tale, bearing the "enunciatory" traces of a single deranged subject, is revealed as mere "discours" rather than an abiding and objective "histoire." The "unnarrated" framing-tale at the end of the film, in which the asylum director – as well as a version of events which valorizes his perspective – now dominate the scene thus functions as a prime example of a "meta-language." As a meta-language it comments upon the other perspective as upon an "object-language" and "frames" the inner tale as a mere discourse, underlining its materiality by pointing to those personal or enunciatory traces of the narration which prevent it from being taken as a transparent window on events: it thus "frames" and explains away Francis' tale firstly by disclosing that the asylum really *is* run by a doctor resembling the Caligari-figure of the framed tale, and secondly by intimating that the insane Francis has simply concocted his tale by projecting his hallucinations onto the director. It thereby denies the framed narrative the status of an objective "histoire," rendering it susceptible instead to interpretation as "discourse," while preserving itself by contrast in the form of an ultimate and unassailable truth.

In "framing" Francis, and in subordinating his narrative to the text's final truth, the dominant discourse neatly meshes with the dominating discourse of its central representative figure or "stand-in" – the benevolent analyst/director, who wants now to use his superior discursive power – the ability which he claims to possess of understanding Francis and of interpreting his discourse – in order to "cure" him. In this regard the film adopts a traditional narrative format by aligning the figure who embodies the abiding truth (the analyst/director) with what becomes its final and authoritative discourse (the framing tale) as a neat narrative resolution and a final confirmation of the discursive power-structure which prevails.

## Strategies of subversion: *Caligari* and expressionist counter-discourse

Yet to take the ending of the film merely at face-value and to accept the final closure it appears to offer is effectively to allow oneself as the interpreter to be "framed" by the outer tale and so to read the film as Kracauer does: as a straightforward version of the classic realist text, in which an all-embracing interpretation is handed over ready-made in the final scenes by the dominant discourse to a passive and unquestioning audience. This would be to ignore the various contradictions which are set up but which, significantly, remain unexplained by the framing discourse, and so continue to dispute its conclusion. Is it not the case for example, that the supposedly fantastic events of the Caligari story – firstly the mysterious murders of the town clerk and of Francis' friend, secondly Caligari's insidious power over his somnambulist slave Cesare, and thirdly the question of Caligari's true identity – are not actually *resolved* as such by the final dominant discourse? As we have seen the framing tale merely sweeps these unanswered questions under the carpet, excluding them a priori from consideration, by maintaining simply that Francis is mad and that his ideas are thus not to be believed.

Naturally, one *could* argue from the standpoint of the outer tale that if Francis *is* mad, then he may himself have murdered or imagined murdering Alan, his friend and rival for Jane's love, and that he may have concocted the story of the mad doctor Caligari, perhaps out of resentment against the asylum director. But this would leave unexplained the significance for Francis of several important details from the alleged hallucination. For example, how would the town clerk's death fit into all of this? Similarly, if Francis is merely projecting his story onto other figures at the asylum (such as Caligari, Cesare and Jane), then why doesn't the other key figure Alan also re-appear in the asylum at the end? Furthermore, when the head of the institute hears that Francis is confusing him with an eleventh-century mystic "Caligari," he appears so strangely knowledgeable regarding all the details of this ancient, and surely rather obscure anecdote that it seems as if he is privy to the story in a way which would appear almost to corroborate Francis' suspicions.[45] Clearly, the framing tale's supposed "rationality" is no more compelling and its explanation is actually no more watertight than Francis' "mad" version of

---

[45] Prawer even goes so far as to claim that since Francis does not actually confuse the asylum director with the mystic monk as the director claims, the director is either misdiagnosing Francis or deliberately pulling the wool over his own colleagues' eyes. See *Caligari's Children*, 189–190.

events. Consequently, such unanswered questions continue to function as an irritant demanding resolution.

Where the framing tale fails to explain such lingering questions, it becomes clear that although the film's structure resembles a classic realist text, it also deviates significantly from this conventional format. For as with those subversive moments which Mac-Cabe discovers even in the most paradigmatic of realist texts, the film also contains

elements which escape the control of the dominant discourse in the same way as a neurotic symptom or a verbal slip attest to the lack of control of the conscious subject. They open up another area than that of representation . . . in order to investigate the very movement of articulation and difference . . . [46]

Like the parapraxes or "Freudian slips" which subvert the dominating language of consciousness and attest to the existence of an alternative and oppositional language of the unconscious, certain elements remain outside the control of the dominant discourse, disputing its power to explain and master all, and contaminating and undermining the reality it constructs. In this way those uncanny elements, such as the lingering, unanswered questions which the dominant discourse would "frame" and repress, thus return to haunt it, and by their presence disrupt the smooth surface of the representation revealing its true status as "discourse" merely posing as "histoire."

As we have seen, these subversive moments are associated with an intervention within the logic of realism by the fantastic, which itself figures as the representative of an alternative, irrational and subversive force. For example the skewed architecture and the strange jagged patterns which marked the backdrops of the inner tale, might be comprehensible via the logic of the explanatory framing tale as the "traces of the enunciation," that is, as an indication of Francis' unreliable idiosyncratic perspective or "madness." Why is it then that these fantastic markings and mad distortions are still present in the framing-tale itself – for example on the floor of the courtyard in the asylum of the benevolent director – if this is supposed now to figure as the realm of rationality, science and indisputable "truth"?[47] Their

---

[46] MacCabe, "Realism and the Cinema," *Tracking the Signifier*, 47–48.
[47] The bizarre "expressionistic" patterns are also still present on the wall of the director's office in the parallel-scene in which Francis, like Caligari before him,

presence suggests a conclusion which is central to expressionism and its treatment of madness and rationality: that the two discourses are not, after all, really so distinct and that, contrary to Kracauer's view, neither inner nor outer tale has an ultimate claim on the truth.[48] The inference is that, just as all language is always haunted by its "Other" – like the alternative discourse of the unconscious disclosed in dreams and parapraxes – so here too even the dominant discourse of rationality cannot exist in a state which is ever free of contamination by such fantastic or mad distortions.

A similar duplicity affects the positioning of the spectator, which remains far from stable and dominant within the framing tale. For example, when in the final shot of the film the seemingly benevolent director explains away Francis' discourse and, as if to emphasize his perceptiveness and the clarity of his vision, suddenly puts on his spectacles, do we not share Francis' anxiety – an uncanny sense of the return of the familiar in unfamiliar form – in suddenly recognizing that familiar patriarchal gaze associated throughout the film with Caligari's hypnotic and authoritarian control? At this moment the kindly doctor is suddenly transformed for the spectator back into the Caligari figure. Similar to the attitude expressed by the look of horror on Francis' face at this point, as spectators we surely share the same unnerving sense of witnessing the return of the repressed. Do we not also perceive an ambiguity then in his promise to "cure" Francis, as if it were a veiled threat by the resurrected "scientist" Caligari to practice his diabolical science on Francis, even though we have been reassured by the master-discourse that all has apparently been set to rights and that the "happy ending" is secure?

Through their interruption of the smooth surface of representation these duplicitous and fantastic elements share the same function as that taken on here by the film's major structuring

is overpowered. It is evident that they have been lightly painted over, almost as if Francis' story were being "whitewashed." Yet as with the other moments of contradiction between the two frames, they ultimately serve to strengthen the tension between the two.

[48] Interestingly, Kracauer is again aware of the illogicality of the "expressionist"-style distortions re-appearing in the "conventional reality" at the end of the film. Unwilling again to cope with this duplicity, Kracauer merely observes this fact, and does not back down, but instead faults *Caligari*'s representational power, claiming that the film's "style was as far from depicting madness as it was from transmitting revolutionary messages" (70).

device, the frame-narrative: they foreground and destabilize the act of narration and question the claim of the dominant discourse to exclusive possession of the truth. In this regard we can describe one of the film's central structural effects as the setting in motion of an extended play between the axes of "histoire" and "discours," dramatized by the ongoing process of conflict between the rival discourses. This conflict itself serves to dispute the finality and fixity of any dominant discourse and to question its ability to subordinate and "frame" its rivals.

It is this play with the distinction between "histoire" and "discours" which is thrust into the forefront of the viewer's attention through the very structure of *Caligari* as a "frame-tale," a structure whose central principle is normally that one level of reality narrates and asserts its authority over the next. The opening shot of the film initiates this process of "baring the device" and of problematizing its structure by showing Francis, subject of the enunciation, beginning to tell his tale to a companion. As if this foregrounding of the act of narration were not enough to draw the viewer's attention to this as a problem, the visual images which follow serve to underline it further. Far from always possessing the given and self-evident mimetic quality normally associated with the photographic medium of film – "seeing is believing" – through which, as MacCabe suggests, the visual code is automatically endowed with the aura of objectivity or "histoire," these images are undermined by two further factors.

Firstly there is a prolonged hesitation as Francis' narration gets under way, which foregrounds the very act of narration itself. Elsaesser has observed that acts of narration are commonly emphasized in Weimar silent cinema.[49] Yet here we switch between the two levels of framed and framing tale repeatedly, returning several times to the scene of the narration before the traces of the narrator are finally left behind, and the objective visual dramatization of the story finally liberates itself from the narrator's verbal discourse and takes on the momentum and continuity more reminiscent of the "histoire," with its transparent and unnarrated quality.

Secondly, even when the scene of narration has been left in the past and the full presence of the visual staging of Francis' verbal

[49] Elsaesser, "Film History," 77.

tale takes over, the fantastic quality and what I have termed the "representational instability" both of the plot and the setting – not only the peculiar markings on the painted backdrops but the artificiality of the sets in general – all this remains as a disturbing factor, offering a hint that the world seen here is still merely a subjective landscape. Like the quality of "excess" which characterizes the visual images (such as the bizarre backdrops, their "flat" quality and the melodramatic costume, make-up and gestures of the figures) it is a constant reminder that, unlike the "histoire," the world depicted here is not to be taken as objective reality.[50] Thus the very possibility of "histoire" – the mode of representation central to the classical film narrative – and the existence of any final truth is called into question.

In this way the frame-structure also interrogates the condition of film's most fundamental discourse – the photographic image itself – questioning cinema's valorization of the visual code as its inherently "dominant discourse" – a highly significant move, given that *Caligari* was itself a founding text in the new narrative medium of film. Against the conventional temptation to accept the visual code as photographically objective, given and self-evident – to accept it in other words as "histoire" – the narrative structure reminds us through its multiple framings that there is always another level at which the "given" may be forced to reveal the traces of its enunciation, and at which "histoire" may be revealed as mere "discours."

Unlike the structure of the classic realist text, in *Caligari* the constant overlapping or contamination of one reality by another, the jostling of the rival claims to objectivity, and the mutual displacement of discourses shows that there is no single discourse which can reveal the truth as it "really" is, no neutral standpoint which would offer an undisputed perspective on the real world. In other words, despite the way in which the film seems at the end to encourage the spectator to cast aside the perspectives provided by Francis' tale for the seemingly authoritative and stable truths offered instead in the world dominated by the asylum director, given the constant slippage between the two levels, and the contradictions which their mutual interference produces, this final fram-

[50] Noel Burch describes *Caligari* in these terms in an article, "Primitivism and the Avant-Gardes: a Dialectical Approach," rpt. *Narrative, Apparatus, Ideology*, ed. Philip Rosen (New York: Columbia University Press, 1986), 483–506.

ing becomes a deeply ironic gesture. For the neat closure which the framing story at the end of the film seems to promise (and the correspondingly stable and cosy "positioning" it offers the viewer) can only be upheld by an interpretation prepared to overlook the obviously subversive and fantastic elements of the film, to suppress the process of mutual undercutting staged by the two frames, and to ignore the constant conflict between "histoire" and "discours" which the very structure of the film plays out.[51]

Referring again to MacCabe's model, we can say in conclusion that the film merely takes up the structure of the classic realist text, only then to reject it by problematizing – through the contradictions which it then introduces into the conventional format – precisely the kind of pat interpretation of the real which such a structure normally encourages. It is only by ignoring these inbuilt contradictions – as Kracauer does – that one may continue to take the final frame of *Caligari* at face value, as a transparent window on the truth.

In this sense of course, the interpretation is itself set up or "framed" by the film's characteristic structure. Whichever of the two perspectives one adopts, it will be the wrong one. For given the interplay between the two narrative components, any interpretation which privileges one side of the frame to the exclusion of the other (as in Kracauer's reading) is itself responsible for limiting the scope of the text. And while the attempt to see these two realms as completely unrelated paralyzes their productive conflict, the attempt to valorize for example the final framing tale over the framed tale of Francis' narrative reduces the film to the conservative message found by Kracauer in the last scenes. Such an approach is evidence of the (rather dubious) underlying hermeneutical conviction that a ready-made meaning – a "figure in the carpet" – lies waiting to be discovered within the text. And given such an approach, the search for meaning will always be limited to those interpretative possibilities already formulated explicitly by the text.

To the extent that a particular reading of the film itself remains

---

[51] Kracauer himself cannot succeed finally in ignoring the fundamental ambivalence or "duplicity" of the film. Besides the "perversion" of the original nonconformist plot which he places in the forefront of his interpretation, he later introduces, almost as an afterthought, a "double aspect" of the film, in which "Caligari's authority triumphs with a hallucination in which the same authority is overthrown" (67).

fixed at the level of the framing tale, it must in a sense repeat the narrative's gesture: it is forced to uphold that interpretation of reality which is embodied by the asylum-director (the framing-tale's "stand-in") and to exclude the rival perspective embodied by Francis (who then becomes the untrustworthy narrator of what amounts to a series of mere hallucinations). Through its acquiescence in the authority of that dominant discourse which prematurely closes off meaning by suppressing alternative perspectives, such an interpretation thereby reproduces precisely the central act of closure or "framing" which the film, as a radical frame-narrative (or "subversive" text) ironizes and undercuts in its very form.

## *Caligari* and counter-discourse

Given the perspective I have offered here on *Caligari*'s relativization of certain dominant epistemological assumptions (such as the dichotomy between madness and rationality), the director's confident positivist assertion in the final seconds of the film that, having discovered the basis of Francis' confusion of identities, he now knows how to cure him, is surely no less wild, unfounded and irrational a claim than any of those voiced by the "madman" Francis. With his exaggerated confidence in his psychoanalytical powers the director appears in fact no less deluded than Francis, and seems to inhabit a reality which is equally uncertain – typically it differs only in respect of the ballast lent to it by his positivist sense of self-assurance. In this respect he fully embodies the confident rationalist – a common figure in the genre of the fantastic, as we have seen – for whom reality is always uncomplicated, clear-cut and controllable – at least until his or her logical and reasoned explanation of uncanny occurrences is proved wrong by the more powerful duplicity of events.

By the end of *Caligari* then the asylum-director's world of rationality and sanity – like the film's "outer" frame (to which this rational perspective corresponds) – is seen as so thoroughly undermined by its uncanny Other – a phenomenon registered not least by the interventions of the grotesque and the fantastic – that it can offer no safe refuge, no "outside" from which to view events "objectively." It is clear then, that a purely "realistic" reading of the text – such as the kind that Fredric Jameson believes is fundamental to the modernist text in order to re-establish its underlying realist substratum – would be confounded at every turn, since *Caligari's* central principle is that indecidability which denies the very basis for such a realistic perception of clear identities and differences. The bid to "frame" the indecidable and pin it down in the narrative is analogous to the "kindly" director's attempt to frame the inexplicable within a rationalist mode in order to fix it: the result is the upsurge of the fantastic which resists a logical reading, and the virulent growth of that duplicity which subverts any framing, undermining the very distinction upon which rests the dichotomy between sanity and madness, science and sideshow.

While the "madness" which characterizes the framed tale is carried over into the scenes of the supposedly "rational" framing story – witness the strange markings on the floor of the asylum courtyard – the principle of indecidability has become a dimension of the representational system itself: we cannot even be sure if the space is actually a courtyard or a hall – the differences between "inside" and "outside" are again representationally "indecidable."[52]

Given the film's fundamental duplicity it is perhaps not even so much a question of the "virulence" of the irrational infecting the rational, as Elsaesser maintains,[53] but rather that *Caligari* simply collapses all distinctions between the two. Thus the very notion of an "outside" is questioned. There is no longer any place "beyond" the various versions of madness on either side of the frame from which the contradictions might be resolved. For the film reorganizes the conventions of time and space and turns the fictive "world" into a dreamlike landscape in which the possibility of a distinction between identities and realities is preempted.[54]

---

52 See Minden, "Politics and the Silent Cinema," 294.
53 Elsaesser takes up this notion of the "virulence" of the internalized conflict which subverts the process of containment ("Social Mobility," 23). By contrast Nancy Ketchiff (in "Dr. Caligari's Cabinet: A Cubist Perspective" *The Comparatist* 8 [May 1984]: 7–13) maintains that the "acknowledgment of the fictive nature of the story . . . introduces an ironic mode that is not compatible with German Expressionism"(9). This observation ignores the duplicity and ambiguity which form an essential component of the expressionist poetics of counter-discourse.
54 For this reason Minden is inconsistent in suggesting that the "visionary mode of expression . . . is ultimately subordinated to the objective authority under attack" ("Politics and the Silent Cinema," 293). Where the possibility of a distinction between the inside and the outside is subverted – as indeed he himself believes is the case – then the notion of any subordination of one to the other surely becomes questionable also.

It is this inability to maintain such rigid and rationalistic distinctions which – extending far beyond its strategies of representational destabilization – characterizes the text as a counter-discourse: a progressive means for questioning both the dominant epistemology and the institutionalized conventions of signification underpinned by it.

If it is true as we observed in the chapter on melodrama that an hysterical complex, finding no outlet in conventional means of expression, returns on a different (bodily) level, then the text too displaces that which cannot be accommodated within the framework of a realistic discourse of representation.[55] In *Caligari* those fears and desires which cannot be expressed and pursued through conventional realist narrative or logic are taken up by the text's indecidable elements such as the fantastic and the grotesque. They are given a structural "correlative" for example in the form of the sleeper Cesare, who becomes a walking hysterical symptom, a *mise-en-scène* of anxiety and desire. But beyond this they are not so much "represented" per se in the film's content as rather embodied and simulated in its *form* as a dimension of its system of representation, emerging in its significant gaps, fissures, deferrals and repetitions. Like the uncanny (and the unconscious) these subversive elements are "represented" only to the extent that they escape the rational control of conventional signification. Yet as Colin MacCabe points out they should not be viewed as mere *moments* of rebelliousness but rather as full-scale "strategies of subversion," forming a "systematic refusal of any such dominant discourse."[56] For it is at that point where conventional representational discourse fails to accommodate the unspeakable, and where the codes of realism consequently begin to falter and to become highly unstable, that the fantastic and the duplicitous emerge in the expressionist avant-garde as forms of counter-discourse opposed to the language and logic of rational explanation.

[55] On hysteria and narrative structure I refer again to Geoffrey Nowell-Smith, "Minelli and Melodrama," 113–118 (esp. 117).
[56] MacCabe, "Realism and the Cinema," *Tracking the Signifier*, 48. In direct contrast to my argument here, Mike Budd sees the film as "systemically unstable rather than subversive" (25). However, this analysis relies upon an extremely restrictive understanding of *Caligari's* "system," marginalizing its unstable elements as mere aberrations of a film that "comes to resemble a well-functioning machine, each part fitted perfectly to the next" (12). See Budd, "Moments of *Caligari*."

## Conclusion. Expressionism and Weimar silent film: forms of oppositional discourse

Commentators have attempted to approach the relationship between the expressionist movement and Weimar silent cinema in a variety of ways.[57] One of the most persuasive perhaps is Thomas Elsaesser's argument that the expressionist "quotes" in *Caligari* for example are part of a "self-consciously 'artistic' impulse" (68) behind the film, and constitute the attempt to appeal to a bourgeois audience which might otherwise look condescendingly upon the new medium of film. He sees this impulse as a direct response and intervention in the so-called "Debate on Cinema" ("Kinodebatte")[58] in which many contemporary critics took up a similar standpoint that was prejudiced against the photographic medium of film as a low mimetic form, since it was seemingly "not 'worked over' by the shaping intelligence of the 'artist'" (71). Consequently the introduction of expressionist stylistic features constituted in one sense an emphatically aestheticized practice, "a self-conscious attempt at bourgeois cinema" (68). At the same time the prominent expressionist style created a distinct and separate niche for German cinema, differentiating the "product" from commercial US film (77).

Drawing upon Elsaesser's argument, Mike Budd describes *Caligari* in terms of a "commodity form" (19) which adopts a "carefully limited version of Expressionism" (13). Furthermore he consequently describes the structure of *Caligari* as conforming largely to the model of the classical narrative in which "expressionist elements could be bolted onto a realist narrative," even though this produced an "uneasy mixture" with "textual discrepancies" (22, 23).

Now in the light of the foregoing analysis of *Caligari* the very notion that it might be feasible to extrapolate a sanitized and

---

[57] Silvio Vietta's short article "Das Expressionistische am deutschen Stummfilm," is one of the few which succeeds in analyzing German cinema of the 1920s concretely in terms of the more influential recent methodological approaches to expressionist literature and art, such as the changed conditions of perception in the metropolis (34); the reduction of characters to synecdoches (35); the translation of the dynamic and disjunctive language of expressionism into camera movement (35); the similar use of distorted perspectives and spaces (34); the contrast between light and dark (34–35). See *Literatur und Stummfilm*, ed. S. Vietta and K. Tröster (Mannheim, 1980).

[58] See Anton Kaes, *Kino-Debatte* (Tübingen: Niemeyer, 1978).

"limited" version of expressionism and attach it to the main body of the film, leaving the text uncontaminated and intact as a fundamentally realist narrative, becomes highly questionable. If there is truth in Walter Benjamin's thesis that with the emergence of mechanically reproducible works of art such as film the "aura" of creative originality and uniqueness – which still adheres to bourgeois (and especially organic) works of art – is destroyed,[59] then the attempt to bestow upon the mechanical and photographic medium of film the artistic aura pertaining to the bourgeois aesthetic could surely not be achieved by "bolting on" an intrusive, fragmentary and thoroughly disruptive form of oppositional discourse which is the essence of expressionism. For as we have seen, it is precisely this "aura," the sense of an "artistic" work created by a "shaping intelligence" – such as the classic realist text's connotations of illusionism and aesthetic mastery, or the organic work's sense of a rounded, compositional whole – which the progressive and avantgarde oppositional aesthetics of expressionism set out to subvert with its various forms of disruption and montage. If indeed the expressionist elements of *Caligari* are "bolted" on, then only in the sense that, like the montage, they serve to emphasize the bolts and joins, thereby pointing to the artifice of the construction and differentiating the text from the "real." Rather than producing a commodity form – whose central aesthetic feature is always the ease with which it can be consumed – expressionism's function in *Caligari* is to create a work more akin to a montage, an inorganic and disjunctive text in which the "loose narrative ends" are explicitly *not* tied together for the spectator.[60]

As Elsaesser has observed there is a particular emphasis throughout Weimar cinema on "specular relations" (73), that is, on acts of seeing, surveillance and fascination, and these are linked to a specific and central function in these texts, namely the attempt to account for "the authority, origin, and control of the act of narration" (65). And indeed my analysis of *Caligari* bears out Elsaesser's comment that this emphasis on vision serves as a metaphor for relationships of control and power, such as "family and oedipal conflicts" (70). He also observes that Weimar cinema foregrounds the artistry of the work, over and beyond its mere

[59] Walter Benjamin, "The Work of Art in the Age of Mechanical Reproduction," *Illuminations*, ed. Hannah Arendt (New York: Schocken, 1969), 217–252.
[60] Budd, "Moments of *Caligari*," 41.

photographic capability, by means of a "profusion of nested narratives, framed tales, flashbacks, *en-abîme* constructions and interlacing of narrative voices" (65).

Notwithstanding Elsaesser's observations however it is important to stress that these particular emphases on narrative and specular relations in Weimar cinema are also related specifically to the oppositional and avant-garde functions of expressionism. If the classic realist text and classical narrative film feign neutrality and transparency (as MacCabe maintains) by disguising the ideological means through which they impart a sense of authority and truthfulness, then it is this element which expressionism's oppositional discourses deconstruct. For the irrational and unquestioned forms of social authority are embodied not only by patriarchal figures such as Caligari – as has been amply documented in the wealth of research on the familiar expressionist themes of rebellion and oedipal struggle – but are also present less conspicuously as an ideological and discursive mechanism in conventional systems of representation.

We can briefly summarize the ways in which these counter-discourses operate against such institutionalized authority as that of the representational system. Firstly the visual code – "seeing is believing" – is destabilized, for example by the unsteady backdrops, by the collapsing of conventional spatio-temporal distinctions (such as inside vs. outside) and frequently by the lack of a clear and unifying compositional center. Secondly the spectator's vicarious sense of omniscience is undermined where the text withholds the possibility of a pleasurable sense of recognition (and thus cognitive mastery) of the familiar. Thirdly, far from fleeing the epistemological crises of the period (through sublimation, aesthetic escapism, or similar "affirmative" means) the film instead invokes the fantastic and the grotesque in order to simulate a "crisis of perception and phenomenality" (clearly related to the broader contemporary social problematic) in which it incarcerates the spectator. Fourthly, the empowerment of the viewer by identification with a dominant specular position (such as with Caligari's hypnotic and castrating gaze) is undermined by "counter-surveillance" – the return of the gaze – and by the decentering and re-delegation of the controlling masculine point of view to such unstable figures as Jane and Cesare. Finally, by foregrounding various acts of narration *Caligari* signally refuses to "efface the marks of the enunciation," and so denies the imperceptible and anonymous narrative authority associated in the classic realist text with the visual code and with its narratological equivalent, the "dominant discourse." Contrary to Budd's contention, the film's complex cross-cutting and editing techniques signally *fail* to produce a sense of overall "continuity and stability" (25) – analogous to Lukacs' "covering over" – and unlike the model of the classical narrative film (with which Budd frequently aligns *Caligari*), its various codes of decor, lighting, acting etc., are scarcely "transparent" and "self-effacingly subordinate to narration" (10), especially when one recalls the exaggerated and excessive quality of the stylistic elements of expressionism and their disruptive and unsettling impact upon the film.

As Elsaesser claims, the foregrounding of narrative devices such as flashbacks and frames, or (to use the formalists' distinction) the emphasis on the "plot" (the work's rearrangement of events) rather than on the "story" (the original order in which the events occurred)[61] may indeed have the effect of forcing the spectator "to attend to the artistry of the work,"[62] and thereby raise the "high-cultural" cachet of the film. Yet this artistry does not figure merely as an end in itself, or as an aesthetic indulgence. For as with the historical avant-garde, the text simultaneously ensures that where it enjoys a state of aesthetic autonomy by liberating itself from the conventional constraints of illusionism and of representation, this autonomy now takes a form which is "ideologically charged."[63] If the premise of the formalists' distinction is a fundamental belief in rationalism, causality, and the conventional space-time continuum, which allows the decoding of the story with "each event coming in the order in which it would occur in real life and the events bound to each other in a cause-and-effect relationship,"[64] and if this is what makes it possible to decode the plot and so discern the text's underlying pattern, then *Caligari* is characterized both by its suspension of such logical interpretative constructions and by its disruption of any rationalistic sense of assurance.

---

[61] Boris Tomashevsky, "Thematics," *Russian Formalist Criticism*, 66–67. See also the editors' commentary, 25.
[62] See Tony Bennett, *Formalism and Marxism* (London: Methuen, 1979), 25.
[63] Hohendahl, "The Loss of Reality," 92.
[64] Editors' commentary, *Russian Formalist Criticism*, 25.

More than merely foregrounding the artistic arrangement of events by complicating them as "plot," the film's structure of indecidability interrogates the ideological assumptions behind the representation of the rationalist continuum of time, space and causality. In reorganizing the imaginary temporal and spatial relations its crucial dimension of indecidability ensures that, like the dadaists' avant-garde creations, its "objects do not return from their alienation."[65] In other words the text ultimately resists a simple re-coding back into everyday logic (such as that of the dominant social discourse), and resists the notion that there is a "real" or "natural" order of truth which may be recovered through the work. And in resisting this rationalist re-coding while projecting its own indecidable reorganization of the conventional time-space continuum, it foregrounds the fundamentally discursive and artificial nature of all such conventions, exposing their ideological status as merely naturalized constructions rather than the unmitigated truth they purport to be.

[65] Brecht, "[Notizen über V-Effekte]," *Gesammelte Werke*, 15 (Frankfurt: Suhrkamp, 1967) 364.

# 7

❖❖❖❖❖❖❖❖❖❖❖❖❖❖❖❖❖❖❖❖❖❖❖❖❖❖❖❖❖❖❖❖❖❖❖❖❖❖❖❖❖❖❖❖❖❖

# Conclusion. Postmodernism and the avant-garde

❖❖❖❖❖❖❖❖❖❖❖❖❖❖❖❖❖❖❖❖❖❖❖❖❖❖❖❖❖❖❖❖❖❖❖❖❖❖❖❖❖❖❖❖❖❖

### Towards a poetics of postmodernism: simulation, parody, and history

I want to conclude by outlining some of the links between post-modernism and the expressionist avant-garde, and by discussing some of the central issues defining the various cultural formations of the modern and the postmodern period.

The modernist movement is characterized by its all-encompass-ing fascination with innovation and "the shock of the new." As Habermas has noted in a key essay in the debate on postmodern-ism, "Modernity – An Incomplete Project," from the time of the dispute between the "Ancients and Moderns" the term "modern" has regularly expressed "the consciousness of an epoch that re-lates itself to the past of antiquity, in order to view itself as the result of a transition from the old to the new."[1] Modernism similarly constitutes itself primarily in relation to the tradition it simultaneously shrugs off, that is by making "an abstract opposi-tion between tradition and the present." Consequently, it defines itself by negating a past seen as extending up to all but the "dernier cri." For the "distinguishing mark of such modern works is 'the new' which will be overcome and made obsolete through the novelty of the next style" (4). Paradoxically it is this

---

[1] In *The Anti-Aesthetic: Essays on Postmodern Culture*, ed. Hal Foster (Port Towns-end, Washington: Bay Press, 1983), 4. Also published as "Modernity versus Postmodernity," *New German Critique* 8.1 (Winter 1981).

sense of being authentically "modern" and independent of the past that now articulates the work's claim to belong to the "classics."

Walter Benjamin's key observations with respect to modernity and its aesthetics – regarding the "loss" or "atrophy" of experience in the modern metropolitan world ("Erfahrungsverlust"), and the work of art's loss of "aura" in the era of its mechanical reproduction – open up a new perspective on this question of modernism's drive for innovation.[2] From Benjamin's perspective we can view modernism's fetishization of newness for example as a means of restoring to the shrunken or reified modes of experience in modernity a renewed sense of wonder with respect even to the most banal aspects of life. And modernism's "hyper-realistic" or "magnifying-glass" style of representation which observes the most minute details of everyday life, and which demonstrates its infinite sensitivity towards the slightest reflexes of consciousness and the intricate processes of cognition, can thus be understood as a response to the experiential impoverishment Benjamin describes. Its innovative attempts at registering the impact of the real upon consciousness thus confer upon the normally mundane and contingent aspects of modern life a renewed sense of wonder.[3] At the same time modernism's emphasis on originality and innovation seeks to restore (or at least compensate for) both the decline of the "genial" inventiveness of the artist and the work's loss of aura. However, if as Benjamin maintains, the sense of aura associated with the ritual and cultic quality of traditional art have the effect both of distancing art from everyday life and of fostering the sense of its autonomy from the social sphere, then his optimism regarding the prospects for a progressive "de-auraticization of art" clearly applies less to modernism, with its more hermetic and self-absorbed aestheticism, than to the avant-garde and to its strategies of desublimation and de-aestheticization.[4]

[2] Walter Benjamin, "The Work of Art in the Age of Mechanical Reproduction," 217–252.
[3] On this point, see also Astradur Eysteinsson, *The Concept of Modernism* (Ithaca: Cornell University Press, 1990), 126–127. I am indebted here both to Eysteinsson's commentary and to the particular constellation of theoretical texts he invokes.
[4] On the question of Benjamin's concept of the "de-auraticization of art" see Martin Jay, "Habermas and Modernism," *Habermas and Modernity*, ed. Richard J. Bernstein (Oxford: Polity Press, 1985), 126–128.

Fredric Jameson has argued similarly that in "classical Anglo-American modernism" there is a "strategic emphasis on innovation and novelty, [an] obligatory break with previous styles."[5] This modernizing stance, the urge to "'make it new'" derives from the need "to produce something which resists and breaks through the force of gravity of repetition as a universal feature of commodity equivalence" (136). In other words, Jameson views modernism's emphasis on innovation as a response to the "repetitive structure" characterizing the "commodity production of consumer capitalism" (135). If, as has been suggested, modernism also defines itself by setting itself off from the encroachments of mass culture, then this further role of innovation makes it a crucially important feature.

Firstly innovation contributes in particular towards modernism's cultivation of a high-cultural profile of "obscurity and hermeticism,"[6] and it thus becomes a central means by which modernism differentiates itself from the formularized and consumption-oriented generic formats typical of mass culture's commodity aesthetics. However, innovation is also associated with an endless series of accelerated self-renewals in reaction to further encroachments from outside of its high-cultural bastion as modernism attempts to preserve its separateness and autonomy. And in the face of the enormous changes brought about in the culture and society of modernity by the material determinants of consumerism, modernism's rather desperate response – its endless and spiralling cycles of innovation – is testimony to its lack of awareness (or possibly to its consummate lack of interest) regarding the manner in which these social and institutional forces determine its position and function, and affect its own social differentiation – as can be seen from its ignorance or disavowal of the institutionalization of art.

Secondly, modernism devotes its innovative energy to a massive overhaul of the outmoded or exhausted stereotypes it has inherited, in the hope that the renovation of formal and linguistic structures will have a correlative or "knock-on" effect and so renovate the structure of the life-world too. For as Jameson notes, there exists the belief in modernism that "a change in style will

---

[5] Frederic Jameson, "Reification and Utopia in Mass Culture," 136.
[6] Linda Hutcheon, *A Poetics of Postmodernism. History, Theory, Fiction* (New York and London: Routledge, 1988), 41.

help us to see the world in a new way and thus achieve a kind of cultural or countercultural revolution of its own."[7]

By contrast to the avant-garde's critical and rebellious drive then, modernism's iconoclastic edge is directed essentially against the outmoded and traditional techniques of its predecessors, so that rather than criticizing art and its conditions as a whole – the function which in Bürger's opinion defines the historical avant-garde – the aim of modernism's drive for innovation is primarily to distance itself merely from previous modes and fashions of art. As a consequence, modernism ends up not by critiquing the bourgeois society from which it emerges, but as Jochen Schulte-Sasse notes, by becoming instead "the cultural complement of modernity"[8]: its frequent fascination with technology, with being up-to-date and with using the most advanced and innovative formal means available to it – what Linda Hutcheon calls its "[f]aith in the rational, scientific mastery of reality"[9] – are testimony both to the "complementary" character of its relationship to its own historical period, as well as to its rather passive and uncritical nature.

Jameson, for example, sees the relationship between modernism and modernity as marked by "an aestheticizing reaction against the sordid realities of a business civilization."[10] And as Alex Callinicos has also observed, modernism frequently takes over from aestheticism the "concept of art as a refuge from alienated social life" with the result that it has "a propensity to treat reality as an occasion for aesthetic experience."[11] This "aestheticizing reaction," or what Callinicos refers to as "Modernism's primarily aesthetic relation to the world" (49), stems from the particularities of the heritage of modernism: on the one hand it has its origins in aestheticism and in a form of aesthetic autonomy which denies or represses the real, while on the other hand it emerged within an historical period in which the harsher social aspects of capitalism in late modernity were all too apparent – historical factors which by contrast were of central

---

[7] Jameson, "The Ideology of the Text," *The Ideologies of Theory*, I, 68.
[8] Jochen Schulte-Sasse, "Carl Einstein; or, the Postmodern Transformation of Modernism," *Modernity and the Text*, ed. Huyssen and Bathrick, 42.
[9] Hutcheon, *A Poetics of Postmodernism*, 28.
[10] Jameson, "The Ideology of the Text," 68.
[11] Alex Callinicos, *Against Postmodernism. A Marxist Critique* (Cambridge: Polity Press, 1989), 55, 53.

importance for example for the naturalists at the beginning of the modernist period.

Typically modernism attempts either to flee from history or pretends to stand outside of it completely. Consequently it often seeks in the unity of art a kind of formal redemption from the discontinuities of the modern world. T. S. Eliot believed for example that "in the mind of the poet these experiences are always forming new wholes" and observed a tendency in modernism to seek refuge in myths as "a way of controlling, of ordering, of giving shape and significance to the immense panorama of futility and anarchy which is contemporary history."[12] Joseph Frank discovers a similar yearning for order in modernism's underlying reliance on the organic and on a "capacity to form new wholes, to fuse seemingly disparate experiences into an organic unity,"[13] a capacity culminating in its characteristic tendency both to sew the text together through a complex of internal references and correspondingly to de-emphasize or even suspend reference to the outside world. To be sure modernism's minute dissection of the everyday world and of the human psyche renews the understanding of our habitual modes of perception and communication, and – in its epistemological effect at least – may be described in Eysteinsson's terms as "an anarchic force attacking and even severely undermining our social order . . . " (26). Nevertheless, modernism's interest in the real world is often very narrow and specific, and frequently arises only as a means to more formal or hermetic ends. Eysteinsson, for example, concedes that the "modernist preoccupation with human consciousness" is not motivated by "a mimetic concern with the human environment and social conditions" but may be seen instead as an "inward turn" which itself "negates outward reality" (26). Hence Jameson's observation (referred to above) that "modernism is not a new thing in itself, but rather something like a cancelled realism, a realism denied and negated and *aufgehoben* in genuinely Hegelian fashion . . ." – a devastating criticism given modernism's defining urge for innovation.[14]

These two inherited features of modernism – its unproblematic

---

[12] T. S. Eliot, "Ulysses, Order, and Myth," *Selected Prose of T. S. Eliot*, 247, 177.
[13] Joseph Frank, "Spatial Form in Modern Literature" *The Widening Gyre: Crisis and Mastery in Modern Literature* (New Brunswick: Rutgers University Press, 1963) 10.     [14] Jameson, "The Ideology of the Text," 68.

and unreflected adoption of aesthetic autonomy and its character-istic mode of reworking but simultaneously negating realism – are reflected in modernism's central assumptions. Firstly in separating itself off as an autonomous cultural discourse modernism operates from the belief that it possesses a perspective which is external to, and independent of, the realities to which it purports to respond. Secondly, modernism frequently takes for granted, in a similarly unreflected manner, that its systems of language, thought and representation are "neutral" mimetic implements. Consequently its goal of renewing those outdated or worn-out formal techniques which it inherits frequently rests upon the similarly unreflected assumption that, in Jameson's sense, this renovation will lead in turn to the re-creation of the realities to which they correspond.[15]

However, with the advent from *within* modernism of more progressive forces, culminating in the radical expressionists and the other cultural formations of the historical avant-garde, these unreflected assumptions are revealed as deeply problematic. Rather than simply "renewing" the inherited rhetorical, represen-tational and conceptual apparatus – the dominant discourses of art – the avant-garde instead deconstructs its clichés. This distinc-tion is vital. For example, the poetry of the "expressionist revol-ution" does not intend to "renew" or "update" the idealistic Romantic discourse it inherits (such as the familiar cosmological tropes of God, heaven and stars) but, as we have seen, aims instead to "parody" or to "de-aestheticize" them in order to question both the position of such ideas within the conceptual vocabulary of the period, as well as their role within affirmative culture as a whole.[16]

---

[15] See ibid., 68.

[16] T. S. Eliot's *The Waste Land* is a modernist variation on the avant-garde strategies of montage and re-writing. Although his confrontation with a discursively pre-determined world appears very similar at first glance, in actuality it is motivated by very different interests from those of the expressionists. As Eliot's essay on "Ulysses" makes clear, he is concerned above all to discover (or impose) a degree of "order" with regard to the chaotic modern world and its "immense panorama of futility and anarchy." As a consequence his extensive use of quotation constitutes the attempt to *graft* his own discourse onto those classical texts of the past which have already established a kind of bridgehead in this endeavor. Rather than *overturning* and casting aside these older, founding discourses – as the avant-garde would do – he resurrects them and clings nostalgically to the norms they embody. As one commentator points out, "Eliot found his own voice by first reproducing that of others – as if it was only through his reading of, and response to, literature that he could find anything to

It is also important to note that the avant-garde's discursive techniques, such as its re-writing of the recurrent images, the rhetorical clichés, and the ideological stereotypes of a previous cultural paradigm, aim primarily at the thorough-going critique and deconstruction of such orienting discourses rather than the establishment of a new and competing linguistic or formal-technical norm: it is a defining feature of the historical avant-garde that it is precisely *not* interested in creating an alternative "meta-narrative" or "master-discourse."[17] At the same time, its deconstruction of the hidden ideological content behind these stereotypes points both to the lack of neutrality characterizing the inherited system of representation and the inability of the writer from within the discursive constellation in which he is enmeshed to adopt a position "outside," from which he might comment upon society. This is one of the common modernist presuppositions described by Jochen Schulte-Sasse, who cites Thomas Mann's central strategy of "irony" as a prime example of the naive modernist assumption that "the artist can inhabit a place outside of society and the discourses institutionalized in society."[18] Franco Moretti similarly points to this "complicity between modernist irony and indifference to history"[19] as one of modernism's central characteristics:

This is an aesthetic-ironic attitude whose best definition still lies in an old formula – "willing suspension of disbelief" – which shows how much of the modernist imagination – where nothing is unbelievable – has its source in romantic irony. And romantic irony . . . is a frame of mind that sees in any event no more than an "occasion" for free intellectual and emotional play . . . (341)

To the extent that modernism engages or even attacks modernity then, it does so through a disavowal (or ignorance of) its own already institutionalized (and thus sanitized) situation, blissfully

hold onto, anything 'real'. That is why *Ulysses* struck him so forcefully . . ." See Peter Ackroyd, *T. S. Eliot* (London: Hamish Hamilton, 1984), 118. In this sense Eliot's use of previous texts is not a subversion but an *extension* of the aestheticist assumptions at the heart of modernism, in particular the belief in the existence of a separate, transcendent and self-sufficient world of art.
17  Examples of this deconstructive re-writing are the early phase of dada in Zürich and of the earlier, unpolitical phases of both expressionism and surrealism.
18  Schulte-Sasse, "Carl Einstein," 42.
19  Franco Moretti, "The Spell of Indecision," *Marxism and the Interpretation of Culture*, ed. Cary Nelson and Lawrence Grossberg (Urbana: University of Illinois Press, 1988), 343.

unaware of the fact there can be no independent and stable point of view "outside" of the social "text" which envelops all discourse: that there can be no *"hors texte."*

To summarize my argument then, what distinguishes the avant-garde from modernism in general is its institutional awareness: firstly, unlike modernism the avant-garde not only renovates the means but also deconstructs the *ideology* of art, while reflecting upon those social demarcations of culture for which modernism seems to show a complete lack of awareness or interest. The avant-garde sets out to expose and alter art's status as a socially differentiated and segregated mode of discourse, and to make it clear that its position is always mediated by the social mechanisms responsible for the institutionalization of culture. Since modernism signally fails to reflect upon its own position within this organizational differentiation of discourses it is inevitable, as Schulte-Sasse notes, that any critical impact it might have is always already "defused by the autonomous institutionalization of its artistic practice" (42). Modernism's naive reliance on the supposed neutrality of its representational and linguistic media, and its assumption of an external and superior perspective both bear witness to this lack of institutional awareness. By contrast, the avant-garde's goal of overcoming the enforced separation of art and life springs precisely from its insight into what Habermas defines (with Max Weber) as the process of "bourgeois rationalization" responsible for producing this functional differentiation of the separate spheres of social activity.[20] For behind the avant-garde's eccentricities and seemingly meaningless antics in ridiculing, exposing and overthrowing art's rules lies a profoundly meaningful purpose: the interrogation of the historically specific means by which art is mediated and administered by society's dominant cultural discourses.

Historicizing the avant-garde: the institution of art
and the social imaginary

I have argued in this book that what Bürger identifies as the central defining feature of the avant-garde, namely "the sublation of art and life," is itself best understood in a historical manner. As Hardt

[20] Jürgen Habermas, *Legitimation Crisis* (London: Heinemann, 1976), 85.

points out, one cannot use this formula and the categories "art" and "life" unless one also specifies which particular art-form and artistic functions one is referring to, as well as the particular real-life context into which this art is to be integrated.[21] At the same time, with the historical avant-garde the sublation of art and life becomes less important as a concrete goal to be implemented than as a general orienting principle to be borne in mind, as a question to be reflected upon, or even as an aporia to be experimented with and "worked-through." For example in the case of the progressive expressionist writers and artists, the aim is the creation of a new kind of "radicalized" or "ideologically charged" aesthetic autonomy which is wary of the separation of different discursive realms – what Habermas calls the "irretrievable sacrifice of bourgeois rationalization affecting art"[22] – and wary of the affirmative functions which this autonomous status has conventionally entailed. Besides adopting this new cautiousness regarding aesthetic autonomy the historical avant-garde similarly rethinks its central principle: its goal is now the "*cynical*" sublation of art and life. As we have seen, this practice involves reversing the polarity: if the progressive idealism adopted for example by the utopian avant-gardes of the Romantic period attempted to elevate life to the ideal level of art, the historical avant-garde now de-aestheticizes art and so brings any lingering idealist elements down to earth, to the level of the mundane and the material.

The historical avant-garde's heightened social, historical and institutional awareness also expresses itself in the overturning of those artificially static and stable images of experience which are the product of dominant social discourse, and in the interrogation of the normative status of technical-scientific rationality and of what the expressionists see as its systematizing and limiting effects. Characteristically the historical avant-garde intervenes by undermining the normativity of such ordered and seemingly factual modes of organizing experience, and by destabilizing any inherently regulatory and rationalist dimensions, such as the sense of transparency, objectivity and clear-cut "decidability" which inhere in the "classical" system of representation itself.

The historical avant-garde's critical (or ideology-critical) impact lies then in revealing that such organized and ordered images of

---

[21] Manfred Hardt, "Zu Begriff, Geschichte und Theorie der literarischen Avant-garde," *Literarische Avantgarden*, 159.    [22] Habermas, *Legitimization Crisis*, 85.

reality are in fact the product of an arbitrary discursive organization whose function is to create a smooth and efficient social imaginary capable of imposing a continuum of time, space and causality upon the fundamentally contingent and chaotic world of experience. The conventional organic work for example frequently presents experience as ordered, closed and static, and so tends as a result to suspend or even to paralyze further reflection on possible alternatives. Consequently, its limitation is that it has difficulty, as Colin MacCabe observes of the classic realist text, in representing contradictions. The avant-garde text by contrast is characterized, like the "subversive" texts MacCabe describes, by the combative character of its approach to such fixities, by its interrogation of the apparent "givens,"[23] and by its revelation that reality does *not* exist as a "totality." The avant-garde instead reveals reality as a construction that, if perceptible at all, exists as fundamentally irregular, fractured and contradictory, and with the character not of a "totality" but rather what Ernst Bloch associates with "interruption" or "Unterbrechung."[24]

With regard to this dismantling of the real I have argued here that the dominant social discourses, as well as the institutionalized forms of art corresponding to them, have the effect of establishing particular patterns of perception, and of projecting as "reality" the products of these limited and historically specific forms of seeing.[25] This systematization results in what Benjamin, as we have seen, calls the loss or "shrinkage of experience": the restriction of experience to the dominant patterns of organized life in society. It is in this regard that the broader understanding of the avant-garde, for which I have argued in this book, is particularly relevant. For the artists of the historical avant-garde not only attack aesthetic conventions and the institution of art. As Eysteinsson points out, if one goes beyond Bürger's theorization of the avant-garde and studies the manifestos of the various progressive movements, it is clear that

---

[23] On this point see Lyotard, "Vorstellung, Darstellung, Undarstellbarkeit," *Immaterialität und Postmoderne* (Berlin: Merve, 1985), 91–102. Here 97.

[24] See Eysteinsson's important chapter on the "Aesthetics of Interruption," *The Concept of Modernism*, 179–241.

[25] Jochen Schulte-Sasse argues also that Carl Einstein deconstructs reality as a "form of seeing that the civilizing process gradually enforced as a transcendental a priori that therefore had to be overcome." See "Carl Einstein," 48.

their main target, besides the general burden of tradition, is bourgeois life-praxis and conventional language and discourse, which is both laden with the deadening values of the past and susceptible to the ideological manipulations of the present . . . In the case of Zürich Dada for instance [the] avant-gardists aimed their radical semiotic warfare against the sign system of conventional, communicative language . . .[26]

In a sense then, the avant-garde's attack is directed more than anything else against the *bourgeois construction of social reality* in all its guises. The avant-garde exerts a resistance against this restrictive and all-encompassing social imaginary through the development of oppositional discourses or "counter-texts" which explode these constraining experiential constructions, and open them up to alternatives. Examples of this would be the progressive artists' characteristic explorations of illogicality, madness and the unconscious, or the massive expansion of the self through the wholehearted embrace of life-intensity, intoxication and chaos which characterizes many of the expressionists (and perhaps most notably, Gottfried Benn).[27] Through such alternative values the historical avant-garde sets about deconstructing conventional configurations of experience and perception, yet – true to the nature of the "expressionist revolution" which inscribes a permanent and ongoing revolutionary openness into its images – it does so without substituting for the established patterns a new set of fixed values of its own. For it is precisely such a sense of fixity that expressionism's re-writing of the discursive world, its creation of images "under erasure," sets out to undercut.

The avant-garde "bracketing" of reality's seemingly factual social "givens" even extends to undermining the truth-status of the visible: as in *Caligari* for example the empiricist principle "seeing is believing" is frequently overturned. The familiar reliance on those scientific or positivistic values which produce such concrete facticity is revealed as a mode of investigation which only succeeds in legitimizing itself as a master- or meta-discourse by undermining or "framing" all alternative and subaltern perspectives, that is, by virtue *only* of its power as an unquestionable

---

[26] Eysteinsson, *The Concept of Modernism*, 173.
[27] On this point, see Jochen Schulte-Sasse, "Foreword: Theory of Modernism versus Theory of the Avant-Garde." Introduction to Bürger, *Theory of the Avant-Garde*, xliv.

*a priori* – an "irrational" authority.[28] As the example of *Caligari* also demonstrates, in order to counter this self-legitimizing "irrational authority" it is significant that the historical avant-garde does *not* take the conventional route of appealing to an even higher, "more rational" authority via a new master-rhetoric or dominant discourse. Instead, it deconstructs the very notion of "rationality" as well as the distinction between "inside" and "outside" – the difference on which is based the illusion of an exterior, framing, and transcendental perspective, and the myth of an all-powerful "meta-language." And in doing so the avant-garde sweeps aside the clutter of defunct cosmologies and their rhetorical ballast, and purges them in its revolutionary fire.

## Postmodernism and the historical avant-garde: postmodern parody and expressionist re-writing

With the progressive works of the historical avant-garde a series of significant steps is taken which paves the way for the emergence of the postmodernist mode. For if modernism still upholds "the claim to represent, or narrate, the event itself from a position nonetheless exterior to it,"[29] then a central task of the historical avant-garde – and, as we have seen, of the counter-texts of expressionism in particular – is to deconstruct this "outside." By forcibly re-writing the discursively constituted world and undercutting its dominant rhetoric and images from within, the expressionists already produce an insight which later becomes a paradigmatic position in postmodernism: that one is always already enmeshed in the constant circulation of signs, images and discourses, and that in this realm there can be no "outside" or neutral point of view since one's perspective is always already informed and contained by this restricted discursive economy.

Postmodernism challenges the traditional notions of an unaffected, external perspective and of the possibility of originality within this all-embracing pre-written world primarily by means of pastiche or parody. Through their foregrounding of intertex-

---

[28] See Seyla Benhabib, "Epistemologies of Postmodernism: a Rejoinder to Jean-François Lyotard," *New German Critique* 33 (1984): 103–126, here 105; also Axel Honneth, "Der Affekt gegen das Allgemeine. Zu Lyotards Konzept der Postmoderne," *Merkur* 38 (1984): 893–902, here 896.

[29] Bill Readings, *Introducing Lyotard. Art and Politics* (London: Routledge, 1991), 74.

tual relations these parodic forms of art lead, as Linda Hutcheon maintains, to "a vision of interconnectedness" which acknowledges history and the factors of social determination at the same time as it both sees through the fallacy of the "histoire" and recognizes that the "'reality' of the past is *discursive* reality" rather than objective fact.[30]

This acknowledgement of the eminently discursive nature of history and reality is precisely what is involved in the expressionists' forcible re-writing of what they perceive as an already "written" world. This acknowledgement of the discursive construction of the real is often associated primarily with postmodernism. Silvio Gaggi argues for example that,

Art after the sixties often reasserted representationality, but what was represented were things that were already images; that is, art images began to be used as a means of examining the nature of images themselves. And stories and novels began to be concerned with the processes and problems of writing.[31]

As we have seen however, the decisive steps towards this reorientation regarding representationality and the discursive construction of the social imaginary were already taken by the historical avant-garde. Like postmodern parody the avant-garde's response – its strategy of re-writing – denies any claims to objectivity either in the "original" (i.e. the text it re-writes), or in the new, parodic counter-discourses it creates. This produces a level of *self-reflexivity* (another vitally important characteristic of the postmodern) which constantly points to the arbitrariness of the constructed world, yet does so simultaneously in a way, as Hutcheon says of postmodernism "that admits its own provisionality" (13) as well. In other words, like postmodern parody, the expressionist avant-garde's revolutionary re-writing of the world not only reveals the inherent fictionality of all existing cosmologies, meta-languages and master-narratives, but most importantly insists at the same time upon the provisionality of its *own* claims to truth. For example, where the idealist or utopian expressionists might still proceed as if their attempt to seize control of history through their projections of "Geist" and "Menschenverbrüderung" ("fraternity

---

[30] Hutcheon, *A Poetics of Postmodernism*, 24

[31] Silvio Gaggi, *Modern/Postmodern. A Study in Twentieth-Century Arts and Ideas* (Philadelphia: University of Pennsylvania Press, 1989), 20.

of all mankind") were already historical fact, the expressionist avant-garde by contrast is deeply skeptical of creating such new fixities. As a result it tears down the old mythologies as well as their corresponding rhetorical constructs, in anticipation of the postmodern belief, as Hutcheon explains in Lyotard's terminology, that "knowledge cannot escape complicity with some meta-narrative," and that, as a consequence, "*no* narrative can be a natural 'master' narrative: there are no natural hierarchies; there are only those we construct" (13).

What I have argued here is that the expressionist avant-garde in effect prefigures what Lyotard describes as the important "pagan" quality defining postmodern discourse,[32] that is, its reluctance to "seize the high ground" of any epistemological debate, and to avoid creating new meta-languages in favor of the production of what one Lyotard-commentator, Bill Readings, describes as a rather more provisional "series of little narratives."[33] The expressionist avant-garde shares with postmodernism a wariness of nostalgia for any more substantial consolation such as a firm sense of theoretical or cosmological unity. For the turbulent period of history preceding the postmodern – associated not only with the barbarity of great wars and holocausts but with the horrors of totalitarian thought – is testimony enough, as Lyotard says with respect to the dangers of a longing for such unity and totality, "that the price of this illusion is terror."[34]

In this regard the two cultural formations – the expressionist avant-garde and the postmodern – are clearly linked: both by their wariness of all totalizing theoretical constructs – what Lyotard calls "the phantasm of taking possession of reality" – as well as by their corresponding need to wage a "war on totality."[35] They are also related via a common Nietzschean "prehistory" characterized by a sense of skepticism with respect to the relativism of all "Weltbilder"[36] and of all the transcendental signifieds or "grand

[32] Jean-François Lyotard and Jean-Loup Thébaud, *Just Gaming* (Minneapolis: University of Minnesota Press, 1985), 58.
[33] Readings, *Introducing Lyotard*, 73.
[34] Lyotard, "What is the Postmodern?" *The Postmodern Explained* (Minneapolis: University of Minnesota Press, 1992), 16.
[35] Lyotard, "What is the Postmodern?" 16.
[36] For a commentary on this aspect of Lyotard's thought, see Honneth, "Der Affekt gegen das Allgemeine," 899.

narratives"[37] which anchor and legitimize the "meta-discourses" of the modern period.[38] In eroding the sense of fixity which clings to such constructed worlds, both postmodernism and the expressionist avant-garde do not so much intend to create a new "meta-language" as produce the "site of resistance to meta-languages."[39] Even if their strategies involve "the invention of other realities" the goal is not to create a new sense of order to replace the old, but rather to pursue to its furthest extreme this Nietzschean nihilism involving what Lyotard calls the "discovery of the *lack of reality* in reality."[40] Where the avant-gardes have "humiliated and disqualified reality by their scrutiny of the pictorial techniques used to instill a belief in it" (12) they do so in order to fulfill one of the avant-garde's most significant goals: to reveal the extent of art's implication in the creation of the "Weltbild," the particular patterns of perception and experience which substantiate and constitute the real.

Thus the Nietzschean links between the expressionist avant-garde and postmodernism lie in their shared goal of deconstructing some of the guiding principles of traditional Western thought. For example, in as far as the term "postmodern" carries the suggestion that this historical phase occurs "after" the modern period, it also implies a radical break with the entire humanist tradition of thought, and above all with its central tenets: the belief in the unitary Cartesian self, and in the use of reason as a means both of recognizing the world's order and of orienting the self within it.[41] Yet as I have argued above, these are precisely the founding epistemological and ontological principles which are already targeted, subjected to intense scrutiny and ultimately overturned in the Nietzsche-inspired "expressionist revolution." In other words, at this early stage of the historical avant-garde (1910–20) the "post-humanist" principles which will later prove central to the postmodernists are already apparent.

The link between postmodernism and the avant-garde also

---

[37] Lyotard, *The Postmodern Condition* (Minneapolis: University of Minnesota Press, 1984), xxiii.
[38] For a commentary on the notion of "grand narratives," see Benhabib, "Epistemologies of Postmodernism," 104.
[39] Readings, *Introducing Lyotard*, 74.
[40] Lyotard, "What is the Postmodern?" 9.
[41] On the notion of "post," see Gaggi, *Modern/Postmodern*, 18–19. See also Lyotard, "Note on the Meaning of 'Post-'," *The Postmodern Explained*, 75–80.

becomes evident if we bear in mind that it is precisely this rebellious and iconoclastic phase of the modern period – the phase we have equated with the "historical avant-garde" – that Lyotard circumscribes paradoxically as "postmodern," arguing famously that a "work can become modern only if it is first postmodern. Thus understood, postmodernism is not modernism at its end, but in a nascent state, and this state is recurrent" (13). In other words, for Lyotard postmodernism constitutes the ever-changing, radical and revolutionary front of modernism as a whole. This take on Lyotard's formulation points towards the center of my concerns here: what is interesting about the relationship between the avant-garde and postmodernism is not the extent to which the historical avant-garde (and in particular the expressionist avant-garde) "preempts" or "prefigures" the central strategies and paradoxes of postmodernity – an observation that would reduce postmodernism merely to an historical tautology – but rather the extent to which they *both* represent an ongoing process of defining a critical response to modernity. For this critical process consists of the attempt to respond to and deconstruct bourgeois cultural practices without on the one hand becoming merely their "cultural complement" or ideological accomplice, and without on the other hand falling into a merely oppositional or "reactive" relationship, in which the critical text becomes "enmeshed in a fundamental epistemological dependence on the very thing it criticizes."[42]

This wariness of merely ending up as a theoretical supplement, of devolving into the mere "antidote" or "opposition" to the very object it interrogates, is certainly an important factor differentiating the "sophisticated" expressionists from their more passionate, and naively iconoclastic fellow-artists on the idealist or "activist" side of the movement. In essence one could argue that this characteristic feature of the avant-garde expresses a wariness of lapsing into a conciliatory or affirmative form of cultural production against its own intentions to the contrary, and of drifting into a mode of criticism moreover which would risk nailing its colors to precisely those presumptions (such as the presumption of a rational, stable and external point of view) which it needs instead

---

[42] Schulte-Sasse, "Modernity and Modernism, Postmodernity and Postmodernism: Framing the Issue," *Cultural Critique* 5 (1987): 5–22. Here 8.

to question. This is not to argue of course that the expressionist avant-garde refrains completely from creating critical or oppositional forms of art but rather that it does so, as I have argued throughout, in a manner which, through its *internal* forms of self-reflection and self-criticism, takes fully into account both the social limits within which art is produced and received, as well as the institutional predeterminations which limit the oppositional effects of its critical potential.

## The historical avant-garde and Baudrillard's postmodern "age of simulation"

To this extent the criticism most frequently directed at postmodernism – its alleged lack of direct political and ideological engagement – could also be aimed at much of the historical avant-garde, not only with respect to expressionism but also as regards the earlier phases of both the dada and surrealist movements. If we regard postmodernism with Schulte-Sasse as "that movement in the history of art that does not attempt to overcome the separateness of art and life any more . . . [and] accepts the fact that the functional differentiation of society is irreversible" (7), then the origins of this postmodern development towards the acceptance of social "differentiation" and aesthetic autonomy must be traced back directly to the historical avant-garde. For it is here that progressive art first acknowledges the experience of its failure to overcome this separation and attempts to work it through, by developing instead a new, radicalized and adversarial conception of aesthetic autonomy.

Here too art first takes account of its socially differentiated status, and creates strategies capable of responding incisively to this situation by discovering *internalized* forms of criticism (or self-criticism) – such as parody and re-writing – which do *not* presume an external or objective viewpoint (as modernism by contrast tends to do). Rather than continuing to strive for the unachievable goal of sublating art and life, such strategies seem almost to turn this goal of sublation on its head and, with a new cynicism more fully realized in contemporary postmodernism, begin to question the very notion that the two realms are even separate in the first place. For given what Habermas calls the

Conclusion. *Postmodernism and the avant-garde*

"false sublation of art"[43] (such as in the totalitarian state, or in aestheticized politics), and given also the all-encompassing circulation of signs and representations which in modernity inform and contain the real, the differences are increasingly effaced between the world and its "image of the world" ("Weltbild"), that is, between a real-life referent and its artistic image or signifier. Beginning with what Paul Mann calls the "reflexive awareness" of the avant-garde there is a growing sense not only of "the fundamentally discursive character of art,"[44] but also of the equally "written" character of the inhabited "life-world." For the real is now constituted as a constellation of signs and simulacra, whereby the existence of any "original" is opened to doubt – a fact which explains the prominence both of the strategies of parody and pastiche in postmodernism, and of analogous forms of rewriting in the expressionist avant-garde, which displace or defer the notion of "origin."

One commentator, Michael Newman, has even traced the entire development of modern art in terms of this relationship between the parodic text and the "original." He observes for example that the Romantic conception of parody is still oriented toward "the assertion of originality and the sovereignty of the artist-creator"; later forms of parody (which I would associate with the historical avant-garde and in particular with expressionism) then begin to question "the *assumption* of authority and origin, so that the parodic text enacts their displacement or decentering"; finally the postmodern parody takes this decentering even further in as far as it lacks all nostalgia for the "original" and "*begins* with the assumption of the impossibility of authority, origin, full presence and so on."[45]

One might add to this scheme a further observation that bears on the shift within modernity towards the postmodern and towards what Baudrillard has termed "the age of simulation."[46] For if simulation involves "the generation by models of a real without origin or reality" (2), the creation of mere "copies" without the

[43] Habermas, *Legitimization*, 86.
[44] Paul Mann, *The Theory-Death of the Avant-Garde* (Bloomington: Indiana University Press, 1991), 6.
[45] Michael Newman, "Revising Modernism, Representing Postmodernism: Critical Discourses of the Visual Arts," *Postmodernism ICA Documents*, 95–154. Here 141.
[46] Jean Baudrillard, *Simulations* (New York: Semiotext(e), 1983), 4.

268

benefit of an original, as well as the "liquidation of all referentials" (4), then it may be possible to describe the various artistic movements of the period along the following lines in terms of their response to this questioning of origins and reality.

Walter Benjamin identifies what is surely the starting point for Baudrillard's speculations here with his observation (referred to above, 252) that the modern period is increasingly affected by the emphasis on the mechanization of the work of art. This phenomenon develops to such an extent that the work loses the traditional artistic "aura" of originality and uniqueness and is received instead within the framework of a consumer-oriented "commodity aesthetics." The reaction to art's change of status varies widely among the different cultural formations of modernity. As we have seen, modernism for example responds to this disappearance of the "original" and to the effacement of the real-life referent not only by differentiating itself sharply from the reified forms associated with consumerist mass culture and the commodity form (for example through its emphasis on the high cultural status of its hermetically distanced forms), but simultaneously compensates for the loss of "aura" by reasserting with all the more vehemence the notion of newness, originality and artistic innovation[47] – a response amounting in a sense to a new spin on the Classic-Romantic use of the concept of the "genius." By contrast, the artists of the avant-garde and postmodernism both respond to this development by taking the opposite tack: they present the "referent," the object itself, as both the "referent" *and* its artistic "representation" in one – paradigmatically in the "objet trouvé" – thereby questioning not only the conventions of aura and of original artistic creation (as Bürger has shown), but also disclosing the overlaps *already existing* between the two levels of reference (referent–signifier), that is to say, the points at which these levels already begin to "short-circuit" and explode the conventional artistic/representational system.

The strategies of expressionist re-writing and postmodern parody share with the historical avant-garde's aesthetics of the "found object" this goal of *short-circuiting* the representational relationship between the signifier and its referent. Where the avant-garde aesthetics of the "found object" in dada presents the

---

[47] See Jameson, "Reification and Utopia in Mass Culture," 135–136.

"referent" itself as identical to the artistic signifier, so the acts of re-writing in expressionism or of parody in postmodernism similarly assume that both the original and its artistically reworked counterpart belong to essentially the same order, and that since both are discursive constructions within a discursively determined world of "simulations" – as in Baudrillard's model – neither can claim priority as the "original." In both cases the act of representation is questioned since the work actively participates in the constant circulation of images and in the slippage between discourses. Like those expressionist images which emerge, as I have argued, "under erasure" and with this resistance to closure and fixity already as it were "built in," the effect is not only to oppose classical realism and its attempts to "fix" its object mimetically, but in exposing the very attempt to re-present something as "present," the goal is to deconstruct any lingering "nostalgia for presence."[48]

This is the central function of the avant-garde's "oppositional discourses": by undermining the otherwise unquestionable and monolithic "presentness" of the real they not only "humiliated and disqualified reality" by pointing to the "lack of reality" in the real, but with their intense scrutiny of representational techniques they undermined the socially institutionalized dominant discourses underpinning reality, whose function is "to instill a belief in it" (2). Consequently, if it is true, as Jochen Schulte-Sasse maintains, that the postmodern distinguishes itself by no longer attempting to overcome the separation of art and life[49] – an attitude that directly relates to and is prepared by the experiments of the historical avant-garde – then the question arises as to whether this position stems from a kind of nihilistic resignation or simply from the realization that what with the "aestheticization of politics" (Benjamin),[50] the "false sublation" of art and life (Habermas),[51] the increasingly "semioticized" urban landscape of modernity,[52] and the subsequent acceleration of the forces of

---

[48] Lyotard, "What is the Postmodern?" *The Postmodern Explained*, 13.
[49] Schulte-Sasse, "Modernity and Modernism," 7.
[50] Benjamin, "The Work of Art in the Age of Mechanical Reproduction," *passim*.
[51] Habermas, *Legitimation Crisis*, 86.
[52] See Vietta and Kemper, *Expressionismus*, in particular section 2.5.2. ("Das neue Massenmedium Zeitung und die veränderte Struktur der Öffentlichkeit"). See also Georg Simmel, "Die Großstadt und das Geistesleben," *Die Großstadt. Jahrbuch der Gehe-Stiftung* (Dresden, 1903).

simulation, the boundaries between the art and life are in any case already completely effaced.

## Expressionist counter-discourse: re-writing and parody

The central moment in the development of Expressionism as an avant-garde movement is the sense of self-reflexivity that emerges from its confrontation with an already "written" world. Since with the Nietzschean revolution and its relativization of all cosmological belief systems the possibility of an *external* viewpoint is excluded, expressionism develops certain discursive strategies – related, as we have seen, to what is later called "parody" and "pastiche" in postmodernism – which are necessarily aimed at exposing the discursive constructedness of the world and at undercutting this endless circulation of images *from within*. To be sure, the idealist and activist factions of the expressionist movement still respond by giving vent to their nostalgia for the sense of fixity associated with the old stable world of referents and for the continuity provided by the traditional cosmologies and dominant discourses, and like modernism they even resort to creating new mythologies to fill the vacuum. For as Baudrillard writes, "when the real is no longer what it used to be, nostalgia assumes its full meaning. There is a proliferation of myths of origin and signs of reality; of second-hand truth, objectivity and authenticity."[53] But it is precisely in this respect that the expressionist avant-garde differs in its response from its more "naive" counterparts within the movement in as far as it is wary of the nostalgia and sense of order clinging to the old (fictional) systems. As a consequence it makes its goal the attempt to "deconstruct established patterns of perception without hastily replacing them"[54]: this is the message of the "expressionist revolution."

As we have seen, the formal strategies and oppositional discourses by which the expressionist avant-garde develops this deconstructive approach have much in common with postmodern parody which, as Linda Hutcheon writes, "allows an artist to speak *to* a discourse from *within* it, but without being totally recuperated by it."[55] For example my analysis of Döblin's "Murder of a Buttercup" illustrates the way in which the parodic

---

[53] Baudrillard, *Simulations*, 12.     [54] Schulte-Sasse, "Carl Einstein," 43.
[55] Hutcheon, *A Poetics of Postmodernism*, 35.

text can create a set of counter-discourses by performing a kind of linguistic pastiche, a parodic parade of disembodied, authoritarian discourses and gestures. Like the forms of parody typical of the postmodern, the critical impact of expressionist counter-discourses such as Döblin's parodies derives precisely from the manner in which these authoritarian dominant social discourses are addressed and undermined from *within*. For example, what we have termed (after Bakhtin) the "dialogical" and "hybrid" forms of discourse not only refrain from adopting an "outside" or classically "ironic" standpoint, but succeed in forcing contradictory world-views into an ideological collision even within the same syntactical and discursive frame. Similarly the confrontations staged between the mimetic and diegetic poles of the narration undercut the very possibility that a dominant narrative discourse or meta-linguistic position might emerge, by means of which the text could produce an (illusory) sense of control analogous to the classic realist text: instead of adopting an exterior, meta-position the parodic "counter-text" speaks *to* such authoritative discourses from *within* their very limits.

Similarly, as my analysis of *Caligari* demonstrates, although the dominant discourse of scientific rationality frequently inhabits the narrative, and appears to reinforce society's pervasive ideological belief in the possibility of final, indisputable knowledge, the sense of authority attached to the techno-scientific principle is constantly destabilized from within by the overwhelming sense of "indecidability" in the text. This affects the perception of identities, characters and events to such an extent, that the notion of a stable and "outside" perspective, and the construction of a rhetorical, textual or ideological meta-language is always ruled out.

Thus in the expressionist avant-garde the attempt to render reality "definable" by means of realism is always undermined *from within* by a series of similarly "internal," counter-discursive strategies such as the interaction with the fantastic, the grotesque and the melodramatic, or through the subversive effects of the parodic and the dialogical. These counter-discourses point towards those realms excluded by realism's rational and unitary "vision" and marginalized by an organization of experience based on a restrictive, techno-scientific "reality-principle." Thus their goal is not so much to set up an abstract and merely formal opposition to realism as to destabilize both its claims to offer a transparent, inclusive and truthful "histoire" and, by extension, those correspondingly realist discourses through which the social imaginary is constructed.

## Lyotard's postmodern sublime and Habermas' "Enlightenment project of modernity": modernism, mass culture and the avant-garde

In pointing to a marginal realm beyond the limits of the dominant discourse the subversive "counter-texts" of the avant-garde develop a poetics of the "unrepresentable." This category is linked in many respects to a further key concept currently discussed in the debate surrounding the definition of postmodernism – particularly with regard to Lyotard's important intervention – namely the notion of the sublime.

In revisiting and remodeling Kant's aesthetics[56] Lyotard stresses the important differences – already implicit in Kant's formulation of the problem – between the beautiful and the sublime. According to Kant, the beautiful depends upon a consensus of taste, a shared sense of aesthetic value.[57] By contrast to the "restful contemplation engendered by the beautiful" (II,§27: 107) the sublime is associated with its opposite: namely with a tension or "agitation" and with a "rapidly alternating repulsion and attraction" (II,§27: 107). For Kant maintains that the sublime is a response[58] to an object whose "magnitude" or "limitlessness" (II,§23: 90) is such that it overwhelms the power of the imagination to encompass or "represent" it, a monumentality for which only a concept or "idea of reason" can provide a degree of theoretical purchase. In exceeding the limits of representation the sublime is consequently associated firstly with the monstrous and formless,[59] and secondly with that which fails to adhere to the (generally agreed upon) conditions of the aesthetic. In line with

[56] Lyotard's notion of the sublime does not exactly correspond to Kant's conception at all points, as Lyotard himself admits. See Lyotard, "What is the Postmodern?" *The Postmodern Explained*, 14–15.

[57] Kant, *The Critique of Judgement*, Part II ("The Analytic of the Sublime"),§40: 150–154. See also Lyotard, "Vorstellung, Darstellung, Undarstellbarkeit," 94, 97.

[58] It is important to note that Kant emphasizes that the sublime is to be seen as a "response" rather than as an "object" or "cause" *per se*. See *Critique of Judgment* II, § 26: 104.

[59] On this point see Paul Crowther, *The Kantian Sublime: from Morality to Art* (Oxford: Clarendon Press, 1989), especially 100.

Kant's argumentation Lyotard too describes the sublime as "the feeling of something monstrous. Das Unform. Formless. The retreat of regulation and rules is the cause of the feeling of the sublime."[60]

Now just as expressionism, finding itself in a chronically anomic epoch, actively supplements the process of ideological and cosmological fragmentation (or "interruption") which has already been set in motion, so according to Lyotard, in modernity the poetics of the sublime similarly creates a correlative process of "aesthetic anomie": via an emphasis on the sublime, the unrepresentable and the abstract it undermines and interrogates the limits, conventions and conditions of art – one of the most striking examples of which Lyotard finds in "abstract painting since 1910."[61] It is this attempt to produce "indirect, virtually ungraspable allusions to the invisible" (68) – an "invisible" which remains outside the grasp of conventional representational discourses – which then becomes one of the central foundations for the urge to "abstraction" in the modernist period.[62] For although it is true, as Lyotard maintains, that "one cannot represent the absolute . . . one can demonstrate that the absolute exists – through 'negative representation,' which Kant called the 'abstract'" (68). And whereas the artists of the "Romantic sublime" attempted to allude to the unrepresentable and the absolute in their "sujet" as a means of pointing nostalgically to a "lost origin or goal in the distance," by the time the historical avant-garde emerged at the beginning of the twentieth century there had occurred a significant shift of emphasis, with the result that they sought this "unrepresentable" closer to home "in the conditions of the artistic work itself."[63] Let us sketch this development in more detail.

Romanticism demonstrates its continued longing for the presence of the absolute and the unrepresentable with a choice of subject matter that frequently alludes directly to the monumental scenes in which the poets or painters themselves were originally

[60] Lyotard, "Complexity and the Sublime," *Postmodernism. ICA Documents*, ed. Lisa Appignanesi (London: Free Association Books, 1989), 24.
[61] Lyotard, "Presenting the Unpresentable: The Sublime," *Artforum* 20.8 (April 1982): 64–69. Here 68.
[62] See also Lyotard, "The Sublime and the Avant-Garde," *The Lyotard Reader*, ed. Andrew Benjamin (Oxford: Blackwell, 1989), 204.
[63] Lyotard, "Vorstellung," 98.

"transported" by the experience of the sublime.[64] And as Paul Crowther notes, there is as a consequence a whole genre of sublime landscape painting featuring "towering mountain ranges, raging storms, bottomless crevasses, blasted heaths, threatened travellers, etc., etc."[65] The works of Romantic artists such as Caspar David Friedrich belong then to a genre that is, as Lyotard says, "essentially made up of attempts to represent sublime objects."[66]

Although motivated by very different interests, the more politically-oriented idealist and utopian vanguards of the Romantic period set themselves the similarly impossible task of coming to terms, as Christopher Norris observes, with the "virtual transposition of the Kantian sublime into the realm of history and politics." In other words, they take on the task of making rational sense of – and thus making "representable" – the political and revolutionary turmoil of the period and the "very chaos or formlessness of current events . . ."[67] As a consequence, the experience of contemporary reality as a chaotic ferment, combined with the nostalgia it produces for the lost sense of totality – the "presence" deemed capable of organizing this formlessness – result in the utopian projection of those abstract ideals (ideas of reason) most readily associated with the revolutionary period and the Romantics: notions of universal justice, peace, freedom, fraternity, enlightened government and social progress.[68] Where these notions are idealistically projected directly onto the world, they result in that tendency towards illusionism that Kant associates with "Schwärmerei" ("wild enthusiasm") or that *"fanaticism*, which is a *delusion* that *would will some* Vision *beyond all the bounds of sensibility*; i.e. would dream according to principles (rational raving)" (II,§29: 128). Similar to Kant Lyotard describes this tendency as "thinking there is a presentation when there is not."[69]

Now this category of "fanaticism" leads via the sublime towards a further criterion by which we may firstly distinguish

---

64 See Thomas Weiskel, *The Romantic Sublime. Studies in the Structure and Psychology of Transcendence* (Baltimore: Johns Hopkins University Press, 1976).

65 Crowther, *The Kantian Sublime*, 155.

66 Lyotard, *The Lyotard Reader*, 204.

67 Christopher Norris, *What's Wrong With Postmodernism. Critical Theory and the Ends of Philosophy* (Baltimore: Johns Hopkins University Press, 1990), 217.

68 On this point see Norris, *What's Wrong With Postmodernism*, 217.

69 Lyotard, *Reader*, 403.

between different factions within expressionism, secondly further define the avant-garde, and thirdly demonstrate its links to the postmodern. For although it is not mentioned by Lyotard, Kant's further discussion of the "mania" of fanaticism – doubtless motivated politically by his ideological wariness regarding any revolutionary impulses that could result in social change and the possible destabilization of the state[70] – becomes a central factor in his model of the sublime.

Clearly Kant is guided by the belief that it is precisely the fact of the *unrepresentability* (of the idea of freedom for example) – associated in art with the sublime, as we have seen – which acts as a "safeguard": "the safeguard is the purely negative character of the presentation. For the *inscrutability of the idea of freedom* precludes all positive presentation" (II, § 29: 128). Now in the light of my revision of Bürger's theory of the avant-garde it is clear that it is this safeguard of "negative presentation" – also central to Kant's aesthetics of the sublime – which is precisely what is missing in the more "fanatical" works of the idealist and utopian artists of the expressionist period, such as the "activists" ("Aktivisten") or the group that Sokel calls the "naive expressionists." Lacking the safeguard of the unpresentable these artists frequently lapse into what Kant would call a "delirium," "fanaticism" or "enthusiasm," in which, "as an affection, the imagination is unbridled" and as such "may be compared to *mania*," which is "least compatible with the sublime, for it is *profoundly* ridiculous" (II, § 29: 128).

By contrast to the more "ridiculous" outpourings of the "naive" expressionists, what also distinguishes the "sophisticated" expressionists of the avant-garde is a certain sensitivity towards the unpresentable and the sublime. As we have seen, in Kafka's work for example the central categories (such as the "metamorphosis," the "law," the "trial," the "castle") emerge as unrepresentable semantic vacuums rather than objects fully accessible to realism: we recall that in Kafka's uncanny Other of

[70] As Christopher Norris observes, "Kant himself was of course no friend to revolutions, at least in so far as they involved the overthrow of existing monarchical or state structures. Hence no doubt his desire to maintain that crucial separation of realms whereby freedom, progress and justice are held to be ideas of pure reason, and therefore not concepts that could ever be translated into the here-and-now of revolutionary action." See Norris, *What's Wrong With Postmodernism*, 217.

realism the "Ungeziefer" cannot be drawn. At best its metonymic traces emerge, such as "the open door of a dark side-room . . ."[71] The abundance of meaningfulness – the power which Kafka's texts display in organizing a broad variety of anxieties and desires in the minds of his readers – not to mention the real pleasure his audience derives from the skill and artistry involved in his creation of this overwhelmingly enticing possibility of meaning[72] – exists in a profound state of antagonistic tension with the unavoidable sense of existential meaning*lessness* which pervades Kafka's world.

Like the utopian works in those other contemporary cultural formations which emerge in response to late modernity's characteristic anxieties, social concerns and fundamental historical problematics – issues to which Jameson refers in the article "Reification and Utopia in Mass Culture" – Kafka's texts function similarly by arousing a response in his audience linked to its deepest hopes and fears regarding these historical contents. Whereas modernism for example does not so much attempt to "process" these dangerous and unsettling sleeping contents as to offer certain "compensatory structures" which "contain" them, and whereas the "utopian" works of mass culture arouse these elicited responses only in order to "manage" and repress them all the more effectively by channeling them into "imaginary resolutions" and "the projection of an optical illusion of social harmony,"[73] Kafka's work probes the same dormant strata, drawing out lingering doubts and yearnings through his polysemous, if indeterminate, organizational constructs only to *refrain* ultimately from either offering compensation or transformation as a means of "managing" or "repressing" these contents. For although Kafka's work too consists in opening the Pandora's box of modernity, unlike these other contemporary cultural forms, this act of disclosure does *not* lead to sealing it shut all the more tightly. Instead – and this is what distinguishes Kafka's work as "avant-

---

[71] Letter to K. Wolff, October 25, 1915, in Kafka, *Briefe 1902–24*, ed. Max Brod (Frankfurt: Fischer, 1958), 136. (Cited in chapter 5 above).

[72] This bitter-sweet pleasure – characteristic of Kafka's work – appears related to the fundamental mechanism of "subreption" underlying the Kantian sublime: the realization (or revivification) of the potential of rational comprehension as a means of gaining a degree of theoretical purchase on the ungraspable in the very face of its monumentality.

[73] Jameson, "Reification and Utopia in Mass Culture," 141.

garde" – it produces a pronounced and yet unsatisfied longing for meaningfulness, presence and transcendental closure. This is a nostalgic longing related to that projected by the idealists, yet clearly distinguished from them: distinguished firstly by means of Kafka's more "sophisticated" reliance in evoking this longing upon the means of allusion and upon the forms of "negative presentation" associated with the "safeguard" of the sublime and the unrepresentable; and secondly by the fact that Kafka allows these utopian-nostalgic projections to come into being precisely on the condition that they remain paradoxically unfulfilled and unresolved. The longing for meaning is thus regulated and tempered by the single truth determing his texts: the fundamental experience of meaninglessness.

If the "utopian" quality of those texts belonging to Jameson's category of "mass culture" pertains to their "ritual celebration of the renewal of the social order and its salvation not merely from divine wrath, but also from unworthy leadership" (142) then Kafka's works, like those of the expressionist avant-garde in general, are characterized by their attempt – even at the level of their poetics of representation and their sublime or "negative" strategies – to undermine the illusion by which such utopian ideals are projected as certainties: by the productive and dialogical tension between the pleasure in the thought of a higher, meaningful and ideal order on the one hand, and the despair on the other that man is mired in meaninglessness and cannot reach the realm of the meaningful. As in his response to Max Brod's attempt to perceive a sense of hope in the world Kafka's works always offer the sense that there exists "hope, no end of hope, only not for us."[74] Thus rather than defusing and recontaining the desire for change within the compensatory and imaginary resolution of social contradictions – as is the case by contrast with modernism and mass culture – in the works of Kafka and the expressionist avant-garde the tension between the meaningful and the meaningless is heightened and the unbridgeable difference between the two poles is accentuated.

---

[74] "Oh, Hoffnung genug, unendlich viel Hoffnung – nur nicht für uns." Cited in Lukacs, "Die weltanschaulichen Grundanlagen des Avantgardeismus," *Werke IV*, 497.

Revisiting Lyotard's answer to the question, "What is the postmodern?": the sublime as the unrepresentable condition of art

The unresolvable tension which Kant discovers in the feeling of the sublime is translated by avant-garde works such as Kafka's into the creative tension between the "idea" on the one hand and the impossibility of its representation on the other. We have already noted that Kant is wary of the possibility of translating the "idea" into direct political action and social change. It is surely for this reason that he insists firstly that the feeling of the sublime is distinct from the sense of beauty, for which (as Lyotard points out) Kant's point of reference is the notion of "community"[75] (Lyotard reiterates that beauty "demands, and in a sense promises, community"); and secondly that he both insists upon the sublime as the "safeguard" which prevents the projection of false communities while reminding us, as Lyotard observes, that "(n)obody has ever *seen* a society. Nobody has ever seen a beginning. An end. Nobody has ever *seen* a world . . . " (23).

This observation allows us to make a further distinction among forms of progressive writing. For the difference between the idealist and utopian avant-garde on the one hand and the more cynical and sophisticated avant-garde on the other may be gauged precisely in terms of their projection of the notion of "community" and "utopia." Like those Romantics whose sublime consciousness leads them nostalgically to evoke the sublime through landscapes and so on, the idealists similarly intersperse "nostalgic, utopian images of a better, reconciled world into (their) critique of civilization."[76] The more "cynical" avant-gardists on the other hand refuse this consolation, and so emphasize instead their inventiveness in finding new "negative presentations" and alternative means of abstraction by which they can allude to the unrepresentable while simultaneously demonstrating an awareness of the "impossibility of presenting a utopia" or a "future golden state of society." [77]

Lyotard draws a similar distinction between artistic movements in the modernist period by describing two separate emph-

---

[75] Lyotard, "Complexity and the Sublime," 23.
[76] Schulte-Sasse, "Modernity and Modernism," 8.
[77] Schulte-Sasse, "Carl Einstein," 41.

ases within the sublime which can be differentiated according to whether the accent falls upon the "nostalgia for presence" (which he places "on the side *melancholy*, the German expressionists"), or alternatively upon "inventing new rules of the game," which he links with "experimentation" and places "on the side of *novatio*, Braque and Picasso . . ."[78] In the light of my exposition of expressionism, it should be clear that Lyotard's attempt to place the expressionist movement in its entirety either in one category or the other necessarily foreshortens the scope of the concept. For although it is true, as we have seen, that one section of the movement, the idealist-utopian expressionists, may indeed lapse into "nostalgia for presence," this response is not shared by the less "naive" expressionists who belong more properly to the avant-garde. Furthermore, given the urge to abstraction, experimentation, and unmediated expressiveness which drives even the most "naive" of expressionists, it is seldom the case that their nostalgia is simultaneously combined with the creation of the kind of affirmative formal structure Lyotard has in mind, whose "recognizable consistency continues to offer the reader or spectator material for consolation and pleasure" (14).[79]

A second criticism of Lyotard's model at this point is that the work's character as "novatio" is in itself no guarantee that it will not also end up providing formal consolation (as is frequently the case with the products of affirmative culture in modernism) nor that it will avoid aestheticizing its critical content and thus risk defusing its message. Consequently where Lyotard associates the postmodern with the "flashing by" of generations and artistic movements[80] – in other words with innovation or the stylistic updating of art – he appears to be falling back into what is paradoxically an *unhistorical* approach. For he fails to take into account the historical shift in the *function* of innovation – a differentiation central to Peter Bürger's theory, by contrast – a shift from the kind of innovation which functions merely as criticism of the preceding or rival artistic movements, to a more radical form of innovation as artistic *self*-criticism which questions the very basis

[78] Lyotard, "What is the Postmodern?" *The Postmodern Explained*, 13.
[79] Such consolatory "consistency" is more likely to be found for example in certain modes of Romanticism, where its more conventional organic and harmonious forms are frequently combined with just such a nostalgic attitude towards the utopian and the ideal.
[80] Lyotard, "What is the Postmodern?" *The Postmodern Explained*, 12–13.

of art's possibility within its historically institutionalized framework.

As we have seen, Lyotard's most celebrated statement in this regard is that "a work can only become modern if it is first postmodern. Thus understood, postmodernism is not modernism at its end, but in a nascent state, and this state is recurrent" (13). Read in the light of Lyotard's conception of "novatio," this definition appears at first glance to view postmodernism simply as a rather conventional version of the avant-garde, namely as a kind of "advance guard" or "cutting-edge," which merely fulfills "a preliminary task of formal exploration, while the real 'advance' is made by those who transcend the less firm ground of experiment and destructive aesthetics associated with the avant-garde."[81] In other words, postmodernism begins to resemble an iconoclastic and innovatory force that clears an artistic or ideological space for the development of the new, and does so for the same reason that cultural fashions and new movements such as modernism have conventionally attacked their predecessors. It is only when Lyotard specifies the function of the "recurrent" innovatory force to which he refers that his conception of the postmodern as the vanguard or "nascent state" of modernism begins to take on a more substantial and differentiated meaning:

The postmodern would be that which in the modern invokes the unpresentable in presentation itself, that which refuses the consolation of correct forms . . . and inquires into new presentations – not to take pleasure in them, but to better produce the feeling that there is something unrepresentable. The postmodern artist or writer is in the position of a philosopher: the text he writes or the work he creates is not in principle governed by pre-established rules and cannot be judged according to a determinant judgment, by the application of given categories to this text or work. Such rules and categories are what the work or text is investigating. (15)

Lyotard thus carefully excludes those traditional functions of "consolation" (associated with the nostalgic, utopian mode), as

---

[81] Eysteinsson, *Modernism*, 154. Eysteinsson balances his judgement carefully where he warns against "seeing the avant-garde as simply a preparatory stage for the masterpieces of modernism or judging the avant-garde as the only significant revolt, while modernism is merely a classicism in disguise" (178). In his article "The Fate of the Avant-Garde," Richard Chase similarly maintains that "under modern conditions the avant-garde is a permanent movement," *Partisan Review* 24.3 (1957): 365.

well as the kind of formal innovation or "new presentations" (which, as we have observed of modernism, are in danger of defusing the message), since both always risk taking on a purely conciliatory aestheticist function.

In this respect the concept of the sublime becomes important in both postmodernism and the avant-garde as a *counter-concept* to what Marcuse calls "affirmative culture." For the unrepresentable sublime is not only a Kantian "safeguard" against the mania of (Romantic) "Schwärmerei." Just as importantly it now introduces a similar wariness or cynicism towards affirmative culture's attempt to represent, emulate, or anticipate the ideal, the harmonious and the utopian. Furthermore it also shifts the center of the text's concerns away from the "unrepresentability" of God, utopia or the "transcendental signified," and towards art's own internal realms of the "unrepresentable": it begins to interrogate both the "rules" and the unreflected conditions of the possibility of art, and so directs attention towards those similarly unspoken institutional and discursive constraints acting upon the aesthetic sphere.

These "rules and categories" normally remain unrepresented because to question them is to initiate an inquiry and formulate a set of questions which simultaneously place the whole artistic endeavor in doubt:

The pictorial avant-garde, as we have seen, responded to painting's "impossibility" by engaging in research centered around the question, "What is painting?" One after another, previous assumptions about the painter's practice were put on trial and debated. Tonality, linear perspective, the rendering of values, the frame, format, the supports, surface, medium, instrument, place of exhibition, and many other presuppositions were questioned plastically by the various avant-gardes. "Modern painters" discovered that they had to represent the existence of that which was not demonstrable if the perspectival laws of *costruzione legittima* were followed. They set about revolutionizing the supposed visual givens in order to reveal that the field of vision simultaneously conceals and needs the invisible . . . [82]

Here Lyotard clearly equates the postmodern with the "abstract" element of modern art and in particular with the paradigmatically "philosophical" function of the avant-garde: it produces works of the "idea" which probe the very limits, assumptions and condi-

---

[82] Lyotard, "Presenting the Unpresentable: the Sublime," 67. Translation modified grammatically.

tions of art. It is in this respect that the avant-garde/postmodern is not only always ahead of its time but is also always *outside* the realm of art, since it not only questions but *contravenes* its rules and conventions. It both *is* and *is not* art, since it necessarily breaks with the conventional definition of art in order to redefine the rules: "the artist and writer therefore work without rules and in order to establish the rules for what *will have been made*."[83] This is also the reason why the avant-garde has frequently been associated with a new, paradoxical "anti-aesthetics," an aesthetics of the formless, the abstract and the ugly – rather than with the harmonious and the beautiful – and also why it is necessarily linked not with the Kantian sense of beauty as a "shared" or "communal" phenomenon, but with an alternative dimension associated with the sublime. For the avant-garde/postmodern belongs to a field

opened by the esthetics of the sublime – which is not governed by a consensus of taste. Avant-garde painting eludes the esthetics of beauty in that it does not draw on a communal sense of shared pleasure. To the public taste its products seem "monstrous," "formless," purely "negative" nonentities. (I am using terms by which Kant characterized those objects that give rise to a sense of the sublime). When one represents the non-demonstrable, representation itself is martyred. Among other things this means that neither painting nor the viewing public can draw on established symbols, figures, or plastic forms that would permit the sense or the understanding of there being, in these idea works, any question of the kind of reason and imagination that existed in Romano-Christian painting.[84]

To the extent then that both postmodernism and the avant-garde derive from an aesthetics of the sublime they are not ruled by "taste," convention and consensus. Instead, they are forever placing themselves in contradiction to art's conventions by deconstructing the prevailing definitions, conventons and conditions of art as their "unrepresentable" theme.

The avant-garde/postmodern necessarily rests upon an aesthetics of the sublime precisely to the extent that it is forced to reject the aesthetics of beauty affirmed by (and simultaneously affirming) a consensus, a community of taste. The historical avant-garde's call to "shake up the burgher" ("épater le bourgeois") and

[83] Lyotard, "What is the Postmodern?" *The Postmodern Explained*, 15.
[84] Lyotard, "Presenting the Unpresentable: The Sublime," 67.

to create a new rebellious aesthetics of shock draws its significance, as well as its effect, from this rejection not only of the existing community of middle-class attitudes and taste. For it constitutes both a rejection of bourgeois society's particular institutionalization of aesthetic and moral praxis, as well as an ideological abjuration of the social conventions, the shared values, and the dominant discourses which determine the social imaginary. The result is the critical and mutually defining tension between the marginalized avant-garde on the one side and the formations of "high" or "mass culture" on the other: the avant-garde artists reject public taste and fail to "recognize" themselves in the dominant social imaginary, while in turn the larger community of the public for its part ignores the avant-garde or rejects it outright as incomprehensible and foreign.

In summary then, if the utopian works of modernism and mass culture are characterized, as Jameson maintains, by their compensatory or reconciliatory structures – what we have called with Marcuse their "affirmative" character – then in the case of the avant-garde/postmodern by contrast, the inscription into their texts of an awareness of the limits of utopian representation is simultaneously an indication of an essential and defining insight: their ideological consciousness of, and resistance to, the institution of art as the framework which firstly determines the effects and uses of all cultural production, which secondly (in its contemporary form) encourages the creation of illusory modes of compensation, and which thirdly helps to organize experience into an ideologically acceptable social imaginary.

With regard to this awareness of the institutionalization of art in modernity Schulte-Sasse observes that it is precisely "the degree to which artists gained such an insight [that] determines the difference between modernism and the avant-garde/postmodern."[85] If this is so then the historical avant-garde in a sense

---

[85] Schulte-Sasse, "Carl Einstein," 42. I would differ with Schulte-Sasse only with regard to his apparent reduction of the scope of this notion of art's "institutionalization." Rather than indicating the level of historical and institutional self-consciousness, the concept is conflated here with artistic awareness of "the separation of art from life." As he himself shows, even Peter Bürger rejects the goal of sublating art and life ultimately as the single defining feature of the avant-garde. Furthermore it is clearly not an essential feature of the "sublime" awareness associated with the "negative aesthetics" of the unrepresentable linking the avant-garde with the postmodern (which is a central point of departure for Schulte-Sasse's excellent paper).

constitutes an endless series of experiments with what Lyotard calls the "assumptions implicit in modernity,"[86] an ongoing process of interrogation which testifies to this institutional awareness by questioning institutional presuppositions, and by "working-through" the problematic and institutionally-administered relationship between art and life.

If the result is that the historical avant-garde ultimately accepts the irreversibility of art's functional differentiation in society – albeit somewhat reluctantly – then with the transition towards the postmodern this separation is no longer problematic: either the postmodernists accept aesthetic autonomy as a fact of artistic life, or conversely, in the era characterized by simulation and by the aestheticization of politics they see the realms of art and life as already absolutely and irreversibly intertwined. In either case however, the result is the same: postmodernism's unproblematic acceptance of art's status (very different in this respect from the lingering doubts characterizing the historical avant-garde) becomes the central principle and condition from which it begins to operate.

## Desublimation and the sublime: the idealist and the cynical avant-garde

As I have shown, the historical avant-garde is characterized by a self-reflexive mode of criticism which approaches reality as a discursive construction. By demonstrating that language, logic, thought and systems of representation are not "neutral" but are part of the social framework of ideologically tendentious dominant discourses, the progressive cultural formations of the avant-garde reveal the means by which a belief in the "realness" of reality is induced. We should recall that Lyotard describes a similar process of resistance to the real within visual culture as,

the way various avant-gardes have, as it were, humiliated and disqualified reality by their scrutiny of the pictorial techniques used to instill a belief in it . . . [T]he avant-gardes continually expose the artifices of presentation that allow thought to be enslaved by the gaze and diverted from the unpresentable.[87]

---

[86] Lyotard, "Note on the Meaning of 'Post-'," *The Postmodern Explained*, 79.
[87] Lyotard, "What is the Postmodern?" *The Postmodern Explained*, 12.

The paradigm for the expressionist avant-garde's counter-discursive strategies of "disqualification" or "derealization" of the real would be the expressionist painter Franz Marc's self-reflexive problematization of the "blue horses." As we have seen, the violent discrepancy of their "unrealistic" color coding places the image of the horse "under erasure" and reminds the audience not to conflate the representational image with any specific referent. Simultaneously this technique inscribes an "openness" into the image which postpones closure and emphasizes its unfixable and "unpresentable" quality.

I have linked this strategy of undermining such conventional relationships of representation to the avant-garde's general program of "de-aestheticization," and have shown its relation within the anti-aesthetic practices of the period (such as in its subversion of the "consensual" category of the "beautiful") to the tendency to "desublimate" art. In the light of this it is significant that in his discussion of the postmodern Lyotard explicitly criticizes both Marcuse and Habermas for their alleged "confusion" regarding the "Freudian" concept of "desublimation." With regard to the way in which the various avant-gardes "humiliate" and "disqualify" reality with their subversive "scrutiny of the pictorial techniques used to instill a belief in it," Lyotard argues that

if Habermas, like Marcuse, takes this work of derealization as an aspect of the (repressive) 'desublimation' characterizing the avant-garde, it is because he confuses the Kantian sublime with Freudian sublimation, and because for him aesthetics is still an aesthetics of the beautiful. (12)

It is true that there is a lingering traditionalism in Marcuse's aesthetics which is indeed implicitly oriented towards the beautiful. For Marcuse ultimately remains deeply ambiguous with regard to the program of desublimation associated with anti-art – an ambiguity linked to his attachment to the positive side he discovers in affirmative culture. Although he clearly applauds the "subversive, dissonant" tones of contemporary black culture for example, which "give art a desublimated, sensuous form of frightening immediacy,"[88] at other points he openly clings to a more traditional concept of the "work" as an entity whose form is by definition "sinngebend" (or "meaningful") and as such, necessarily produces the effect of sublimation always associated

---

[88] Herbert Marcuse, *An Essay on Liberation*, 47.

with the beautiful: "[the] aesthetic necessity of art supersedes the terrible necessity of reality, sublimates its pain and pleasure . . . " (43–4).

This ambiguity ties into the question regarding the relationship between the aesthetics of the sublime and the avant-garde's strategy of desublimation. Perhaps we can best approach this issue by saying that Lyotard's "derealization" is to the real what desublimation is to the sublime. In other words, if the avant-garde's techniques of "derealization" reveal the "real" to be the product of a set of dominant discourses, representational contrivances, and codes intended to instill a belief in the reality they create, then similarly "desublimation" – which we have described as the central category of the historical or "cynical" avant-garde – follows the logic of the Kantian "safeguard": it prevents the sublime (like the ideal and the utopian) from being presented as if it were real or already "realized."

The avant-garde/postmodern aesthetics of the sublime then is paradoxically a strategy of *de*sublimation. For its function is to counter the idealizing and consolatory effects of sublimation, whereby the latter concept is understood not so much in the strict Freudian sense of a postponement, repression or displacement of *libidinal* goals but rather of *ideological* goals. This progressive aesthetics of the sublime is a program of desublimation geared to undermining affirmative culture's tendency to treat the ideal as presentable (or even as already present) and as a consequence to postpone or suspend its real-life implementation. For if Kant's sublime prevents the creation of "graven images," false gods and utopias by emphasizing the limits of representation, the avant-garde/postmodern reworking of the sublime achieves *its* desublimation slightly differently: it does so by revealing the representation of the ideal and the utopian (or the attempt to anticipate or emulate this ideal realm through harmonious and organic forms) to be an institutionalized compensation operating within the framework of affirmative culture. Like the strategies of "negative presentation" (identified by Kant) which are intended to approach the sublime by indirection as it were, the de-aestheticizing practices of the avant-garde scrutinize the system of representation, check any tendency towards idealization, and thereby preclude the creation of compensatory illusions, consolatory forms or images of harmony. For they produce the effect of desublimation both by tearing away the veils of artifice which create this utopian and idealized imaginary world, and by uncovering and pushing to the forefront instead the underlying banal and de-aestheticized reality normally covered up by the conventional, compensatory modes of affirmative cultural representation.

Thus the "confusion" which Lyotard finds in Habermas and Marcuse derives from the paradoxical nature of the sublime as a means of "desublimation" in progressive modern art. The "confusion" is significant: it is indicative of the clear continuity between the avant-garde's primary strategies of desublimation and de-aestheticization on the one hand, and postmodernism's central category of the sublime on the other.

## Modernity and postmodernity: the counter-discourses of the avant-garde and Habermas' "incomplete project" of emancipation

In his often cited discussion of postmodernity, "Modernity – An Incomplete Project," Jürgen Habermas not only takes issue with Lyotard and with what he sees as the conservatism in contemporary French theory, but discusses in this light the outlook for what he calls the "project of modernity." Surrounded by a postmodern culture dominated by debates regarding the "network of 'post' concepts and thinking – 'post-industrial society,' 'post-structuralism,' "post-empiricism,' 'post-rationalism',"[89] not to mention "post-histoire" and "post-humanism," Habermas responds by taking stock of what remains of the heritage of the Enlightenment in the contemporary world, and by assessing the ways in which the goals and emancipatory potential of this "unfinished project" of modernity have been affected by the entry of society and culture into the phase of postmodernity.

Habermas follows Max Weber in equating cultural modernity with the increasing development of the discursive spheres of science, morality and art, and with their differentiation into separate and independent realms:

The project of modernity formulated in the 18th century by the philosophers of the Enlightenment consisted in their efforts to develop objective

[89] A. Wellmer, "On the Dialectic of Modernism and Postmodernism," *Praxis International* 4.4 (Jan 1985): 337–362. Here 337.

science, universal morality and law, and autonomous art according to their inner logic. At the same time, this project intended to release the cognitive potentials of each of these domains from their esoteric forms. The Enlightenment philosophers wanted to utilize this accumulation of specialized culture for the enrichment of everyday life – that is to say, for the rational organization of everyday social life.[90]

However, with the social separation and the growing autonomy of these individual spheres of human activity the validity of this entire enterprise of modernity has been opened to question. For this social differentiation has failed to lead to the opening up and utilization of the particular forms of knowledge promised by these various specialized fields for practical and social purposes. Instead, the expressionists' nightmare-scenario of an upsurge of irrational authority and the exponential expansion of instrumental logic and rationality – a nightmare later re-visited by Horkheimer and Adorno in the *Dialectic of Enlightenment* – has seemingly come to pass. A culture of specialists possessing a particular form of scientific-technological logic has come to dominate, so that rather than bringing these discourses into closer touch with life, "the distance grows between the culture of the experts and that of the larger public" (9).

In the face of the threat associated with these dominant social discourses it is highly significant that Habermas not only chooses still to defend the Enlightenment project of modernity, but that he does so by pointing to certain projects within the *aesthetic* sphere which appear to offer a possible solution to its central dilemma. The aesthetic programs he envisages are characterized, as one commentator suggests, by their emancipatory potential in being able to "illuminate conditions in the life-world while providing progressive cognitive and moral effects,"[91] and are clearly associated with the central deconstructive projects characterizing the avant-garde as I have described it here. Furthermore it is significant that in elucidating these emancipatory aesthetic goals Habermas not only refers directly to the work of Peter Bürger on the avant-garde, but also frames his investigation in terms related directly to Bürger's central problematic: the growing specialization, separation and development of particular forms of discourse

90  Jürgen Habermas, "Modernity – An Incomplete Project," *The Anti-Aesthetic*, 9.
91  Douglas Kellner, *Critical Theory, Marxism and Modernity* (Baltimore: Johns Hopkins University Press, 1989), 168.

towards autonomy, and the emancipatory possibility of a trans-formation of their autonomous status to bring them closer to life and put them to more socially productive uses within what Haber-mas calls the "hermeneutics of everyday communication" (9). For as Habermas describes it, "The project aims at a differentiated relinking of modern culture with an everyday praxis . . . " (13).

What I want to argue in concluding is that the avant-garde's program of resistance – involving the development of a variety of counter-discourses as part of an oppositional "anti-aesthetics" – is responsible in large part for keeping alive the Enlightenment project of modernity within the aesthetic sphere. For as Bürger observes in response to Habermas' article, even if the avant-garde's attempts to reintegrate art and life did indeed fail ulti-mately, it nevertheless produced a very important set of experi-ments and challenges over and beyond its immediate goal of aesthetic sublation. Firstly in questioning "the legitimacy of the term 'great art work'" the avant-garde liberates possibilities for "free productivity," that is, for a critical impact and a sense of creativity beyond the bounds of tradition and aesthetic conven-tion.[92] Secondly, its creation of a set of counter-discourses, a new rhetoric freed from normative institutional constraints, is itself expressive of a need still prevalent in postmodernity – as Richard Rorty puts it, "a need for the ineffable, the sublime, a need to go beyond the limits, a need to use words which are not part of anybody's language-game, any social institution."[93]

In this respect one can accord the avant-garde a larger degree of success in reintegrating art and life than even Bürger is prepared to do. For as we shall see presently, if it is true, as Habermas and Wellmer maintain, that one of the important social functions of aesthetic experience is that it can be "used to illuminate a life-historical situation" (13) and so lead to a change in what Bürger calls society's "cognitive interpretations and normative orienta-tions" (22), then even though this function is certainly not exclus-ive to avant-garde culture, it is above all the historical avant-garde which, in the modernist period at least, takes up this cognitive

---

[92] Peter Bürger, "The Significance of the Avant-Garde for Contemporary Aesthet-ics: A Reply to Jürgen Habermas," *New German Critique* 8.1 (1981): 19–22. Here 22.

[93] Richard Rorty, "Habermas and Lyotard on Postmodernity," *Habermas and Modernity*, ed. Richard Bernstein (Oxford: Polity Press, 1985), 161–175. Here 174.

function and makes it into its central principle. For to the extent that knowledge is the product of specific rhetorical organizations and signifying practices in society, it is paradigmatically the avant-garde's counter-discourses which have had the important critical function both of exposing the ideological content of the dominant discourses pertaining to the cultural sphere and of subjecting them to criticism by revealing the extent to which it is this discursive ideology that constructs and supports reality.

Consequently the "incredulity towards metanarratives" by which Lyotard defines the postmodern,[94] and the correspondingly "postmodern" awareness, as Bill Readings argues, that art can now no longer naively "aspire to the metanarrativity that would ground a truth claim,"[95] should actually be traced back much further, to the cynicism of the avant-garde, to its experiments with signifying practices and with the conventions of reality-construction, and to its total skepticism with regard to the organization of discursive meanings in society. Like the contemporary practice of deconstruction which also attempts, as Frank Lentricchia notes, to "undercut the epistemological claims of representation," the historical avant-garde seems to bear a similar cynical message – deriving from the same source, Nietzsche – namely, "the news that all hope for securing the 'foundations' of knowledge is futile – that 'foundations' must be replaced by 'abysses,' that 'representations' must always be 'put into question'."[96]

Clearly the avant-garde's Nietzschean capacity for cynicism and critique has its own blind spot. For while "it may tell us how we deceive ourselves . . . it has no positive content."[97] As a consequence of this wariness of holding specific political positions this form of critique comes close to deconstruction's predicament in as far as it takes on board the risks of "quietism" or

---

[94] Lyotard, *The Postmodern Condition*, xxiv.
[95] Bill Readings, *Introducing Lyotard*, 74.
[96] Frank Lentricchia, *Criticism and Social Change* (Chicago: University of Chicago Press, 1983), 50.
[97] Lentricchia, *Criticism and Social Change*, 51. This is also the reason why Habermas views contemporary French thinkers such as Foucault, Deleuze and Lyotard as "neo-conservative" – they critique existing "totalizing" models but offer only "pluralism" in their place, while failing to "preserve at least one standard for [the] explanation of the corruption of *all* reasonable standards." Jürgen Habermas, "The Entwinement of Myth and Enlightenment: Re-reading *Dialectic of Enlightenment*," *New German Critique* 26 (1982): 28. For commentary see also Richard Rorty, "Habermas and Lyotard on Postmodernity," *Habermas and Modernity*, ed. Richard Bernstein (Oxford: Polity Press, 1985), 161–175.

"conservatism by default"[98] – risks which are avoided by even the most politically or aesthetically "naive" of the avant-garde discourses of engagement (such as that of the "aktivists" or utopian expressionists). However, *if* the avant-garde has the effect, like deconstruction, of inducing quietism – or even quiet despair – by presenting as an unavoidable conclusion the idea that all reality is merely an endless series of discursive representations and reflections, and that these images function as an ideological means of obscuring the groundlessness of reality's construction and epistemology, then one should also bear in mind that it is the historical avant-garde – and in particular the expressionist faction among its various oppositional formations – that is directly connected to the most important political developments in modernist culture concerned with ideological demystification, and not least the politically engaged and critically progressive tradition represented by Brecht.

For the Brechtian aesthetic which develops from the foundations of progressive expressionism is, like the historical avant-garde, a form of aesthetic deconstruction which constantly points to the fictional basis not only of its own representational practices but to those of art as a whole, and so in turn reveals those discursive fictions underpinning the ideological signifying practices in society at large. To be sure, Brecht's work differs from what we have seen as the purely "deconstructive" aspect of the avant-garde to the extent that he *does* ultimately hold up a "positive content," a set of epistemological foundations and ideological foundations for pragmatic social change. But as is clear from the differences which emerge between Brecht and Lukacs during the "expressionism debates," these ideological principles are not meant to predetermine and so preempt the work's mimetic relationship to reality (as is the case with Lukacs' "totalizing" approach to the construction both of the real and of the work itself – his twin notions of "Aufdecken/Zudecken" ("opening up/covering over"), nor are they to be presented in the work from the outset as if they upheld a claim to normativity. Instead, Brecht allows the audience to consider, from among the diverse possible outcomes that his plays suggest, those means most likely to produce a solution to the problems depicted.

[98] Lentricchia, *Criticism and Social Change*, 51.

The essential feature that Brecht's poetics shares with the expressionist avant-garde is the attempt to short-circuit or interrupt the text's own representational construction. He does this by undermining the work's illusionism but also by integrating into the text, montage-style, unrevised fragments of the real; alternatively he divides up the narrative into segments which open themselves up more directly and individually to the real (rather than to the text's overall plot or internal tension). This has the important effect of avoiding the creation of the traditional organic or holistic structure which always risks masking existing ideology with a similar structure of its own. For if, as Bloch argues, reality is itself characterized by "interruption," then these adversarial texts of the avant-garde are organized around a recognition of the unavoidable difference between reality and representation, a recognition which precludes the possibility of endowing the construction of the real with the gloss of completeness (which Lukacs saw as the essential realist technique of "covering over").

If the task of the counter-discursive text is to disclose a reality which dominant ideology and its social discourses serve to obscure, then clearly it cannot fall into the trap of itself embodying a totalizing, rigidly demarcated holistic construct. In other words, the oppositional text cannot set out merely to replace ideology's closed construction of the real with yet another, equally organic and totalizing structure.[99] Instead the point is to intervene by defamiliarizing and thus unraveling these holistic "world outlooks" *as* ideological and arbitrary discursive constructions – in Benveniste's terminology, to expose them as "discours" rather than "histoire." For if, as Althusser maintains, ideology functions by concealing the real conditions and relations of existence beneath a system of discourses, images and representations, and if this "imaginary relationship of individuals to their real conditions of existence"[100] acts as a substitute for the real, then it is the imaginary which must be revealed as a construction, and thus opened up by alternative perspectives.

[99] Eysteinsson notes that "the organic 'wholeness' of the literary text may reinforce the latent detachment of literature from other social practices . . ." See *The Concept of Modernism*, 204.

[100] Louis Althusser, "Ideology and Ideological State Apparatuses," *Lenin and Philosophy* (London: NLB, 1971). For commentary see Catherine Belsey, *Critical Practice* (London: Methuen, 1980), 56–63; Paul Q. Hirst, "Althusser's Theory of Ideology," *Economy and Society* 5.4 (Nov. 1976): 385–412.

Now if we describe this social imaginary in terms of Habermas' model, namely as the vehicle for "the reproduction and transmission of values and norms" burdened with the central tasks of "passing on a cultural tradition, of social integration and of socialization" (8), then oppositional cultural formations such as the avant-garde figure as an important means of social intervention – albeit predominantly at the conceptual level of the imaginary rather than on an empirical or pragmatic plane. For as Wolfgang Iser points out, in as far as the literary text mimetically reproduces not "reality" but the *structure* of this imaginary (Iser calls it the "model of reality") the text also "interferes with this structure, for generally it takes the prevalent thought system or social system as its context, but does not reproduce the frame of reference which stabilizes these systems."[101] As a consequence, by aesthetically defamiliarizing and conceptually "suspending" the dominant social "thought system" the literary text is able to "take as its dominant 'meaning' those possibilities that have been neutralized or negated by that system . . . [T]he borderlines of existing systems are the starting point for the literary text. It begins to activate that which the system has left inactive . . . " (72).

Although Iser's observations here are meant to apply to the oppositional potential of *all* literary texts,[102] his model has a particular relevance to the modern period, and especially to the adversarial culture of the avant-garde. For the avant-garde's counter-texts embody a clear shift of the cultural "dominant": the avant-garde not only focuses upon the (perennial) critical function of the literary text as a means of defamiliarizing the social "thought system" or "world picture" (70), but makes this task the very *center* – rather than the by-product – of its concerns. For example although even the classic realist text may also perform the critical and subversive function Iser describes, it nevertheless retains the conventional artifice and ideological pretense of transparency. The counter-text by contrast is completely self-reflexive. For in reproducing and demystifying the dominant system of the real, it turns this strategy of demystification against its *own* construction by simultaneously highlighting its own illusory nature

---

[101] Wolfgang Iser, *The Act of Reading. A Theory of Aesthetic Response* (Baltimore: Johns Hopkins University Press, 1978), 71.

[102] As Astradur Eysteinsson points out, Iser comes close to ascribing "an inherent adversarial function to literature." Eysteinsson, *The Concept of Modernism*, 217.

as an artifically-constructed system. Those "transparent" works which do not reflect on their own practices of representation, although providing insight in Iser's sense into the dominant social "thought system," will not necessarily contribute to our understanding of the processes of signification, nor to our understanding of the way ideology is constructed. To the extent that the self-reflexive text, like the montage, acknowledges its own construction, unravels the process of realism, and initiates the reader into the mysteries of representation, it will also serve as a critical model of social signifying practices in general, with a direct bearing on the construction of ideology and the imaginary relationship of the subject to the social formation.[103]

Important in this regard are those counter-discursive strategies of expressionism which I have discussed, such as its foregrounded artificiality and stylization, as well as its representational instability and excess. In Silvio Gaggi's terms these would constitute the kind of "self-conscious" mode which emphasizes "a recognition and declaration of the inescapable gap between the world and the representation of the world."[104] If the classic realist text is defined by its attempts to conceal this gap – since according to MacCabe its functioning depends "on obscuring the relation between text and reader in favor of a dominance accorded to a supposedly given reality"[105] – this also makes it blind to the rules conditioning its *own* existence. In this respect we must observe in the classical system two significant blind-spots which the avant-garde attempts to overcome: not only what MacCabe calls the classic realist text's inability to "deal with contradictions" in content (49), but more importantly, the serious limits on its capacity for self-reflection, and in particular for reflection upon the contradictions brought about by its own institutional determinations.

This representational restriction, what Gaggi calls "the inability

---

[103] To this extent it is certainly true, as Eysteinsson maintains, that modernism also "contains the rudiments of an adversary culture." See *The Concept of Modernism*, 222. The difference of course, is that modernism generally lacks precisely that historical or political awareness (or even interest) which might prevent this adversarial role from being defused and recuperated institutionally as mere formalism (or as what Benjamin would call mere "technique").

[104] Gaggi, *Modern/Postmodern*, 53. I gratefully acknowledge my indebtedness in this chapter to Gaggi's book, especially with regard to its treatment of the relationship between Brecht and the self-reflexive art of postmodernism.

[105] MacCabe, "Theory and Film," *Tracking the Signifier*, 77.

of the classical system to represent the act of representation" is simultaneously an indication of the particular constraints operating upon the corresponding "classical epistemology" (13), and it is significant that neither the classical system of representation nor its epistemology are left unchallenged by the avant-garde. For as has been noted already, the self-reflexive, anti-illusionistic quality of the avant-garde's counter-texts produce insights not only into their own semantic operations, but into the way that meaning and ideology is created by the signifying practices of society at large.[106] And like the postmodern, which, as Lyotard notes, "inquires into new presentations" in order to "produce the feeling that there is something unpresentable," the avant-garde too sets itself the philosophical task of inquiring precisely into those institutional, social and epistemological conditions of its own existence which are absent or unrepresentable, with the view, as we have seen, that "[s]uch rules and categories are what the work or text is investigating."[107]

In probing and revealing the institutional rules and restraints under which it operates, the avant-garde not only foregrounds the gap between the world and its representation, but undermines the dominance normally attributed automatically to the (supposedly) real by producing the counter-discourses designed to undermine the ideological and representational practices which support this dominance. These oppositional strategies often have a simple goal: the reinforcement of the idea, as MacCabe says, that "[t]here is no neutral place from which we can see the view and where all the points are located. There is no possible language of 'affidavit exposition' that would show the scene 'as it really is'" (43). By demystifying the myth of perspectival "neutrality" the progressive literary text becomes free to re-conceptualize the dominant models of reality, and to re-align and defamiliarize their underlying systems of value in the manner described by Iser. And even though this re-arrangement occurs through a process which is confined initially to a purely *theoretical* realm – that is, confined within the limits of the aesthetic sphere – then unlike those similar moments of critique provided by affirmative culture, the de-aestheticized and desublimated form of the avant-garde text ensures that this negativity is not immediately recuperated, or re-

---

[106] On this point see Eysteinsson, *The Concept of Modernism*, 204.
[107] Lyotard, "What is the Postmodern?" *The Postmodern Explained*, 15.

contained purely as an unrealizable ideal. Instead, this aesthetic reconceptualization becomes important, as we shall see, in providing an emancipatory insight into the construction of the real, and in overturning – precisely at the level of ideology and the social imaginary – what Habermas calls that "false normativity" (5) associated with the dominant social discourses and the organization of the consciousness of time, space and causality.

Following Althusser, Catherine Belsey has argued that ideology functions not only by obscuring the real conditions of existence but by presenting "a set of omissions, gaps rather than lies, [and by] smoothing over contradictions, appearing to provide answers which in reality it evades, and masquerading as coherence . . ."[108] If this is so then the avant-garde's counter-discourses make their starting point the interrogation of this artifice of coherence and closure, and the investigation of precisely those gaps and fissures which ideology and dominant social discourse attempt to cover over ("Zudecken"). As Iser observes,

Herein lies the unique relationship between the literary text and 'reality,' in the form of thought systems or models of reality. The text does not copy these, and it does not deviate from them either – though the mirror-reflection theory . . . would have us believe otherwise. Instead it represents a reaction to the thought systems which it has chosen and incorporated into its own repertoire. This reaction is triggered by the system's limited ability to cope with the multifariousness of reality, thus drawing attention to its deficiencies. (72)

The distinction that again needs to be made to Iser's model with respect to its application to the self-reflexive works of the historical avant-garde is that where the text draws attention to the system's "deficiencies" – what Belsey calls the "gaps" and "omissions" obscured by dominant social discourse – in the case of the avant-garde it does so in a manner which foregrounds not just the *contents* marginalized by the system, but the actual *process of marginalization* itself: in other words, it is the process of signification and its systematic shortcomings (or ideological biases) which become the center of the counter-text's concerns.

To this extent at least the avant-garde fulfills precisely the function that Habermas associates with the renewal of certain emancipatory principles of the Enlightenment through the "pro-

---

[108] Catherine Belsey, *Critical Practice*, 57.

ject of modernity": the task of promoting "communicative action" and "communicative rationality" (8). For if the social process of the "reproduction and transmission of values and norms" is usually influenced by "a form of modernization guided by the standards of economic and administrative rationality" (8), it is the various formations of the avant-garde which have historically provided a counter-weight by promoting "communicative action." This means presenting not only an alternative vision of the real, but also an alternative perspective on the way all such models of the real are constructed. And it is this projection of radical alterity which produces an effect of singular importance for Habermas' project: it interrogates both the social imaginary as well as society's signifying practices in general, thereby producing the possibility of a communicative re-alignment of these discursive constructs.

In generating alternative perspectives and counter-discourses which reveal the social imaginary as a scientific-technological construction this conception of the avant-garde's oppositional stance offers us what Habermas' model still lacks: a set of concrete examples – over and beyond the rather limited instances he himself cites (namely, Surrealism's failed aesthetic revolt, and Peter Weiss' *Aesthetics of Resistance*) – of what one might see as the aesthetic sphere's active participation in the "project of modernity." For these oppositional texts offer a model of the kind of "communicative rationality" which holds the potential to break down the rigid demarcations between different realms of discourse and so overcome "the decisive confinement of science, morality and art to autonomous spheres separated from the life-world and administered by experts" (14), while at the same time reappropriating "the expert's culture from the standpoint of the life-world" (13). If the project of modernity aims, as we have seen, "at a differentiated relinking of modern culture with an everyday praxis . . ." (13) this possibility may be most clearly glimpsed in Habermas' (and Wellmer's) view of the kind of emancipatory aesthetic experience in which

as soon as such an experience is used to illuminate a life-historical situation and is related to life's problems, it enters into a language game which is no longer that of the aesthetic critic. The aesthetic experience then not only renews the interpretation of our needs in whose light we perceive the world. It permeates as well our cognitive significations and our normative expectations and changes the manner in which all these moments refer to one another. (13)

And as Peter Bürger points out in his reply to Habermas, the least one can say about the avant-garde with respect to the project of emancipation in modernity is that the very possibility of a re-linking of art and life in the manner described by Wellmer and Habermas – "is unthinkable without the avant-gardist assault which shook up the aesthetics of autonomy." Consequently if it is true that the avant-garde's program to reintegrate art and life ultimately failed, then clearly it "should not be regarded as a mistake without results,"[109] but rather as an experiment whose impact is still being felt in the present, in the culture of post-modernity.

[109] Bürger, "The Significance of the Avant-Garde," 22.

# Bibliography

Ackroyd, Peter. *T. S. Eliot*. London: Hamish Hamilton, 1985.

Adorno, T. "Commitment." *The Essential Frankfurt School Reader*. Ed. A. Arato and E. Gebhardt. New York: 1978. 300–318.

"Zeitlose Mode. Zum Jazz." *Prismen*. Suhrkamp: Frankfurt, 1955. 144–161.

Althusser, Louis. "Ideology and Ideological State Apparatuses." *Lenin and Philosophy and Other Essays*. Trans. Ben Brewster. London: New Left Books, 1977.

Anz, Thomas. *Die Literatur der Existenz. Literarische Psychopathographie und ihre soziale Bedeutung im Frühexpressionismus*. Stuttgart: Metzler, 1977.

*Phantasien über den Wahnsinn. Expressionistische Texte*. Munich: Hanser, 1980.

"Entfremdung und Angst." *Sozialer Wandel*. Ed. H. Meixner and S. Vietta. Munich: Fink, 1982. 19–21.

Anz, Thomas, and Michael Stark, eds. *Expressionismus: Manifeste und Dokumente zur deutschen Literatur 1910–1920*. Stuttgart: Metzler, 1981.

Appignanesi, Lisa, ed. *Postmodernism. ICA Documents*. London: Free Association Books, 1989.

Bakhtin, Mikhail. *Rabelais and his World*. Trans. H. Iswolsky. Cambridge: MIT Press, 1968.

[Mikhail Bachtin] *Literatur und Karneval: Zur Romantheorie und Lachkultur*. Trans. Alexander Kaempfe. Munich: Hanser, 1969.

*The Dialogic Imagination*. Trans. Caryl Emerson and Michael Holquist, ed. Michael Holquist. Austin: Texas University Press, 1981.

*Problems of Dostoevsky's Poetics*. Trans. and ed. Caryl Emerson. Minneapolis: Minnesota University Press, 1984.

Ball, Hugo. "Kandinsky." Lecture held in Galerie Dada, Zürich, 7 April 1917. Rpt. Anz and Stark, *Manifeste und Dokumente*. 124–127.

Barlow, John D. *German Expressionist Film*. Boston: Twayne, 1982.

# Bibliography

Barthes, Roland. *S/Z*. Trans. Richard Miller. London: Cape, 1975.

Bateson, Gregory. *Steps to an Ecology of Mind*. New York: Ballantine, 1972.

Baudrillard, Jean. *Simulations*. New York: Semiotext(e), 1983.

Baudrillard, Jean and Mark Poster. *Jean Baudrillard: Selected Writings*, Stanford: Stanford University Press, 1988.

Baudry, Jean-Louis. "The Ideological Effects of the Basic Cinematographic Apparatus." *Film Quarterly* 28.2 (Winter 1974–75): 39–47.

Becker, J. M. *Das letzte Gericht*. Berlin: Fischer, 1919.

Belsey, Catherine. *Critical Practice*. London: Methuen, 1980.

Benhabib, Seyla. "Epistemologies of Postmodernism: A Rejoinder to Jean-François Lyotard." *New German Critique* 33 (1984): 103–126.

Benjamin, Walter. "The Work of Art in the Age of Mechanical Reproduction." *Illuminations*. Ed. Hannah Arendt trans. Harry Zohn. New York: Schocken, 1969. 217–252.

"Der Autor als Produzent." *Gesammelte Schriften*, Vol. II. 2. Ed. R. Tiedemann and H. Schweppenhäuser. Frankfurt: Suhrkamp, 1980.

Benn, Gottfried. "Schöpferische Konfession." *Gesammelte Werke*. Vol. 4. Ed. Dieter Wellershoff. Wiesbaden: Limes, 1958.

*Gehirne*. Stuttgart: Reclam, 1974.

Bennett, Tony. *Formalism and Marxism*. London: Methuen, 1979.

Bennington, Geoffrey. *Lyotard. Writing the Event*. Manchester: Manchester University Press, 1988.

Bentley, Eric. *The Life of the Drama*. London: Methuen, 1965.

Benveniste, Emile. *Problems in General Linguistics*. Miami: University of Miami Press, 1971.

Berger, Peter and Thomas Luckmann. *The Social Construction of Reality. A Treatise in the Sociology of Knowledge*. 1966; Harmondsworth: Pelican, 1984.

Bertens, Hans and Douwe Fokkema, eds. *Approaching Postmodernism*. Philadelphia and Amsterdam: John Benjamins, 1986.

Bloch, Ernst. "Diskussionen über Expressionismus." Schmitt, ed., *Expressionismusdebatte*. 180–191.

Bradbury, Malcolm, and James Walter. McFarlane. *Modernism: 1890–1930*. Harmondsworth: Penguin, 1976.

Brecht, Bertolt. *Schriften zum Theater*. Vol. 3. Frankfurt: Suhrkamp, 1963.

"Der Nachgeborene." *Lyrik des Expressionismus*. 249.

Brinkmann, Richard. *Expressionismus: internationale Forschung zu einem internationalen Phänomen*. Stuttgart: Metzler, 1980.

Bronner, Stephen Eric and Douglas Kellner, eds. *Passion and Rebellion. The Expressionist Heritage*. South Hadley, MA: J. F. Bergin, 1983.

Brooks, Peter. *The Melodramatic Imagination. Balzac, Henry James, Melodrama and the Mode of Excess*. New Haven: Yale University Press, 1976.

Budd, Mike, ed. *"The Cabinet of Dr. Caligari": Texts, Contexts, Histories*. New Brunswick: Rutgers University Press, 1990.

# Bibliography

"Moments of *Caligari*." "*The Cabinet of Dr. Caligari*": *Texts, Contexts, Histories*. Ed. Mike Budd. 7–119.

Bürger, Christa. "Moderne als Postmoderne: Jean-François Lyotard." *Postmoderne: Alltag, Allegorie und Avantgarde*. Ed. Christa and Peter Bürger. Frankfurt: Suhrkamp, 1987. 122–143.

Bürger, Peter. *Theory of the Avant-Garde*. Trans. Michael Shaw. Minneapolis: University of Minnesota Press, 1984. Trans. of *Theorie der Avantgarde*. Frankfurt: Suhrkamp, 1974.

"Institution Kunst als literatursoziologische Kategorie. Skizze eine Theorie des historischen Wandels der gesellschaftlichen Funktion der Literatur." *Vermittlung–Rezeption–Funktion*. Frankfurt: Suhrkamp, 1979.

"The Significance of the Avant-Garde for Contemporary Aesthetics: A Reply to Jürgen Habermas." *New German Critique* 8.1 (1981): 19–22.

Burch, Noel. "Primitivism and the Avant-Gardes: A Dialectical Approach." Rpt. *Narrative, Apparatus, Ideology*. Ed. Philip Rosen. New York: Columbia University Press, 1986. 483–506.

Cahill, Frank. *The World of Melodrama*. University Park: Pennsylvania State University Press, 1967.

Calinescu, Matei. *Faces of Modernity: Avant-Garde, Decadence, Kitsch*. Bloomington: Indiana University Press, 1987. 100–104.

Callinicos, Alex. *Against Postmodernism. A Marxist Critique*. Cambridge: Polity Press, 1989.

Carroll, David. *Paraesthetics. Foucault, Lyotard, Derrida*. London: Methuen, 1987.

Carroll, Noel. "The Cabinet of Dr. Kracauer." *Millenium Film Journal* 1. 2 (1978): 77–85.

Chase, Richard. "The Fate of the Avant-Garde." *Partisan Review* 24.3 (1957): 363–375.

Cixous, Hélène. "Castration or Decapitation?" *Signs: Journal of Women in Culture and Society* 7.1 (1981): 41–55.

Clément, Catherine. *Miroirs du Sujet*. Paris: Editions du Seuil, 1975.

Cohn, Dorrit. *Transparent Minds. Narrative Modes for Presenting Consciousness in Fiction*. Princeton: Princeton University Press, 1978.

Crowther, Paul. *The Kantian Sublime: from Morality to Art*. Oxford: Clarendon Press, 1989.

Denkler, Horst. *Einakter und kleine Dramen des Expressionismus*. Stuttgart: Reclam, 1968.

Dierick, Augustinus. *German Expressionist Prose*. Toronto: University of Toronto Press, 1987.

Döblin, Alfred. *Aufsätze zur Literatur*. Ed. Walter Muschg. Olten and Freiburg: Walter Verlag, 1963.

"Die Ermordung einer Butterblume." *Prosa des Expressionismus*. Ed. Fritz Martini. Stuttgart: Reclam, 1970. 102–115.

Dreitzel, Hans Peter. *Das gesellschaftliche Leiden und das Leiden an der*

# Bibliography

*Gesellschaft*. Stuttgart: Enke, 1968.

Duytschaever, Joris. "Eine Pionierleistung des Expressionismus: Alfred Döblins Erzählung *Die Ermordung einer Butterblume*." *Amsterdamer Beiträge zur neueren Germanistik* 2 (1973): 27–43.

Eagleton, Terry. *Literary Theory*. Oxford: Blackwell, 1983.

"Capitalism, Modernism and Postmodernism." *New Left Review* 52 (1985): 60–73.

Edschmid, Kasimir. "Expressionismus in der Dichtung." *Die neue Rundschau* 29. 1 (1918. Bd. 1. Märzheft): 359–374. Rpt. Anz and Stark, *Manifeste und Dokumente*. 42–55.

Egbert, D. D. *Social Radicalism and the Arts*. New York: Knopf, 1970.

"The Idea of 'Avant-Garde' in Art and Politics." *Literarische Avantgarden*. Ed. Manfred Hardt. Darmstadt: Wissenschaftliche Buchgesellschaft, 1989. 44–65.

Eliot, T. S. "Hamlet and His Problems." *Selected Essays, 1917–1932*. New York: Harcourt Brace, 1932. 124–125.

"Ulysses, Order, and Myth." *Selected Prose of T. S. Eliot*. Ed. Frank Kermode. New York: Harcourt Brace Jovanovich, 1975.

Elsaesser, Thomas. "Film History and Visual Pleasure: Weimar Cinema," *Cinema History/Cinema Practices*. Ed. Patricia Mellencamp and Philip Rosen. The American Film Institute Monograph Series. 4. Frederick, MD: University Publications of America, 1984. 47–84.

"Tales of Sound and Fury. Observations on the Family Melodrama." *Monogram* 4 (1972): 2–15.

"Social Mobility and the Fantastic: German Silent Cinema." *Wide Angle* 5.2 (1982): 14–25.

Eykman, Christoph. *Denk- und Stilformen des Expressionismus*. Munich: Francke, 1974.

Eysteinsson, Astradur. *The Concept of Modernism*. Ithaca: Cornell University Press, 1990.

Fokkema, Douwe and Elrud Ibsch. *Modernist Conjectures*. London: Hurst, 1987.

Foster, Hal, ed. *The Anti-Aesthetic: Essays on Postmodern Culture*. Port Townsend, Washington: Bay Press, 1983.

Frank, Joseph. "Spatial Form in Modern Literature." *The Widening Gyre: Crisis and Mastery in Modern Literature*. New Brunswick: Rutgers University Press, 1963.

Frank, Leonard. *Der Mensch ist gut*. Zürich: Max Rascher, 1918.

"Der Irre." Rpt. Anz, ed. *Phantasien über den Wahnsinn*.121–25.

Freud, Sigmund. "Das Unheimliche." *Imago* 5 (1919).

*Totem und Tabu*. 1913. Frankfurt: Fischer 1956.

Frühwald, Wolfgang. "Kunst als Tat und Leben. Über den Anteil deutscher Schriftsteller an der Revolution in München 1918/1919." *Sprache und Bekenntnis. Festschrift für Hermann Kunisch*. Ed. Wolfgang Frühwald and Günter Niggl. Berlin: Dinker, 1971.

# Bibliography

Gledhill, Christine. "The Melodramatic Field: An Investigation." *Home Is Where The Heart Is*. London: BFI, 1987.

Gaggi, Silvio. *Modern/Postmodern. A Study in Twentieth-Century Arts and Ideas*. Philadelphia: University of Pennsylvania Press, 1989.

Garten, H. F. *Modern German Drama*. 1959; London: Methuen 1964.

Grimstead, David. *Melodrama Unveiled: American Theater and Culture, 1800–1850*. Chicago: University of Chicago Press, 1968.

Habermas, Jürgen. "Bewußtmachende oder rettende Kritik." *Zur Aktualität Walter Benjamins*. Ed. Siegfried Unseld. Frankfurt: Suhrkamp, 1972.

"Herbert Marcuse über Kunst und Revolution." *Kultur und Kritik. Verstreute Aufsätze*. Frankfurt: Suhkamp, 1973. 345–351.

*Legitimation Crisis*. London: Heinemann, 1976.

"Modernity – An Incomplete Project." *The Anti-Aesthetic: Essays on Postmodern Culture*. Ed. Hal Foster. Port Townsend, Washington: Bay Press, 1983. 3–15. Also published as "Modernity versus Postmodernity," *New German Critique* 8.1 (Winter 1981).

"The Entwinement of Myth and Enlightenment: Re-reading *Dialectic of Enlightenment*." *New German Critique* 26 (1982): 13–30.

Hamann, Richard and Jost Hermand. *Expressionismus*. Munich: Nymphenberger Verlagshandlung, 1976.

Hardt, Manfred, ed. *Literarische Avantgarden*. Darmstadt: Wissenschaftliche Buchgesellschaft, 1989.

"Zu Begriff, Geschichte und Theorie der literarischen Avantgarde." *Literarische Avantgarden*. Ed. Manfred Hardt. Darmstadt: Wissenschaftliche Buchgesellschaft, 1989. 145–171.

Hasenclever, Walter. *Geschichten, Dramen, Prosa*. Ed. K.Pinthus. Reinbek: Rowohlt, 1963.

Hausmann, Raoul. "Rückkehr zur Gegenständlichkeit in der Kunst." *Dada. Eine literarische Dokumentation*. Ed. Richard Huelsenbeck. Hamburg: Rowohlt, 1984. 113–115.

Heilman, Robert. *Tragedy and Melodrama: Versions of Experience*. Seattle: University of Washington Press, 1968.

Hermand, Jost. "Expressionismus als Revolution." *Von Mainz nach Weimar*. Stuttgart: Luchterhand, 1969. 298–355.

Heym, George. "Umbra Vitae." Pinthus, ed. *Menschheitsdämmerung*. 39–40.

"Der Irre." Rpt. Fritz Martini, ed. *Prosa des Expressionismus*. Stuttgart: Reclam, 1970. 140–155.

Hirst, Paul Q. "Althusser's Theory of Ideology." *Economy and Society* 5.4 (Nov. 1976): 385–412.

Hoddis, Jakob van. "Morgens." Pinthus, ed. *Menschheitsdämmerung*. 168.

Hohendahl, Peter Uwe. *Das Bild der bürgerlichen Welt im expressionistischen Drama*. Heidelberg: C. Winter, 1967.

"The Loss of Reality: Gottfried Benn's Early Prose." Huyssen and

# Bibliography

Battrick, eds. *Modernity and the Text*. 81–94.

Holland, Norman. *The Dynamics of Literary Response*. New York: Oxford, 1968.

Honneth, Axel. "Der Affekt gegen das Allgemeine. Zu Lyotards Konzept der Postmoderne." *Merkur* 38 (1984): 893–902.

Huelsenbeck, Richard. "Der neue Mensch." *Neue Jugend* 1 (23 May, 1917): 2–3. Rpt. Anz and Stark, eds. *Manifeste und Dokumente*. 131–135. *En avant Dada*. Hanover: Steegeman, 1920.

Huelsenbeck, Richard, ed. *Dada. Eine literarische Dokumentation*. Hamburg: Rowohlt, 1984.

Hüttner, J. "Sensationsstücke und Alt-Wiener Volkstheater. Zum Melodrama in der ersten Hälfte des 19. Jahrhunderts." *Maske und Kothurn* 21 (1975): 263–281.

Hutcheon, Linda. *A Poetics of Postmodernism. History, Theory, Fiction*. London and New York: Routledge, 1988.

*The Politics of Postmodernism*. London; New York: Routledge, 1989.

Huyssen, Andreas. *After the Great Divide: Modernism, Mass Culture, Postmodernism*. Bloomington: Indiana University Press, 1986.

Huyssen, Andreas and David Bathrick, eds. *Modernity and the Text: Revisions of German Modernism*. New York: Columbia University Press, 1989.

"Modernity and the Experience of Modernity." Huyssen and Bathrick, eds. *Modernity and the Text*.

Ihekweazu, Edith. "Wandlung und Wahnsinn. Zu expressionistischen Erzählungen von Döblin, Sternheim, Benn, und Heym." *Orbis Litterarum* 37 (1982): 327–344.

Iser, Wolfgang. *The Act of Reading. A Theory of Aesthetic Response*. Baltimore: Johns Hopkins University Press, 1978. Trans. of *Der Akt des Lesens*. Munich: Fink, 1976.

*Prospecting: From Reader Response to Literary Anthropology*. Baltimore: Johns Hopkins University Press, 1989.

Jackson, Rosemary. *Fantasy: The Literature of Subversion*. London: Methuen, 1981.

Jacquemin, Georges. "Über das Phantastische in der Literatur." *Phaicon* 2. Almanach der phantastischen Literatur. Ed. R. A. Zondergeld. Frankfurt: Suhrkamp, 1975. 46–50.

Jameson, Fredric. *Fables of Aggression. Wyndham Lewis, the Modernist as Fascist*. Berkeley: University of California Press, 1979.

"Postmodernism, or The Cultural Logic of Late Capitalism." *New Left Review* 146 (1984): 52–92.

"Reification and Utopia in Mass Culture." *Social Text* 1 (Winter 1979): 130–148. *The Ideologies Of Theory. Essays 1971–1986*. 2 vols. Minneapolis: University of Minnesota Press, 1988.

"Beyond the Cave: Demystifying the Ideology of Modernism." Rpt. *The Ideologies of Theory*. Vol. 2. 115–32.

# Bibliography

"The Ideology of the Text," *The Ideologies of Theory*, Vol. I. 17–71.

Janouch, Gustav. *Gespräche mit Kafka*. Frankfurt-on-Maine: Fischer, 1951.

Jay, Martin. "Habermas and Modernism." *Habermas and Modernity*. Ed. Richard J. Bernstein. Oxford: Polity Press, 1985. 125–139.

Kaes, Anton. *Kino-Debatte*. Tübingen: Niemeyer, 1978.

Kafka, Franz. *Briefe 1902–1924*. Ed. Max Brod. Frankfurt-on-Maine: Fischer, 1975.

*Gesammelte Werke*. Ed. Max Brod. Frankfurt: Fischer, 1983.

Kant, Immanuel. *The Critique of Judgement*. Trans. J. C. Meredith. Oxford: Oxford University Press, 1982.

Kanzog, Klaus. "Alfred Döblin und die Anfänge des expressionistischen Prosastils." *Jahrbuch der deutschen Schillergesellschaft* 17 (1973): 63–83.

Kayser, Wolfgang. *The Grotesque in Art and Literature*. Trans. Ulrich Weisstein. New York: Columbia University Press, 1981.

Kellner, Douglas. *Jean Baudrillard. From Marxism to Postmodernism and Beyond*. Stanford: Stanford University Press, 1989.

*Critical Theory, Marxism and Modernity*. Baltimore: Johns Hopkins University Press, 1989.

Kemper, Hans-Georg. *Vom Expressionismus zum Dadaismus: eine Einfuhrung in die dadaistische Literatur*. Kronberg/Ts: Scriptor Verlag, 1974.

Kermode, Frank. "The Modern." *Modern Essays*. London: Routledge, 1971.

Ketchiff, Nancy. "Dr. Caligari's Cabinet: A Cubist Perspective." *The Comparatist* 8 (May 1984): 7–13.

Klabund. "Ironische Landschaft." *Lyrik des Expressionismus*. 208.

Kleinschmidt, Erich. "Roman im 'Kinostil.' Ein unbekannter 'Roman'-Entwurf Alfred Döblins." *DVjs* 63. 3 (1989): 574–586.

Knapp, Gerhard. *Die Literatur des deutschen Expressionismus: Einführung, Bestandsaufnahme, Kritik*. Munich: Beck, 1979.

Kokoschka, Oskar. *Mörder, Hoffnung der Frauen, Einakter und kleine Dramen des Expressionismus*. Ed. Horst Denkler. Stuttgart: Reclam, 1968.

Kornfeld, Paul. "Der beseelte und der psychologische Mensch." Rpt. Anz and Stark, eds. *Manifeste und Dokumente*. 222–238.

"Nachwort an den Schauspieler." *Die Verführung*. Rpt. Pörtner, ed. *Literaturrevolution 1910–1925. Dokumente, Manifeste, Programme*. Darmstadt: Luchterhand, 1963.

Kurtz, Rudolf. "Programmatisches." *Der Sturm* 1 (3 March 1910): 2–3. Rpt. Anz and Stark, eds. *Manifeste und Dokumente*. 515–518

Kracauer, Siegfried. *From Caligari to Hitler: A Psychological History of the German Film*. Princeton: Princeton University Press, 1947.

Kreuzer, Leo. *Alfred Döblin. Sein Werk bis 1933*. Stuttgart, 1970.

Krull, Wilhelm. *Prosa des Expressionismus*. Stuttgart: Metzler, 1984.

Lacan, Jacques. *Ecrits*. London: Tavistock, 1977.

Laplanche, J. and J.-B. Pontalis. *Vocabulaire de la Psychanalyse*. PUF: Paris, 1967.

# Bibliography

Lentricchia, Frank. *Criticism and Social Change*. Chicago: University of Chicago Press, 1983.

Leonhard, Rudolf. "Die Politik der Dichter." *Die weißen Blätter* 2.6 (1915): 814–816. Rept. Anz and Stark, eds. *Manifeste und Dokumente*. 363–365.

Lichtenstein, Alfred. "Sommerfrische." Rpt. Pinthus, ed. *Menschheitsdämmerung*. 63.

"Nebel." Rpt. Pinthus, ed. *Menschheitsdämmerung*. 59.

"Landschaft." *Lyrik des Expressionismus*. 209.

"Nachmittag, Felder und Fabrik." *Lyrik des Expressionismus*. 73.

"Die Fahrt nach der Irrenanstalt I." *Lyrik des Expressionismus*. 166

Links, Roland. *Alfred Döblin. Leben und Werk*. East Berlin: Volk und Wissen, 1965.

*Alfred Döblin*. Munich: Beck, 1981.

Lodge, David. *After Bakhtin. Essays on Fiction and Criticism*. London: Routledge, 1990.

Lohner, Edgar. "Die Problematik des Begriffes der Avantgarde." Hardt, ed. *Literarische Avantgarden*. 113–127.

Lukacs, Georg. "Es geht um den Realismus." Schmitt, ed. *Expressionismusdebatte*. 192–230.

"Franz Kafka oder Thomas Mann?" (in section "Die Gegenwartsbedeutung des kritischen Realismus.") *Werke IV*. Neuwied: Luchterhand, 1971. 500–550.

"Die weltanschaulichen Grundlagen des Avantgardeismus." *Werke IV*. 467–499.

Lunn, Eugene. *Marxism and Modernism: An Historical Study Of Lukacs, Brecht, Benjamin, and Adorno*. Berkeley: University of California Press, 1982.

Lyotard, Jean-François. "Complexity and the Sublime." *Postmodernism ICA Documents*. 19–26.

"Defining the Postmodern." *Postmodernism ICA Documents*. 7–10.

*The Differend: Phrases in Dispute*. Theory and history of literature 46. Minneapolis: University of Minnesota Press, 1988.

"Vorstellung, Darstellung, Undarstellbarkeit." *Immaterialität und Postmoderne*. Berlin: Merve, 1985. 91–102

"Presenting the Unpresentable: The Sublime." *Artforum* 20.8 (April 1982): 64–69.

*Immaterialität und Postmoderne*. Berlin: Merve, 1985.

"The Interest of the Sublime." *Of the Sublime: Presence in Question*. Trans. J. S. Librett New York: State University of New York Press, 1993. 109–132.

*The Postmodern Condition: A Report on Knowledge*. Minneapolis: University of Minnesota Press, 1984.

*The Postmodern Explained*. Minneapolis: University of Minnesota Press, 1992.

"Rules and Paradoxes and Svelte Appendix." *Cultural Critique* 5 (1987): 209–219.

"Sprache, Zeit, Arbeit." *Immaterialität und Postmoderne*. Berlin: Merve, 1985. 35–54.

*The Lyotard Reader*. Ed. Andrew Benjamin. Oxford: Blackwell, 1989.

Lyotard, Jean-François and Jean-Loup Thébaud. *Just Gaming*. Minneapolis: University of Minnesota Press, 1985.

MacCabe, Colin. *James Joyce and the Revolution of the Word*. London: Macmillan Press, 1979.

*Tracking the Signifier. Theoretical Essays: Film, Linguistics, Literature*. Minneapolis: Minnesota University Press, 1985.

"Realism and the Cinema: Notes on Some Brechtian Theses." *Screen* 15.2 (1974): 8–26. Rpt. *Tracking the Signifier*. 33–57.

"Theory and Film: Principles of Realism and Pleasure." *Screen* 17.3 (1976): 7–27. Rpt. *Tracking the Signifier*. 58–81.

Maclean, H. "Expressionism." *Periods in German Literature*. Ed. J. M. Richie. Wolff: London, 1966.

Marc, Franz. "Der Blaue Reiter." (1914). Rpt. *Manifeste Manifeste. 1905–1933*. Ed. Diether Schmidt. Dresden: Verlag der Kunst, 1956.

Mann, Heinrich. "Geist und Tat." *Pan* 1.5 (1910/11): 137–43. Rpt. Anz and Stark, eds. *Manifeste und Dokumente*. 269–273.

Mann, Paul. *The Theory-Death of the Avant-Garde*. Bloomington: Indiana University Press, 1991.

Marcuse, Herbert. "The Affirmative Character of Culture." *Negations*. Trans. J. Shapiro. Boston: Beacon, 1968.

*An Essay on Liberation*. Boston: Beacon, 1969.

*Counterrevolution and Revolt*. Boston: Beacon, 1972.

Martini, Fritz. *Prosa des Expressionismus*. Stuttgart: Reclam, 1970.

Marx, Karl. *Critique of Hegel's Philosophy of Right*. Cambridge: Cambridge University Press, 1970.

McHale, Brian. "Free Indirect Discourse: A Survey of Recent Accounts." *PTL: A Journal for Descriptive Poetics and Theory of Literature* 3 (1978) 249–287.

"Change of Dominant from Modernist to Postmodernist Writing." *Approaching Postmodernism*. Ed. Hans Bertens and Douwe Fokkema. Philadelphia and Amsterdam: John Benjamins, 1986: 53–78.

*Postmodernist Fiction*. London: Methuen, 1987

Meixner, Horst, and Silvio Vietta, eds. *Expressionismus, sozialer Wandel und kunstlerische Erfahrung: Mannheimer Kolloquium*. Munich: W. Fink, 1982.

Merton, Robert K. *Social Theory and Social Structure*. New York: Free Press, 1968.

"Social Structure and Anomie." Merton, ed. *Social Theory and Social Structure*.

"Continuities in the Theory of Anomie." Merton, ed. *Social Theory and*

# Bibliography

*Social Structure.*

Metz, Christian. *The Imaginary Signifier: Psychoanalysis and Cinema.* Trans. Celia Britton, Annwyl Williams, Ben Brewster and Alfred Guzzetti. London: Macmillan Press, 1982.

Meyer, Hans. "Expressionismus und Novemberrevolution." *Spuren* 5 (1978): 10–13.

Minden, Michael. "Politics and the Silent Cinema: *The Cabinet of Dr. Caligari* and *Battleship Potemkin.*" *Visions and Blueprints: Avant-Garde Culture and Radical Politics in Early Twentieth-Century Europe.* Ed. E. Timms and P. Collier. Manchester: Manchester University Press, 1988. 287–306.

Moretti, Franco. "The Spell of Indecision." *Marxism and the Interpretation of Culture.* Ed. Cary Nelson and Lawrence Grossberg. Urbana: University of Illinois Press, 1988.

Müller-Salget, K. *Alfred Döblin. Werk und Entwicklung.* Bonn: Bouvier Verlag H. 1972.

Müller, Robert. "Die Zeitrasse." *Der Anbruch* 1. 1–2 (1917/18). Rpt. Anz and Stark, eds. *Manifeste und Dokumente.* 135–38.

Murphy, Richard. "The Poetics of Hysteria: Expressionist Drama and the Melodramatic Imagination." *Germanisch-Romanische Monatsschrift* 40.2 (1990): 156–170.

"The Expressionist Revolution: The Re-Writing of the Discursive World." *The German Quarterly* 64.4 (1991): 464–74.

Neumann, Gerhard. *Franz Kafka. Das Urteil. Text, Materialien, Kommentar.* Munich: Metzler, 1981.

Newman, Michael. "Revising Modernism, Representing Postmodernism: Critical Discourses of the Visual Arts." *Postmodernism ICA Documents.* 95–154.

Nietzsche Friedrich. *Werke.* Frankfurt: Ullstein 1969.

Norris, Christopher. *What's Wrong with Postmodernism. Critical Theory and the Ends of Philosophy.* Baltimore: Johns Hopkins University Press, 1990.

Nowell-Smith, Geoffrey. "Minelli and Melodrama." *Screen* 18.2 (Summer 1977): 117–118.

Ogburn, William F. "Cultural Lag as Theory" (1957). *On Culture and Social Change.* Chicago: University of Chicago Press, 1964.

Paulsen, Wolfgang. *Expressionismus und Aktivismus, eine typologische Untersuchung.* Bern and Leipzig: Gotthelf, 1935.

"Expressionism and the Tradition of Revolt" *Expressionism Reconsidered.* Houston German Studies Vol. 1. Ed. G. B. Pickar and K. E. Webb. Munich: Fink, 1979.

Pascal, Roy. *From Naturalism To Expressionism: German Literature and Society 1880–1918.* New York: Basic Books, 1973.

Perkins, Geoffrey. *Contemporary Theory Of Expressionism.* Frankfurt-on-Maine: Peter Lang, 1974.

# Bibliography

Petro, Patrice. *Joyless Streets. Women and Melodramatic Representation in Weimar Germany*. Princeton: Princeton University Press, 1989.

"The Woman, The Monster, and *The Cabinet of Dr. Caligari*," Budd, ed. *"The Cabinet of Dr. Caligari": Texts, Contexts, Histories*. 205–217.

Picard, Max. "Expressionismus. Ein Vortrag." *Die Erhebung* (1919). Rpt. Anz and Stark. *Manifeste und Dokumente*

Pickar, G. B. and K. E. Webb, eds. *Expressionism Reconsidered*. Houston German Studies Vol. 1. Munich: Fink, 1979.

Pinthus, Kurt. "Versuch eines zukünftigen Dramas." *Schaubühne* 10.14 (2 April 1914): 391–394. Rpt. Anz and Stark, eds. *Manifeste und Dokumente*. 680–683.

"Rede für die Zukunft." *Die Erhebung. Jahrbuch für neue Dichtung und Wertung*. Ed. A. Wolfenstein. Berlin: Fischer 1919. Rpt. Rothe, ed. *Der Aktivismus*. 116–133.

Pinthus, Kurt, ed. *Menschheitsdämmerung. Ein Dokument des Expressionismus*. Reinbek: Rowohlt, 1983.

Pörtner, Paul ed. *Literaturrevolution 1910–1925. Dokumente, Manifeste, Programme*. 2 vols. Luchterhand: Neuwied, 1960.

Prangel, Matthias. *Alfred Döblin*. Stuttgart: Metzler, 1987.

Prawer, S. S. *Caligari's Children: The Film as Tale of Terror*. Oxford: Oxford University Press, 1980.

Rank, Otto. "Der Doppelgänger," *Imago* III (1914): 97–164. *The Double: A Psychoanalytic Study*. Trans. and ed. H. Tucker, Jr. Chapel Hill: North Carolina University Press, 1971. Trans. of *Der Doppelgänger, eine psychoanalytische Studie*. Leipzig, 1925.

Readings, Bill. *Introducing Lyotard. Art and Politics*. London: Routledge, 1991.

Renner, Rolf Günter. "Kafka als phantastischer Erzähler." *Phaicon* 3. Almanach der phantastischen Literatur. Ed. R. A. Zondergeld. Frankfurt: Suhrkamp, 1978. 144–162.

*Die Postmoderne Konstellation. Theorie, Text und Kunst im Ausgang der Moderne*. Freiburg: Rombach, 1988.

Ribbat, Ernst. *Die Wahrheit des Lebens im frühen Werk Döblins*. Münster: Aschendorff, 1970.

Rodrigues, Olinde. "L'artiste, le savant et l'industriel." *Oeuvres de Saint-Simon et d'Enfantin*. Aalen: Otto Zeller, 1964. 207–213. Rpt. Hardt, ed. *Literarische Avantgarden*. 13–16.

Rorty, Richard. "Habermas and Lyotard on Postmodernity." *Habermas and Modernity*. Ed. Richard Bernstein. Oxford: Polity Press, 1985. 161–175.

Rosen, Philip. *Narrative, Apparatus, Ideology*. New York: Columbia University Press, 1986.

Rothe, Wolfgang. *Der Aktivismus*. Munich: DTV, 1969.

*Expressionismus als Literatur. Gesammelte Studien*. Munich: Francke, 1969.

# Bibliography

Rumold, Rainer. *Gottfried Benn und der Expressionismus: Provokation des Lesers, absolute Dichtung.* Monographien Literaturwissenschaft 52. Konigstein/Ts: Scriptor, 1982.

"Introduction." *The Ideological Crisis of Expressionism: The Literary and Artistic German War Colony in Belgium 1914–1918.* Ed. Rainer Rumold and O. K. (Otto Karl) Werckmeister. Columbia, SC Camden House, 1990. 1–18.

Russell, Charles. *Poets, Prophets, and Revolutionaries: The Literary Avant-Garde from Rimbaud through Postmodernism.* New York: Oxford University Press, 1985.

Ryan, Judith. "Each One as She May: Malanctha, Tonka, Nadja." Huyssen and Bathrick, eds. *Modernity and the Text.* 95–109.

Samuel, Richard H., and R. Hinton (Richard Hinton) Thomas. *Expressionism in German Life, Literature, and The Theatre, 1910–1924.* Philadelphia: A. Saifer, 1971.

Schickele, Rene. *Die weißen Blätter* 3 (1916). 1. Quartal, 135–136. Rpt. Anz and Stark, eds. *Manifeste und Dokumente.*

Schmitt, Hans-Jurgen, ed. *Die Expressionismusdebatte. Materialien zu einer marxistischen Realismuskonzeption.* Frankfurt: Suhrkamp, 1973.

Schreyer, Lothar. "Der neue Mensch." Rpt. Anz and Stark, eds. *Manifeste und Dokumente.* 140.

Schrimpf, W. "*Faust* als Melodrama? Überlegungen zu einer Bühnenfassung von 1815." *Euphorion* 81 (1987): 347–352.

Schulte-Sasse, Jochen. "Carl Einstein; or, the Postmodern Transformation of Modernism." Huyssen and Bathrick, eds. *Modernity and the Text.* 36–59.

Schulte-Sasse, Jochen. "Avant-Garde." *International Encyclopedia of Communication.* Oxford: Oxford University Press, 1989. 162–166.

Schulte-Sasse, Jochen. "Foreword: Theory of Modernism versus Theory of the Avant-Garde." Introduction to Bürger, *Theory of the Avant-Garde.*

Schulte-Sasse, Jochen. "Imagination and Modernity: or the Taming of the Human Mind." *Cultural Critique* 5 (1987): 23–48.

Schulte-Sasse, Jochen. "Carl Einstein; or, The Postmodern Transformation of Modernism." Huyssen and Bathrick, eds. *Modernity and the Text.* 36–59.

Schulte-Sasse, Jochen. "Modernity and Modernism, Postmodernity and Postmodernism: Framing the Issue." *Cultural Critique* 5 (1987): 5–22.

Shelley, "Preface to Prometheus Unbound." *Shelley's Poetry and Prose.* Ed. D. Reiman and S. Powers. New York: Norton, 1977.

Sheppard, Richard, ed. *Expressionism In Focus: Proceedings of the First UEA Symposium on German Studies.* New Alyth: Lochee Publications, 1987.

Shklovsky, Victor. "Art as Technique." *Russian Formalist Criticism. Four Essays.* Trans. L. Lemon and M. Reis. Lincoln: Nebraska University Press, 1965. 3–24.

# Bibliography

Silberman, Marc. "Industry, Text and Ideology in Expressionist Film." *Passion and Rebellion. The Expressionist Heritage.* Ed. Stephen Eric Bronner and Douglas Kellner. South Hadley, MA: J. F. Bergin, 1983. 374–383.

Simmel, Georg. "Die Großstadt und das Geistesleben." *Die Großstadt. Jahrbuch der Gehestiftung.* Dresden, 1903.

Smith, James L. *Melodrama.* The Critical Idiom 28. London: Methuen, 1973.

Sokel, Walter. *The Writer in Extremis; Expressionism in Twentieth-Century German Literature.* Stanford: Stanford University Press, 1959.

"Brecht und der Expressionismus." *Die sogenannten zwanziger Jahre.* Ed. R. Grimm and J. Hermand. Bad Homburg: Gehlen Verlag, 1970.

*Franz Kafka. Tragik und Ironie.* Frankfurt-on-Maine: Fischer, 1976.

Sorge, J. *Der Bettler. Werke in Drei Bänden.* Ed. Hans Gerd Rötzer. Nürnberg: Glock und Lutz von Hans. Gerd Rotzer, 1962–67.

Stadler, Ernst. "Der Spruch," Pinthus, ed. *Menschheitsdämmerung.* 196.

Stoker, Bram. "The Censorship of Fiction." *The Nineteenth Century.* (London; September 1908): 481.

Ronald Taylor et al., eds. *Aesthetics and Politics.* London: New Left Books, 1979.

Taylor, Seth. *Left-Wing Nietzscheans: The Politics of German Expressionism, 1910–1920.* Berlin and New York: W. de Gruyter, 1990.

Terdiman, Richard. *Discourse/Counter-Discourse. Theory and Practice of Symbolic Resistance in Nineteenth-Century France.* Ithaca: Cornell University Press, 1985.

Todorov, Tzvetan. *The Fantastic. A Structural Approach to a Literary Genre.* trans. R. Howard. Ithaca: Cornell, 1973. Trans. of *Introduction à la littérature fantastique.* Paris: Editions du Seuil, 1970.

*Einführung in die fantastische Literatur.* Trans. K. Kersten, S. Metz and C. Neubaur. Munich: Hanser, 1972.

*Mikhail Bakhtin: The Dialogical Principle.* Trans. Wlad Godzich. Minneapolis: Minnesota University Press, 1984.

Toller, Ernst. *Prosa, Briefe, Dramen, Gedichte.* Reinbek: Rowohlt, 1979.

Tomashevsky, Boris. "Thematics." Lemon and Reiss, eds. *Russian Formalist Criticism.* 66–67.

Trakl, Georg. "Elis" and "An den Knaben Elis." Rpt. Pinthus, ed. *Menschheitsdämmerung.* 100, 101.

Trommler, Frank. *Sozialistische Literatur in Deutschland. Ein historischer Überblick.* Stuttgart: Kröner, 1976.

Unger, Erich. "Vom Pathos. Die um George." *Der Sturm* 1.40 (Dec. 1910): 316. Rpt. Anz and Stark, eds. *Manifeste und Dokumente.* 118.

Van Hoddis. "Weltende." Rpt. Pinthus, ed. *Menschheitsdämmerung.*

Vietta, Silvio, and Hans-Georg Kemper. *Expressionismus.* Munich: W. Fink, 1975.

Vietta, Silvio, ed. *Lyrik des Expressionismus.* Tübingen: Deutscher Taschenbuch-Verlag, 1976.

# Bibliography

"Das Expressionistische am deutschen Stummfilm." *Literatur und Stummfilm*. Ed. S. Vietta and K. Tröster. Mannheim, 1980. 33–36

Vietta, Silvio, and Horst Meixner, eds. *Expressionismus: sozialer Wandel und kunstlerische Erfahrung*. Munich: Wilhelm Fink, 1982.

Watzlawick, Beavin and Jackson. *Pragmatics of Human Communication*. New York: Norton, 1967.

Weber, Samuel. "The Sideshow, or: Remarks on a Canny Moment." *MLN* 88 (1973): 1102–1133.

Weiskel, Thomas. *The Romantic Sublime. Studies in the Structure and Psychology of Transcendence*. Baltimore: Johns Hopkins University Press, 1976.

Wellmer, Albrecht. "On the Dialectic of Modernism and Postmodernism." *Praxis International* 4.4 (Jan 1985): 337–62.

Werner, Renate. "Das Wilhelminische Zeitalter als literarhistorische Epoche. Ein Forschungsbericht." *Wege der Literaturwissenschaft*. Ed. Jutta Kolkenbock-Netz, Gerhard Plumpe and Hans-Joachim Schrimpf. Bonn, 1985. 211–231.

Willett, John. *Expressionism*. London: Weidenfeld and Nicolson, 1970.

Williams, Raymond. *Marxism and Literature*. Oxford: Oxford University Press, 1977.

Wolin, Richard. "Modernism vs. Postmodernism." *Telos* 62 (1984–1985): 9–30.

Wordsworth, "Observations Prefixed to the Second Edition," *Lyrical Ballads*. Ed. T. Hutchinson and E. de Selincourt. Oxford: Oxford University Press, 1950.

Zimmermann,Werner. *Deutsche Prosadichtungen unseres Jahrhunderts*. Bd. 1. Düsseldorf, 1966.

Zmegac, Viktor. "Alfred Döblins Poetik des Romans." *Deutsche Romantheorien*. Ed. R. Grimm. Frankfurt: Fischer-Athenäum, 1968.

# Index

abstraction, 3, 14, 17, 19, 91, 95,
135–36, 154, 160–3, 171,
177–78, 183, 193, 221, 274,
279–80
*see also under* expressionism;
Sokel, Walter
Adorno, Theodor W., 42, 191,
289
aesthetic autonomy, 10, 27, 29–34,
36, 40–41, 47, 69, 78, 249, 252,
254, 256, 259, 267, 285, 299
*see also under* Bürger, Peter;
modernism
aestheticized politics, 28, 33, 268,
285
aestheticism, 1, 6–7, 9, 30, 33, 36,
65–66, 116, 254
affirmative culture, 9–11, 16, 28,
30–35, 37, 40, 45, 48, 78, 99,
108, 156, 232, 256, 280, 282,
284, 286–88, 296
*see also* Marcuse, Herbert
alienation, 17, 54, 113, 130, 132,
134n.108, 165, 250
*see also under* avant-garde;
*Ichdissoziation*
alienation device ("*V-effect*"), 19,
138
*see also under* Brecht, Bertolt

Althusser, Louis, 98, 133, 134n.106
ideology, 293, 297
anomie, 152, 178–9, 203, 210
and "aesthetic anomie," 274
*see also* Merton, Robert K.
Anz, Thomas, 100n.45, 118n.79,
130n.99, 151nn.17, 19
atrophy of experience
(*Erfahrungverlust*), 17, 252,
260
*see also* Benjamin, Walter
*Aufdecken/Zudecken* (opening
up/covering over)
*see under* Lukács, Georg
aura, 21, 32, 40, 203, 240
*see also under* Benjamin, Walter
author as producer
*see under* Benjamin, Walter
autonomy of art
*see* aesthetic autonomy
avant-garde
as aesthetics of
meaninglessness, 23–24,
24n.43, 25–26, 26n, 94, 102,
141, 196, 277–78
alienation as device, 79, 91,
100–1, 250
*see also Ichdissoziation*; Brecht,
Bertolt

# Index

as counter-discourse, 47–48, 54, 57, 78, 83, 106n.56, 108–9, 115–16, 127, 130, 136–37, 182, 185, 195, 200, 202, 245, 261, 263, 270, 272–73, 290–91, 294, 296–98 *see also under* counter-discourse

cynical sublation of art and life, 34, 39, 60–61, 67, 106, 259

as de-aestheticized art, 32–33, 66, 259

desublimation and de-aestheticization in, 34, 37, 39–40, 59–60, 67, 159–60, 210, 252, 286–88, 296

epic structure, 20–23, 81, 84, 175

history of the term, 35

manifestos, 260

vs. modernism, 3, 5, 11, 29–30, 32, 47–48, 105–6, 256–58, 281n; *see also* modernism: relation to avant-garde

montage, 13, 15–16, 18, 20, 22, 24, 58n.26, 64, 80–82, 97, 140–41, 154, 175, 247, 256n.16, 295

vs. organic structure, 14, 19, 23, 25–26, 58, 70, 79–80, 83, 137, 196

relation to postmodernism, 264–67, 269, 276, 281–84, 287, 296, 299

ready-made, 23, 79

recoding, 62, 93–94, 97, 105, 250; *see also* expressionism: re-writing

reintegration of art and life; *see* sublation of art and life

romanticism, 35, 38, 58, 61, 153, 156, 179, 259, 274

self-criticism, 8–9, 47–48, 267, 280

self-reflexivity, 263, 267–68, 271, 284n, 285, 294–97

undermining of dominant cultural codes, 71, 256

undermining of institution of art, 10–11, 15, 26n, 139

Bakhtin, Mikhail, 122n.89, 193, 200

carnival, 100n.47, 214, 228n

"character zone," 124

"heteroglossia," 136–37

"hybrid" or "double-voiced" discourse, 123–25, 136, 194, 272

definition of, 126, 129

monological vs. dialogical, 89, 186–87, 194, 200, 272

verbal-ideological systems, 200

Ball, Hugo, 52–54, 68n.50

"Kandinsky," 151

Barthes, Roland, 195

"the readerly" ("*lisible*"), 232

Bateson, Gregory, 102n.49

Baudrillard, Jean, 269, 271

simulacrum, 268, 270

Becker, Julius M., 18, 90n.35, 172, 174

Beckett, Samuel, 113n.68

Belsey, Catherine, 83n.16, 134n.106, 293n.100, 297

Benhabib, Seyla, 262n.28, 265n.38

Benjamin, Walter, 13, 45n, 252n.4, 270

"aura," 247, 252, 269

"The Author as Producer," 12, 32, 39–40, 108

"tendency" vs. "technique" (*Tendenz* vs. *Technik*), 12–13, 15–16, 32–33, 42, 70, 203, 295n.103

"atrophy of experience" (*Erfahrungsverlust*), 17, 252, 260

Benn, Gottfried, 17n.29, 41, 43, 45–46, 46nn.92–93, 55, 57n.22, 75–76, 89–90, 96, 102n.50, 127, 130, 136, 141, 227n.33, 261

315

# Index

Benn, Gottfried (*cont.*)
  *Brains* (*Gehirne* ), 18n, 101–2,
    104–5, 107–13
  "Morgue poetry," the, 61, 109
Bennett, Tony, 249n.62
Benveniste, Emile, 134n.106,
    231n.39
  *histoire* vs. *discours*, 139, 185, 231,
    232–34, 234n, 235–36, 238,
    240–42, 273, 263, 293; *see also*
    Metz, Christian
Berger, Peter, 152
*Bildung* (identity-formation), 17;
    *see also* Schiller, Friedrich
Bloch, Ernst, 14–16, 51n.9, 59,
    116n.75, 203
  interruption, 14, 137, 184, 260,
    293
Brecht, Bertolt, 56, 171, 250n, 292,
    295n.104
  alienation device ('V-effect''),
    19, 138
  epic theater, 13, 21, 42n.84,
    79–81, 135n.108, 140, 154 *see*
    *also* Tableau
  interruption, 173
  montage, 293
Brooks, Peter, 144, 146, 149–50,
    152–3, 155n.26, 158–59, 173
  "desacralization," 145, 147–48,
    151, 178
  *The Melodramatic Imagination*,
    146n.7, 161n.38, 162n.40,
    179
Budd, Mike, 245n.56, 246, 249
Bürger, Peter, 1–8, 10, 12, 16, 18,
    25–27, 32, 34, 36n.69, 37, 41,
    50nn.6–7, 64, 70, 78, 97, 106,
    141, 254, 258, 260, 261n.27,
    269, 276, 280, 284n.85, 289–90,
    299
  aesthetic autonomy, 6, 11, 27–29,
    33
  organic, 15, 57, 94, 233
Burgher, the (*der Bürger*) *see*

expressionism: critique of the
    burgher

*Cabinet of Dr. Caligari, The*, 95,
    204–30, 234–35, 237, 238n.47,
    239–49, 261–62, 272
Calinescu, Matei, 5, 35n.64
Callinicos, Alex, 254
carnival, 100n.47, 215, 229; *see also*
    *under* Bakhtin, Mikhail
Carroll, Noel, 204n, 220, 220n
cinema-style (*Kinostil*) *see under*
    Döblin, Alfred
Cixous, Hélène, 157
classic realism *see* classic realist
    text
classic realist text, 65, 82–83, 93,
    105, 107, 116, 119, 126–8, 139,
    152, 207, 234, 242, 247–48, 260,
    294–95
  definition of, 80–81, 81n.10, 232
  and counter-discourse, 85,
    99–100, 248 *see also under*
    expressionism
  and dominant discourse, 83–84,
    104, 115, 117, 121, 127–9, 137,
    231, 232, 233, 235–41, 243, 245,
    249, 256, 262, 270–72, 284–85,
    287, 291
  as meta-language, 122, 230–33,
    236, 265
  vs. the "subversive" or
    avant-garde text, 15, 64,
    91–92, 126, 138, 156, 233
Clément, Catherine, 226
Cohn, Dorrit *see* narration:
    psycho-narration
correlative *see* objective correlative
counter-discourse
  definition of, 99, 103, 293
  and expressionism, 99–100, 176,
    272, 295
  and the avant-garde, 47–48, 54,
    57, 78, 83, 106n.56, 108–9,
    115–16, 127, 130, 136–37, 182,

316

# Index

# Index

reintegration of art and life *see* sublation of art and life

representational instability, 19, 207, 218, 220, 226–7, 241, 295

revolution *see under* expressionism

re-writing, 40, 57–58, 60–61, 65–66, 71, 261–63, 267–70; *see also* expressionism

romanticism, 35n.66, 36, 62, 106, 164, 268, 280n.79

and the sublime, 274–75, 279

*see also under* avant-garde

Rorty, Richard, 290, 291n.97

Russell, Charles, 106

Russian formalism, 85

story vs. plot, 249

*see also* defamiliarization; Shklovsky, Victor

Schiller, Friedrich, 6, 20

concept of *Bildung*, 17

Schulte-Sasse, Jochen, 4, 48n, 254, 257–58, 260n.25, 261n.27, 266n, 267, 270, 271n.54, 279nn.76–77, 284

scopophilia, 227

self-reflexivity

*see under* avant-garde

semantic vacuum, 169, 181, 194, 198–200, 216–17, 276

semiotic excess, 173, 175, 195, 198n.42

Shelley, Percy B., 36n.66

Shklovsky, Victor

"Art as Technique," 85n.23, 223

Silberman, Marc, 204n

Simmel, Georg, 270n.52

*Simultangedicht* (simultaneous poem), 14; *see also* expressionism

social imaginary, 14, 128, 294, 297–98

socialization, 17, 98, 113, 135, 137, 294; *see also under* Althusser, Louis

Sokel, Walter, 3n.7, 21n.36, 42n.83, 49n.2, 70n.53, 73n.62, 75n.3, 86, 86n.27, 89, 91, 95, 116n.74, 119, 193, 201n, 222, 276

"abstraction," 90, 160

"objective correlative," 90, 221, 224

Sorge, Johannes, *The Beggar* (*Der Bettler*), 90n.35, 157–58, 161, 170n.57

Stadler, Ernst, 55

Stark, Michael, 151n.17

*Stationendrama* (stations-of-the-cross drama), 20n.35, 57n.23, 80, 161, 164, 172; *see also under* expressionism

Sternheim, Carl, 42n.84, 161, 161n.39

*Stilwandel; see* stylistic transformations

Stramm, August, 68n.50, 143n

stream-of-consciousness, 45n.89, 47, 91–92, 105, 107, 121; *see also under* modernism; narration

Strindberg, August, 20

stylistic transformations (*Stilwandel* ), 70

subjectivity, 172, 199

and bourgeois identity, 135, 226

construction of, 16, 17; *see also Bildung*

crisis of, 225–26; *see also Ichdissoziation*

decentering of, 17, 18, 133, 206, 221, 224, 227

destabilized, 20, 132, 220, 224, 227n.33, 229

and displacement of identity, 216

doubling and supplementarity of self, 131, 206, 209, 213, 221–22, 224, 226, 229

dramatization of, 90n.35, 148–49, 170, 174, 192, 199–200, 224